The Masculine Self in
Late Medieval England

The Masculine Self in
Late Medieval England

DEREK G. NEAL

The University of Chicago Press

CHICAGO AND LONDON

DEREK NEAL is assistant professor of history at Nipissing University
in North Bay, Ontario, Canada. His research interests include
gender, sexuality, and religion in late medieval and early modern Britain
as well as the role of fictional literature in historical analysis.

The University of Chicago Press, Chicago 60637
The University of Chicago Press, Ltd., London
© 2008 by The University of Chicago
All rights reserved. Published 2008
Printed in the United States of America
17 16 15 14 13 12 11 10 09 08   1 2 3 4 5

ISBN-13: 978-0-226-56955-0 (cloth)
ISBN-13: 978-0-226-56957-4 (paper)
ISBN-10: 0-226-56955-1 (cloth)
ISBN-10: 0-226-56957-8 (paper)

Library of Congress Cataloging-in-Publication Data
Neal, Derek G.
The masculine self in late medieval England /
Derek G. Neal.   p.   cm.
Includes bibliographical references and index.
ISBN-13: 978-0-226-56955-0 (cloth : alk. paper)
ISBN-13: 978-0-226-56957-4 (pbk. : alk. paper)
ISBN-10: 0-226-56955-1 (cloth : alk. paper)
ISBN-10: 0-226-56957-8 (pbk. : alk. paper)
1. Masculinity—England—History—To 1500.   2. Men—England—Social life
and customs.   3. England—Social life and customs—1066–1485.
4. England—Social conditions—1066–1485.   I. Title.
HQ1090.7.E85N43   2008
305.38′82100902—dc22
2008009929

In memory of Helen Waddington (1968–2003)
whose own interest in gender nourished her
lifelong concern for others

Contents

Acknowledgments

ANY LONG-TERM project incurs many debts, and personal and professional kindnesses are the most pleasant debts to record. At an early stage Anna Dronzek pointed me toward courtesy literature. Juliet Sloger provided advice about romances (and the invaluable TEAMS Web site). My archival research in England during the summer of 1999 was funded by a Faculty of Graduate Studies and Research Fellowship from McGill University. The professionalism of the staff at Canterbury Cathedral Archives, at the Borthwick Institute of Historical Research in York (now the Borthwick Institute for Archives)—particularly that of Philippa Hoskin and David Smith—and at the Public Record Office (now the National Archives of the United Kingdom) at Kew, London, made my work during that trip much easier. The hospitality of Donna Sharp in Exeter, Adam and Elizabeth Tegetmeier in Bradford-on-Avon, the Clow family in London, and David Wilson in York made it pleasant as well. An early version of chapter 1 might never have become my first published article but for Katherine French, who persuaded me to present it at the Sixteenth Century Studies Conference (Cleveland, November 2000), and Gordon Desbrisay, who heard it there and urged me to submit it for publication. Michael Diamond, Jacqueline Murray, Susie Phillips, and Lisa Perfetti all provided copies of their published and unpublished papers. I particularly thank Gary Shaw for permitting me to read his book, *Necessary Conjunctions,* while it was still unpublished, and Sandy Bardsley and Sara Butler for providing copies of their doctoral dissertations.

Portions of chapters 1 and 2 were previously published, in different form, as "Suits Make the Man: Masculinity in Two English Law Courts, c. 1500"

(*Canadian Journal of History* 37 [2002]: 1–22), and are used by permission. Portions of chapters 2 and 3 were previously published, in different form, as "Husbands and Priests: Masculinity, Sexuality and Defamation in Late Medieval England" (in *The Hands of the Tongue: Essays on Deviant Speech*, ed. Edwin Craun [Kalamazoo, Mich.: Medieval Institute Publications, 2007], 185–208), and are used by permission. Other portions of chapter 3 were previously published, in different form, as "Masculine Identity in Late Medieval English Society and Culture" (in *Writing Medieval History*, ed. Nancy F. Partner [London: Hodder Arnold, 2005], 171–88), and are used by permission.

My parents, Wilbert and Edeltraud Neal, never failed to ask (especially at Sunday dinner) after the progress of this study, and I know they share my satisfaction at its completion. Gwenda Wells, a true friend since my first year at McGill University, opened her home to me on numerous overnight visits to Montreal after I had moved to Ottawa. She also unwittingly inspired chapter 4 of this book when she lent me a recording of La Nef's musical performance of the Perceval story. Shannon McSheffrey gave me crucial interpretive and practical advice, particularly on archival research, guiding my introduction to the easily bewildering world of the medieval ecclesiastical courts. She also generously provided copies of her transcriptions of important London court records.

This book's gestation spanned the transition, challenging for me as for any scholar, from doctoral candidate to assistant professor. I am grateful for the interest and kindness shown by all my colleagues in the Department of History at Nipissing University, and for the helpful staff of Print Plus there. I must also thank Douglas Mitchell, Timothy McGovern, and the rest of the editorial team at the University of Chicago Press, as well as the two anonymous readers who reviewed the manuscript. Of course, I assume responsibility for any errors that remain.

Nancy Partner was an insightful, responsive, straightforward, and respectful research supervisor while I was her doctoral student at McGill University and has continued to be a helpful mentor and valued friend ever since. From her, I have learned challenging ways of thinking about many things, history being only one of them.

Steve Mazey's witness to my historical career long predates this project. I owe my (relative) mental health to his presence in my life, and my debts to him are greater than I can record here.

Note on Primary Sources

ALL QUOTATIONS from primary sources, whether Middle English, French, or Latin, appear here in modern English. Unless otherwise indicated, these translations and modernizations are my own. The original text has only been included where the point under discussion depends on vocabulary, phrasing, or some other rhetorical feature.

INTRODUCTION

———— ✳ ————

I ONCE met a senior historian of modern America, a man who was a specialist neither in gender nor in the Middle Ages. When I told him that I studied masculinity in late medieval England, he smiled indulgently. "Ah," he said. "Swordplay."

On a different occasion, I was speaking with a woman, the owner of a bed-and-breakfast in Seattle. She had not studied history, but she had her own opinion about what masculinity might have meant in late medieval England. Unlike the U.S. historian, she did not smile, but responded curtly: "Power and status. What else would it mean?"

Those two remarks are probably pretty representative of the associations and attitudes called up for most people (inside and outside the academy) by the phrase "medieval masculinity." One person might imagine short-tempered men quarrelling outside the village tavern: touchy about petty insults, jealous of their women, showing off. Another might see the governing hand of the household patriarch, sometimes open in fatherly generosity, sometimes wielded in chastisement against wife and children. The famous "double standard," subjecting women but not men to severe sanctions for sexual misbehavior, would not be far from many minds. Nor would the celibate priest, whose sexuality we imagine being either vented in illicit liaisons with parish girls, or sublimated into cruel misogynist rhetoric.

As my Seattle interlocutor sensed, all these concerns have something to do with the relation of maleness to power and control, wielded in abusive or beneficent ways. The concept of patriarchy, the institutionalized, self-sustaining power of men over women, has been the usual means of thinking about this relation of maleness to dominance. The impatient tone of the Seattle woman's rejoinder signaled her suspicion that I was involved in a project deflecting questions of gender away from questions of power dynamics: Why do men ever do what they do, especially to women, if not to gain "power and status"? And why bother to investigate something to which we already know the answer?[1]

This book's response to that comment is, "All right, but what power and what status?" Power to do what, status measured by what standard? Certainly, medieval evidence amply documents the advantages medieval men enjoyed, and the learned culture of the Middle Ages consistently argued for male superiority. But the social advantages enjoyed by many men gave them power not only over women but also over inferiors of other kinds: children, servants, and social inferiors. Women themselves might exercise different measures of such power over their own social inferiors, regardless of sex. Moreover, masculine positions might involve not just the control of one person over another, but also, as with the celibate priest, the command of self over self. The hierarchies of medieval Europe were too complex for us to equate masculinity solely with power and domination, or with the need or desire for them, or the expectation of the exercise of them.

The comment of the male Americanist was revealing in its own way. For him, the combination of "masculinity" and "Middle Ages" signaled conflict between men. And that was conflict of a particular kind: involving swords, not fists, it evoked chivalric duels and therefore one of the most familiar images of medieval culture, with all its aristocratic and romantic trappings. Calling it "swordplay," rather than sword fighting, in turn, suggested that the conflict, however damaging, was not a fight to the death, and that it had a ritual context giving it significance. Its outcome probably reflected on the combatants in some way. So the conflict was both serious and not serious. It was a performance, where something was acted out. Someone else might stress that "play" invokes leisure, the freedom to expend bodily energies of strength for pleasure, not for the sake of one's own survival or the profit of others. A modern observer of fights between men might note with bitter irony that "swordplay," that is, fighting for pleasure, hence taking an enjoyment in aggression, has long been taken as a general male tendency with possibly damaging consequences but also potential payoffs. That same observer would probably note the metaphorical association of "swords" as phallic symbols, extensions of the male body with penetrating and wounding potential. And a queer theorist, or even just a psychoanalyst, might point out the homoerotic possibilities reposing not far below the surface of an interaction between men where aggression, tension, excitement, pleasure, and phalluses coincide. All of these elements, in their different ways, come up in the following pages.

But the indulgent smile that accompanied "swordplay" had something to tell us too. It suggested the function that the medieval era serves for many people in the twenty-first century: a period whose arcane and perplexing conflicts provide entertaining contrasts to the gravity of the modern world. By implication, then, the Middle Ages are not really very important or very serious. And this attitude is not confined to popular perceptions; anyone who works on slander or sexuality can testify to the mirth that quotations from his or her primary sources will provoke at an academic conference, even among people who have devoted their careers to this same era. Matters as serious as bloodletting conflict, or moments of crushing humiliation, somehow become quaint and funny when they have happened to medieval people and are described in their language.

Anyone can tell what is going on here, of course: when we laugh at the Middle Ages, we affirm our modernity. We all think we know that Jakob Burkhardt, Johan Huizinga, and Norbert Elias were misguided when they implied that medieval people were psychologically less complex or less developed than we are, or that they had no concept of the individual self, or that they were creatures of the infantile id, prone to capricious storms of emotion and ungoverned by civilized restraint. Yet we cling to these ideas (or parodies of them) more than we think. The distinction between modernity and premodernity is a powerfully self-defining one for us, and so we have deep interests in refusing to recognize certain aspects of the human condition in the past, even when that refusal robs us of a vocabulary for understanding the people who lived in those societies. The way we choose to study premodern identity, therefore, becomes crucially important, and identity is exactly what the array of associations and roles rehearsed above (fathers, priests, fighters) are really about.

Why have these matters ended up in a book? The answer in fact connects directly to the background of criticism and politics from which my suspicious Seattle critic was speaking. The study you are reading is about men, but it owes its existence to women both past and present.

Masculinity would not have become the subject of serious historical research, beginning in the early 1990s, without at least two preceding decades of scholarship about the history of women, most of which was the work of women historians inspired by feminist criticism. That lineage is especially important for our knowledge of the social setting of this book, the mid-fourteenth to early sixteenth centuries in England. Building on the techniques of the new social history developed in the mid-twentieth century, historians of medieval and early modern women's experience examined new kinds of evidence, and analyzed it in new ways, to reveal the many intricate factors in premodern social life that defined both the restrictions and the qualified possibilities in women's lives. Gender was not just the norms dictated by jurists and theologians, or the stereotypes of prescriptive and imaginative literature, but inherent in the interactions of far more humble people revealed in urban, manorial, and ecclesiastical records. This was evidence that told us about marital patterns and sexual behavior, about the gendered division of labor, about the contours of personal reputation.[2] Historians of women thought and wrote about power and hierarchy in ways not delimited by broad-brush definitions of wealth and social class. They thereby revealed a much more detailed world of premodern life as ordinary people most often lived it, in the places where they most often lived it: the rural village and the small urban community. The newest work on premodern communities, bringing together categories of gender and culture with traditional social history, would be unimaginable without this legacy.

Not long after this gendered social history became available, beginning in the late 1980s, historians interested in gender began to follow the lead of their counterparts studying gender in other humanistic and social-scientific disciplines. Literary scholars and theorists had debated the relationship of sex to gender; anthropologists, social psychologists, and sociologists had realized that the position of women and the discursive meanings of femininity were not explicable solely with reference to an all-powerful monolith called "patriarchy."[3] Male experience and the meanings of maleness, it turned out, were complex and culturally variable, which meant they might be historically variable as well. Historians thus turned to masculinity with a new theoretical tool-kit that the pursuit of women's history had honed and refined.

The adoption of masculinity as an interest in gender history happened across the historical profession, and as with women's history two decades earlier, there was a back-to-front effect, as the first and most numerous studies focused on the nineteenth and twentieth centuries.[4] Perhaps this was because the modern era, past but accessible, seemed the most obvious source of present-day aspects of gender: social arrangements, public discourse, and interiority. After Freud, the study, indeed the naming, of sexuality as such, marked an entire realm of human existence as modern and gave it a modern vocabulary. Michel Foucault, who cast a long shadow into the 1990s, had cast regulatory regimes as a constitutive feature of modernity and had linked that theme to sexuality. As a result, historians of the premodern era had to grapple with the applicability of categories and analyses derived from kinds of evidence that were scanty or nonexistent for the period before the nineteenth century.

Within that part of the premodern that we vaguely call "medieval," there is an additional set of problems. As their professionally defined name implies, the "early modern" centuries are assumed to possess their quotient of protomodernity. However, there is never the sense that anything starts in the Middle Ages—that it has something to offer to current debates, or even that what is unique about the period has its own authority. Nobody looks for evidence of the "medieval" in the modern or examines the modern through medieval categories, except (sometimes) medievalists. And this is particularly significant for the study of medieval identity. As Nancy Partner has put it, we have trouble recognizing medieval people as possessing "depth, complexity and individuality" because "'medieval' has come to mean the opposite of those qualities, at least as regards persons."[5] And it is exactly "as regards persons" that this book aims to consider the male population of England between Black Death and Reformation.

THE TERM "medieval" covers a very large span of time and refers simultaneously to very different societies. At the same time, until very recently, scholarship on masculinity, particularly in history departments, was the province of a rather small number of writers scattered across the field. It is understandable, therefore, that the historiography of medieval masculinity thus far consists largely of small-scale contributions collected together in multiauthored volumes.[6] These collections bring together, in variable proportion, the work of historians and literary scholars, an indication of the importance of literary criticism in the study of premodern masculinity. They show, however, little cross-fertilization between history and literature, a gap I try to address in the present book. The field's first monograph, by Ruth Mazo Karras, appeared only in 2003, and its focus and approach are fundamentally different from mine.[7] Elizabeth Foyster and Alexandra Shepard have addressed the late sixteenth and early seventeenth centuries in England, but this is the first full-length and nationally specific study of masculinity for the period before 1530.[8]

Gender history seeks to understand what sexual difference meant in past societies. Sensibly understood, that means not just the cultural associations, the symbolic values, which societies cast in the terms of sexual difference, but also the way those values became manifest in the lived experience of men and women. In this case: what did it take to be known as a man in late medieval England? And how can the historian set about finding an answer?

I realized very early on that the answer did not lie in one of the chief ways masculinity has been apprehended in historical terms: the recurring idea that societies, and/or the men in them (depending who is telling the story), experience a "crisis of masculinity" under certain historical conditions. Those conditions usually involve any alteration in the perceived security of men's social, and especially economic, roles. A survey of the literature reveals that these crises have happened rather too often over recent centuries, with no apparent resolutions, for the concept to have much use.[9] It is also suspicious that no one has revealed a crisis of masculinity in England during the period I examine (roughly 1350–1530), even though the social conditions of that era seem ideally suited to cause one: significant demographic disruption, economic decline in the towns, the abandonment of traditional masculine regulatory associations in village life, and cultural and political change under an increasingly pervasive royal bureaucracy. The idea of "masculinity" at issue in these claims of crisis is largely a metaphorical one standing for conservative social and moral values and serving rhetorical purposes in social critique, contemporary or modern. It treats masculinity as a feature of society and fails to make a convincing link to lived experience.

If the "crisis of masculinity" is not a suitable concept for considering masculinity historically, then what is? Looking for the relation between cultural expectations and lived experience led me to consider masculinity as identity—as something in which individuals had a stake. And this drew me to George Devereux's theory of the "double discourse." Gender identity, like all phenomena of the human experience, has both social and psychological aspects. We can roughly understand the social as "exterior" and the psychic as "interior" dimensions, or "frames of reference." While their influences on identity are interdependent, society and psyche demand separate attention. The frames are complementary, but one sees different things through them, and the more attention one pays to the first, the less one can pay to the second at the same time. They are not susceptible to analysis by the same conceptual tools, nor can the historian employ the same sets of evidence for both.[10] So the book begins with the "outside" social world, which generates the kind of evidence more familiar to most historians, and proceeds logically toward the "inside" realm of the mind and personal identity.

My focus throughout is on the most ordinary men accessible: not always an easy goal. This is not another book about knights and chivalry. At the same time, when the best surviving collections of personal letters come from gentry families, it would be silly to exclude them. Thus, this book tells the reader a lot about townspeople and gentry and the better-off peasants who were able to leave their traces in historical records, very little about the aristocracy, and not as much about the rural masses as I would like.

The social frame of reference looms large in this study; evidence from a variety of sources soon makes apparent how much a masculine identity in late medieval England depended on a social presence. Being a man meant being present, visible, accepted among and interacting with a community of other males in the formal and informal structures of a man's immediate community: the marketplace, the guild hall, the manor court, the vestry meeting. Manhood, to use a more medieval word, was reserved for adult males, but adulthood in itself was not enough. Rather, the values of mature social masculinity were those that enabled a man to maintain his place among his peers without encroaching on, or endangering, theirs. Regardless of how many disputes arose, the homosocial nexus or community of men was supposed to get along, in a way that was (though not literally cooperative) mutually sustaining rather than destructive. Modern associations of masculinity with control, dominance, or competitive, aggressive actualization of self fail to convey the texture of the late medieval masculine world. Chapter 1 sketches that world and explains why I believe that English culture at this time saw guile, trickery, or craft, especially but not necessarily where it led to dishonest dealings with others, as essentially incompatible with masculinity. In contrast, a social manhood involved "trueness": an open and uncomplicated honesty wherein a man's outward expressions corresponded to his inward intentions.

It is not hard to see how a society that valued stable relations among male peers would have valorized this kind of transparent honesty. But there was more to a mature social masculinity than this. The literal home base for a man's social identity was his household. It was the tangible form of his place among his peers. From the household, a man looked outward to his peers and was open to their scrutiny. Chapter 2 argues that for a man to behave irresponsibly with respect to household and property diminished a masculine identity—whether that meant wasting his own money, abusing his servants or tenants, sleeping with his neighbor's wife or daughter, allowing illicit sex in his house, or battering his own wife into a coma. A household identity showed how a man would behave among his peers: whether he would respect them and what was theirs and deal with them fairly. I refer to this set of concerns under the rubric of "husbandry," to underscore how the marital status of husband and the word's other contemporary meaning of "good manager" were closely related in a masculine identity.

My analysis of this kind of evidence shows us a form of masculine identity we can describe as a social self (not a term I invented; see chapter 1 below). The social self was a primary identity in late medieval society where community was so important. Everyone, male and female, had a social self, and no two were exactly the same. Social rank, regardless of sex, accounted in part for its size and shape. Yet a masculine social self was symbolically much larger, more rounded, and more visible than a feminine one; it took up more social space. We can imagine it as a three-dimensional but amorphous figure whose distinctive shape is formed through the pressures of all the other social selves around, above, and below it—and its own reactions to those pressures. Getting compressed, flattened out, or stretched thin diminished masculinity, but so did a too-aggressive expansion or protrusion that threatened to damage the self's closest neighbors. This imagery just underscores the way that individual identity came through relation to others; it was not precluded by it.

But there is a lot about masculinity that does not fall under the themes I have discussed so far. I realized that I had to consider the male body and its meanings in their own right, for several important reasons. First, the masculine values of "husbandry" had a lot to do with self-restraint or self-command. A man clearly demonstrated that self-command with respect to the body and all of the appetites and passions the body generated. The careful moderation of sexual passion positively augmented a medieval social masculinity, partly because of the disruptive effect of extramarital sex on relations between male peers. Demonstrated genital sexual activity was neither the center nor the linchpin of a masculine identity. Consequently, even a celibate clergyman had investments, arguably crucial ones, in the values of husbandry and mature masculinity. Judging by their disputes, clergy were just as concerned as laymen with defending their place among male peers. So it seems clear that the social masculinity of the late medieval clergy was fundamentally the same as that of laymen, despite their celibacy.

As chapter 3 explains, however, the body has a significance beyond the outwardly social. In fact, it is a crucial link in my argument's movement further inward, conceptually, toward more personal and interior aspects of identity. This only makes sense, really, for the premodern world, where external physical features could be taken to indicate or express essential internal traits of individual character and temperament. Masculinity was one such physically expressible feature. The male body was more on display during this period, due to changes in men's attire, than ever before. And as far as their means permitted, men seized on versions of these revealing, exaggerating styles no matter how many preachers sermonized against them. I do not think they were primarily dressing for women. Rather, the clothes displayed both wealth and a desire to be in fashion (a new concept). In both ways, they affirmed a man's social presence among others. And the masculinity of that presence was underlined precisely because only men could wear such clothes or undertake such a performance. Surely, the awareness of being on display expressed masculine self-confidence; it confirmed the way the wearer felt about himself as a man and the way he wanted his male peers to perceive him.

Clothing was not the only way that an individually perceived masculinity could run afoul of normative prescription. As we see in legal and extralegal records, both laymen and clergymen might have felt the need to obey a standard of masculinity that was plainly at odds with the sober and moderate ideal I described initially. Modest control over the body in all its expressions, including speech, supported a prudent and responsible masculinity by making it more socially credible. Yet for self-control to be meaningful, one had to have something to control. Especially (but not only) among young men, masculinity could demand the open indulgence of bodily appetite (in drinking, fighting, and illicit sexual acts) just as powerfully as authority might insist on its strict restraint. So even in a patriarchal society, masculinity might not necessarily mean adherence to patriarchal authority. Significant in itself, this complicating factor makes it all the more appropriate to make some effort to conceptualize an interior masculine subjectivity for the late Middle Ages—a subjectivity that is something more than just the reproduction in miniature of a society's disciplining instructions.

Where, however, to begin? And what should we look for? The records of social life reveal what people did, and only tangentially why they did it, or what they wanted. When they do reveal these things, what we get are conscious intentions. Interiority, however, is just as much concerned with what the subject wants unconsciously: wishes, desires, dreams, which have not met the censoring authority of perceived cultural demands. To understand masculinity, we need to get a sense of the particular set of unconscious wishes and desires that may characterize a masculine identity.

We find these things in a not-so-obvious place: fictional literature, as I argue in chapter 4. In this final chapter, I interpret a variety of late medieval romances to sketch out a generalized template for masculine subjectivity. Many romances dramatize the struggle of a central male character to establish himself in a masculine social identity. Guided by psychoanalytic theory in its recent revisions, I take the interpretation one step further to explore how the romances also dramatize the psychic conflicts inherent in a masculine gender identity. For example, the young Perceval, in the romance that bears his name, leaves home to follow feats of arms and join an all-male cohort, against the protests of the mother who kept him away from that world. *Sir Perceval* is more explicit than most romances in making masculinity depend on a turning away from feminine (maternal) influence toward a milieu centered on an idealized paternal figure, with whom the central character therefore identifies. But versions of the same program turn up in many other romances. Not coincidentally, this basic plot structure is the same as the revised psychoanalytic scheme of masculine gender identity formation: a disidentification, in early childhood, with the femininity of the mother and a new identification with the father. (Remember, these processes are unconscious.) What is the connection?

In an era of literary history long before realism, the contents of fiction exist in, at best, an oblique relation to social reality, and it makes most sense to treat them as fantasy, as expressing something that lived reality cannot admit. Putting the question this way leads us logically to psychoanalysis, because it is the most powerful theory explaining how what is latent (unconscious, and thence often repressed) gets transformed, in dreams and fantasies, into a conscious, manifest expression. The romances function like dreams: dreams that solve problems and deal with conflicts that are too difficult for conscious life. The powerful simplicity of their narrative structure, and their sense of magic and mystery, both derive from the fact that they reflect deep and prevalent fantasies in their culture of origin. Those fantasies reside in, and work for, a kind of generalized unconscious—what I call the literary subject.

Many of the problems in the romances involve desire, a form of need: need for attachment, for closeness, for the possession of powerfully attractive objects, masculine and feminine. I have already mentioned how the masculine social self depended for its existence on relation to other social selves. Analogously, modern psychoanalysis tells us that the individual or private self can only exist in relation to others as well. But the romances fantasize desire and need out of existence, either by denying them or by guiltlessly killing off their objects; these texts close the masculine subject off, effectively denying that a subject exists in relation to others. In psychoanalytic terms, this subject is deeply narcissistic, either dealing with its objects solely as extensions of itself (as if created for its own needs) or repudiating them completely. It is especially noteworthy, and understandable, that such a masculine *private* self should be a baseline fantasy in a society where masculine *social* identity demanded exactly the opposite: incessant day-to-day relation, dependency on others, at least the appearance of transparency and a lack of secrets, and very little true privacy. This is not to say that the society created or "caused" the fantasy, but rather that it did nothing to counter it, and in fact reinforced it.

Moreover, although I have presented these interior, psychological meanings of masculinity last and at the end of a progression, I am emphatically not saying that they are the essential meanings to which we reduce all the others. Rather, they complete a fuller and more rounded account of the way masculinity worked in a historical context. In both social and psychic frames, masculinity in late medieval England was significantly defensive; conscious vigilance kept the masculine social self in balance with its most important others, male peers, while equally vigilant unconscious defenses kept a masculine private self together. Those aspects of identity interacted in a way that reflected the world late medieval men inhabited—a world we have indeed lost, but not as long ago as we might think.

———— ✳ ————

CHAPTER ONE

False Thieves and True Men

MASCULINE IDENTITY FORMATION IN A SOCIETY OF STRESSES

ENGLAND after the great plague of the 1340s was not a warrior society, not a capitalist society, not a secular democracy, not a "feudal" society, not a hunter-gatherer or nomadic society, not a society of widespread industrial employment (or chronic underemployment). It was a society of complex social stratification, itself shifting in small ways over the period 1350-1530; of considerable economic insecurity; of cultural transformation, especially with respect to literacy and discourse; of great inequality of wealth. Even very common people might be very mobile (because they had to be); a smattering of education, at the very least, reached possibly a large number of them. Town merchants, urban patriciate, and rural gentry were intermarrying, blurring the bounds between urban and rural society. In general, mobility, flexibility, and change were well within the reach of more people than we would commonly think.[1] In other words, late medieval England was no more susceptible to interpretive reduction to a set of sociological rules than any society that succeeded it. Consequently, generalizations about the way its inhabitants confronted their world are on shaky ground from the beginning.

The same applies to the meaning of masculinity. Here, in addressing the social and cultural context supplying this study's evidence, I want to give a sense of how certain features of the world surrounding male subjects might have worked to shape the formation and maintenance of a masculine gender identity, in its social and private dimensions. These features—trends, customs, and practices—impinged on men particularly at crucial life stages, during adolescence and young adulthood, when they were being socialized into the community of men that would be their most significant lifetime frame of reference. They represent *man*hood, understood quite literally. As such, they bore most heavily, perhaps, on men of the lower and especially middling orders of village and town.

All social historians of the Middle Ages share the frustration that the sources tell us the least about the largest part of the medieval population, the peasantry. But, despite the problems involved in trying to say anything very specific about rural subjects masculine or feminine, our analysis still benefits from a vision that builds them in, so to speak, from the beginning and is willing to admit the considerable variety of their world. The towns contained far fewer people, but the modes of life possible within them were so significantly different (and documented in such comparatively generous detail) that they demand equal attention.

The suggestions I can make about the meanings of manhood determined and shaped by constitutive features of these environments are necessarily speculative and not amenable to direct empirical proof. Sometimes, however, the view is worth the risks of the climb to the lookout.

THE UNKNOWN MAJORITY

First to the country, and village society. Despite research by several generations of social historians, the true variety and breadth of this world remain difficult to grasp, and it is too easy to retain a flat, stereotypic view. But peasant society encompassed a wide variation in wealth and living standards; it was not hived off from the strata "above." Its inhabitants were more mobile and interacted more with the worlds of their social superiors (and their urban neighbors) than we tend to think. For men especially, though most destinies were humble on the scale of the realm's total social reach, there were quite a few of them possible.

L. R. Poos's study of Essex after the plague provides a good example, albeit a special one, of the rural world in which late medieval subjectivities formed. In Essex at this period, most landholdings were small, and there was a high proportion of people who could not sustain themselves on their own land (and, of course, many more who had none) and who therefore had to work for wages.[2] Among the wage earners were, first, servants: usually people in their teens and twenties, who were probably resident in a household and worked for a year or so in each before moving on. They had a high rate of migration among village, town, and country, perhaps even venturing to London, before saving up enough to settle down on their own small holdings. These young migrants were likely the children of the more prosperous smallholders. A high proportion of all adolescents and young adults would pass through this stage, which was just that: a stage, not a livelihood. Yet there were many others still who worked for wages throughout their adult lives; these Poos classifies as laborers. Essex in general seems to have had a high rate of migration (albeit not random and not over very long distances), and only a minority of persons were resident in the same place throughout their lives. A more recent review, though admitting methodological problems, concludes, "It is clear that proportions of households containing servants were generally high" in England and supports the existence of "life-cycle service," in both town and country. Poos's conclusions have been substantially supported by the further research of P. J. P. Goldberg.[3]

In the fourteenth and fifteenth centuries, therefore, social identities—the sense of self in relation to the rest of the world—were not necessarily formed with reference to a static, close-knit, kin-heavy, custom-bound community, even if many people did eventually settle in just such a place. Instead, perhaps as often as not, they were shaped by disjuncture: by departure from the parental home and likely from the parental village; by separation from immediate family and the necessary renegotiation of one's stance in relation to new authority figures, a succession of parent substitutes in the form of masters and mistresses. It meant, as well, the knowledge that this way of living was not unusual, that there were thousands of others one's own age away from home, living the same way. Among them were those one might meet, befriend, fight, or possibly later marry. In all, it sounds like a pattern of life one today would more instinctively associate with urban rather than rural rhythms. The newer research shows that those worlds might not be so far apart.

Age, more immediately perhaps than social class, structured this unstable and insecure world for both sexes. Within it, both boys and girls had to manage adolescence with its emotionally and physiologically fraught changes. Male adolescence, with its vital phases of group socialization, puberty, genital sexuality, and wider responsibility, poses challenges in any society. It is a defining stage for conflict of three principal kinds: socialized contest with peers; engagement with hierarchical and containing pressures; and comparison between self-knowledge and increasingly well-perceived, sharply defined, and effective social requirements. All three of these are and were part of the negotiation of a social self. For male youths, the terms of competition and struggle, mostly against other men, would be set at this stage.

Identity involved awareness that the unsettled stage of moving about was temporary, but also that it was necessary to what came next. That was true both for girls, who might be saving money to get married, and for boys, in whose futures marriage figured as a more distant but almost as indispensable a milestone. Gender identity entailed, in addition, awareness of the difference in those futures. Security was not something either sex could reasonably count on. But for male youths, who experienced a wider range of occupations and environments even as servants, the disjointed and unpredictable quality of late adolescence was especially meaningful. It prefigured the schizoid nature, equal parts competitive conflict and fraternal trust, of the homosocial nexus into which it served to socialize them.

Historians have debated, for several generations now, the effects of the Black Death on all the European societies it touched. In England as elsewhere, despite the great mortality, the subsequent changes were not always drastic and were certainly not universal.[4] Their effects varied greatly by region and between different social status groups. The formulas students have learned for years—that the plague brought about freer access to land through depopulation, prompted the lower orders to challenge authority, and paved the way for the Peasants' Revolt of 1381—can no longer be resorted to with quite the same assurance. Yet, despite the variation (some areas, e.g., Havering in Essex, having been previously so overpopulated that the first plague did not lead to vacant lands), we are still left with undeniable evidence of some changes, especially in rural society.[5]

In sketching out a social context for masculinity, it is more helpful to think broadly. The specific details of actual changes in population levels, wages, rates of violent crime, or economic growth are less important here than the kind of society they comprise. And in combination, the different scraps of evidence we can put together suggest that much less was certain, or secure, in England socially throughout the fifteenth century than had been the case before the plague. Life did not change greatly in its outward forms, its broad structures; the social hierarchies and patterns of authority of 1350 endured remarkably little altered (given all of the pressures on them) to 1530 and after. At the small scale, however, especially in the local community to which most ordinary people primarily related, little shifts accumulated; everyday ways of doing things, which had been taken for granted generations before, gradually faded, disappeared, or changed out of recognition.[6] The idea that this amounted to change in ordinary social relations as well is not new, having been argued by Ambrose Raftis and his intellectual heirs since the late 1960s.[7] But the social historians who hypothesized such change were not, until very recently, interested in gender, and they certainly did not conceptualize masculinity as something to prompt questions about the communities they studied. Making their conclusions speak to issues of masculinity is therefore an act of interpretation in itself.

With respect to masculinity in rural society, perhaps the most intriguing indicators of change are the customs of pledging and tithing. As far as we can tell from the limited number of villages thus far studied, these might represent a primary means for young men to enter the larger homosocial group and negotiate their place within it. Pledging made pairs of men responsible for one another's behavior. If a court adjudged one liable for the consequences of misconduct, the other was to guarantee that the offender would carry out the court's orders to make good; if he failed to do so, the court could come after the pledge instead.[8] Tithing involved larger groups, responsible for peacekeeping, in which boys could first be enrolled as early as age 12. When a youth committed a crime against the peace, his tithing group was responsible for bringing him to the view of frankpledge and could be amerced if he did not show up. Tithing was not only a rural phenomenon; records of tithing groups survive from towns as well.[9] Yet in the village, where there was a smaller range of associations to belong to, it was arguably more important. This enrollment must have signified a certain substance within the community.[10] Thus, the male adolescent, the protoman, acquired a group identity within a larger group. And because only men could become members of tithings, an entire array of social agency, which women could not share, was open to them (hence, certain kinds of conflicts and alliances would not directly involve women). The masculine identity achieved through becoming a pledge, or being sworn into a tithing, was a social one, marking the individual's arrival in a community of peers. And this was, undeniably, an identity inseparable from community, from the group. In this context, the village man's identity was bound up with both recognized status and particularity. Being a *man* meant being responsible for specific male others and knowing that they were in turn responsible for him.

This special belonging, a complex of role, responsibility, and commonality, was reserved for males, but not guaranteed to them. In the overall trajectory of a life, it was only a first step, and it was itself inseparable from regulation and hierarchy. The custom would have allowed older men to regulate the younger and would have fit quite easily into existing

hierarchies of wealth and age. It was certainly not an attainment of equality with peers, only of comparability. It is important to stress, too, that this
group identity did not preclude individual identity or the possibility of deviance. Entering such a group meant answering to its rules, which did not
appeal to everyone; we know that some men refused to find a pledge.[11] It was
only one facet of a social masculinity, to be placed alongside more individual
achievements: marriage, fatherhood, property acquisition or endowment.[12]
Responsibility for subordinate others was built into the household roles of
husband and father, but these were capacities not necessary to tithing or
pledging. The point is that the achievement of manhood in the village was
not necessarily any simpler than in other contexts (town, gentry, nobility)
that we tend to regard as subtler and more varied. What we can reasonably
describe as men's *need* for the fraternal bond of the group came from multiple
sources, beginning with pure material survival but answering also to deeper
psychological needs. It constituted one kind of pressure, and circumstances
might dictate few possible alternatives, few choices other than conformity.
But group identity served to structure individual identity, not to extinguish
it or render it irrelevant.

Tithing and pledging alone, meaningful as they are, cannot universally
illuminate the rural world of the fifteenth century. Olson found that after
the plague, the use of pledging (and of other old village customs) virtually
disappeared in Ellington and Upwood. This may have been because it was
no longer suited to the changed village situation: lower population, more
mobility, perhaps (one infers) less predictability. Evidence about tithings
seems slow to come up in other studies of rural communities. In the Devon
village of Yarcombe, men were still organized into tithings between 1420
and 1455, but the custom was dropped at Havering in 1497 and on several
other Essex manors in the 1480s.[13] So this was not a custom that necessarily
survived the entire period. It is all the more unfortunate, then, that there is
so little other eloquent evidence.

The extinction of pledging and tithing at different times in different
communities points toward the variety in rural life across the country. But
fascinating as such customs are, they may be nearly as important for our
purposes here in their absence as in their presence. The disappearance of
a system formally binding men to each other must have meant, one suspects, that social manhood in the village came to mean something different
later. Raftis termed the disappearance of pledging "the most striking breakdown in the communal discipline," concluding that "villagers now no longer
wished to support one another in this fashion."[14] Even where pledging did

endure, the extant records may suggest that social relations still changed, as in one village where by 1526 the most important relationships between individuals seem to have been not horizontal within a status group (as seemed to be the case pre-1348), but vertical, suggesting the development of status-structured affinities.[15] With social masculinity no longer depending so much on belonging to a community of peers, perhaps other markers (marriage, fatherhood) simply assumed greater importance. It is tempting, from the modern perspective, to think of the breakdown of normative structures as liberating, as facilitating individual agency. But we should be wary of such a conclusion. Where one form of authority loses hold, another often takes up the slack. At Warboys, bylaws and fines filled the regulatory gap. McIntosh argues provocatively that local courts increased their surveillance and punished misbehavior more rigorously after the mid-fifteenth century.[16]

More choice also means less certainty, more insecurity. The man of the period of economic change, or decline or contraction, whatever we choose to call it, had to be prepared for more possible variation to enter his life than his grandfather might have encountered. Poos's Essex sounds like a place where just such a transformation might have happened, especially since, of all parts of England, it best seems to fit the classic postplague transformation pattern. It appears certain that depopulation pushed down rents and gave rural workers increased wages. It is somewhat harder to generalize beyond that, because of the disjointed nature of work for the vast majority of these rural inhabitants. But we also know that Essex had high rates of nonconformance to manorial regulations and other forms of nonconformity, and was of course the seat of not only the Peasants' Revolt of 1381, but also smaller rebellions in the fifteenth century. While the first plague led to little change at Havering, subsequent attacks both depopulated the manor and brought in newcomers from outside, many of whom in turn did not last long there. Something similar happened at Warboys; not only did many of the older families disappear, but there was by 1360 a "marked increase in violence," much of it against officials.[17] This sounds like a rural society whose stresses and relative disparities tended to favor mobility, change, and breaks with tradition rather than the opposite, on the part of the disadvantaged orders.[18] But plagues and rebellions are big, disruptive changes. There is also much slower, more gradual and patchy change. And with change there is also continuity. Increased social mobility for some, and uppity peasants in some counties—even when peasant resistance extended to open rebellion as in 1381 and the 1450s—did not mean that deference in everyday situations necessarily changed, and "by the middle of the fifteenth century a new demographic and economic equilibrium had become established which took much of the former heat out of inter-tenant and landlord-tenant relations."[19] Blanchard's study could be an example of how social change did not necessarily mean increased personal flexibility or mobility, but a different relation to peers. Still, the transformations must have induced some consciousness of a difference with the past and of the obsolescence of certain aspects of traditional manhood.

MANHOOD IN THE TOWNS

The evidence from rural society may be inconclusive, but it is highly suggestive. While customs of pledging and tithing were primarily meaningful in rural settings, the patterns I have discussed have their analogues in town and city. We should, first of all, not envision these worlds as too strictly divided. Small towns were in many ways more like larger towns, in their social texture, than like rural villages. People came to them from the countryside just as they went to the larger centers, and might find in them a variety of occupations and entertainments, possibly a school, and a "meeting place between country dwellers and a wider world."[20] When we take into account the mobility of the period, we realize that the special features of town life (diversity, opportunity, advanced division of labor, specific forms of sociability) were not restricted to residents of the largest centers.

Urban youths found their identities structured by life stage in an even more elaborated, ritualized fashion than their country cousins. The importance of skilled trades in towns made apprenticeship an additional layer in urban youthful masculinity. Servants were everywhere, both male and female. In the early fifteenth-century town, "most adolescents were probably in service with others."[21] The apprentices were a more purely homosocial group. Apprenticeship, and originally even its succeeding stage of journeymanhood, represented a prolonged state of effective adolescence and subordination to paternal substitutes, including susceptibility to corporal punishment.[22] Apprentices in York, Beverley, and Hull in the fifteenth century generally served terms of five to seven years and would not enter the freedom of the city until their early to mid-twenties.[23] This stage seems only to have lengthened as time went on. In Wells, for example, the average length of service increased from about seven years in the fifteenth century to eleven in the sixteenth.[24] Among the many significant restrictions on apprentices, the prohibition of both sexual behavior and marriage theoretically created a condition of enforced chastity, in which they were to spend their most sexually pent-up years.[25]

Apprenticeship could be a rite of passage drawn out almost to the point of losing its transitional quality. Once again, manhood for this fairly ordinary sector of English society was a matter of achievement. The cruel irony of the later part of the period was, we may fairly assume, the increasing doubt about what exactly was being achieved, as economic contractions not only encouraged longer periods of apprenticeship, but also made it less and less likely that apprentices would ever become masters. Still, it does not seem that the culture of urban youths in England ever went to the extremes of the German journeymen of the sixteenth century, for whom sexual misbehavior was the prime taboo among a large, significantly disenfranchised underclass. The very existence of the York journeymen in the fifteenth century as an organized group is shadowy, and they seem to have been easily suppressed by the masters (though they caused those masters undeniable anxiety). Subordinate men in England were sufficiently disciplined by other authorities that they did not need to censure themselves.[26]

Although the world of male youths was regulated most importantly by men and aimed at preparing its initiates to interact and compete with men, it was not a rigidly same-sex environment. Neither in town nor in country life were women routinely separated from the company of men. The relative liberty of young men and women among the nonelite classes in England to meet and choose sexual (and, likely, marriage) partners now seems clear, considering they lived amid the general northwest European regime of life-cycle service and late marriage.[27] Certainly, this was a very different world from Florence in the same period, where young men, whose own marriages might still be more than a decade off, could resort only to each other for their social needs, and to prostitutes and male youths for sexual ones.[28]

We can probably assume, though, that the pressures of the postplague years did not open the same possibility of transformation and variation in masculine opportunity in the towns that may have obtained in the countryside.[29] Exactly how, indeed, whether social life in the towns changed after the plague remains murky. Most research on late medieval urban history has focused on changes in population and economy, and even on those subjects, years of debate have not achieved much of a consensus from the ambiguous evidence. Plague mortality in the towns was probably high, but the visible decline of the towns, in terms of falling population and decaying structures, often did not occur until decades later, after towns had been losing their living residents to the newly less crowded countryside. Nor does the evidence from all towns agree. What this changed situation (where it *was* changed) may have meant for urban social relations remains largely still an unasked question, though Christopher Dyer asserts that "the hierarchy was not changed fundamentally."[30]

To point out the extreme recentness of the cultural valorization of youth may seem like stating the obvious. But in England as elsewhere in premodern Europe, immaturity slanted the meaning of maleness toward the negative to a degree now unfamiliar. The rawest testaments to the importance of *physical* maturity are usually hidden from us by the late Middle Ages. The related vocabulary, however, is eloquent. In medieval England, the words for "young or immature male" and "untrustworthy male," "male of no account," blurred easily together. "Boy" is not to be understood as meaning "male child" before the fifteenth century, and its original meaning of "servant" or "person in a menial position" shifted into a term of increasingly vague abuse—but one applied only to men. In fact, it is hard to find the word "boy" in a nonderogatory or noncondescending sense before the sixteenth century. At the same time, "knave," a common word to designate male children, had a clearly insulting quality when applied to adult men; its dismissive and diminishing connotations were apparent in the Middle Ages.[31] (The concepts for "woman" and "girl" or "maid" are not complementary at all; even where "maid" implies service, it is not derogatory, and of course where it denotes virginity, it is a positive term.)

In both urban and rural society, manhood was an age-dependent form of masculinity. This meant that tensions always existed between competing models of masculinity: between the riotous and the sober, the self-indulgent and the moderate, the youthful and the mature, the unformed and the formed.[32] The mature ideal was the one privileged by social institutions, religious and secular; the disruptive energy of male youth could be equally necessary in defining a masculine identity in formation. This tension was ancient and continued to characterize English (and European) society for long afterward. It was particularly embedded in the late Middle Ages, en-coded in custom.[33] One could argue that the tension possibly increased over the sixteenth century: population grew, and the economy continued to shift, but the social distances between privileged and less privileged men in close association, between unformed men and the men charged with forming them, only increased.

While maturation was necessary for the achievement of manhood, it was not sufficient for it. The passage from boy to man was not a simple matter of chronological age; English custom and law both spoke in contradictory voices about the age of maturity anyway, various ages between 12 and 21 granting various adult rights and responsibilities.[34] Nor were there cultur-ally universal ritual declarations to mark the transition. Instead, achieving manhood depended on milieu, on life path: "For most people in the Middle Ages . . . the transition from childhood to a working career did not imply maturity in other ways."[35] The social and institutional boundaries of adolescence and adulthood were blurry for both sexes. But there was no corresponding *process* for girls. Womanhood did not depend on entering any real or symbolic community of other women. Part of the reason, of course, is that the status of "woman" brought with it no substantial rights or privileges. The most important factors distinguishing women from one another, in terms of their engagement with the world, had nothing to do with age— particularly since, in many legal senses, women might remain in the position of dependent children for much of their lives.

Becoming a man certainly opened more opportunities than becoming a woman, but we need to be cautious in our conception of how much broader that mature range of action was. Graduating from subordinate youth, in a strongly stratified society, could not mean autonomy in the modern sense; Karras's statement that full manhood "required maturity, independence and financial success" needs some qualifying.[36] Masculinity could not correspond to an unalloyed, untrammeled pursuit, expression, or expectation of self-actualization, because that was simply not available to anyone. This appears more sharply from later evidence, as Alexandra Shepard has recently explained. By the late sixteenth century, the prescriptive ideal of economic self-sufficiency and mastery was simply out of reach for many men: the growing ranks of subservient wage laborers and household servants, or apprentices and journeymen with diminished chances of becoming masters. Moreover, women's economic activity made female contribution often significant, so that even supposedly autonomous married men might not be solely responsible for their households' solvency.[37] Both of these factors are obvious continuations of the late medieval situation, thrown into heightened relief by economic changes of the sixteenth century. Positions of dominance and authority were relative, and so the spheres where individuals could exercise freedom and agency ("instrumentality"), were highly restricted. Karras's repeated recourse to the terms "dominance" and "dominate" in describing the essence of medieval masculinity is therefore inadequate.[38] A sense of oneself as a man cannot have been a matter only of proving one's independent mastery of women or other men.

Yet, conceiving medieval people as mired like flies in molasses, within an immobilizing hierarchy, and hence lacking expectations of anything different, is not a useful alternative. The clearest, most appropriate lens through which to view the matter is the concept of *service*, identified by Rosemary Horrox as "the dominant ethos of the middle ages." In Horrox's formulation, service can be roughly defined as any relationship of dependence described by mutual interests. People throughout the social spectrum experienced it in some form, from the most ceremonial sinecures or the most abstruse definitions (even the king had to serve God and was bound by oath to serve his people), to the most menial physical labor.[39]

Passing through one form, one stage, of service enabled a man to undertake another; that is the nature of a deferential and hierarchical society. If he aspired to anything, it was to move upward within, not to escape, a hierarchy of service. There were usually limits on his movement, but with luck and planning, he might not exhaust them in his own lifetime, or that of his descendants. My use of the masculine pronoun here is deliberate; part of being a *man* was a publicly recognized access to that broader range of limits. Both men and women, of course, served others. But men had access to a greater variety of service roles and were useful to their superiors, their masters, in a wider range of ways. For most women, the defining moment came when marriage anchored their service in the home, and to one man. For most men, it came—often also with marriage, but not exclusively—when the balance of their social identity shifted: when their service, in effect, became anchored *outside* the home (which was usually also a workplace) and became a matter of negotiation in the structures of the wider community, among an array of other men. This was a balance between horizontal and vertical social links, a minutely graded series of interpersonal connections, which took account of very small advantages and favors to play off larger ones. To state that "the apprentice was less than fully a man *because he worked for another*" pulls social masculinity out of its context; even masters, despite their greater freedom, had to serve others.[40]

All this sounds like an argument that late medieval England required men to "know their place." But that banal statement of the situation does not sufficiently convey the distinctiveness of masculine identity. By understanding this social world as scaffolded by service, we counteract the blurring effect of that inescapably too-rough modern conception of status hierarchies, see what possibilities a premodern masculinity might contain. The *smallest* increments of status, those that defined one's immediate surroundings, were more important in the process of an individual life than the broad categories (peasant, merchant, gentry, noble) in which historians now think.

Status definitions were not the only limits on personal agency, of course. Late medieval England was laced through, perhaps increasingly, with regulatory forces, against which individual deviance would eventually collide. (It was *laced*, rather than *walled*; with sufficient agility one could slip through the web for quite some time, but one would probably trip up before long.)

Some such forces were concrete and formal, such as the many legal juris-dictions honeycombing the realm. Others were less tangible, like the weight of the "common voice," the censuring or sanctioning capacity of the local community, which circumscribed individual reputations. Still others were discursive, such as the rhetoric of preaching, which sought to cultivate a moral capacity in individual hearts. These different kinds of regulation—sometimes distinct, often overlapping—constituted one-half of an equilib-rium entered by all members of society.

Regulation means more than limitation. It also means the setting of standards, within which individuals measure themselves against their peers. After all, before improving on one's position, one first had to secure it as it was. The interpersonal clashes making intramasculine competition part of the historical record demonstrate men's defense, through their society's institutions and discourses, of a niche, a *place*. The social dimension of a masculine identity depended on this exercise.

LIVELIHOOD, REPUTATION, AND CONFLICT

"Thou art an arrant strong thief. I get my goods truly, but so dost thou not, in for thou hast a saddle to ride to the Devil upon to fetch money."[41] According to witnesses in a defamation suit, this is what defendant John Goodhyn, a Somerset man, said to plaintiff John Horssington on a June day in 1515. Five centuries later, we are left with a flickering glimpse of a moment of stress between two men, one of many such quarrels to land in various parts of the justice systems of late medieval England. This conflict was about words and about livelihood, and that is obvious; it was also about selfhood and gender, and that is not so obvious. It signifies a moment like many others wherein, under the attentive gaze of their neighbors, ordinary individuals marked out their sense of themselves.

While that sense of self depended on many things, gender has to be re-garded as one of its central anchors. Every society presents its members with a set of meanings imputed to biological sex, and every individual, male or female, must respond to those meanings in tracing the route of his or her life. This traffic between the prescriptions of culture and the conscious or unconscious responses of the individual is the most sensible way of con-ceptualizing gender—as a dynamic, with dimensions both "inside" and "out-side" the individual: "Society provides a great deal of "reality" in ready-made form—reality in the form of institutionalized role expectations as well as authorities, agencies of social control, and agencies of adjudication. At the same time, society's reality is never superimposed in a total way on the individual; every person makes something unique of the social reality he or she experiences."[42]

The two sides of gender always interact, yet remain conceptually distinct. No theoretical approach can adequately address both dimensions simultaneously. In the same way, the more precisely one observes sociological phenomena, the further the psychological recedes from view, and vice versa. Since both modes of understanding are necessary, the study of gender as an aspect of identity therefore calls for a "double discourse": an equally concerted and subtle attention to both sides of the conversation, acknowledging that both interior life and cultural patterning require their own appropriate frames of reference.[43]

This discussion therefore begins with the outward, socially legible face of masculinity. Historians, especially, tend to be most comfortable with this side of gender, being accustomed to seeing social life as *social* and as documented by behavior, especially misbehavior. Handling the record of behavior seems less problematic for historians than that of the psyche, because the interpretive move that takes the reader past naive literalism seems mostly to be a matter of description in context: explaining the wider processes and pressures (usually cultural or political) that determined the reasons for the record's existence. This is reading gender through *documents*, rather than *texts*. Documents seem (at first glance) to contain, however buried, some degree of "factualness," and although we need to be somewhat more adventurous in our approaches to grasp the essence of gender-as-meaning, this is at least a place to start. No one could deny that sexual difference underpins some important social divisions through the powerful meanings for which it serves as a substrate, even in the early twenty-first century. Yet the inescapable socialness of premodern society, the fact that individuals could only thrive within a carefully sustained framework of community interactions, loaded the social aspect of identity, of being a person, with even more crucial importance.

In turn, the structural and cultural elements of late medieval English society (law, custom, discourse), beginning with the language itself, declared that personhood was a masculine state. In English, "man" could mean a male adult, as it does now, encapsulating the powerful cultural association of masculinity with maturity. In the poem titled by its Victorian editor "The Mirror of the Periods of Man's Life," "man" quite definitely means "male." The life stages described in the text are modified by the possessive "his"; the subject "he" is advised to go to school, to "Oxford, or learn law," and the twenty-year-old is tempted "at the tavern to make women merry cheer." Not only does the poem figure mankind as male; the choices and temptations enumerated therein were not those of female persons, of any age. Lechery's advice is that "you recklessly scatter your seed." Envy is cast as overambition: "Keep your foothold, and seek to pass by the best." At thirty, the man boasts he is "full of manhood and might"; manhood here is definitely a male sense of power and strength, not humanity.[44]

Confusingly enough, though, "man" could also mean "human being" in general, a connotation that only became uncommon in the late twentieth century. More strikingly, "manhood" could mean "the qualities and characteristics of male adults," either actual or ideal; it could mean "the state of being adult and male." *Or* it could mean "humanity," the quality of being human, or (substantively) "the human race," as we might now put it. Though grammatically genderless, the English language still conflates maleness with a default setting for humanity: the baseline norm. If the category "man" overlapped with "human being," with all the virtues that distinguished humans from the rest of Creation, little was left that was positive, having any substance, for the category "woman" to contain. Concepts and values keyed to sexual difference (manly/womanly, male/female, masculine/feminine) thus inevitably cast the feminine in terms of lack, insufficiency, and subordination. There is neither need nor room here to detail the well-known social bases and manifestations of women's second-class status, but one might keep in mind their limited rights in property and before the law. Manhood and legal-social personhood were crucially intertwined. Being masculine, being manly, depended on being a man in society.

An entire body of written evidence developed around this particular requirement. Much inner conflict, played out in behavior, occurs when individuals experience disjuncture between their knowledge of themselves and their reflection in their immediate outside world. This is the province of reputation, whose borders appear when breached through public insult. Reputation could be defended in any number of ways. In that act of defense, a measure of the plaintiffs' subjectivity (mediated, of course, by scribal translation and formal convention) becomes legible to us. To show how this works, I offer here readings of some representative disputes—not the florid outbursts that led to violence or bloodshed, but more mundane, slow-burning, complicated quarrels over the social faces of men's lives: good name, household order, the shifting complex of community relations, as recorded through legal actions in two very different, but important, late medieval courts. When John Goodhyn called John Horssington a "thief," they were men living in a society where power and authority were profoundly identified with maleness. And when Horssington decided to take Good-hyn to court, he engaged a legal system where men comprised the vast majority of the litigants and one hundred percent of the staff. Before masculinity caught the attention of gender studies, this would have seemed unremarkable, merely a fact of patriarchal life. It is that, and also more. It allowed Horssington, and the scores of men like him who litigated over conflicts like this, to draw on deep-laid linguistic and cultural meanings of masculinity, a code mutually understood among men.

Most late medieval people negotiated their lives in a local world that made intrusive and ubiquitous interpersonal demands: a world of gossip and nosy neighbors, literally and figuratively thin walls, customary obligations, and a constant and inescapable consciousness of one's precise relation, current and potential, to whomever held whatever degree of power or influence, great or small, in church or guild or town or county or royal court. If the arguments against the existence of a premodern private subjectivity make any sense at all, it is in this context. Modern privacy, especially in the sense of extensive control and choice in one's contacts with others, was impossible to achieve, and so this cannot have been the primary defining aspect of identity for the vast majority of people. The more pertinent unit of subjectivity for us to consider is, as David Gary Shaw argues, the "social self" (a term of the early sociologist George Mead): that "bundle of perceptions held about an individual by a social world."[45] Shaw's heuristic helps to overcome not only the problem of the generally irretrievable private premodern self, but also rigid and anachronistic distinctions between individual and society. While demarcated by social relations, the social self is still a self, illuminating "how different similar lives can be."[46] I would add that this does not mean premodern Europeans had no concept of the individual or conceived their own identities solely in terms of belonging to a group. Social pressures did not seal premodern persons into a limited range of inflexibly formed identities. Their shape was in motion, formed by push and pull, between inside and outside, psyche and culture. The social self was what defamation suits sought to protect.

Some courts reveal this more consistently than others, and I have focused here on two: the diocesan consistories, representing the church courts, long the forum for moral regulation, and the court of Chancery, to which persons despairing of justice in their local courts petitioned. Both these courts produced plentiful and detailed written records. At this level, lawyers were involved, and litigation was not cheap, which means that the very poorest and most marginal men are not represented in the suits. But neither, as far as we can tell, was the world of these courts exclusively that of the wealthy or powerful. For this, there is more than one reason. The middling orders, in fact, had the most to gain or lose in terms of reputation. They could afford to take greater risks than the poorest, but at the same time were far less insulated from the consequences than were the great nobles and upper gentry.

My use of legal records to get at such a question may seem at first both unremarkably obvious and oddly naive. Premodern legal sources have long attracted many historians who do not specialize in legal issues, as they document aspects of life where gender operated: marriage, sexual (mis)behavior, honor, reputation. And yet recent scholarly opinion has emphasized a healthy suspicion toward legal documents. Are they not, after all, discursive products of those disciplining and punishing regimes of official power responsible for the very illusion of subjectivity? Are they not as determined by fictive intentions and rhetorical techniques as the most outlandish romances? How credulous must one be to think they represent anything like reality?

There are several reasons not to be put off by these entirely valid cautions. First, legal records are especially important for masculinity, not only because they document specific behaviors and reactions to them, or because they express social codes. Rather, they are a site of significant cultural work. Catherine MacKinnon, writing in 1983, was able to envision even the late-twentieth-century state as "male in the feminist sense."[47] More than twenty years later, her phrase sounds too blunt, but it has provocative force for the historian. Masculinity must enter our understanding of men's relationships, not only with one another, but also with their societies' institutions. Serving as they did not only to frame disputes but also to enshrine them in writing, the law courts probably loom the largest among the institutions available for the negotiation and reinforcement of masculinity as the baseline of a social self, and they did so because they spoke a masculine language. If gender describes in part the social vocabulary of sexed personhood, whose meaning is contained and supported by public discourses, then the medieval law courts must certainly be "gendered" masculine. Nor should we be tempted, by intoxication with watered-down Foucault, into abandoning them because they bear the stamp of Power, an attitude that not only cuts out the equally Foucauldian concept of resistance, but also applies rather dubiously to the particular juridical systems on which I draw here.

Finally, in an interpretive move to be developed through the rest of the book, I argue that attention to the fictional qualities of nonfiction documents guides us toward an analysis that foregrounds the discursive and linguistic dimensions of gender. Such an approach has more in common, perhaps, with modes of interpretation more often found in literary studies, wherein language transmutes latent meanings into manifest expressions. Applying this method in historical analysis helps us to connect social and behavioral manifestations with a defensible model of premodern subjectivity. This priority has guided my selection of documents; in studying the defamation suits, I have concentrated on surviving witness depositions. Depositions come mostly from suits at the instance of individuals, so my approach does leave out an entire class of prosecutions (the "office" cases). But this restricted scope has real strengths. Unlike the terse entries of office cases, depositions allow close reading. And instance cases are valuable because they describe limits; they show us what men who could afford it felt worth taking to court.

A brief comment on method here: Charles Donahue, Jr., leery of the temptations of the "interesting" but unrepresentative case in church court records, warns against undue attention to deposition evidence, which (because of its formulaic and tendentious nature) cannot be taken as literal documentation of lived reality. Donahue advises historians who use legal evidence to emphasize quantitative rather than textual analysis, looking for statistical patterns leading to conclusions that apply more generally.[48] While Donahue's concerns are understandable, they are also unnecessarily limiting. There is no reason why the conclusions of "macro" quantitative analysis and of "micro" textual analysis cannot together contribute to a useful synthesis (and "together" need not mean "in the same study"). Moreover, Donahue's preferred approach is only partially useful to address questions about gender, whose fundamentally discursive aspects we cannot quantify. As for the "interesting case," we cannot afford to ignore any possibly valuable piece of evidence, no matter how atypical, given the rarity of documents that speak in even the most oblique fashion to the experience of ordinary medieval subjects. Episodes—stories—are not like statistical "outliers," those data at either extreme of a numerical range that one discards before performing a chi-square test or calculating an average. The extreme and the atypical show us what is possible in a society, the limits of its capacities, and what has to happen for certain forms of experience to be accommodated. Keeping a sense of proportion and perspective is the responsibility of any thoughtful reader. So I have no qualms about using the "interesting case"; indeed, the more interesting, the better.

FALSE THIEVES

By modern standards, the masculine insult vocabulary of defamation suits seems odd. If asked what insults men are likely to offer one another, most of us—drawing on our own observations—would probably name terms that are in some way sexual.[49] In late medieval England, however, we see very few defamation suits brought over accusations of cuckoldry, and only one has ever been traced to an imputation of sodomy.[50] Suggestions of sexual passivity, incapacity, or incompetence are quite absent, and yet one suspects that such insults were probably not any less offensive 500 years ago than they are today. On the contrary, perhaps they failed to surface in court because men dealt with them informally. It would be unwise to speculate about the specific means without the evidence. But we have to keep in mind the limitations of the evidence we do have. Suing for defamation is a formal treatment of speech offenses; these suits, technically, reacted to repeated, premeditated rumor, which according to canon law had to be intended to damage the victim's reputation. Words blurted out in anger were not *supposed* to form the basis of a suit.[51] As often happens with rules, this one seems to have been tested with some frequency. Nevertheless, defamation suits may largely exclude an entire species of masculine reactions to injurious words: the immediate defense against an insult. It stands to reason that sexual mockeries could fall into that group. In 1512, a London plaintiff's witness, prodded in a kind of cross-examination, admitted that "one bad word requires another."[52] Taking the next step, turning insult into defamation, required some sober assessment and reflection, not to mention budgeting: the channeling of emotional drive into cognitive process. Bringing a lawsuit has never been a matter of impulse. Only really serious injuries would warrant it.

We know from other times and places, including our own, that dishonor through words can lead to physical conflict between men. So it would make sense to seek an answer among the records of petty assaults, including those leading to homicide. Unfortunately, the medieval English criminal records are not very forthcoming about provocation, verbal or otherwise. They usually simply describe the assault and say what was done with the offender. Moreover, English law was not favorable to those who committed violence and claimed provocation through verbal insult.[53] Individuals' defenses of their own actions, including provocation, have almost totally disappeared from the historical record of crime, if in fact they were taken down in the first place. The English records, though vast in their general surviving volume, are somewhat inferior in this regard to some that remain from France or the Mediterranean world.

The sex-linked patterns in ecclesiastical defamation suits have long been known. Women, who toward the end of the sixteenth century increasingly constituted the majority of plaintiffs, were primarily concerned with allegations of sexual looseness.[54] But unless there was some complicating circumstance, such suggestions very rarely exercised men, who far outnumbered women among plaintiffs down to 1530. John Frenssh of London, for example, sued in 1472 only *after* his alleged fornication (with more than one woman) had landed him in a civic jail.[55] In a 1475 London case, the defense invoked sexual behavior in trying to discredit a witness named Thomas Carpenter, allegedly a common adulterer who had been punished for sleeping with two women. But he was also declared to be a destitute pauper: a person of no account.[56] Both these examples, with numerous others, involve (as even these brief statements show) a number of other masculine concerns besides sexuality itself. The record of male litigation in this era over sexual aspersions as such is largely a silent one, with the occasional provocative exception. This does not mean that sexual behavior had no consequence for masculine honor, but the subject of masculine sexual reputation is best reserved for consideration a little later.

John Goodhyn, with whom we began, was not original in flinging the word "thief"; that was in fact the insult most commonly taken to church courts by late-medieval men, at least on the evidence of the six best-documented dioceses.[57] Before the late fifteenth century, this term always appears as a specific accusation of theft ("you stole such-and-such"), in line with the original canon-law definition of defamation: the public and injurious imputation of a crime carrying temporal penalties. Only in the later fifteenth century did nonspecific accusations ("you are a thief") begin to be actionable.[58] Perhaps, then, a more pragmatic explanation exists for the absence of certain sexual insults for men: such slurs simply were not actionable under the canon law that governed defamation suits, since they were not accusations of punishable crimes (although an accusation of sodomy, punishable by a church court, would have qualified, even before its Henrician criminalization). But by the early sixteenth century, regardless of legal theory, church court defamation practice had undergone a near reversal. Partly under enforcement of Praemunire legislation, common-law courts took over accusations of offenses punishable at common law, and general slurs came to constitute the only kind of defamation regularly sued in the church courts. These institutional changes have generally been discussed in terms of legal history: in particular, the power relationship between the ecclesiastical and the expanding secular courts.[59] I think they are equally important in having changed the terms of legal discourse on an issue on which language and gender so clearly converge. Church court defamation suits by men now bristled with words like "whoreson," "whoremonger," "perjurer," and the all-time favorite, "thief."

The usual explanation of these patterns has been, rather vaguely, that men sued over insults that injured their standing in the public fora of work and commerce.[60] Perhaps male honor was grounded in livelihood. Shaw comments, "Commercial slanders attacked the basis of much urban honor and the reputation upon which your livelihood was founded."[61] Certainly John Goodhyn, in emphasizing that he earned his living "truely," drew the lines of insult thickly around work and fair dealing. Livelihood often cemented a man's relations with his social equals; they might be established and defined through kinship and marriage, but they were enacted through work. If slander cost a man people's trust, he could quickly find that the intricate network of relations sustaining him within the community crumbled in a sort of cascade reaction. Trust could make the difference between eating and not eating.

This may only be part of the picture. Some recent work on Britain around 1550–1700 has begun to question and refine the perceived sharp division between the bases of male (public, nonsexual) and female (private, sexual) reputation, showing that men might well be at great pains to limit public knowledge of their (hetero)sexual misdeeds, and that women might defend their names in terms of livelihood. Such studies demand of us subtler thinking about both evidence and interpretation. Yet these scholars employ the far richer surviving legal records of the Elizabethan and seventeenth-century courts, with which medieval evidence is difficult to compare.[62] Further, while this approach shows us the effects men feared, it does not explain how slander would produce the necessary mistrust among those who heard it. In order to understand that, we must examine defamation as a social and linguistic phenomenon more closely, moving from its most literal to its most metaphoric significance.

Particularly with the earlier suits, where allegations of theft are specific, it seems difficult at first to see the connection to gender. The defamatory utterances, often not given in direct quotation, seem really only to tell us what was said to have been stolen, and in this there is considerable variety: a hat, some yarn, some fruit, the iron chain off a plow, a horse, a knapsack containing ten pounds sterling, and on and on, with no discernible pattern. I would argue, though, that even at this most elementary level there is more to be said. Certain objects do come up more than once. This may reflect simple practical realities, such as how easy some things were to steal undetected, or how valuable something was considered to be and hence "worth," in a sense, defaming someone over. The latter group might include substantial sums of money, gold, jewelry, or large livestock such as cattle, sheep, or horses, all of which come up with some frequency. Small objects of low to moderate value would fit into the first category: pears and plums, figs and raisins, or chickens. These are the kinds of things a poor person might steal, possibly someone who was hungry.

Accusation of theft is not a simple matter. Alleging a substantial theft paints the slandered person as an abusive plotter: someone with whom to be wary of entering into transactions, someone not to trust. Calling someone a petty thief is different. In the small medieval community, a petty thief would be a person of no account, someone with no social self. Consider the chicken: small, plentiful, easily carried off and consumed, and something just valuable enough to make its loss credibly injurious. Joan Reason, for example, landed in court for saying that Robert Smyth had stolen and sold or disposed of her hen and chicks. Smyth had supposedly also taken the goods of another man, but attention quickly focused on the chickens. Both witnesses, while adducing different information, stressed that the story had made the rounds of intimate conversation: it was commonly told, in Smyth's presence, in the taverns of Scholden (Kent), and John Arnold had heard it in his own house.[63] The imagined act of stealing is only the tip of the matter. Both kinds of allegation would have a more devastating effect on someone with social ambitions, someone who was negotiating the tricky world of social competition and relations, whose position was not yet secure (and few people of the middling orders could claim true security, even in contemporary terms).

The horse thief stands in contrast to the chicken thief in the kind of injury possible to a masculine social self. Indeed, Maddern found that livestock, especially horses, featured prominently among the items for which East Anglian juries were most likely to hang thieves.[64] Accused of having slandered John Aleyn as the thief of a horse, a cow, and some cloth, John Uffynton was able to retaliate by claiming Aleyn had a history of shady dealings around horses. Uffynton's "exception," his objection to the witnesses, tried to show that Aleyn was already of ill repute, that his history as a horse thief was known and discussed, and that consequently nothing Uffynton had said could have injured him further. The witnesses retold three previous episodes, dealing with events several years in the past. The more probably scandalous of these claimed that Aleyn had tried to sell as his own a horse that had been in his care. When the horse's owner wanted to reclaim it, Aleyn had fled to sanctuary in a monastery. Robert Hawe, the witness who told this, had apparently functioned as a mediator, effecting an agreement for nonprosecution between Aleyn and the owner (via a servant).[65]

The amounts of money involved in these incidents were not trifling. For his part in the affair, Robert Hawe was paid one noble: six shillings and eightpence. (Hawe omitted to mention that he had been paid; that information came from a different witness.) This is the same amount Aleyn himself had supposedly paid a "man of Thanet," the owner of (possibly) a different horse, as compensation. (Actually, Aleyn gave the man a cow worth ten shillings and got fortypence change, the difference from a noble, in return.) The agreement reached in the monastery was that Aleyn would pay the man he had wronged twenty shillings—fully one pound—not to be prosecuted, though whether he ever did pay, Robert Hawe did not know. In the third incident, Aleyn was supposed to have paid John Walter *thirty* shillings to avoid prosecution over Walter's horse found in Aleyn's enclosure; Walter's widow implied that this had remained unpaid at Walter's death in 1410. (Since she claimed the theft had taken place in 1404, the Walters seem to have been rather patient in waiting for Aleyn to get the money together.)[66]

Aleyn, Uffynton, and their group must have been among the more substantial members of the small town of Sturrey, in Kent (today, an easy bus ride east from Canterbury). One suspects from the case that Aleyn's position may have been more precarious than that of those he wronged. If the depositions actually do refer to three different incidents in three different years (and do not simply reflect the witnesses' imprecise and contradictory memories), Aleyn took considerable risks with his reputation and life for the not-very-secure payoff of selling a stolen horse, though we cannot know his assessment of the competence of local authorities and his relationship to the local justices and jurors. The episode, in a modern analogy, seems reminiscent of the junior Wall Street junk-bond dealer or insider trader who gets in over his head. At first, we have a little trouble imagining just who Aleyn could have been, that he would stoop to stealing horses but also credibly have access to significant sums of money. The word "shady" thrusts itself at us: someone whose dealings, resources, connections are never quite clear (though how extensive such things could have been and remained unknown in a place the size of Sturrey seems doubtful to us today). What puzzles us a little is the consequent bad reputation of which Aleyn was already supposed to have experience, or, at least, the way that is spun in the case. One wonders how there could have been any doubt about a previous defamation, unless it was not generally known—or known among the right sort of people. The first witness for Aleyn, expanding a little on formula, says that John continued and "persevered" in these words among the "good and worthy people," just as another witness *for* Aleyn said he had been defamed among the "common and middling" people of Sturrey.[67] The case suggests, indirectly, some facts of life in the premodern small community. Potential, or suspected, "robbers" or "thieves" did not vanish anonymously into some criminal alternative world, whisked away and dealt with by a taken-for-granted criminal justice system. Either they left town or they did not, and if not, then everyone had to face them every day.

THE LANGUAGE OF THE COMMON VOICE (AND FAME)

Accusations of thievery attacked a masculine social self by diminishing it, reducing the symbolic space it occupied in a constellation of other social selves. There are different ways of imagining this aspect of social identity. In the text and context of these defamation suits, the relevant medieval word is *fama*. To be de-*famed* was to have one's *fama* damaged. Yet *fama* was not only a part or characteristic of an individual. It was inseparable from the spoken word, as implied by the stock legal phrase *vox et fama*, "common voice and fame," on which all witnesses had to comment. In a way, then, *fama* belonged to others as well. It connected a subject to others, both as a lifeline and as a tether on which either side could pull to its own advantage. Men and women both guarded their *fama*, but in a very real sense, men, whom everyone expected to interact more publicly and to whom more social possibilities were open, had more to guard. Masculine *fama* was larger and more variegated than the feminine variety. Defending one's masculine honor meant holding one's place (not being yanked out of it) and preserving the possibility of improving on it.

Surely, though, any insult would have done as well as "thief." Indeed, I will later consider how other kinds of verbal slurs might have functioned against the masculine social self. The more pressing objection to answer is probably a pragmatic one. If an allegation of theft were taken seriously, the reader may be thinking, the plaintiff would be guilty (depending on the value of the stolen goods) of a felony subject to severe punishments, including death. We therefore have to consider how a defamation suit in the church court might relate to criminal prosecution, or the prospect thereof, in the secular courts. I have not found a clear and general answer to this problem. But a church court suit would likely not serve well to protect anyone against determined criminal prosecution, given the length of time required in the different systems. (Using defamation suits defensively, to deflect *genuine* complaints of theft, was, in contrast, a possibility prohibited by Parliamentary statute.)[68] Conceivably, too, where someone had dropped or disproved a criminal accusation yet the unsatisfied accuser continued spreading rumors, a defamation suit would be worthwhile. These suggestions are conjectural in the absence of specific examples.

One Canterbury case, however, does begin to reveal the consequences of a false accusation. In 1416, Thomas Austyn sued Isabella Laybrooke for declaring publicly that he had stolen a pear and an apple from Thomas Broyle's garden and then "applied" the stolen fruit "to his own uses." This comical overstatement introduced a frightening situation. Austyn's witness John Brys, when asked whether Austyn had been defamed amid the good and worthy, declared that it could not be otherwise, because Austyn was arrested and taken to the prison called Speche Hows in Canterbury High Street, where Thomas Broyle moved a civic charge against him to the sum of ten marks.[69] Surely that amount far exceeded the fruit's value, and we are left to surmise, as often, that the episode marked the culmination of some long buildup of grievances between the two men.

Note, though, that a pear and an apple, rather than a horse or a sack of silver, landed Austyn in the town jail. Criminal courts may have been harshest on—that is, most likely to hang—repeat thieves of large-value items. Maddern found that in East Anglia, at about the time of these suits, "the hanging value of stolen goods seems to have been well above the 12d. limit which defined capital felony from amerciable trespass. Over half the defendants [in her sample] were said to have stolen goods worth over half a pound. Clearly this was not the minor pilfering of temporary necessity."[70] In London, "if a thief was a first offender and not a member of what were regarded as the criminal classes, the goods were often valued at less than 12d in order to give him another chance."[71] Maddern suggests that juries' harshness to high-value thieves functioned to protect the richer members of local society—not against the poor, but against their immediate social inferiors, who sought to usurp "the outward signs of their status."[72] Maddern does not adequately demonstrate that such thieves did in fact rank as she has described them. But the suggestion raises intriguing possibilities. Perhaps Isabella Laybrooke deliberately chose trifling items with which to slander Thomas Austyn, knowing that it would inconvenience and humiliate him as a petty thief, but not endanger his life; the stakes in this quarrel were not *that* high.

If we step outside the church court for a moment, another example shows similar animosities at work. It also introduces the next important point, that accusations of theft needed not be explicit, and that they carried a power extending beyond their literal meaning. Around 1470, an anchor belonging to Thomas and Margaret Gylys of London went missing—"Whereupon," as their petition to Chancery states:

> A neighbour of Thomas (your humble beseecher) told Margaret that one John of Moore had brought an anchor on the New Year's day at night to a certain house beside the Tower of London (John of Moore is noted & named to be a suspect person in such matters), to which Margaret said that it was told her that John of Moore was a false harlot; for which said languages and words John of Moore affirmed a plaint of trespass against Thomas Gylys in the Tower of London and caused him to be arrested.[73]

If Moore was, as the Gylyses claimed, a "suspect person," he might have had a hard time in an above-board defamation suit, since a plaintiff needed to have been of honest reputation in order to have *fama* to lose. Margaret did not specifically accuse Moore of theft, but in responding to her neighbor's hints, she repeated a current-day slur. We should mark that slur without getting misled by the word "harlot," which then had a broader, often nonsexual, meaning. The modifier "false" is the more important part of the phrase.

Community relations were under special pressures in London, with its dense population, social mixing, and presence of many non-English people. Among the witnesses there for Richard Faques, plaintiff in a defamation suit in 1511, was a Venetian-born printer and stationer, Julian Notary, who quoted Alice White as follows:

> I pray you, good man Faques, let me have my money. For ye have my money, the which I lost, and that was taken from me and conveyed out of my bag. For ye have it, as it is showed me by a sooth sayer. For he shows me that there was a man in our company that hath a blemish in his face, which he saith has it, and there was none but you that hath any such token.[74]

Notary's English wife, Anna, reported that on a different occasion, when she was in the street passing the Whites' shop, Alice had called to her and asked to speak with her. In the shop, Alice then told the story of the soothsayer and asked Anna: "I pray you, show Richard Faques thus, and desire him that I may have it [the money] again, and that he let it be cast in some corner in my house, or in my garden privately, for else I will trouble him for it."[75]

Alice White never actually called Richard Faques a thief, nor did she say explicitly that he had stolen her money. But her meaning was unmistakable, and her highly unusual reference to a soothsayer reinforced it in a subtle and revealing way. Faques's thievery was so crafty, Alice suggested, that only her psychic friend could detect it. And the soothsayer revealed more than the act; he exposed the "truth" about Faques, that inner falseness betrayed by the "blemish" in his face. Alice was pretending to be tactful when she requested that Fawkes return the money secretly, but she violated any supposed confidence by saying all this to Anna Notary, with servants in the room. (Anna rather unconvincingly claimed that she *thought* the servants had not overheard them.) No wonder Anna said she was *exosa*, very reluctant, to be the bearer of such a message.[76]

The exact circumstances of this case are uniquely its own. As a story, however, it shares some important thematic elements with other defamation suits. Alice White's reference to Richard Faques's face was an oblique variant of what other defamers of men invoked more directly. "Thou false gleand thief, sayst thou that thou beat not me?" said John Rayner in 1424 Yorkshire, while in Norfolk in 1505 William Saxmundham defended his alleged defamation of Peter Melton thus: "He said ill to me, he called me gleyed-knave."[77] *Gleand* or *gleyed* means "side-glanc[ing]," or in modern terms, "shifty-eyed." This is how a thief looks out at the world: planning, watching, assessing, as if casing the joint.[78] In the dispute between John Aleyn and John Uffynton, described above, what set the whole series of memories in motion was Uffynton's verbal challenge to Aleyn, rendered in Latin as "Deponas capucinum tuum quia respicies ut fur et latro": Take off your cap, for you look like a thief and a robber.[79] "Look like" here nicely covers both the transitive and intransitive connotations of *respicies ut*; Aleyn resembled a thief because he "looked" like one under his cap.

For its part, the "corner of the house" to which Faques would have to return the money recalls a York case of 1406, wherein William and Matilda de Malton found it necessary to disprove rumors that they had stolen a valuable horse from John Cookfield, rector of Thormandby. The case is provocative in the roles it assigns to man and wife, respectively. Cookfield apparently said that William had taken the horse with Matilda's "advice and express consent," and that while William had actually led the animal away, Matilda was the one who informed him about it and told him where a bridle was to be found. And where had that bridle been? Hanging in a "certain dark corner," as one of the witnesses said Cookfield had told her. So according to Cookfield, Matilda was the brains behind the job, and although the legal language positions her as her husband's accessory, the implication is the reverse. William is both subordinated to and identified with his wife's feminine guile.[80] Corners, dark places, the hidden, the subtle are not masculine spaces.

This scheme is most graphically drawn in Thomas Katerik's 1512 suit against Alice Pykman. Katerik was a servant of the landlord of Alice and her husband John. Witnesses claimed that Katerik had come to Alice's house to confiscate some livestock because she and her husband had not paid the rent. Alice was provoked to angry words. According to the first witnesses, she said, "What, will you drive away my beasts? You come more like a thief than a true man."[81] The next witness, elaborating this contrast, claimed she said: "You deal like no true men, to come thus in at my back gate, and to distrain my cattle; if you had dealt well by me, you would have come in at my front door."[82]

Alice Pykman knew the weight of the words that she had been accused of speaking. When questioned, she claimed that the rent was not due, and that she had barred the gate against Katerik because she thought he would try to get into her house through the windows to take away other movable property in addition to the three cows he was driving before him. Moreover, she claimed she had said nothing beyond "then you do like no true men."[83] I suspect that she, or her proctor, used this phrasing because it was just vague enough to make its defamatory value uncertain, even under the emerging rules in the London consistory. The juxtaposition with thievery, or with doors and windows, made it too dangerous.

The contemporary imprint of masculinity thus emerges through the meta-phoric imagery of the house and yard: real men do not slip in through the back gate; they con*front* things, at the front door. Even defamations for spe-cific thefts are always for stealthy, hidden theft: *furtive surripuit*, "stealthily took away," is the standard Latin phrase, and for good reason; the relation between the English words (stealth/steal) mirrors the Latin (*fur* [thief] / *furtive*). Of course, this similarity reflected in part the ancient priorities of English law. Even "the early codes see the difference between an open and a concealed act (as in the original distinction between manslaughter and mur-der, for instance, or robbery and larceny) as being far more crucial than that between a premeditated and an accidental one."[84] But although both kinds of crimes were still crimes, no one ever seemed to defame a man as a thief by claiming that he walked up to the defendant and snatched something out of his hands. Robert Sedle, as he recalled his conversation with a Canterbury defendant, had been explicit on this point. Sedle had, he said, remarked to Richard Laurence, "I heard that you said that William [Salter] took away a chain belonging to Henry Newelond." Laurence affirmed that he had said so. Sedle then asked, "How did he take it, stealthily or not [*furtive vel non*]?" and Laurence replied, "For certain, he took it away stealthily, and I'm willing to prove that, because I saw how [William] was carrying off a chain signed with Henry's sign, and he carried it from [Richard's] boat to his house."[85]

This rather stagey account of a conversation was obviously shaped to highlight the most slanderous aspersions; there could almost have been a wire on Sedle. But in its very tendentiousness, it reveals the most defamatory issue: stealth and furtiveness. The implied distinction here is not really between men who steal things and men who do not. Rather, it is between two gendered meanings. The thief, by definition a sneak thief, is merely the most common personification of unmanliness. As Philippa Maddern observed in the writings of fifteenth-century commentators, "manly knights . . . met their enemies 'out in the open field' or 'in the midst of the field'; they did not sneak up and attack treacherously and furtively."[86] The redoubtable Norfolk gentlewoman, Margaret Paston, warning her husband to beware a suspected enemy in 1448, wrote: "I know well he will not set upon you manly, but I believe he will start upon you or on some of your men like a thief."[87] We begin to see why the Chancery petitioner Davy Johns, bemoaning his unjust imprisonment, chose to emphasize that the oppressive sheriff of Wiltshire "right piteously leaves him in prisons among thieves." Though not perhaps the most dangerous, these were the most tainting companions for the reputation of a respectable man like Johns.[88]

Thievery represented not only stealth but also deceitfulness. English culture treated with extreme suspicion the wilful presentation of things as something other than what they "really" were. Thieves were, often explicitly and always by suggestion, *false* thieves, and "false" was an adjective liberally used against men, who could also be false "harlots," "extortioners," and "heretics." (Female "whores" were more often "strong," a mere intensifier.) A witness said that John Horssington had provoked an insult by telling John Goodhyn, "Thou art a false harlot," to which Goodhyn retorted, "I would the falsest of us both were hanged."[89] In 1495 London, "Thomas [Austen] said to Thomas Lowson . . . 'Thou callest me false man behind my back, why do you say so?'. And the other Thomas replied . . . 'Nay, I called you not false, but ye be a false man to me in your dealing.'"[90] "Edmund Wilkins was a false and an untrue man" was enough to provoke a suit in Norwich in 1521.[91] And of course, one who lies is also false. Two days before the Wilkins case, the Norwich court heard that "John Breise said that Richard Barker 'was a false knave and falsely forsworn.'"[92] The unmanliness of false speech in particular was a long-lived construct. Two centuries later, Joseph Addison remarked:

The great Violation of the Point of Honor from Man to Man, is giving the Lie. One may tell another he whores, drinks, blasphemes, and it may pass

unresented; but to say he lies, tho' but in jest, is an Affront that nothing but
Blood can expiate. The Reason perhaps may be, that no other Vice implies a
Want of Courage so much as the making of a Lie; and therefore telling a Man he
lies, is touching him in the most sensible Part of Honor, and indirectly calling
him a Coward.[93]

Addison's analysis was directed at his elite Augustan audience, for whom
cowardice violated a ritually demonstrated "Honor" among upper-class
equals. Unfortunately, the middling orders of 1500 had no comparably acute
commentator on such matters, so we are left to conjecture. I think they would
probably have agreed on the seriousness of slandering a man as a liar, but
not because it made him a coward. After all, fear was part of ordinary social
relations for all but the most powerful, and middling folk had not the luxury
of bravado; lawsuits were risky, but "Blood" endangered even more. Rather,
they would have recognized in Addison's comment just the familiar deep
horror of falseness in men. That continuum of subtlety, hiddenness, and
falseness, on which we find the Maltons' "dark corner" and the craftiness
of Richard Fawkes, eventually reaches our Somerset quarrel. One of the
witnesses there heard Goodhyn call Horssington a "heretic." Falseness in
religion *and* business, then, took shape in that "saddle to ride to the Devil
upon," signifying the kind of forbidden craft only witches employed.[94]

TRUE MEN

The vocabulary of falseness sketches, in negative, the valorized image of premodern masculinity: the "true man." There is no exact modern equivalent
for this meaning of "true." It encompasses "honest," "loyal," "faithful," and
"open," connotations that have largely dropped from the word. Today
we distinguish it from the slippery but somehow comprehensible concept
"real man." This, I argue, is a modern distinction. In 1500, a true man was
a real man was a man who was true. In effect, the "true man" was a premodern *species,* to the point that "trueman" could eventually be rendered as
one word.[95] The meaning of "truth," Richard Firth Green tells us, began
to shift significantly in the late fourteenth century. Its then-newest senses,
those conveying "conformance to fact" and "reality," as we understand
them today, were gaining currency, in competition with older connotations
of honesty. Green suggests, "An intellectual sense of *true* preceded that of
the noun *truth.*"[96] And a word's different meanings can be distinguished at
one cognitive level while remaining intertwined at another. In about 1448,

John Downyng, who leased a property called Wood Mill from the Pastons, complained to his landlords about one William Sybbesoun. Downyng described Sybbesoun as "a strong thief to Wood Mill, for truly he and his wife have procured my servant and my goods, that is to say wheat and rye by the bushel and the half, as thiefly and as un-truly as he might do." This, said Downyng, was "great hurt to me truly." Sybbesoun occupied the close that Downyng held, "so that I gained nothing by it since the time that I came there, and I pay eight shillings a year for the close. And he has been the man which I have trusted right much, and in all this time he has bribed and stolen away my goods, and I knew it not until I sent my servant in to see about it." Downyng asked for help and judicial warrants quickly, "for I know well if he hears of it he will withdraw himself and hide."[97] Sybbesoun was literally a thief because he stole Downyng's crops, and also because he alienated the loyalty of Downyng's servant. These actions were "truly," *really,* done (and "truly," *really,* damaging), and yet they were also done "un-truly," that is, *stealthily and dishonestly,* hence "thiefly." Like the thief he was, Sybbesoun could not be trusted, neither to honor the trust Downyng had placed in him, nor to face his accusers. Instead, he would *hide,* just as he had pulled off his hidden theft. A late-fourteenth-century poem complains that England "at one time was called the jewel of kingdoms, the flower of manhood," but that presently, "Lechery, sloth and pride—these are what England obeys, since truth was set aside."[98]

Masculinity, "true" manliness, emerges from the sum of such evidence as signifying an uncomplicated honesty: openness, manifest veracity, a surface meaning that is the only meaning. The word "truth," and the idea of trueness, had an ancient cultural lineage in English that bore especially on masculinity because of its connection to public discourses deriving ultimately from its oldest meaning of integrity to one's word, honoring the oath: honesty. Indeed, the oath retained great cultural strength even while, as Green argues, its legal evidentiary power was being undercut by the growth of written record.[99] Joan Selson, a Somerset woman, was sued by Nicholas Gyllyng, who accused her of spurning him for another man. Joan was recorded as declaring: "If Nicholas Gyllyng be a true man, he is my husband and I am his wife."[100] These words, quoted by a consistory court witness in Wells in 1514, were used as evidence that Joan had promised to marry Nicholas. Joan's comment may have meant, "If Nicholas is honest about it, he is married to me," or "If Nicholas is true to his word [and, by implication, not cheating on me], we are man and wife." She also meant, "If Nicholas is a real man, he will honor our contract and marry me." Like most marriage cases, this one turned on the pledging of "troth," a word concept semantically underlying "truth." A "true" man was one who honored his oath. But a man who honored his oath was also a "real" man, because only a man who respected the homosocial code enough to deal openly, guilelessly with other men (or, in much more restricted circumstances, with women) could establish a masculine social self and be accepted as a "real man": a "true man" in the modern sense. Displayed by fictional characters and historical actors, knights, servants, and tradesmen, this may be one valence of masculinity not varying with social status.

In effect, trueness opposed not only deceit itself, but all excessive complication and subtlety, all craft and cunning, and by extension, all looking below the surface of things. Elizabeth Clere wrote to the Pastons in the mid-fifteenth century about a man named Stywardesson who was trying to regain her good favor and forgiveness. He approached her on Easter (playing on the holiness of the day), but she did not trust him, because he answered her with "many crafty words," which was "untrue language."[101] Contemporary Winchester schoolboys found "wit is treachery" among their Latin translation exercises, along with "Gift is Judgeman and Guile is chapman." A couple of generations later, other English schoolboys would have read "Truth needeth no painted or colored terms," and then (within a scant few pages of each other) "He did not prove himself a true man to me," "He is double or a variant man," and "He was shamefully mocked when his subtlety was spyed."[102] A cheerfully unsubtle Middle English tale deals with Gamelyn, a young man of exemplary strength. He is strong both physically and, in the poem's terms, morally: he keeps his word and trusts people, because he has no "guile." His evil older brother is therefore able to fool him in their first conflicts. Even later, Gamelyn is tricked because his brother appeals to Gamelyn's sense of honoring an oath. Having rashly "sworn" that he would physically bind Gamelyn, the brother asks to bind him so that he not be "forsworn"—and Gamelyn consents. For such credulity, the text might have set Gamelyn up as a fool, but instead he is its central character and eventually its demonstrated hero.[103] At Havering, Essex, in 1383, John atte Hach claimed that Thomas Burgh "regularly stood outside the doors and windows of John's house, listening to his secrets, and then defamed him to other men, 'so that John has lost the friendship of his neighbors'; for this John claimed damages of 20s."[104] Note that revealing secrets aggravated the offence. After all, if John had embarrassing secrets, Thomas had only revealed his true character (assuming, as seems reasonable, that the defamation sprang from the secrets). Why, in a community-minded environment, would someone who revealed truths not be rewarded rather than prosecuted? The community recognized something like privacy and needed to discourage those who would pry beneath the surface.

IDEAL AND REALITY

The opposition between thief and true man remained in conventional use past the seventeenth century. It appears in Shakespeare (e.g., "'Tis gold which makes the true man kill'd and saves the thief; nay, sometimes hangs both thief and true man").[105] Samuel Johnson's *Dictionary* listed it as current in 1755. Distrust of subtlety and guile became something of a constant in English culture. Evidently, the prizing of trueness, what Lionel Trilling considered under the term *sincerity*, considerably predated the mid-sixteenth-century political and social developments that Trilling thought were responsible for it.[106] Though it is hard to speculate about reasons for this cultural trait, Richard Firth Green points toward the connection between culture and literacy. Under the older English "folklaw," evidence had to be "public, tangible, and incontrovertible."[107] The evidence I have presented here suggests that in such a context, "true" *had* to mean "open" or "patent." Italian society, dependent on written record far longer, placed less emphasis on a man's sworn "word" as the ground of fact. Consequently, "trouthe" in the English sense—that which is sworn to—had less social authority.[108] Perhaps, then, in Italy, open trueness could not become identified with social masculinity in the same way. At any rate, with the important, rule-proving exception of Robin Hood, the English had not the same fondness for the trickster, the duper of peers, the sneak seducer as seems evident in some other European literatures. Jane Austen had the undeniably masculine Darcy declare, "Whatever bears affinity to cunning is despicable." In 1728, Benjamin Franklin, echoing the culture that underlay his own, described a virtuous ideal man whose plain, even ragged homespun clothing, devoid of all artifice, echoed the fact that "he always speaks the Thing he means."[109] By the nineteenth century, Ralph Waldo Emerson "had no doubt that sincerity was the defining quality of the English character.... 'We will not have to do with a man in a mask,' he perceives the English to be saying.... The English, Emerson tells us, are blunt in expressing what they think and they expect others to be no less so."[110] The gendered conception of space in the Victorian home might rely on the same principle: "The drawing room was seen to enforce caution and dissembling on men's speech where there should have been manly directness."[111] And the theme crops up in modern evidence in some of the strangest places. Apparently, pre–World War II soccer-playing styles in England "also mirrored wider working-class male solidarities. There was no room here for 'fancy dans' or, indeed, for the deviousness and dishonesty associated . . . with the 'feminised' foreign traditions of playing the game."[112]

The insults that drove men to the law courts converged, therefore, on a deep psycholinguistic node with great cultural significance. So the sense of injury that prompted litigation over allegations of falseness was, at its root, an injury to masculinity. The insult reached far below the social surface for both the victim and his neighbors, lending critical force to their actions. That deep-rootedness might not seem obvious at first. But the simultaneous existence of related manifest and hidden meanings is neither a twentieth-century invention nor foreign to medieval culture. Biblical exegesis depended on latent meanings attached to open expressions, as Augustine of Hippo explained in the *Doctrina Christiana*.[113] The same dynamic underpins the vocabulary of literary criticism; allegory and metaphor, for example, make no sense otherwise. Modern linguistics, too, makes a distinction between "surface" and "deep" structure: as Noam Chomsky noted, "the surface structure is often misleading and uninformative and our knowledge of language involves properties of a much more abstract nature, not indicated directly in the surface structure." And in dreams, it is argued, deep structures are organized into manifest forms using transformational processes analogous to those of language.[114] Within the human mind, where language, emotion, and cognition converge, the perceptions of the conscious mind encounter cultural attitudes encapsulated in language, itself thrusting its roots well below consciousness. Such interior processes underpinned and generated the motive energy of the more obvious social dynamics of insult. This explanation is not incompatible with the idea that lay masculinity depended on economic reliability.[115] Material consequences were not unimportant: quite the contrary. But for a man to be called "false thief" did not mean that others would now think he went around stealing things. Nor did the accusation work because (or just because) it meant that he would now sell fewer shoes than someone else. It was much more insidious precisely because it was not defined in terms of what he did or did not *do*. What mattered was what he *was*. (A petition of 1433 asked that those who profited by thieves and "common women" no longer be considered "worthy of truth nor to bear witness of truth"; tainted by association, their oaths should no longer have value in court.)[116] For reasons they would probably be hard pressed to explain, his neighbors now perceived him as a diminished man;

his social self had shrunk. There was something wrong with *him*, and that was what he must disprove. The need to do so makes more sense, makes him more of a human being, if we credit him with sufficient interiority to evaluate and resent the mismatch between his social self—that "bundle of perceptions," now grievously (or unjustly) altered—and his private self.

THE LEGAL RHETORIC OF MASCULINITY

These lawsuits do much to trouble simplistic notions of gender polarities in premodern England. I suspect that despite years of nuanced studies, gender is still most commonly seen in terms of an opposition of strength and weakness, or of dominance and submission. This cannot be the whole story in a deferential society, where prescribed responses to social status determine attitudes to power. The dynamic I am proposing instead, between positive masculinity (true, open, straightforward) and negative unmasculinity (false, hidden, tricky), is confirmed and refined by the evidence of petitions to Chancery.

With their direct appeal to legal authority, Chancery petitions seem tailor-made for the kind of analysis made famous by Natalie Zemon Davis: attention to the "fictional" aspects of the documents, that is, how components are selected, or omitted, to make the kind of story that will suit the purposes of the author.[117] But this takes some careful handling. Not much is to be gained by ringing postmodern changes on the open supplicatory gestures of the Chancery petition form, a formal falling to the knees through phrases like "meekly beseecheth," "humbly showeth," "poor orator," and "gracious lord." The petitioner's abject helplessness, before both a powerful oppressor and the chancellor's mercy, is assumed *a priori* by formal convention. So petitioners to Chancery had to find a more subtle language to cast themselves in the desired terms, through the lawyers who drafted their requests.[118] This language builds on the patterns I have outlined. Chancery petitioners frequently draw attention to their oppressors' guile and craft, an arsenal of deceit that no honest man can engage; "subtle imagination" is a favorite condemnatory phrase.[119] Defendants are forever seen trying to evade the proper channels: they refuse bail to release the plaintiff, undermine juries, fail to show up for arbitration hearings. So they are not only devious but unreasonable, in a society where reason was a masculine attribute. This applies even to a case where the petitioner is the one accused of assaults and menaces.[120]

In my first example, from the 1520s, one man claims that another has stolen his goods and abducted his wife. But our ability to understand this as a straightforward case of violent harassment is complicated by the petition itself. The file in fact contains two petitions, two versions of the same events, both brought by the same man, but telling different stories. In one, Edward Divrych complains that Walter Lankeforth "entered into" his house at Tavyton in Devon and "from thence conveyed your said Orator unto the Castle of Lydforth within the said county and there imprisoned him by the space of 14 days or more." Lankeforth then ransacked Divrych's goods and chattels, to the value of 40 pounds "or more," and "also from this at the same time took one Alice, wife to your said Orator, and conveyed her to such place as he liked, and so continually keepeth her still as his concubine," threatening Divrych with death if he "once come near her or took any suit against the same Lankeforth."[121]

The second version is a little longer and more colorful, but not necessarily more complete. There is nothing here about Divrych being imprisoned. Instead, Lankeforth "came upon him . . . with force and arms, that is, to wit, sword, buckler, and other weapons defensible against the peace, intending to have murdered your poor orator, and . . . broke and entered into the house of your said suppliant, and took his wife, and used her unlawfully at his pleasure." Then, a surprising shift: "Soon after that, the said Walter and the wife of your said suppliant condescended, appointed, and between them agreed to break up a coffer of your said suppliant's." A detailed list of things they took follows, including "certain writings and Bills obligatory wherein certain persons stand bounden unto your orator in several sums of money." Divrych takes pains to draw attention to these documents again as the petition ends; they are discussed far more than the other stolen goods or, for that matter, the wife, who in this version has no name.[122]

The two stories differ in more than the sequence of events. The first version I described is a narrative of oppression in which Divrych is a passive victim: a mere "husbandman," as he describes himself, made destitute by the mysterious and threatening Lankeforth, who appears out of nowhere, imprisons Divrych, and takes away "all the goods and chattels," plus Alice. Divrych stresses, even more than petitioners usually do, that fear for his life keeps him from living in his own house, and that he is now too poor to sue Lankeforth at common law. The language is simple, sticking to a main sequence of events. In the second version, we have a very different Edward Divrych: he calls himself a tucker, a man with a trade (albeit not an exalted one), who by implication opposes this honest status to Walter Lankeforth's known bad reputation. Lankeforth, who has no descriptors in the first version, in the second has become a "yeoman, a riotous person and evil disposed." Divrych the tucker is a man of means, a creditor to no small degree. His main concern is to recover those bills. Even though Lankeforth intended to murder him, there is no mention of fear or poverty. And befitting such a man, the language becomes precise and legalistic: the attack took place on the twenty-third of July; Lankeforth came "with force and arms" to "break and enter," classic legal phrases that precisely categorize the criminal offense; he took the wife "unlawfully" and keeps her "contrary to the law of holy church and the law of this land," where the husbandman only invokes "God's laws."[123]

Two distinct strategies of masculine self-creation through a legal instrument are the result. Edward Divrych the tucker is aware: he knows the law, he knows there was a conspiracy to rob him, he knows in detail what was stolen. He is not a dupe, but a man prepared to exercise his rights. Edward Divrych the husbandman's posture of helplessness underscores his honesty and good intent; he would go after his wife, if only he could. Both strategies serve, in part, to elide any speculation about the wife's own agency in all this, though that is exactly what we are bound to wonder. We may never have any other evidence about the untold "real" story: a story, perhaps, of an unhappy marriage, a wife's relationship with a man more powerful than her husband, some outstanding debts, and a husband left to recover what he could without revealing himself as a hoodwinked cuckold. We may never know which version is earlier, whether one is a draft, whether the second followed the failure of the first, or whether both were prepared at the same time to see which sounded better or to provide a fallback option. It does not matter. A gendered reading brings out the masculinity of these narratives, both in the subjects they create and in the way they sideline a woman's role to make this a matter between men. And this would be true even if the tucker's and the husbandman's tales turned out to be among those "legal fictions" in which the common law of the fourteenth and fifteenth centuries increasingly dealt, requiring parties to make creative claims in order to get their cases into court.[124] Gender is written into the fictions. Being alert to the careful fashioning of that masculinity facilitates our retelling of "what happened" because it allows us to read in negative. When someone loudly calls our attention to one thing, it may be to distract us from something else.

The pragmatic objection to these readings would be that litigants' concerns simply echoed legal definitions. Covert theft was a recognized crime, as were breaking and entering, lying in wait, or coming with "force and arms." This is perfectly true. It was also greatly convenient for male litigants. Whether in the church courts or Chancery, cultural and legal meanings reinforced each other, underscoring on more than one level the significance of masculinity. Of course, women used the law to defend their reputations and property, but for women, no matter how virtuous, law and language simply did not cooperate in the same way. Trueness, so essential for masculinity, did not completely lack meaning for premodern femininity. But "true women" existed in English culture only as special examples. The contexts in which women could defend themselves as true, or be praised in those terms, were very restricted. Legal definitions and cultural misogyny worked together to obscure women's agency in the documentary record: in Chancery petitions that react to false accusations of rape, the woman is always said to have made the accusation at the instigation of some other man, reflecting not only most women's legal nonpersonhood, but also the contemporary notion of woman as too intellectually vacuous and instrumentally weak to have done such a thing on her own.[125] The wife of the parasitic William Sybbesoun, apparently as thievish as he, elicited no special comment from the Pastons' outraged tenant. In more ways than one, the fault was not hers.

Ironies abound here. For the moment, we note that the narrative techniques shaping these masculine personae (selection, omission, screening, allusions) are the exact functional analogues of craft, subtlety, and guile, those feminine-gendered qualities, perhaps deplored in the same documents that employ them. The whole process therefore depends on a kind of contract between petitioner and petitioned, a tacit understanding that certain things are to be left unsaid, hinted at. This agreement seems to say: "Tell me a good story, and I will overlook the holes in it that we both know are there— the parts we both know you're not telling. If your story is good enough in itself, I will give you what you want." This saves the appearance of honesty, with no meaning beneath the surface, whose importance for masculinity we have already seen. Observing this is much easier than thinking that medieval chancellors, and their staff, were so credulous as not to notice obvious inconsistencies. Neither must we credit them with some mysterious logic, which we, looking back from the "modern," therefore cannot appreciate.

That leads us to a broader, social-cultural irony bearing directly on the importance of trueness. Maddern has suggested that the famous letters of the Pastons hint at a shift in values over the fifteenth century. In the older system, wherein outward actions were most important, "true" (i.e., honorable) *intentions* could justify crafty and duplicitous *acts*. The newer values held integrity to mean faithfulness to one's inner moral convictions; "heart's ease" comes up in the letters as a factor in deciding a course of action. Such "oneness," a publicly observable agreement between inner intention and outer expression, meant a consequent frowning on those who were "double" (which was exactly the word Elizabeth Clere chose to describe the crafty Stywardesson).[126]

What Maddern identifies as an older ethic is detectable in some other sources still circulating in the Pastons' time. A sermon exemplum tells the story of a royal justice who killed his rapist nephew after having "drawn him to him with fair words." The nephew had previously escaped punishment for his offense. The uncle did not number the killing among his own sins on his deathbed, claiming that he "did it not for wrath and vengeance, but...for equity of rightful behavior." He was exonerated when the eucharistic host flew into his mouth despite the bishop's refusal to administer it to him.[127] In the romance *Amis and Amiloun,* the title characters' loyalty and fidelity to each other matter more than their relationships to anyone else: wives, children, superiors, even arguably to God. Their bond ("friendship" seems too weak a term), signified by a cementing oath, stands above all other considerations, even moral ones. No problem has a straightforward solution—except for the simple principle that the protagonists' bond is to be honored at the expense of all else. Hence, one man can help the other to get out of a lie, enter a tournament under false pretences, even kill his own children in order to end the other's misery. Trickery, for example, seems not to be unmasculine here, because it is put at the service of maintaining the integrity of the masculine oath and bond.[128]

Romance literature, however, offers only fantasy solutions, which we should understand as the fulfilment of wishes unrealizable in real life. It could be that, as Maddern suggests, the "true man" had recently gained in his long-held significance. The more interesting reality, however, is that despite that possible change, it was no easier in the fifteenth century than before to act out the ideal in real life. If anything, the various pressures on the middling and gentry orders meant that guarded self-presentation, crafty appraisal of one's enemies, and even some pushing and fudging in the legal system were inescapable strategies, especially for the men on whom most of this public life devolved. In the surviving letters of the Paston, Stonor, and Plumpton families, such calculated dealings are taken for granted.[129] This suggests a contradictory, and probably neurosis-inducing, state of existence. Men needed to maintain the *appearance* of honest guilelessness while at the same time watching their backs, deploying all available means, often not above board, to maintain every small advantage. There was great potential for backfire. William Plumpton's servant Greene wrote to him with the bad news that a man whom Plumpton had paid to get writs of *supersedeas* had deceived him. Plumpton could not, however, sue the miscreant to recover his money, because "the matter is not worshipful."[130]

Despite the ubiquity of such underhanded dealings, open and visible responses to verbal injury had their definite uses. Defamation itself was not necessarily open only by virtue of being spoken aloud and known after the fact among neighbors. It might deliberately address an imagined audience. In 1517, witnesses at Exeter quoted John Love's slander of Richard Somervyll in such terms: "thou art a strong whoreson thief—a Rope to hang him," "false horse thief—get a halter, hang him up," "thou whoreson thief—a rope to hang thieves."[131] In these phrases we can almost see Love turning from Somervyll to call out to whoever was watching. A response to slander might need to be equally demonstrative or gestural. One bad word may sometimes have called for another; at other times, however, it called for something more formal and elaborate. I close this chapter with some illustrative examples of conflicts wherein the very action of bringing a lawsuit may have been important for its own sake, beyond redressing the potential injury of slanderous words.

In *Chylton and Smyth c. Wylmyngton* (Canterbury, 1416), none of the three witnesses considered the two joint plaintiffs to have been defamed by a rumor that they had burglarized a church. Nobody believed the idea, they said; "all the neighbors" thought it was false.[132] Why, then, would Chylton and Smyth have bothered to sue? Assuming the witnesses' perceptions were accurate, and the defense had not suborned them, the motivation cannot have been to guard against erosions of trust among credulous neighbors. Instead, perhaps the point was to make the recognized gesture of responding to an insult. Bringing a suit could be as much a posture, a symbolic act, as a practically intended one. Showing that one was willing to take the time and spend the money showed how "big" one was, the substance of one's masculine social self. The London woman "who called an alderman a thief when he complained of untidiness outside her house" was surely not referring to any specific alleged act. But most likely she landed in prison not only because she uttered the word, but because she wielded it against a man of substance.[133] Was she really worth bothering with? Was his honor not sturdy enough to withstand such an assault? Again, the gesture of response may have been more important than any actual injury.

The two related suits that Richard Knapton brought against Joan Mudde and her husband Roger in 1527 show how multilayered a dispute between men over speech could be. Against Joan, Knapton claimed she had accused

him of having a child through an adulterous affair and then of being impli-
cated in the child's death. It is entirely typical that a slander alleging a man's
sexual irregularity should only come to court when there is something else
involved: in this case, a "criminal accusation" was a direct consequence of
the sexual misbehavior. But Knapton's positions (the formal list of points
at issue in the case) in fact separate Joan's defamation into three separate
groups. Vague slurs like "harlot" and "Lollard," in the first position, carried
minimal risk of legal sanction and, one would think, were the least substantial in terms of credible injury to reputation. The bastardy allegation was
placed by itself in the second position, indicating perhaps that the sexual
behavior (punishable by a church court, but not incurring criminal penalties as infanticide would) was worth considering on its own. Last came the
more serious, but more outlandish and perhaps less credible accusation that
Knapton had abandoned his bastard child to be torn apart by swine.[134]

So much for Joan. Knapton sued Roger Mudde for a different slander,
which was not sexual. Unlike the positions against Joan, those against Roger
claim *only* vague slurs with no supporting context: "false heretic," "lewd
knave," "harlot," and "Lollard." The witnesses had nothing specific to
say about these, but testified to a more substantial verbal offense. Robert
Cartwright had heard Roger say to Knapton, "False churl, you deal falsely
with my wife, but I'll take care of you without having to lay hands on you."
The "false dealing" was not sexual. Rather, Cartwright said that "[Mudde]
was provoked to call him so because the said Knapton caused the wife of
the said Roger Mudde to be suspended out of the church."[135]

In both cases, Knapton was being accused of shifty, underhanded dealing:
concealing a bastard and trying to squirrel away the evidence of his misdeed,
in the first; pulling legal strings in the other. Even if everyone knew the
accusations to be untrue, it was still worth Knapton's while to show that he
would not stand for them. The tenor of the suit against Roger suggests that
Knapton was spinning Roger's statement as a revenge slur—which itself,
interestingly, involved falseness in dealing with the law. Roger's own claim
speaks to the rights of the husband concerning an injury to his wife. Within
the supposed defamation, we see Roger in turn defending his own social
self, of which his wife formed a part. (The second witness, blurring the two,
reported "whether it [i.e., the false citation] was served of Roger Mudde or of
his wife he can not tell, but he says it was served of one of them."[136]) Roger's
additional comment, "I'll take care of you without having to lay hands on
you," pushed the tension higher and evoked a different masculine discourse.
It demonstrated that Knapton's injury was *worth* personal attack, but that

he had sufficient self-command to restrain himself. This self-command was a careful assessment of strengths and weaknesses, along with a face-saving posture of standing up for oneself: rational, sensible, and protective.

The important thing was to leave no doubt that an injury would be answered.[137] Saying this in a public place, with "the more part of the parish" present, Roger Mudde was able to take the advantage of making public something that was technically private. Exposing hidden treachery (perhaps, in addition, by suggesting that Knapton had tried to strike at him through his wife rather than face-to-face), while presenting himself as open and fair in his "dealing," as responsible for his wife, and as prepared to respond yet reasonable and rational, Roger took the stance of the consummate *man*. Unfortunately for the Muddes, regardless of the community's opinion, the church court sided with Knapton, and both husband and wife were ordered to pay costs. The point, nonetheless, stands: both plaintiffs and defendants reveal gendered motivations in defamation suits. Where the gender in question was masculine, there was perhaps a wider choice of discourses on offer from which to draw.[138]

Both the church courts and Chancery help to qualify the role of the dynamic between institutional structures and individual subjects in producing gender in premodern England. They show us to what extent masculinity was produced through language, and in what relation to the law: the words that offend, the words that can or cannot be brought to court, the way words must be put together to be used in court. The individual provides the impulse setting the process of litigation in motion, but the institution—the law—defines the terms. It sets the rules of grammar and syntax; within these, the litigating subject creates a script that defines himself. When the rules of legal discourse change, the script will necessarily change too. This happened in ecclesiastical defamation cases after 1450. The jurisdictional changes of those years meant more than a shift in power between church and secular courts. Defamation continued to be prosecuted in the church courts over the course of the sixteenth century, and the volume of cases increased rather dramatically. New possibilities for negotiating masculinity had opened up. Reputation, understood less with respect to specific actions and more in terms of character, became more important to more people. When they saw they could litigate over something, they did (it became easier to perceive certain injuries as worth fighting), to the point that by the early seventeenth century, jurists were discussing measures aimed at cutting down on such business.[139]

Fifteenth-century English society was still marked by lordship, by the exercise of arbitrary and informal power through links of patronage and clientage. The expanding formal justice system was still only one among several alternatives available for the redress of grievances. But the law courts refined, restated, and reinforced the values of the surrounding culture, the beliefs held by individual minds. That "mass of beliefs" adding up to masculinity depended on perceptive assessment and social self-presentation—and equally on the more hidden places where language and emotion met. Late medieval English culture may have prized masculine guilelessness and transparency, but the interior supports for that ideal tended more toward obscurity, subtlety, and contradiction: qualities the human mind often displays, no matter how culturally shunned.

———— ✳ ————

CHAPTER TWO

Husbands and Priests

HUSBANDRY (I):
POLLERS, EXTORCIONERS, AND ADULTERERS

Trueness and falseness traced the sensitive zone of the masculine social self at its points of contact with others. Masculinity meant that a man claimed at least a certain minimal presence among his peers. In other words, the values of positive masculinity permitted a modicum of social cohesion between men. Trueness did not guarantee perfectly harmonious cooperation, but it provided a regulatory standard for social relations, a standard invoked especially when men pursued disputes.

Those disputes, in turn, were themselves subject to a regulatory standard. The community of burgesses in late medieval Wells, as described by Gary Shaw, seems to have most prized a willingness to compromise one's individual ambitions and desires for the sake of the group's stability. The community guided its members to limit disputes: not to sue fellow burgesses outside the borough's own court, to enter and abide by arbitration, and so on. The rewards for doing so, for playing the game, could be considerable. Penalties imposed by the borough court, for example, were relatively mild compared to those one courted by trying to circumvent it. The hierarchy of the community did not, however, tolerate insubordination that led to disrespect, defined as "a stubborn and proud heart" or "wilfulness."[1] Within this system, the masculine social self had to know its limits, even as it sought to expand within them.

Moderation, self-restraint, and self-control all shaped the dimensions of masculinity I call "husbandry." This word seems most appropriate not only because it evokes the married state, which so defined mature men's social identities, but also because it usefully brings together a variety of themes most often known by other names. Husbandry included being a "husband" in the modern sense, but also in the now archaic sense of "manager," one who both orders and sustains.[2] The prudent and honorable management of property and household dependents was central to husbandry. It also involved the rule and limitation of the self. In these aspects, "husbandry" means almost the same thing as "governance," the word more often used by historians. I prefer "husbandry" for this broad concept because "governance" has too many modern connotations of top-down rule and dominance, which remain no matter how much one explains the idea of "governance of self." "Husbandry" includes governance, but also puts a strong emphasis on management, care, economy, and prudence.[3] It also implies respect for one's own, which is ultimately a form of self-knowledge. These aspects of husbandry strongly affected a man's place in the social world of men. Good husbands, like good fences, made good neighbors; they also made good masters and good servants.

A verse from the year 1513, deploring the abuses of the times, imagined a future era of justice when "True men might live without vexation; Pollers, promoters, had no domination."[4] In light of my previous attention to the meanings of "true," this text is thought provoking. Its opposition of "true men" to "pollers" is not immediately clear to a modern reader. In searching to understand it, we discover an entire range of meanings, which complement and extend those explored in the previous chapter. Investigating this range takes us a long way around, but the central theme is substance: getting it, having it, losing it, lacking it. Especially in the tangible form of property, substance, and the concerns surrounding it, lent a richly physical significance to the masculine social self.

Substance

When John atte Helde supposedly said that John Loket had stolen a large sum of gold and silver from Thomas Garynton's room at Canterbury, that was not the end of it. Two witnesses both quoted Helde as claiming that Loket had been, in effect, nobody before accomplishing these thefts: that he could not have bought one pair of trousers, or that he was of "no reputation at all." Helde allegedly even said that Loket had gone mad from stealing Thomas Garynton's goods, or perhaps from possessing them.[5]

We can depart from these shreds of slander to trace lines of masculine social identity continuing logically from those in the previous chapter. Helde had dealt his alleged victim a double blow. He tried to erase Loket's place in the community (he is nobody, he has no history) and then to expose whatever status Loket had achieved as false, based on theft. Both these moves, connected to a lumpishly tangible bag of gold and silver, show in what unsubtle fashion a social self depended on the visible signs of substance in property, movable or otherwise. I prefer "substance" to "wealth" here, because "substance" gives a better sense of the way that property provided a kind of minimum requirement for masculine social existence. Candidates for mastership in the late medieval town, for example, might require evidence both of goodness and of goods.[6] Such a person would become one of the "good and worthy" whose opinion counted when a court considered the people among whom a plaintiff's reputation might have been damaged, and we should note that the word for "worthy" here, *gravis*, also meant "weighty"—serious, and literally "substantial." Certainly, wealth always helped. Yet one could be a man, just not a very big man, without being wealthy. One could not, however, be a man without substance. There was a level below which one's lack of material resources put one out of the running, cut one off from the most basic homosocial networks.

The frightening possibility of one's social self slipping away through material ruin was perhaps most immediate in the volatile urban environment. More detailed surviving late medieval testimony to the crucial importance of property comes, however, from those who had more of it. The Paston, Stonor, and Plumpton families were all members of the gentry at different levels, and thus certainly count as elites in the total social scale. Still, even a study that aims to keep more ordinary people in view cannot avoid the famous collections of their letters, simply because contemporaneous letters from more humble social strata are virtually nonexistent.

The gentry provide an exaggerated illustration, like a magnified photograph, of the contemporary investment of masculine substance in property, an equation operating also on their social inferiors. It may seem unnecessary to point out the concern of landed families that the estates that sustained them—their "livelihood," in the eloquent medieval term—be well managed and handed down intact. But I would like to dwell a little on this somewhat obvious theme to show how their property anxieties inevitably assimilated substance to masculinity. Because customs of inheritance and land tenure favored males, the management of property normally fell to men; occasions when it did not were expected to be only temporary expedients. Coming into property marked a masculine life stage (after all, it usually was contingent on the death of a father or another male authority). Concerns over the use, misuse, acquisition, and disposition of property became, by implication, part of a broader and metaphorically physical image of masculinity.

Naturally, where income and status came from land, land always ranked first among the forms of property. Margaret Paston wrote to her more reliable younger son, John III, in 1472: "And the Duchess of Suffolk's men say that she will not depart from Heylesdon near Drayton; she would rather depart from money, but that would not be worshipful for you, for men would not then respect you. Therefore I would advise you to have rather the livelihood than the money ... money is soon lost and spent while livelihood endures."[7] Mismanagement of property troubled Margaret deeply. A year earlier she had scolded her older son, John II, who had succeeded to his father's estate and sold off part of it for the cash return: "I would not wish for a thousand marks that people would think you were inclined that way ... for everyone would think it was through your own misgovernance."[8] To give up land for money made it look as if one were in need of money. It meant turning a stable and securely masculine form of substance into a volatile, promiscuous one to be spent. In a sense, money belonged to no one.

But one could not do without money, either, as John II replied in his own defence. He knew this to be true because he had often been short of it in the past. As a young man, John II joined the king's retinue, and his consequent risky and expensive absences strained his relations with both parents. Part of the strain was financial. Surrounded by more powerfully connected young men, John II needed to cut the figure of their equal, and he wrote to his father, John I, for more money. In 1461, John Russe wrote on John II's behalf to advise the patriarch: "Unless he has money in his purse so he may reasonably spend among them, they will not respect him; and there are gentlemen's sons of lesser reputation that have ten times as much ready money as he does."[9]

In truth, being able to spend liberally on the right things was an essential part of propertied masculinity, and it was obligatory for responsible, conservative fathers just as for possibly reckless sons.[10] John II's courtly ambitions may have made his father nervous, but there were decided risks in the alternatives. During a period when John II was not mixing with the great, someone (most likely Robert Cutler, vicar of Caister) advised John I that having John II at home without visible occupation was causing talk, including suggestions that John I was too cheap to get his son set up properly.[11] More generally, measured liberality cemented relations with great and small. That was part of what "livelihood" was for. At one point in the romance *Partonope of Blois,* the hero Partonope takes leave of his lover Queen Melior to revisit his homeland.[12] Knowing there are political troubles at home, Melior advises, "Prepare for arms and knighthood, and make sure you lack no manhood" (2406–7). This "manhood" must, in classic fashion, involve liberality: "Make sure to give generously; don't worry about where to get the goods; you will have enough from me" (2408–10). And she later sends supplies and gold to aid him.[13] Much later, this pays off. Partonope gives generously to his former enemy Sornegour and his men, once they come on side, and is praised as "manly, courteous, and generous." These recipients "prized him above all others in manhood, generosity, and courtesy" (4853, 4865–66).

In contemporary literature like *Partonope,* we see preoccupations about substance and property dramatized alongside other discourses of masculinity we have come to recognize. The tale of *Gamelyn* does so rather simply and directly. A youngest son cheated out of his inheritance by his false and conniving older brother, Gamelyn regains it essentially through brute strength and full-on assault, turning the tables on his opponents. It transpires that Gamelyn's brother has not only cheated Gamelyn of his inheritance, using it up; he has also kept the profits for himself and not extended liberal generosity and hospitality to their friends and associates as he ought. Upon gaining the upper hand, Gamelyn sets out immediately to correct this social blunder by giving a great feast—using first his brother's share of the property, by way of revenge. This is done openly, broadly; Gamelyn breaks open the gate that his brother has shut fast.[14]

The romance *Sir Amadace* tells a more complicated story of an overspending knight who loses and then regains his social self. At the beginning of the surviving text, Amadace's servants are urging caution and moderation, but Amadace subordinates those values to liberality. He descends into poverty as a result, leaves the court to avoid his creditors, and comes upon a mysterious chapel where a woman sits beside a dead man's stinking corpse. The widow explains that her husband cannot be buried because of his debts, unpaid at his death. Amadace spends the last of his own money to bury the man. He later meets an unnamed White Knight, who helps Amadace but binds him in an oath to share all future gains with him. Amadace then experiences the windfall of a convenient shipwreck and returns to court with money to spare. At the story's resolution, the White Knight turns out to have been the dead man, released from his unburied state. In effect, the White Knight comes calling for his payment, but forgives Amadace of it once Amadace shows his willingness to honor the oath.

Having enough to spare, so that one can sacrifice a bit, is an issue of substance, of material presence, and therefore of masculine social self. Amadace's very traditional, ultimately impractical, and therefore by implication aristocratic, liberality in spending on the dead is rewarded. (He is not made to suffer a great deal in his "poverty.") It brings Amadace honor, but not in a quite logical way. Rather, he has to reenter society through gaining its outward symbols: wealth, material substance. The rest can follow. The test of his oath shows that his honor is true in the most conventionally social sense.[15]

This was fantasy. Sustainable real-life liberality requires prudent management, probably an impossible balance to maintain perfectly: another of those masculine dilemmas. Margaret Paston warned John II, "I want you to beware of giving large gifts and rewards ... for when you need help, they [the recipients] will not be so ready to help you out of what they have. . . . I would wish you to put yourself in his power as little as you may; for if you do it shall be very well remembered hereafter."[16] Social connections established by friendly spending turned all too easily into obligations, as the margin between expenses and revenues could become very narrow. People like the Pastons and Plumptons were always in danger of running behind on their expenses and alienating their creditors, some of whom might easily be their social inferiors, the "servants" (in the broad sense of service I invoked in the first chapter) on whom they depended.[17]

The most prudent way to sustain a credibly masculine social self, then, was through moderation in the treatment of one's own material resources. Miserliness and reckless spending could both ruin a man, make him dwindle into insignificance. This important theme of moderation and self-restraint will resurface repeatedly as my analysis continues. Where substance was concerned, there was, however, another side to the coin. Yoked to the conservation of one's own substance was a more subtle discourse demanding respect for that of other men.

Pollers and Extorcioners

Margaret Paston's warning to John II, quoted above, to beware of overgenerosity in giving gifts, came in the context of another concern. At about the same time, Margaret also advised her son, "Your livelihood has been these two years in such trouble that you cannot profit by it, nor can you take from it without hurting your tenants."[18] As with all landholders, the Pastons' use of their property affected those who depended on them. To abuse or oppress one's social inferiors, for whom a good master ought to care, made one guilty of an offense all too pervasive in late medieval society. The relevant word here, I believe, is "extortion," whose meaning was broader in the late Middle Ages than now. To mark it off as different, I will use a common fifteenth-century spelling rather than the current one. *Extorcion* included the modern sense of applying threats to exact material gain, but extended logically beyond that to encompass all unjust uses of advantage, particularly to deprive or deny another of what was his by right.

Again the masculine pronoun is deliberate, as *extorcion* seemed to be a concept most applicable to masculine spheres of action. Because the ethic of moderate, prudent, and well-governed husbandry was defined as essentially masculine, the *extorcioner* who departed from the standard also departed from social manhood. In the modern mind, masculinity is commonly associated with the indulgence of appetite, with an aggressive realization of self; to be manly is to take what one wants. However, aggressively self-gratifying masculinity dismayed late medieval people who anxiously upheld the value of masculine self-restraint. William Wayte, one of the Pastons' friends, wrote in 1451 concerning some local enemies, "I wish there were a thousand good manly men to cry out against Tudenham, Heydon, Prentys, and Brygge for their false *extorcions*."[19] Men were both the principal extorcioners and those most likely to invoke the topos against each other, though women's voices could articulate it also to useful effect. William Wayte advised John I to orchestrate a public outcry against the Pastons' enemies in the town of Swafham, so that "all the women of the same town be there also and cry out against them also and call them *extorcioners*."[20] Here, the shaming intent of the female chorus was to emphasize how far short of respectable masculinity the offenders had fallen. The relationship between landlord and tenant was especially suited to generate extorcion either perceived or achieved: choosing his words carefully, a London defamation suit witness claimed in 1513, "I called you not *extorcioner*, but I said it is a pity you should oppress the poor tenants."[21] The symbolic vocabulary with which we are now familiar came to bear on these situations. Some of Robert Plumpton's tenants complained they were being slandered as "untrue people of their hands, taking goods by means of untruth," but that actually, certain others were oppressing *them* and living off their goods without contributing anything. Such offenders, extorcioners by implication, sought to increase their own substance by encroaching on that of honest men.[22]

The Plumpton tenants' complaint was the kind of distress that late medieval criticism of such unfair consumption sought to analyze.[23] The Wycliffite *Lay Folks' Catechism* covers extorcioners under the fifth commandment, which prohibits killing, because those who oppress poor folk slay not only their bodies but their souls as well, by causing them to curse and blaspheme. In addition, those who "waste their goods in gluttony, drunkenness, pride, and lechery, and in other vanities" are as bad as thieves, discussed here under the seventh commandment against theft. Such overconsumption deprives poor "men" of their living, their "livelihood," the taking of which makes the taker a "thief and a murderer." In a Wycliffite way, the text envisions such oppression as the theft of inheritance—figured in masculine terms as the extended patrilineal body. Theft here is largely construed as oppression, though cheating servants who do not provide work worth their wages are also scolded.[24] At the end of the section, extorcioners form part of a trio together with moochers and robbers (those who steal "secretly" and openly, respectively), who break the seventh commandment. Naturally, a religious discourse cast theft as sin purely because it was theft, whether committed by force or by trickery. Yet we cannot disconnect these ideas from cultural suspicion of false stealth. The section on the deadly sin of covetousness lists the wrong means of getting things as "by sacrilege or simony, stealing, falsehood, or usury, or other guilery."[25] The "Speculum Vitae," a pastoral treatise of the late fourteenth century, does not use the word *extorcion* in the following extract, but condemns that form of oppression in terms that connect it to other sins of a particular kind: "And it is just the same as physical murder if men spiritually slay a man; that is, when a man enviously holds a deadly hate against another in his heart, or slanders him early or late behind his back, with injurious words and sayings. And anyone that takes livelihood, that sustains life, away from one that needs it, may be considered a man-slayer."[26] Envy, backbiting, slander: these all align by association with stealth and falseness, not as obviously as theft, but unmistakably with the same general flavor.

The experience of extorcion formed the backbone of the stories told in petitions to Chancery and shaped their rhetorical strategies. The narrative intent in a petition to Chancery is to emphasize the petitioner's innocence, on the one hand, and the arbitrary injustice of the injuries to him, on the other. Sometimes the extorcion being protested was literal. In 1448, a youth of seventeen, named Roger Wodecoke, from the Cornish town of Bodmin, suffered a bizarre assault. Roger claimed, in his petition to Chancery, that two men had taken him from "a place called Brynne Water 5 miles [to] the town of Tregoss," where Richard Tregoss, a squire, "bound the head of Roger with a woven string [till] the string broke" (meaning, I think, that he tightened it), "and after bound him with another string till it broke, and then he took a frailing cord and bound him about the head till the blood came out of his eyes and his nose, and then with the end of the same cord bound his hands behind him" (which would have pulled his head back), "and beat him on the cheeks and with a knife cut off his left ear, to the great shame and destruction of Roger."[27]

Roger begins his petition by stating his tender age and claiming that he was in "God's peace and that of our sovereign lord the king" on the Saturday before the feast of the Translation of St. Thomas the Martyr. Dating the incident this way associates Roger with Thomas Becket, a blameless victim of a violent assault to the head, and suggests the impiety of his assailants, that they should inflict such an outrage with such a day approaching. From the Translation of St. Thomas, we then move to the literal translation of Roger from Brynne Water to Tregoss. The assault has three stages of increasing brutality (binding, beating, cutting), and the binding is itself split into three: Richard uses first a woven string, then "another" (bigger, I think), then the frailing cord (a cord big enough to hold together a "frail," or a basket made out of rushes), which doesn't break, because it is the third. Roger is trussed up, his throat exposed like a ritual sacrifice—rather like Isaac, son of Abraham. No angel, however, stays Richard's knife, and the story slams to a stop, as if its own narrative energy had driven it into a wall. Still, it is not quite exhausted; after the usual phrases requesting help, the petition asks for just punishment of this "extorcion," surely a word carefully chosen to reflect the twisting that wrung blood out of Roger's eyes.

So for all the apparent randomness of its events, Roger's story is in fact carefully proportioned for maximum effect. Well-tuned narrative gears propel its linear movement toward a climax, and its allusions do not clutter or weigh it down. In fact, the entire form is an allusion; this is a Passion story, complete with a Man of Sorrows.[28] The point of all its narrative elaboration is to highlight the impossible conflict between a subordinate immature male and his superior in rank and life stage. It is particularly significant that the form of extorcion at issue is an attack on the body. As an adolescent and legal minor, Roger had no substance to call his own aside from his own physical body, and even that was debatable. To become truly a man was to achieve a social embodiment. Richard's assault not only cuts, literally, into Roger's very physical existence, but it strips away part of his social self as well: by cutting off Roger's ear, Richard has marked the youth as a thief. Shame and destruction, indeed; a lot more than flesh was sliced away on that summer morning.

Polling, Cutting, and Loss of Substance

With his knife at the ready, Richard Tregoss personified the "pollers" condemned in the couplet I quoted at the head of this chapter, with whom extorcioners were, for all practical purposes, identical. "*Extorcioners* gape for poor men's goods" and "Polling and oppressing of good men must be avenged" were on adjacent pages of one early sixteenth-century schoolbook.[29] The word "poller" has, in a postagricultural society, largely lost its currency. Its most recent common meaning had to do with removal of the horns of cattle. In the fifteenth century, it was used to mean all manner of shearing or cutting, including barbering. Through this connotation of cutting off or shearing away, it became semantically aligned with the meanings of *extorcion*. Tonsured clerics, their hair literally shorn, might become living puns: one Norfolk clergyman assailed another in 1523 with "Thou art a false polling priest and a shaver, for thou hast used polling, but I will not be polled and shaved on thee."[30] Where clerics' secular involvements incited conflict, "polling" was a concept too tidily versatile to pass up. "I am sorry that ever I served any such poll shorn priest," Robert Pellet allegedly said of the prior of St. Mary's Hospital in London, about 1513, amid a dispute about money owed to the priory.[31] In a symbolic reversal and condensation, the one who bears the signs of poll*ing* thus becomes the embodiment of the poll*er*. But the word's connotations of abuse were not restricted to clergymen, as we learn from the petition to Chancery of John Southwell, servant of a London draper, in about 1475. Southwell's master, we are told, "took great displeasure" against him, commanding the young servant to "poll" the hair off his head. Whether this meant a total shaving or simply a haircut, the point at issue is a subordinate male's control over his own body. Southwell thought "that he was as other servants be and ought for to be," and refused to shear his locks—whereupon, he said, his master convinced a London alderman to authorize Southwell's arrest and imprisonment. Southwell attributed the episode to his master's "malicious appetite," emphasizing the trespass, through ungoverned desire, of one literal or symbolic masculine body upon another.[32]

Property was the most tangible nonfleshly form of the substance comprising this masculine body. Men could experience its waste or loss like the emaciation of muscle, or as the expenditure of a masculine essence, like semen depleted through unguarded sexual indulgence. (The explicit association of the one masculine substance with the other found expression in a fourteenth-century schoolmaster's classroom lesson: a man suffers loss in coition "since money I pay out, and good humor from my own body I spill out.")[33] Lack of self-governance also allowed the masculine social body to contaminate or tear away the substance of other such bodies, as in the rapacious and unjust greed of the "extorcioner" or "poller." In 1513 Essex, William Giller took exception to being called not only "false *extorcioner* and poller" but also "great bellied whoreson" or, possibly, "draff bellied churl."[34] The impact of these insults was likely not restricted to a slight on physical appearance. Great bellies become great for many reasons, but one (certainly in medieval terms) is that they have been filled with good things, possibly those belonging to others. This was the same masculine body Lyndal Roper characterized as "a volcano of drives and fluids which constantly threaten to erupt, spilling outwards."[35] But the damaging energies, of course, pulled inward (polling, consuming), just as they spilled outward.

Oppressing one's inferiors was bad in itself, but in the homosocial world, it damaged a man's reputation because it additionally indicated an untrustworthy attitude toward his peers. The same could be true of poor husbandry of one's own, of the man who "cares not what he spends" or "spends without any measure."[36] It is difficult to understand why else John Topcliff should have sued John Grenehode (Ripon, York diocese, 1381) for imputing to him the "crime" of prodigality. Grenehode apparently alleged that Topcliff was not only a "false man," but a "public and common waster of goods" who had "prodigally consumed and wasted the large part of his goods in wicked and profane uses," and who would indeed waste any quantity of wealth he was able to attain.[37] Given that Topcliff had the right to dispose of his own property, the defamation is hard to perceive unless we grasp the implication of needless waste for his relations with others. The prodigal waster could easily turn into the poller or extorcioner who looked to the substance of others once he had run through his own. Topcliff's lawyer claimed that Grenehode was aiming to derail Topcliff's plans to marry one Emma Erle. A man of Topcliff's status (squire to the archbishop of York) sought a wife who could augment his social endowment, and that meant Topcliff had to get on with Emma Erle's male relatives, as they would have been keeping an eye on whatever property she brought to a marriage.

We should interpret amid a discourse of husbandry John atte Helde's peculiar comment, with which we began, that John Loket's thievery drove him out of his mind. It was a moralistic gloss aimed, like the slight to his social status, at pushing Loket out of the category of people who counted: if a nobody tries to become somebody through shady means, this is the result one can expect. (*Insanum* could cover quite a wide range of observable behavior.) One implication is that Loket reaped the reward of social presumption enacted through unmasculine covertness. The more eloquent possibility, however, is that *insanum* refers not only to the loss of Loket's mind, his mental self-command, as a result of the theft, but ultimately, through a rhetorical displacement, to a more intrinsic deficiency of self-command. The supposed theft was only the ultimate manifestation of a significant failure of masculinity: Loket's lack of respect for homosocial relations, his willingness to trample on his male peers through his desire to grab more (more money, more property, more attention, more prestige) than his fair share—or at least what Helde considered to be Loket's fair share. Once again, a little imaginative speculation is appropriate. Helde's rather wild accusation of theft sounds like the fantasy of a frustrated man, envious of his fellow's success. Late medieval social mobility might be very capricious, in both directions.

Adulterers

The dangers of poor husbandry became especially clear precisely where men were concerned as husbands in the modern sense. Wives counted as substance and, arguably, as property. Peter Idley, in his "Instructions to his Son," deals with the good treatment of a wife in the course of about 60 lines. The emphasis is not on unyielding control, but on benign handling, with an appeal to the son's sense of his own best interests: his life will be easier if he gets along well with his wife, as this will induce her to treat him well. Most importantly, it means she will "keep thy goods, and neither waste nor spend them."[38]

True husbandry is called for here: the wife is valuable property, and as the mention of "goods" suggests, the ideas about her are inseparable from those about property, despite the pious inclusion of references to Adam and Eve and Paul's letter to the Ephesians. Idley's ostensible contrast between patrimonial lands and goods, given by family, and a wife given by "thy Lord eternal," is undermined by the very juxtaposition: it is obvious Idley knows that wives and "temporal goods" are, in his culture, lumped together, and so it makes sense to talk about them at the same time. The end of that stanza bears this out: "Where love is stable God ever sends prosperity and wealth and good increase." A good marriage is good resource management. And as with patrimony, that acquired resource is figured, here explicitly, as part of the husband's own self:

> She is part of your body, remember this,
> And it would be shameful for you to despise your own flesh,
> Or hurt it in any way;
> Never befoul your own name,
> Do not use unclean words, for shame![39]

Of course, in Christian marriage, two become one flesh. But here (as in law and custom), that mostly happens by absorption: the wife becomes part of the husband, not vice versa.

Like other forms of masculine substance, wives were vulnerable to encroachment. Here, the offensive masculine body was a literal one. In considering men's adultery alongside other examples of poor husbandry, my object is to recontextualize it and tone down the buzz that the concept arouses in the modern mind, which focuses on the sexual aspect. Certainly, I would argue, male adultery could be a serious matter in the late Middle Ages, but its seriousness had most to do with the discourses of husbandry: adulterous men were like pollers and extorcioners, misgoverning themselves and so encroaching on the substance of others.

A London woman named Elizabeth Montagu sent a rather pathetic petition to the chancellor in the late fourteenth century, complaining that her husband Thomas had so wasted and misspent his goods in the course of his adultery with a woman named Margaret, that Elizabeth herself was in danger of being imprisoned for debt.[40] The metaphorical dimensions of Elizabeth's discursive strategy should be familiar by now. The male body of Thomas, unproductively wasting its sexual energies in adultery for the sake of personal indulgence, becomes by implication identified with the property, the estate, which is also being frittered away and wasted. Thomas's private, physical body and his public, symbolic body, the body which cuts a figure for him in the social world, have become one. As the wronged wife, Elizabeth used Chancery's concern for material injury to construe this adultery as an offense against her, since it put her in material danger. But male adultery was probably more commonly understood as an offense against other men.

Any act of adultery, of course, involves at least three or four central characters, of which historians have probably most neglected the male adulterer. A historical sense informed by feminism finds it intuitively easy to see the masculine significance of cuckoldry, which involved an unfaithful wife.

Imagining men offended by women escaping their control is not difficult, and to be fair, it does seem to sum up the common premodern perception of both cuckold and adulteress. Men's adultery, in contrast, brings us up against the famous "double standard." The obsessive premodern restriction of female sexual behavior has been well documented in historical scholarship. It leaves one to imagine, through easy binary contrasts, a paradoxical cartoon vision of male sexuality: indulged with impunity and yet (or therefore?) in the larger picture strangely unimportant.

Historians of medieval sexuality have not so much created this impression as failed to supply any sustained corrective to it. Ruth Mazo Karras discusses the relative weight in medieval culture given to men's versus women's sexual transgressions, using mainly pastoral literature (*Dives and Pauper*) with a smattering of church court evidence. Men and women were charged and purged in *ex officio* cases at an equal rate, but the partners of "whores" were not accused. She concludes that lay and clerical (by which she means learned religious discourse) models differed on sexual behavior generally, but that they diverged most strongly on that of men. For example, it seems possible that lay opinion tended to excuse simple fornication, which the church condemned (albeit ambiguously).[41] Yet from this kind of comparison we lack a sense of the range of possible lay opinion.

Shannon McSheffrey's analysis of London court evidence is probably the strongest statement yet to emerge in criticism of the "double standard." In the context of documented prosecution of men for illicit sexual behavior by London church and civic authorities, McSheffrey explores the case of a prominent physician whose wife had unusual success in suing her adulterous husband for a judicial separation, and argues that men's extramarital liaisons could draw censure from their peers and harm their reputations:

> Respectable people shunned men charged with sexual misconduct: when Anastasia Reygate accused Thomas Hay of committing adultery in the home of a local bawd, witnesses reported that many people, including his wife, avoided his company and there was a good deal of murmuring against him. Similarly, when William Boteler told people that John Stampe had carnally known Joan Folke, the "status and good fame of both Joan Folke and John Stampe were greatly injured."[42]

McSheffrey's assessment, which has influenced my own, casts the consequences for adulterous men in terms of the premodern code of "governance": "Men also had to guard against public sexual misbehavior if they wanted to retain good reputations. Their governance, like that of women, could also be related to their submission to proper authority, but men's rule was much more frequently self-governance. Sexual misbehavior that showed their lack of control of themselves, their misgoverned state, could result in disreputability and ill fame."[43]

The patterns McSheffrey identifies are best understood in the wider concentric contexts I have mapped out so far. For a married man to sleep with another man's wife was probably worst of all, directly violating the substance of another man. But for a married man to fornicate with an unmarried woman was not much better. In fact, the woman's marital status likely made little difference concerning the male adulterer, because most women, married or unmarried, formed part of some man's social substance, whether as wife, daughter, or ward. (One exception, of course, was the prostitute, who as "common woman" belonged to everyone and no one.) Here, the issue at stake was homosocial cohesion. Within that nexus, the adulterer risked his vital connections, his credit. That credit had value both among his peers and also hierarchically within a logic of service. Bad husbandry of one's own interests, which included allowing them to jeopardize those of others, called into question one's ability to further those of a master or patron.

Such a network was the very conduit of reputation, common voice, and fame, which took shape in the testimonies of court witnesses. Here, a lack of substance could be damning: "Disreputability was frequently connected with poverty, honesty with substance."[44] In 1510, a Norfolk witness felt obliged to stress that Richard Richardson was of honest reputation despite his poverty.[45] And so a favorite tactic among litigants trying to discredit their opponents' male witnesses, through the legal process of "exceptions," was to invoke poverty. But this was not all: such allegations often associated sexual and social forms of disrepute. In chapter 1, I mentioned Thomas Carpenter of London, reputed to be both a multiple adulterer and a pauper. In 1491, London exception witnesses testified to an even more extensive and lurid combination of sexual and nonsexual misbehavior with respect to John Waldron, as McSheffrey describes.[46] Indeed, we learn of William Boteler, who sexually slandered John Stampe and Joan Folke (see above), from exception witnesses who also said that Boteler had slandered another man as a thief.[47] Exeter exception witnesses in 1517 were asked about both the poverty and adultery of one male witness there. In another case, they had to depose as to the possible drunkenness, pauperhood, adultery, and swindling of George Mason. William Ashe, yet another Exeter witness, reportedly got his servant girl pregnant *and* did not pay her the money he had promised her for her marriage. Thomas Daishper had a suspicious woman in his house *and* was also a perjurer.[48]

Perhaps these examples help to explain why alleged adultery by itself rarely formed the basis of a man's defamation suit in this period, at least at the level of the consistory.[49] Even where men's adultery (or fornication) appears uncomplicated by suggestions of nonsexual disrepute, it needed to have some extreme feature besides the act itself. William Langford, said some Exeter witnesses, was reputed to live in adultery with a woman, not just to have slept with her once or twice.[50] Recall John Frenssh of London, who not only got caught, but had been carrying on with two women.[51] McSheffrey's statement, that "as with women, sexual impropriety in men was seen as part of a complex of generally bad behavior," is valid, but perhaps implies too much equivalence in the situations of the two sexes.[52] For women, sexual honor was the linchpin, without which the entire structure of a social self collapsed. Men's sexual (mis)behavior, unlike women's, had little meaning unless it could be related to the other parts of their social lives, in which it was a secondary factor. It reflected, as I have said, on their "credit," and hence on the trust that bound them to other men. The worth of public testimony, called in question by legal exceptions, was precisely that kind of trust.

The patterns I have argued from late medieval evidence accord, to a certain degree, with those identified in some modern anthropological studies. David Gilmore, in his synthesis of worldwide research, provides examples from far-flung societies wherein masculinity is identified with provision and demonstrable generosity with respect to resources. The "big man" is expected to share wealth, the unmanly man consumes more than he produces.[53] The temptation here is to a kind of functionalism: societies valorize fairness with resources and censure dishonesty and greed regarding them, in order best to support the community as a whole. We should probably resist this interpretation for the small traditional societies that Gilmore describes, and certainly for fifteenth-century England. In the English context, there were too many socially elaborated variables, too much cultural texture, for husbandry to reduce to resource conservation for the good of all. The community or complex of men, the homosocial nexus, was as much a belief as a reality—shifting and rolling like logs underfoot, snapping from horizontal to vertical frames as its male constituents sought to manipulate it for themselves.

HUSBANDRY (II): THE HOUSEHOLD FROM INSIDE

Only a partial understanding of masculine identity results from observing collisions and invasions between masculine selves, as in the previous section.

We now need to explore how the same values of husbandry, which kept different selves in manageable relation, functioned within the boundaries of a man's social self, in the form of his household. This was a matter of married life. In the Middle Ages, and for long after, marriage cemented a man's social identity as certainly as it secured and made respectable a woman's. Marriage meant that a man became the head of a household, and so it granted an authority that subordinate men, such as servants and apprentices, lacked. It made his children, products of his sexual relations, legitimate, and secured the transmission of his property.

However, given the centrality of marriage to social relations in premodern societies generally, medieval evidence provides an ironically and frustratingly restricted view of it. We might expect a rich fund of information to issue from the many records concerning marriage in the ecclesiastical courts. There, indeed, business to do with marriage frequently outweighed all other kinds in sheer volume. Yet legal action over marriage is surprisingly inscrutable where legible codes of gender are concerned. The vast majority of actions are suits to enforce marriage contracts, hinging largely on the exchange of words of consent. Because such contracts themselves, if properly witnessed, were binding, the motivations of the parties were of marginal interest. In other sources, more personal perspectives on the emotional and affective dimensions of marriage, whether anticipated or achieved, are also lacking. Such intimate details did not enter the letters of the well-to-do English families whose letters I have discussed. The Celys and Pastons did consider marriages, but as we might expect, they concerned themselves with matters of material substance and logistics. We do not learn directly how the men of the age felt about getting married, about their relations with their wives and children, or about their ways of deciding how to deal with problems. As is usual when we have to depend on legal sources, we learn most about marital relationships only where something went wrong within them. I left off with this theme, discussing how men's adultery imperiled one side of a husbandly identity, the side facing outward from the household. In complementary fashion, the sexual or even nonsexual misconduct of a wife threatened the other side, that concerning the management of one's own.

Adulteresses

Wives who strayed sexually have grabbed historians' attention because in thinking about these matters, anyone with even a passing knowledge of premodern culture wants to refer to cuckolds. Scholarship on the early modern

period especially has taken up the cuckold as the signal figure of dishonored masculinity, the emblem of men's failed control over women. While
suspected or confirmed infidelity by wives does surface importantly in late
medieval evidence, I would prefer to get away from the "cuckoldry" framework in discussing it. One reason is that the evidence simply does not
support the idea that men feared above anything else becoming, or being
known as, cuckolds. The insult "cuckold" does appear in church court evidence, but relatively infrequently. In addition, it hardly ever appears on
its own. We can better understand the importance of women's adultery, I
think, in the larger context of husbandry, and we learn this by observing
what was at stake in the variety of possible responses to it.

In dealing with an unfaithful wife, the most extreme of the formal options available to a man was to reject her by suing for a legal separation *a
mensa et thoro*, "from board and bed." However, suits *a mensa et thoro* were
comparatively rare, and those claiming adultery rarer still. Expense (a simple
factor) and embarrassment (less simple, and deserving further discussion)
may account in part for the rarity. More important, though, was the fact that
this was a separation, not a divorce in the modern sense, which did not exist.
Neither party separated by this means, which was the only means available
where adultery was the cause, could marry again during the lifetime of the
other. To end his marriage through a judicial separation would cost a man
his husbandly status. He might retain his property and livelihood, but the
separation would cast him into an ambiguous social zone, neither bachelor
nor married man, oddly on the fringes of normal transactional structures.
He would have to rely on servant women and female relatives for everything
a wife would have done: childcare, management of household provisions,
help running the shop or the manor house. (In the late-marriage regime
of England and northwestern Europe, a wife's role in the household was
especially essential, because "there was no other resident adult female who
could assume her functions.")[54] If the marriage had produced no legitimate
children, the situation was even worse, for now there was no near prospect
of any. Inability to marry also cut off a significant route to accumulat-
ing further wealth and to moving up in the world: in short, to full social
masculinity.[55]

Separating such practical considerations from the factor of shame or embarrassment, as our reductive modern minds tend to do, may introduce a
false distinction. To be suddenly deprived of a wife was to become dependent on others, particularly female others. In itself that kind of temporary
dependence cannot have been shameful; the many widowers of medieval

England must have experienced it, perhaps more than once in their lives. Where the cause was not death but an adulterous wife, however, help must rarely have come without pious contempt or well-meaning pity, in the faces and words of one's neighbors and kin, male and female. One could either meet those faces every day or risk everything by going somewhere else—not a promising alternative. Status and wealth did not insulate a man from these consequences. On the contrary, they exacerbated them: the better off he was, the more he had to keep track of, and the higher profile he needed to maintain. Not having a wife to manage the larder and give the servants orders, and not having a wife to bring to the fraternity feast—each contained their complement of social agony.

To pursue a separation must have been a last resort, very carefully considered. As with the physical amputation of a limb, one could only have entertained it where the wife had become as gangrenous flesh on her husband's social body, threatening its very survival. A female Yorkshire witness in the early sixteenth century was discredited as just such a woman, because she left her husband and impoverished him, wasting his goods, to go with another man.[56] Draining away her husband's substance might well make a wife worth cutting off. It is hard to verify such reasons exactly, because of the courts' construction of the grounds for separation. If a plaintiff claimed adultery, it was adultery that needed to be proven, and other aggravating factors were not strictly relevant. The little we do know about the management of marital problems by the church, however, suggests that less serious cases would probably have resulted, at an earlier stage, in admonitions from some clerical authority (whether the couple's parish priest or the official of some lower church court) for the guilty party to do penance, behave, and not offend again. The church had no interest in frustrating the aims of holy matrimony. But sometimes there was no other remedy. For a wife's adultery to prompt such a step, it would need to be flagrant, unrepentant, notorious, and probably repeated over a long period of time.[57]

Of the many shades of shame and dishonor prompting a husband to decide how to deal with infidelity, notoriety was probably foremost. Did he know his wife was an adulteress? More importantly, did everyone else know it? Or did he merely suspect her? The distinction was blurry in a society where the "public voice and fame," not necessarily the truth of a rumor, determined the validity of a defamation case. But a line must have been drawn somewhere. Calling for formal authority to intervene only became worthwhile when the situation could no longer be kept from public knowledge, when rumor was already rife. This applied not only to the last resort of a separation, but also to the less drastic sanctions, such as a citation to answer to the charge of adultery in the church (or, as in London, civic) court. If it was strictly a matter of rumor, an innocent woman (and her husband) could aim to silence malicious gossip by compurgation in the church court.[58] If unable to clear herself, she would have to do public penance and perhaps pay a fine. The shaming publicity would, a husband might hope, make her think twice about further transgressions. It would also preserve the marriage, albeit unhappily. Even this, however, represented a significant disclosure, and from a husband's viewpoint, it was better to prevent or cut short a wife's adultery before knowledge could leak out. It was terrible to seek a separation, and it was distinctly uncomfortable to see one's own wife summoned into the archdeacon's or commissary court, no matter who had caused that to happen. Both these options, however, were preferable to doing nothing, and especially better than being seen doing nothing. A husband had to judge for himself, and quickly, at what point he needed to act.

That decision depended, in part, on how surely a husband knew about his wife's actions. There could be no surer sign than to find the parties *in flagrante delicto*, or even together in a suspicious manner. In such a case, the husband who did not act ran a severe risk of even worse consequences. Nevertheless, the legal records show us that even the outraged husband who attacked his wife's sexual partner did not act with impunity. Just as with verbal provocation, English law did not excuse a deliberate killing incited by an injury to marital honor. That did not mean that husbands could never get away with it. In her study of domestic violence in medieval England, Sara Butler relates the fictional strategies that allowed a murderous husband to plead self-defense within the common law's accustomed definitions.[59] Juries' possible willingness to make such allowances may indicate a cultural standard wherein a husband could properly direct his anger at the man who had violated his household. (It is significant that in Butler's main example, the adultery took place in the family home, and the wife's lover entered the house by stealth.) Actual homicide was, however, an unusual extreme, and the probably more numerous instances of mere assault motivated by such marital situations have not yet received a conclusive analysis. A husband best avoided such risks altogether by dealing with his wife within the household. The question of just how he chose to do this moves our discussion on to some slightly different themes.

Richard Elkyn, of Harwich in Essex, had to answer a church court's questions regarding his treatment of his wife Agnes in July 1513. His responses concerned events that occurred not long after Agnes gave birth to a child. Three different issues were at stake here in what seems to have been an accusation of marital cruelty by Agnes, and we can roughly reconstruct the questions the court must have asked about each in turn. In effect, Elkyn was answering the efforts of his wife's counsel to establish not only that she had been injured, but also that she was blameless. A question about the child she bore was surely aimed to show she had not shirked her conjugal debt. Elkyn parried that attempt by claiming the baby was not his, and that Agnes herself had confessed as much. Shortly after Agnes left childbed, the couple had an argument about who should pay the nurse who had looked after Agnes. In response to a somewhat murky remark by his wife, Elkyn admitted he had threatened her with a table knife and said, "Ah, whore, it would be a good deed to cut off your nose." But he insisted he had not struck Agnes with the knife, only with his fist, as he had done twice previously. Elkyn also claimed he had seen, with his own eyes, Agnes having sex with a priest named Richard Strowte. This was three weeks after the birth of the child.[60] Elkyn thus justified, by implication, the physical force he had used against his wife by alleging that she had been sleeping with the priest: a sacrilegious act that also would have offended cultural standards of purity surrounding women's bodies, as Agnes would not yet have undergone the postpartum ritual of "churching." Indeed, he admitted he had told Agnes that it would be no offense to kill both her and her supposed lover. Though he was careful to insist that he had not tried to kill his wife, Elkyn thus communicated, intentionally or not, his remorseless anger at the idea of her infidelity.

The two witnesses called were both men in their twenties: one a chaplain, the other a carpenter. These young townsmen were respectable by occupation but still relatively small fry in the community. In describing Elkyn's jealous attitude, both cited the words of a more established man, Canon Roger Winton, to the effect that Elkyn had declared a desire to take Agnes to a room and force her, by whatever means necessary, to confess her guilt. The chaplain, Andrew Colby, added that Elkyn had claimed his feelings were validated by one of his peers. One John Kynttermester, in Elkyn's account, had "advised" Elkyn that to cut off Agnes's nose, or even to kill her and Richard Strowte if he saw them together suspiciously, would be to do well.[61] Whether Kynttermester actually said this or Elkyn made it up to support his own attitudes, the meaning was clear: Elkyn felt that the wronged husband had carte blanche to revenge himself on a suspected adulteress. Agnes's witnesses, of course, did not cite this attitude approvingly. For them, it showed how likely Elkyn was to abuse his wife, to attack her without just cause. We would be inclined to suspect some exaggeration on their part had not Elkyn himself, in his own responses, betrayed just such a degree of menacing jealousy.

As witnesses, the chaplain and the carpenter needed all the help they could get (as they had done in quoting Canon Winton), because even in their sympathetic testimony, it does not appear that Agnes had experienced unreasonable physical injury by the standards of the age. In fact, neither witness could truthfully say he had seen Agnes injured at all. Colby the chaplain had only seen her fall to the ground, Elkyn's threatened knife attack frustrated by the heroic "matrona" Agnes Barbour. Barbour had told the second witness, John Alan the carpenter, of another attack where Elkyn threw Agnes against a wall, but Alan had only heard the thump from next door. Agnes's counsel needed to show that Elkyn was the kind of man who would exceed reasonable force in dealing with his wife and who struck her out of harsh anger, not in a moderated spirit of correction. And it is beyond question that such ideas of "reasonable force" governed thinking about men's physical treatment of their wives in the late Middle Ages and for long afterward. One measure of reasonableness was provocation, of which a wife's infidelity was only one kind. A husband's witnesses might cite a woman's disobedience, her sharp tongue, or her lecherous nature as grounds for a husband's use of quite severe physical force. Even where a husband "fiercely or inappropriately beat" and "excessively or indecently castigated" his wife, the court commanded the wife in future to obey her husband.[62] Was infidelity, however, the worst kind of provocation? Did an adulterous wife, by the standards of the day, deserve whatever she got from her husband? Can we go further to say that a husband, to preserve a masculine social self, "had" to beat his wife in such circumstances?

Perhaps she did; perhaps he did. Where the wife's adultery had become common knowledge, the man's choice to have a beating also become common knowledge might be one strategy to show, just as in dealing with insults, that one had responded. But in such a case the adultery would need to be certain, beyond a doubt. Jealous imaginings were not enough; if they were, the witnesses for Elkyn's wife would not have used them as evidence against Elkyn.

A man like Richard Elkyn had to answer to two competing discourses of masculinity, analogous to the different cultural standards of masculine sexuality we can identify in medieval Europe.[63] One discourse, formally supported by church and law, privileged responsible moderation: husbandry. The other, cruder one located manhood in control and in being seen to get what one desired. Sometimes the two discourses conflicted; sometimes they coincided. The former was the more powerful, and no man with a modicum of social substance—with anything to lose—could err by staying on the right side of it. Negotiating the demands of a cruder masculine discourse was a trickier business. A Richard Elkyn might feel that his satisfaction of these simpler, blunter requirements outweighed other concerns, only to find that his male peers thought otherwise. And when that public, formal discourse spoke to you, you could only reply in its language. Nor was it to your advantage to bring the one language to the other. Some months before Elkyn was questioned, the Londoner Robert Bek underwent similar examination. Bek confessed to considerable physical maltreatment of his wife Anna, extending to throwing her down the stairs and also striking her with a sword (though with what part of the sword, he could not tell). Like Elkyn, he admitted to threatening but not striking Anna with a knife. Unlike Elkyn, however, he declined to name the reasons: he was provoked "for certain causes," "for certain causes of a great unpleasantness," for "just and legitimate causes"—which, however, he now "blushes to express." The cause comes out in a witness's statement that as he raised his knife against Anna, Bek declared that were he not prevented by the fear of God, he would mark her as a whore and wound her mortally.[64]

These were harsh and rash words, but at the same time adroitly chosen, whether by Bek himself or by the witness who wanted, in part, to protect him. They stopped just short of a literal threat. John Heywerd, the witness, commented nevertheless that it would be best to separate Anna and her husband so that nothing worse could happen to either of them, and one gets the sense that Bek had exceeded the limits of his neighbors' respect.[65] Even such a man, regardless of how he privately felt, needed to play the part expected of a reasonable husband. Hence the claim that he had acted with just cause, of which he was nonetheless ashamed. (He was ashamed of the cause, not of his actions.)

Considering husbands, wives, and extramarital sex inevitably raises reminders of honor, a concept modern anthropology has theorized (especially with respect to sexual matters) with reference to cultures outside northern Europe, and particularly in the Mediterranean.[66] In such societies, much more extreme dichotomies of honor and shame result in extreme anxiety over both female virginity and cuckoldry. Illicit sexual behavior by women dishonors both their male guardians and their own natal families.[67] Violent reprisals against such women (extending, in a number of modern countries, to murder approved by the woman's own family) may be tolerated, indeed demanded, as the only way to expunge the stain of dishonor.[68] Quite apart from the many differences between such societies and medieval England, it is worth noting that even though the anger of the jealous husband, when sufficiently disguised, could be tolerated under English law, the tolerance had important limits. It did not embrace murder or maiming. If medieval England did have something like an "honor" discourse of masculinity, that discourse did not govern the realm's most powerful institutions. Men defending their actions did not invoke "honor" or claim that their wives had "dishonored" them. That standard shadowed the other, never quite out of view but never attaining hegemony.

Clearly, some "domestic violence," as we now term it, was acceptable, but some was not. The limits are difficult to define; however, a recent anthropological study of violence against women in different cultures has come up with a useful vocabulary, making a distinction between wife beating (physical assault of a limited nature) and battering (more extreme assault causing serious injury, resulting in a lasting disability, or endangering the victim's life). Societies that explicitly condone beating may strongly censure battering, and may have low rates of battering.[69] The English legal evidence is obviously almost completely about battering, and we know that officially, there were few sanctions against beating. Medieval England's equivalent of the modern "battering" concept was narrow and only applied after the fact. Attempted murder, as evidenced by threatening with a weapon, might do it; so might beatings that actually broke bones.[70] Butler identifies a topos among some female witnesses, the displacement of eyes from their sockets, as a fictionalized exaggeration signifying the extremity of the attack.[71] Verbal abuse, too, might aggravate the injury. But since no definition of "reasonable force" was reliable, husbands had wide opportunity to judge for themselves what they felt necessary in any given situation.

Indications exist that where men's treatment of their wives had violated the norms shared by law and community, the husbands' social selves would suffer: "When George Softley of the vill of Latton in Essex beat his wife Alice so greatly that 'she was thereby in peril of her life,' his behaviour was described as 'shameful and unmanly.'"[72] As with the adulterers and fornicators I previously mentioned, doubt fell on the testimony of John Saunderson because he had badly treated his wife and, in fact, thrown her out of the house. Saunderson had appeared in a local court as a result, raising the possibility that his actual prosecution tipped his reputation over the edge.[73] Whether or not there was extra shame for the wife batterer in having been caught, the official mark of the court verified for everyone that Saunderson had gone too far. Other examples bring us closer to the individual perspective. Men might sue for defamation over allegations of such cruelty. In 1492, William Boller was defamed as having beaten Joan Playter, the daughter of the defamer, so badly that she died.[74] Thomas Banburgh of Norwich sued Simon Warner in 1500 for saying that he "was and is a false and unkind man with his wife, for he beat & threw her down a pair of stairs & set his foot on her breast & took and pulled her by the arms till the wind was out of her body and so she died, and then he said 'Will you die for this?' and took his fist and beat her about the head."[75] These were examples of extreme cruelty and literally inhuman treatment: Warner may also have said, "[He] set his knee on her breast as one would break a goose breast."[76] The rarity of defamation suits arising from such accusations of wife battering suggests that only when the abuse was this severe could it tarnish a man's reputation. Of course, a beating that actually caused death was a criminal offense. Note, too, that these allegations were precise; to be called a beater of women or wives in a general way did not prompt a lawsuit. The significance, however, went beyond the risk of criminal prosecution. It might take in masculine sensitivities to matters other than excess brutality. According to another witness for Banburgh, Warner had taken the posture of revealing a dirty secret: "All men know not how she died, for he was her death."[77] Such a brutal death would be unlikely to escape the coroner's notice or anyone else's—even in a town the size of Norwich, neighbors were never far off—and so Warner's remark might have represented that ever-unwelcome action of putting into words what everyone already knows but would rather not face, depending especially on Banburgh's social status.

We need not exclude sympathy for women from the equation altogether, as a strict concept of husbandry tends to do. People might be stirred up against a wife batterer through ordinary humane pity for his wife. However, less vicious beatings did not stimulate that pity, so men were concerned with more than whether or not they were known as brutal. Rather, such ill treatment of a wife represented abuse, waste, in effect, of the precious substance that was uniquely a man's own. A man so reckless and imprudent was not trustworthy and could not expect to keep up his social "credit." The record of John Alan's testimony against Richard Elkyn concludes, in eloquent simplicity, with the comment that Elkyn did not know how to guard the well-being or safety of his wife because of his disordered mind and extreme imprudence: his lack of sense, to gather together the Latin deposition's meanings.[78] To give a woman a mark she would bear outside the household, or to threaten such a thing, was also too much, unless the cause was beyond doubt. Thus, to call a wife "whore" in front of others, or to threaten to cut off (or, as in one Canterbury case, to bite off) her nose, was to turn the household inside out and make it vulnerable.[79] A whorish wife could not bring credit or enhancement to her husband, so to cripple her thus without cause was the same as to deal her a blow making her incapable of valuable labor.

Wives and Servants

Because wives formed part of their husbands' symbolic substance, they could be subsumed also within their husbands' social selves. In 1414, in Canterbury, John Lincoln and John Cottyng jointly sued John and Margaret Melle in the consistory court over an accusation of theft. The alleged thieves, however, were not the plaintiffs, but their wives. Denise Lincoln and Katherine Cottyng had supposedly eaten a hen belonging to John Marche.[80] As usual, legal and social factors combine to complicate our interpretation of the case. The sticking point is the legal status of married women, who as *femmes coverts* were not legal persons and could not be sued at common law. Yet married women could and did sue in their own names in the church courts over defamation and marital issues. There are several possible interpretations here. Perhaps Lincoln and Cottyng, legally responsible in the case of a theft by their wives, wanted to clear their own names to avoid criminal prosecution. Or the husbands may have felt obliged to protect their wives' honor, injured by an allegation of theft. Why, though, did the wives not sue on their own behalf in the church court? Was that considered legally permissible but socially not right? Would a married woman suing in a case like this, independent of her husband, be doing something somehow derogatory to her husband's authority? Or conversely, would a husband appear to be failing in his familial duty if he "left" his wife to defend herself in court, instead of stepping forward in her place?

These possible explanations neither exclude each other nor preclude the most important and overarching motive. A thieving wife was an injury to her husband's social self, and hence the husbands here were protecting male honor. On one level, in fifteenth-century terms, wives stole chickens because their husbands were not governing them properly. At a higher level of abstraction, a wife's identity was subsumed in her husband's; hence her actions, good or bad, regardless of legal definitions, reflected directly on him. The wives fit within the husbands' social selves, and misbehavior by wives injured husbands, because it indicated poor husbandry. In a very direct and material way, a married woman's theft amounted to trespass, in the modern sense, on the substance of others. What we see here is very similar to those cases in the borough court of Wells, around the same time, where an injury to his wife might prompt one man to sue another. The injury need not have been physical: "Stephen Skinner's complaint against William Pedewell was simply that he had spoken abusively to Mrs. Skinner. That was enough of a trespass."[81]

As usual, we need to distinguish intent from effect. The husbands who brought the case suffered a presumable sense of injury. Yet neither witness said that Lincoln and Cottyng had in fact been injured by the accusation that their wives dined on a stolen chicken. Walter Taylor said there had been no injury, and Alice Yepyswych did not comment. (This is noteworthy in itself. Perhaps people did not believe a woman could judge accurately whether a man had been defamed or not, so she was not asked.) But at any rate, even a claim that a wife's misbehavior did not automatically injure her husband's reputation indicates that this was at least a feasible situation in cultural terms. Of course, Taylor's reasoning remains unknowable. Perhaps he was a friend of the accusers, the Melles, though as usual he claimed no prejudice; perhaps the two women involved were of unimpeachable behavior and no one would have believed they would steal a chicken. Or again, perhaps no one believed that the husbands, Lincoln and Cottyng, would have allowed it to happen. It is also worth noting that nobody actually called the women thieves: the court asked this specifically and got a denial from Walter Taylor, who however "believe[d] that he [John Melle] said it with ill will."[82] (Even by this point in the testimony, Margaret Melle has disappeared; no one seems to care what she did or did not say, or how her role differed from that of her husband.)

Husbands needed to foster and manage their other household dependents just as they did wives. This responsibility was not just a matter of self-definition; different levels of legal jurisdiction enforced it. Men could be fined for "fostering" or permitting certain sexual or otherwise suspicious behavior in their houses, and they might sue for defamation against rumors that they had done so.[83] Children would seem the most obvious example of household dependent. As in the matter of marriage, however, the sources are silent on most aspects of fathers' relationships with their dependent children, those within the household. (Even when children grew up and interacted as adults with their fathers, little more emerges.) Fathers safeguarded their children's welfare, of course, and prosecuted those who abused them. But the sources tell us little about how real-life fathers dealt with their own children outside of such rare and extraordinary situations: what degree of affection they expressed for them, what extent of punishment was considered reasonable. We have more information about husbands' dealings with their servants, because these relations fell to a greater degree under the regulatory surveillance of law and custom. Late medieval England may have been a patriarchal society, wherein fatherhood was a pervasive metaphor; ironically, however, from its historical record, we can know its men better as masters than as fathers.

Servants represented the extremities of a masculine social self. This meant that unjustified injuries to them were in some ways injuries to their master. It also meant that one husband could attack another through his servants:

> [Servants] were only appendages of their master, without a separate identity worth acknowledging. . . . Assaulting them occurred more casually than striking a burgess, but it was not precisely acceptable. If it had been, it could not have been a charge in court that a servant was beaten or otherwise interfered with. The sure lesson, however, is that it was only unacceptable when the *wrong* person hit them. . . . Only their master or his agents could *beat* them with ethical correctness. . . . No one was ever charged with having *spoken* roughly either to or about a servant. . . . It was impossible to insult one, but to strike one was to insult a burgess who would have to stand up for himself-as-servant.[84]

Servants therefore could be the very human borders through which their masters defined their own respective territories against each other.

The generalizations here apply to servants of a menial kind, who had no identity outside of their relation to a household master, though we shall later see how the wider symbolic ethic of service admitted the same discourse. Shaw's comment distinguishing between servants and wives ("Servants were on the bottom of protected society; barely worth notice and treated rather like chattel, regardless of their sex. The place of burgesses' wives, however, was considerably more nuanced.") is guided by his borough court evidence, which did not permit servants to figure as agents.[85] In a wider context, it needs a little qualification. Servants' dependent and peripheral identities did not mean that they mutely assented to all masterly arrogations or abuses of their value. Servants had a clear idea of what was fair in a master-servant relationship and were prepared to stand up for it.[86] But neither servants nor wives were protected from physical punishment properly administered, by the terms of the day: that is, for the right reason and by the right person (and in the right manner).

Placing such chastisement under the modern rubric of "domestic violence" may not be a useful move in studying this society, where the infliction of physical pain and injury marked most relations of superior to inferior and extended to judicial penalties. Sara Butler remarks, "That men chose to reassert their masculinity in the home through violence argues that it was a vital component of general late medieval expectations of masculinity, and that these conceptions of gender identity were both internalized and widespread."[87] Yet to term wife beating, or battering, an assertion of masculinity through violence is perhaps to emphasize the wrong things. True husbandly masculinity consisted in the measured application of force, with good judgment guiding one to apply it only when necessary—but, when necessary, not to shrink from using it. This was the paternalistic dimension of husbandry: the parent who failed to discipline an errant child was a bad parent, just as was the parent who beat a child excessively. And dealings with wives and servants were more or less equated. In a letter to the Pastons in 1450, the vicar of Sporle reported on his request for help on behalf of "Herré Halman," who was amerced for beating a servant and a serf (a "bondman" of John I) badly enough to draw blood. The provost hearing the complaint seemed to make light of it: "Frances [Costard] said again that he might not chastise his man so. My master said he had done so many times; and I said it was done for evil will. My master [the provost] mocked Frances and asked him if a man might not beat his own wife."[88] Again, the standard of acceptable force could be quite elastic.

Disputes between masters, and those between their servants, easily blurred one into the other, as we learn from a fifteenth-century petition brought by Richard Smyth of Buckinghamshire. Smyth first claimed that on "the 11th day of August last past," "John Anneys, servant unto Robert Rufford, squire" had attacked his servant, William Hamond. Smyth went on to say that he "would not allow William to go out of his place except to labor there, to safeguard his body and to avoid more hurts that might follow." The next day, Anneys returned with other "malefactors," "lay in wait" for Smyth's other servants, and attacked them, pursuing the fleeing servants to Smyth's house—"at that time there being William Hamond laboring in his shirt, who was hurt before by John Anneys and others; and then John Anneys with others there, seeing William laboring in his shirt, fell upon him and would have slain him. And then he fled from them and they followed him into the hall of your Orator." There Hamond, Smyth claimed, forced to defend himself, killed his attacker Anneys with a "pesehoke." But the story did not end there; the conflict between servants was only the first phase. Now the masters, in consequence, met face to face: "Robert Rufford came to your beseecher's house with others and assaulted your beseecher there, breaking up his gate . . . saying that he was causer thereof, whereas he never knew it till it was done, and was not present there. And there he would have slain him had he not fled into a chamber for the safeguard of his life." Abusing an arrangement made by a mediator (the proctor of Charterhouse), Rufford then got Smyth imprisoned in Aylesbury jail.[89]

The last occurrence, an unjust imprisonment "charging that he [Smyth] should not be mainprised," was the proximate reason for the petition. But it was in Smyth's interest to sketch out the full quadrangle of animosities linking himself, Rufford, and the servants Anneys and Hamond, because it allowed him to cast himself as the good master (a variety of the good husband) and Rufford as a species of abusive extorcioner. The image of Smyth's honest servants, attacked "as they came out of the field with their carts," fleeing and leaving behind the visible emblem of their labor as they "forsook their carts" and the hard-earned cargo within them, is a little masterstroke of scene painting. It serves as prelude to Anneys's repeat attack on Hamond, this time as Hamond was "laboring in his shirt"—near naked, in other words, and defenseless. In typical fashion, the text stresses that Hamond had no choice but to wound Anneys in his own defense. This fatal altercation, we note, happened in the hall of Smyth's own house: not only under his roof, but in the most public room, where he presented himself socially as head of the household. It was the same house in which Smyth the good husband had tried to protect Hamond, not letting him leave it.

Invading this space, Anneys the servant was like an extension of his powerful master's symbolic body, and so that master, Rufford, follows him into the story just as a body would follow a probing hand. Though Smyth himself seems not to have been badly off, to have a house with a "hall," he calls attention to his opponent's superior social status ("squyer"), which by implication Rufford had abused. Here, as in the case of Edward Divrych and Walter Lankeforth, there was no shame in a subordinate position occupied respectably by those whose lot it was to be subordinate.[90] The weakness and vulnerability of Hamond the servant did not make him contemptibly unmanly; they pointed up the unconscionable aggression of Anneys and Rufford. Smyth's role was to defend against such abuse as best he could, and beyond that to trust in the further superior authority of royal justice.

The expectation that masters would protect their servants underlay court cases such as Shaw reports, like the archdeacon of Northumbria who got into a fatal fight over a threat to his servant, or the servants who got beaten by the servants of other men: "On both sides it was natural for a master to take offence when his servant was threatened and for a servant to reciprocate."[91] It also appears in a supposed piece of deception about which Laurence

White petitioned Chancery in about 1474. White's enemy, John Cusake, foiled in his original false indictment against White, resorted to another false claim of trespass in which he "caused" Robert Gregory, "common purveyor of our Sovereign liege lord the king's house," to report that White had attacked Cusake: "Robert Gregory said then that John Cusake was his servant, whereas the contrary is true."[92] An injury to Cusake as "servant" would have been an injury to Gregory as "master," both allowing a new suit to proceed and giving a different commonly understood frame for the legal action.

Because servants not only extended but also reflected the social selves of their masters, good husbandry meant defending them not only from physical attack but also from defamation of character. Edward Hampden wrote to Sir William Stonor on this point in 1478, after he heard of Stonor's "displeasure" and harsh words against Hampden's servant. It seems Stonor was relying for his accusation on the report from a third party connected to Stonor, named Harry Gorton, who had accused Hampden's servant of the very substantial theft of £5. Hampden advised Stonor, "If it can be proved, he shall abide the uttermost of the law: but I believe that they will find ill will behind it. But (take no displeasure, Sir), I would advise Harry Gorton to hold his tongue there, and have a worse tale than this proved on him, or else you may say that I am false." Stonor's own words were also at issue: "Moreover, I heard that you called him a thief: by my truth, I do not know him as one, nor would I ever keep one." Hampden's next sentence collected the values and meanings of true and husbandly manhood and brought them to bear on the dispute: "It amazes me that such a worshipful man as you would slander any poor man so, for the words of such a 'double' man as Harry Gorton. I shall prove before him that he does you more dishonor than good service." This was a bold rebuke, justified perhaps only by family ties, and certainly not by social condescension, as the continuation shows: "Cousin, I and all mine shall do you service; and I trust to do you better service in one hour than shall lie in his power to do all the days of his life.... If he were not your servant, he would well know, and shortly, that his dealings were not good. It is for your sake and not for his own that he is favored so long."[93]

Hampden was Stonor's inferior, though not by much; his relations with Stonor fit within that wider social hierarchy of service. His criticisms of the poisonous Gorton invoke the meanings of the extended masculine self in its full relational significance: Gorton would never be tolerated if he were not the servant of a "worshipful" man like Stonor—who, in slandering another man, was behaving as ill befit his status. Hampden appealed to Stonor's sense of husbandry in casting the servant as the victim. But anyone could see he was equally concerned to protect his own reputation, threatened not only by Stonor's remarks but also by Gorton; he hoped to move against Gorton by appealing to the bigger man, Stonor. Stonor's social superiority prevented Hampden from speaking as sharply as he might otherwise have done against an injury to one of his own: he had to tell Stonor that if his own servant "has offended you in any point, I shall put him under no man's correction but yours."[94] At the same time he must have suspected that to speak in defense of his man, without offending social hierarchy, might gain him favor with Stonor. I do not mean to suggest that Hampden's motivations were completely callous; he might well have genuinely liked and trusted his servant. But even what we would understand as a benevolent concern was inevitably self-interested precisely because his servant was part of his self.

That self encompassed, and might in fact override, the much smaller husbandly self of a servant, even in matters we now consider private. Just such a situation, in the London of Richard Elkyn and Robert Bek, comes to our notice by an unusual route. On a late December evening in 1512, neighbors in the parish of St. Stephen Coleman Street heard a terrible racket of howling and crying. Richard Browne was beating Ellen, his wife. Ellen's sister, Joan, marched to the house of John Parish, a leather dealer, who was relaxing by the fire after supper with his wife and their guests, two men of Parish's trade. According to one of them, Thomas Leeme, Joan shouted from the hall door: "Master Parisshe, speak to your servant yonder, Richard Browne! For he will kill my sister his wife yonder, for that whore's sake, Maude Jacklett your servant."[95] Unfortunately for Joan, Maude was also in the room at the time and later sued Joan for defamation: the only reason we know about the wife beater Richard Browne in the first place.

Whatever the intriguing and unknowable reason why Joan blamed Maude (whore or not) for her sister's beating, and whether this was the first such attack or simply the last straw, Joan identified John Parisshe, Browne's master, as the man to do something about it. She expected Parisshe to be responsible for his servant's behavior, and that responsibility might involve quite a wide span of action. The other dinner guest remembered Joan's words to Parisshe as more directive and less polite: "Parisshe, take home that knave thy servant that has married my sister."[96] The publican John Hey, who lived in a room above the Parisshes, also remembered Joan calling for Parish to "come out and bring your man home."[97] As they represented Joan, at any rate, she had no trouble imagining a servant's household as morally enfolded within that of his master, even where he was not resident within it (not an unheard-of situation).[98] The master's discipline could penetrate his servant's own husbandly territory. Aiming to harmonize rather than raid, such intervention was conceivable, if perhaps unusual.

None of the witnesses relate Parisshe's own reaction. And we do not know whether he rose reluctantly from the fire to do what Joan asked. But in this situation, he had more than one servant to be concerned about. We may well wonder how a mere serving woman like Maude Jacklett was able to afford a lawsuit. My strong suspicion is that Parisshe himself bankrolled it. For the servant who did not live under his roof to be battering his wife was one thing. For another servant, a woman still in the house at eight at night, to be known as a "whore" was quite another, a more serious aspersion on Parisshe's own husbandry, particularly because Joan seemed to be suggesting that these two servants of the same master had been carrying on illicit sexual relations together. This would be a doubly serious stain. Joan Foster called on one idea of good husbandry to overrule the bad husbandry of her brother-in-law. Instead, or perhaps in addition, Parisshe himself may have deployed a different variation on the same theme. Being a good-enough husband did not necessarily mean keeping everybody happy. It meant looking out for the most importantly exposed flanks of a masculine social self.

PRIESTS VERSUS HUSBANDS, PRIESTS AS HUSBANDS

As interdependent as marriage and household were, and as much as they together undergirded masculine social selves, they did not exist in a simple additive relation. We now need to consider what masculinity might have meant for the important minority of men who, by definition, could not marry.

The number of recent statements on the masculinity of the medieval clergy is small. Most, in varying measure, share a belief that the celibacy of the clergy set them significantly apart from laymen. JoAnn MacNamara and Lyndal Roper have claimed that changes in the regulation of clerical marriage and sexuality prompted crises of masculinity in both eleventh- and sixteenth-century Europe. R. N. Swanson and P. H. Cullum both discuss sexuality as a kind of masculine behavior, along with physical violence, prohibited to the clerical estate. Placing active sexual behavior at the center of gender identity, this theory maintains, in effect, that clergymen could prove neither private nor social masculinity, to self or to peers, without sexual experience. Clergymen, in this view, lived out a defining and essential life difference from laymen, which they could not bridge in any practical way. Swanson in fact argues that the clergy consequently inhabited an identity of "emasculinity," a "third gender."[99]

Reifying gender into "genders," to the point of counting "them," is never a good idea, and Swanson in particular suffers from a suspect and very thin theoretical base. Still, such arguments are understandable given all that we know about the centrality of sexuality in the human psyche, and its particular visibility in masculine discourse. Men who were forbidden to have sex or to marry must, we imagine, have had difficulty maintaining a masculine gender identity, especially in relating to laymen. In medieval society, did people view the celibate clergy as unmanly, effeminate, or incomplete because they did not live as laymen did—because they did not copulate, marry, have children, fight for sport, carry weapons? Did that also mean that clergymen's private gender identities were in doubt—that they struggled with the knowledge that they were men in male bodies, with male desires?

Although scholarly opinion has so far said "yes" to both questions, I think an accurate answer is a matter of balance and requires an especially careful weighing of evidence. We do have writings from churchmen who despised sexual desire and seem to have loathed their own bodies' apparent freedom from conscious control, as manifested in spontaneous erections and emissions—men who longed to be free from what they saw as the yoke of carnal temptation.[100] These eloquent testaments come usually from a minority of learned clerics. A more broadly based class of evidence comes from the abundant discourse on clerical sexual misbehavior: the church's injunctions against it, discussions among churchmen on how to prevent or deal with it, and proceedings in the ever-handy ecclesiastical courts against those who had fallen into it.

The place of sexuality in gender identity deserves nuanced attention free from careless assumptions. So do the differences between clergymen and laymen in their approaches to sexual matters, which also influenced their social relations. Nevertheless, the argument for clerical masculinity as a problem by definition, as necessarily insufficient, needs more careful qualification at several levels. Sexuality neither begins nor ends with genital sexual acts culminating in orgasm: wishes, fantasies, and desires, conscious, unconscious, displaced, and sublimated, form the broader texture of an individual sexuality throughout an individual life. Desire, excitement, pleasure: these can reach many sources and objects by many paths, not necessarily direct. The desire not to have desire can be as powerfully directive as desire for a tangible body. In sport and combat, men anticipate (desire, fear) a form of physical excitement with its own complement of pleasure and release. Complex forms of pleasure can come as easily from pleasure's denial, postponement, or opposite, as in ascetic or penitential practices of self-mortification.

All these experiences have a physical and private aspect, but they also are social: reputations can rest on them. In that totality, through the meaning they gain through association with one sex or the other, they are gendered. In further combining desire, excitement, and pleasure with the meanings of the sexed body, they can qualify as sexual in a broader, nongenital sense.[101] Moreover, the wondrous ability of the human unconscious to eroticize literally anything, not just tangible objects, but abstract concepts as well, means that the powerful energy of gendered sexuality can reside in the needs and satisfactions of social life. In this section, I show how many of those social experiences clergymen had in common with laymen, and consequently how many of the same aspects of masculinity applied to them. The lives of clergymen directly paralleled those of laymen in many respects. While the two kinds of men might conflict, they might as easily act in each other's interest; they were all men living in the same communities and making their way along social networks that often intersected. If we are to believe that masculinity meant something to the celibate clergy, we need to consider it in a much broader frame, not solely defined by genital sexual acts. Because that frame takes in most aspects of social life, much of what I rehearse below may seem obvious. Its very obviousness, however, may be what has kept it out of most recent analyses.

Clergy in English Society

In the fourteenth and fifteenth centuries, very little separateness existed in English society between lay and clerical spheres. The boys who would be men in those worlds experienced that porousness from their boyhood. It seems extremely unlikely that any boy later to become a priest, or even a monk, experienced a childhood and adolescence different in any significant way from that of his social peers who would remain laymen. Child oblation was long extinct. In the schools that most obviously served the church's needs, boys who owed their education and lodging to the church formed little communities. Even there, they were not kept from mixing with their fellows. No one assumed that they would necessarily become clergymen, though many did. The undeniable distinctiveness conferred by the first tonsure at minor orders was the beginning of a possible separate path, not the marker of its culmination: in Exeter from 1420 to 1455, out of 4,100 ordinands to the first tonsure, only about 1,200 became priests. The system of canonical ages, up to 24 for ordination to the priesthood, allowed many places to stop before any vow of celibacy became necessary. Many young men put off the commitment to major orders until as late as possible. My point here is that even those young men who felt a true vocation, and who were determined to become priests, surely had not grown up thinking of themselves as different from their male peers; they had been raised as boys, educated among other boys, and brought up to the expectation of a social manhood.[102]

Entering religion as a career involved the same debts and family ties as embarking on any other path to a livelihood. Young men who sought ordination might profit from bequests enabling them to study; they were not all from the wealthiest families. Parents might desire their child to "find a vocation, and lead an affluent and respectable life, in the direct service of the Church.... A merchant's son could maintain his economic position without risk, and improve his social and moral standing."[103] These were unremarkably masculine aspirations. Moreover, the late medieval church itself had, on balance, more mechanisms and practices that diminished distinctiveness than those that maintained it. Dispensations to scholars commonly allowed them to proceed to orders before the canonical age. Frankly material and careerist motivations consequently entered a process that may not have required of ordinands any actual evidence of a spiritual vocation. Indeed, the minor order of holy-water clerk was designed for the support of grammar-school students.[104] The most important factor, however, was the pervasive and inescapable importance of patronage and competition, which bore on anyone with clerical ambitions in ways at least as complex as those on which laymen depended. Although the situation varied over time and between localities, there were never enough benefices for those who wanted them. All the evidence suggests that the career prospects for newly ordained priests in late medieval England were not a great deal more encouraging than those awaiting newly minted humanities PhDs in twenty-first-century academia. The "immense increase during the later medieval period in lay control over clerical careers" meant that priests needed to use their contacts with laymen to their own benefit, and to the disadvantage of their competitors, especially if they wanted the security and social advantage of a parish living.[105] It was relatively easy to be ordained, and to obtain title from a religious house or perhaps a lay patron, but becoming beneficed was a massive hurdle. The patrons who guaranteed title were very rarely the same ones who presented to a living. It might take years for an ordained priest to gain a benefice of his own. Malcolm Burson found that in the archdeaconry of Exeter, the mid-fifteenth-century span between ordination and presentation extended up to twenty-three years; moreover, "most of those who waited a long time for their first benefice seldom achieved much note in ecclesiastical affairs."[106] According to Virginia Davis, those priests who succeeded in obtaining benefices, and especially those who later advanced to high ecclesiastical office, often already had their benefices assured them at the time of ordination. Davis is also emphatic that it was rare for clergy to be able to work their way up to presentment; if one were not presented very soon, one would very likely remain unbeneficed for the rest of one's career.[107]

Priests lived within hierarchical structures that were inescapably masculine, whether it was the structure of the church itself or the structure of lay society, within which the church existed, and which sustained it in many practical ways.[108] They were, at some level or another, in a dependent relationship to other men: sometimes patrons could be women, of course, but not usually, and men far outnumbered women in the experience of any individual cleric. Once a cleric had a position, the nature of his homosocial engagement simply altered a little; it did not diminish. In day-to-day life, "patronage" was a matter of many small practices, many short performances. Margaret Paston, referring to a friar who "claims Oxnead," grouped such a set of relations together in one phrase, reporting worriedly that the friar "hath my lord of Suffolk's good lordship and he [Suffolk] wants to be his [the friar's] good lord."[109] A Norwich defamation case of 1512 was even more explicit, as one priest allegedly said to another, "You are a false priest and a false flattering priest and a false tale teller, and you have misinformed my lord Fitzwater and the Lady his mother about me, so that through your sinister information they are not contented with me."[110]

Relations with laymen, on laymen's terms, were central to a cleric's social existence. It could hardly be otherwise in a society where the average glebe contained one hundred acres of land, involving clergy not only in landlord-tenant relationships, but also in the grain market.[111] Burson's fine, and unfortunately never published, study of Exeter archdeaconry explains the extent and normalcy of such relations for the parish clergy, in which "the sacerdotal function was not considered to exclude participation in the ordinary course of human life." The involvement of parish clergy in "ordinary agrarian life" involved not only farming, but also owing suit to manorial courts. Clergy might "offend against the lord" alongside other villagers. The

livings that gave them their status involved them in very material and practical transactions: confessors' duties included discovery of community offenses, and in Ipplepen in 1439, the vicar "swore an oath to use a variety
of persuasions, including the confessional, to assure the proper payment of
tithes and obventions to the impropriators." Wills show that many priests
acted as godparents, especially to children "destined for a religious life."
Priests maintained an "economic and administrative" involvement in the
affairs of the gentry, and they might be significant creditors: Walter Robert
"canceled debts of £20 from the earl of Devon."[112] Elsewhere, Eleanor
Townshend employed John Clyf, rector of East Raynham, Norfolk, "as a
servant—and perhaps also as a private chaplain—instead of allowing him
to reside in his rectory."[113] Although Lady Townshend was apparently the
one who broke the rules, we must wonder what a complex situation this
may have been, and what combination of ambition, pressure, and lack of
choice prompted John Clyf to agree to it. Denis Brearley, deploying testa-
mentary evidence and lay subsidy rolls, gives a sense of a humbler parish
vicar: Richard Depyng maintained many connections among substantial
people in the parish and acquaintances with other priests for some distance
around.[114]

The secular side of ordinary clerical life is most evident with respect to
the parish clergy, but was just as important in the communities of secular
clergy found in cathedral cities such as York and Lichfield. A cathedral
community involved many laymen: servants or retainers in direct contact
with the clergy, along with the suppliers and tradesmen or craftsmen who
covered their physical needs. It also contained many men with one foot in
the Church and the other in the World: the canon lawyers, the "swarms
of household chaplains, notaries, unattached and would-be chantry priests,
scribes, school- and choir-masters as well as other clerks and *litterati* who
formed the clerical underworld of the late-medieval cathedral."[115] The very
economic structure of medieval communities reinforced and demanded such
interaction. At Lichfield, despite the desire of the dean and chapter to keep
city and close separate, they could not afford to remain so, the city especially.[116] In turn, the cathedral community was, in the social lives of its
inhabitants, analogous to the late medieval monastery. Even the regular
clergy were hardly cut off from the laity in late medieval England, as claus-
tration by this time was far from strict. A 1511 visitation of the Canterbury
houses amply demonstrates the porous boundary. At Faversham, women
had easy access to the cloister and spoke with monks in the nave; at Dover,
the bishop enjoined the monks not to go into the town and chat with the
inhabitants. (As Mary Bateson recognized long ago, the record reveals little

evidence of significant moral laxity.) Just as the world might come to the cloister, so might the reverse occur. Intelligent and lucky men from the monastic houses could get permission to attend university, with a view to improved future preaching and instruction. The Benedictine students from Ely who attended university at Cambridge had a special hall there, but we cannot assume that this kept them apart from other students. These men were a select minority. Yet they were an example of the degree to which even priests who did not achieve high political office or the position of lords spiritual might still need to participate in the secular world. This is not to deny the possible monastic stresses of isolation and self-denial. Where such pressures had come to seem intolerable, however, safety valves were available, more generously to men than to women. Unlike nuns, who might apply for transfer, monks could also request to hold a secular benefice, with or without cure of souls, which in effect released them from vows of poverty and obedience. The gendered nature of such a solution, pointing the male religious toward the social world of masculine interaction, provides yet another indication of the pervasive masculinity of male clerical life.[117]

The everyday and unremarkable quality of this lack of separation emerges from the records even where that closeness led to conflict. In the summer of 1511, a quarrel took place amid a game of bowls in the garden of a London house, where a priest named John Thorpe was playing and drinking alongside the laymen. Thorpe sued Edmund Wytton in the church court for assault, claiming Wytton had thrown a drinking mug at his head and cut his face.[118] Wytton protested to the examiner that Thorpe had not been dressed as a priest in this gathering. We may safely discount, given this tiny London parish, Wytton's fishy argument that he therefore did not know Thorpe was a priest. Still, even Thorpe's witnesses admitted that Thorpe had been dressed down, only in jacket and tunic, for the purposes of the game. They did not report this with any sense of wrongdoing. Alongside the observations, in sundry ecclesiastical records of clergymen who misbehaved while fraternizing with laypeople, we should keep in mind the many uneventful and unrecorded instances when such socializing caused no trouble at all: the priests who had a drink at the pub or played football, and who did not gossip, get drunk, get into fights, or make passes at women.

Conflict

Having to live in the secular world could, of course, lead to involvement in very secular kinds of conflict. Clergymen shared with laymen the need to be prepared for such disputes and the ability (savvy, means, resolve) to defend themselves within them. A parish priest's local profile made him an actor in the affairs of his locality, and the very connections to local elites that had secured his position also embroiled him in the contentious business of those elites. In the Pastons' Norfolk, the troubles of 1451 included an encounter between Lord Scales and the people of Swafham before the Earl of Oxford, in which "my Lord Scales gave the parson of Swafham great language . . . and there was great language between Blake the bailiff and the priest of Tudenham." William Wayte, the letter writer, noted approvingly that "the parson answered my Lord Scales manly in the best way."[119] The priests were expected to participate fully in the business at hand—and they could expect to get as good as they gave.

Such mutuality applied to far less elevated kinds of conflicts as well. While Edmond Wytton denied having hurt John Thorpe with a drinking mug, saying a witness had prevented him from throwing the "bowl" he had at hand, he did protest that the priest had provoked him: Thorpe, he said, had called him a cuckold. Wytton's witnesses disagreed; one claimed that Wytton had first insulted Thorpe as "lewd priest" and had received "knave" as a response from the cleric. Wytton's claim of provocation assumes it was credible that a cleric would utter a crude insult, just as Thorpe's own witnesses have him answering one; conversely, if a priest talked like a layman he could expect to face the same consequences. A priest often would need to talk like a layman, literally or figuratively. It was the social *lingua franca* of the world that both inhabited.

Just as the church courts regulated lay morals, clergymen were not immune from prosecution (by laymen or clergymen) within secular courts. The verbal slander that prompted a 1488 ecclesiastical defamation suit brought by the vicar of Winthorpe (probably Lincolnshire) against Alice Birdall seems to have originated in a lawsuit that Alice and her husband John brought against the vicar in temporal court.[120] Clergymen used the same legal strategies as laymen, even to sue each other. For that matter, they used the same illegal strategies. About 1470, the parson Thomas Smyth petitioned Chancery against another priest, Philip Appowell, whom he claimed had picked a verbal and physical fight with him, evaded the arbitration to which they were bound, and then sued him in the temporal court of Winchelsea, claiming a debt of £40. In Smyth's petition, the clerical status of both men scarcely figures in the narrative of bullying and legal subterfuge, complete with a claim that Appowell and his treacherous "man of law" had come to Smyth's church "with great power and maintenance of soldiers."[121] A society regulated by institutions in which clergymen and laymen made use of the same discourses in masculine conflict was not one marked by significantly different models of social masculinity. A generation later, John and Joan Schawe of Coventry complained that the abbot of Combe and his gang had robbed Joan of some valuable goods and then entangled husband and wife in an impressive series of legal maneuvers in high ecclesiastical and secular courts.[122] The masculine self-enhancement to be gained through such conflict with laymen did not escape the consciousness of clergymen, either: William Paston I remarked that his adversary the friar "made a great boast of the suit that he has against me."[123]

It was not just a matter of clergymen being worldly and, thus, corrupt. Beneficed priests with livings entered a relational dynamic concerned with property, and they faced laymen and other priests on that account. The concerns surrounding their beneficed positions over property rights and income might themselves be the subjects of conflict, possibly violent. To find disputes over tithes is not very surprising. Early-fifteenth-century evidence suggests that tithe squabbles happened more frequently between priests, for whom tithes constituted income and represented influence, than between priests and laymen. A hundred years later, an example of such conflict surfaced in Chancery. The parson of High Unger, Essex, claimed that another priest and his "servants" had attacked him. Thomas Wybard, not "contented" with verbally insulting the priest, had sent these "other ill-governed and riotous persons" to assail him while he was carrying the tithe (which the assailants took) from Wybard's field.[124]

Moreover, the language in such quarrels might fit patterns that we have already noted. In 1529, Robert Buttre denied that he had called Robert Hardyng "false whoreson," "false crafty priest," and "whoremaster priest," claiming instead he had said "that he crafted my farmhold from me."[125] Note the role of falseness and craft in both the admitted and repudiated phrases. The real world exposed priests' social masculinity to the same regime of defamation that I outlined with respect to laymen in chapter 1. William Brodehede, chaplain of Ludgarsale, was defamed in 1493 as a thief and a maintainer of thieves.[126] About twenty years later, a churchwarden of St. Martin in the Fields (then on the outskirts of London) testified that he and his colleagues had hired the chaplain William Spynke to sing matins. When they asked Henry Went, in the church itself, for his share of Spynke's salary, Went retorted, "What, you maintain thieves? Have you put in a thief to be morning mass priest?" Everybody spilled out into the churchyard, where Went then said to Spynke, "You are a strong thief and a rope shall break your neck."[127] Spynke sued Went just as any layman might for a similar slander.

William Spynke could count himself lucky that his dispute had not taken a different turn: the vicar of Linkinhorne, Cornwall, was murdered on the highway in 1411 following a dispute with parishioners about the provision of a chantry priest.[128] Nothing exempted clergymen from even the most violent kinds of intramasculine conflict. They themselves could be the perpetrators as easily as laymen. Neither the reasons nor the results were necessarily special or complex. In 1414, the chaplain John Benyngton sued Nicholas Chelmyngton for assault in the church court of Canterbury. Benyngton's witnesses asserted that the fault was Chelmyngton's, but their own depositions belie them: the chaplain, a poleax in his hand, threateningly approached Chelmyngton and demanded to know why he had behaved badly toward a fellow chaplain of his. Chelmyngton responded, "What's it to you?" He warned that the priest was courting a punch in the mouth, tried to get the weapon, and in the resulting scuffle struck Benyngton while they were both on the ground, drawing blood.[129] The influence of institutional conventions in shaping legal stories, familiar from chapter 1, allowed Benyngton to be the victim despite his aggression, and despite the likely status of a poleax as an offensive rather than defensive weapon. He was a cleric on whom, under canon law, laymen must not lay "violent hands"; blood was drawn, and he was on the ground when Chelmyngton pressed his advantage by striking him further. In terms of an ideal clerical standard, a fighting priest was not very defensible. Yet the witnesses' unspoken attitude was that the law should judge the chaplain in the terms framing any other masculine conflict. It cannot have helped matters that, during the Hundred Years' War, bowing to the Crown's national security concerns, the English Church had suspended the prohibition against the arming of clergymen. That prohibition was never officially reinstated even after the war, a fact that can only have further diminished their self-distinction from laymen. The Chelmyngton case provides an interesting contrast to a similar quarrel that Cullum describes, in which lay jurors portrayed a layman who killed a priest as the victim of the priest's armed attack. Cullum's example dates from 1287, when a cleric who carried weapons was much more clearly in the wrong. The insistence in *Dives and Pauper*, that "the only case in which priests may bear weapons is 'to frighten off thieves when they travel by perilous routes,' and even then 'they ought not to strike,'" was out of touch with late medieval reality.[130]

Such quarrels might also, however, easily originate in the very material and occupational concerns of the clerical life. In 1524, Thomas Cooke, vicar of North Newbald (near Hull), allegedly grabbed the chaplain John Watson and tried to pull him out of his choir stall at the church. Watson had been the previous vicar and had resigned the living to Cooke following arbitration of a dispute between Watson and a parish bigwig. Along with the living, Cooke succeeded to an unresolved debt owed to Watson regarding the dilapidation of the vicarage. He was supposed to settle with Watson about this within three months of taking up the job. The two priests' recorded versions of events begin to diverge at this point, but it does appear that Watson never got his money.[131] Given all this, readers may, as I did, find it surprising that Watson had not been the one to assault Cooke. Even without knowing more of the context, however, we can understand that a scuffle like this probably represented the conclusion to a long story. The very dependence of clerical jobs on patronage and local connections meant that they must also have easily become wrapped in successive layers of jealousy and resentment, drawing on every tension at every link in the chain of neighborly affinities. Negotiating this minefield would have yielded a self-concept made up of the same priorities and anxieties determining the contribution of laymen's livelihoods to their social selves as men.

By the terms of masculine livelihood, a cleric who was not true to his vows, or who abused the privileges deriving from them, conceivably became as "false" as the metaphorical thief. The Norwich consistory heard in 1521 that William Corbett had much damaged the reputation of Thomas Thrower by saying, "You are a wretch, it is a pity that ever you were made priest, you betray confession."[132] The secrets of the confessional were a sensitive clerical responsibility. To reveal them was to offend not only against God and the church, but also against secular standards of trust; as the betrayal of a confidence, such disclosure was analogous to breaking an oath. The offense was understandable in much the same terms as dishonest relations in business. Betrayal of confession featured in 1512 in perhaps my northernmost example, when the rector of Crosby, Cumberland, claimed that three men had defamed him by saying he had defamed someone else—from the pulpit, no less.[133] The pulpit, of course, was an essential prop in the theater of a cleric's reputation; words spoken there could not be more public. One Norfolk priest allegedly used it in 1512 to tell his parishioners that another priest was a liar.[134]

In the same decade, the case of William Robynson, the vicar of Littlebury, Essex, vividly displayed the role of secular concerns in a priestly identity. Robynson sued a man who claimed he had misused the pulpit to cast aspersions on the temporal court of the bishop of Ely. The alleged defamer, James Edwards, had loudly objected to the vicar's warning from the pulpit that perjurers were by definition excommunicate. In relating this to "my lord's court," Edwards was referring to an accusation of unlawful entry (with, by implication, the intent to steal) made in that temporal court against the vicar Robynson. One witness, in fact, said that the vicar had explicitly mentioned the charge, calling it untrue.[135]

Before the audience of the assembled parish, Robynson and Edwards were engaging in an impromptu debate, in which they invoked themes of secular masculinity as they chose: Was the priest demonstrating his own honesty in reacting boldly to a false charge, or was he abusing his status to cover up his own thievish proclivities? Such concerns meant that priests as well as laymen were to shun falseness. Richard Belby, the vicar of Winthorpe, originally accused Alice Birdall of calling him "false priest." She would admit at first only to "You are an untrue priest in your saying." The lawyers, however, agreed that "false whoreson priest" was the phrase at issue, and the witnesses' statements all mention "false" with either "whoreson" or "whoremaster." These bare phrases, laden as they were, gained their power through their circumstantial context. Alice shouted them out in church, as Belby was in the midst of celebrating mass. Indeed, said one witness, Belby was administering the consecrated host: the very moment when his parishioners made literal contact with the most mysterious, defining, and distinctive part of his social self.[136] To call that false, whatever the implied reason, was to strike at the root of his social existence.

The Social Meaning of Celibacy

Celibacy had meaning for priestly masculinity in several ways, more of which we will presently explore. In everyday social relations between men, however, its meaning resided in the literal and ritual context I have just described. The vow of celibacy was a primary feature distinguishing priests in their professions from laymen, and so to break that vow was to cast doubt on one's own social identity: to become a "false priest." This is the negative side of the question. Its positive counterpart was that a reputation for being "clean"—that is, free of licentious tendencies—could be very helpful in a priest's career. Richard Page recommended two successive chantry priests to the Stonor family in these terms. Page wrote in 1479 that the friar Hugh Fabri, "whom I have always owed my very good will and favor to, and so do Appleton, Martyn, and all the gentlemen in our parts," was "a good priest, and a clean." When Fabri wanted to leave three years later, Page praised the next candidate, Robert Tybe, as "an honest priest and good, and a clean living man." Yet the priests' exemplary chastity, their moral worth, and what we might today term their "on-the-job performance" were indistinguishable from their social worth, itself defined by service. Fabri's appointment, said Page, would be "to the great comfort of all the gentlemen in these parts; and as well, you shall have the daily prayer of a good priest"; Tybe would be "a sure bedeman to your mastership, and do you as good service as will any priest in Kent."[137] Celibacy operated within this masculine world as an extreme form of the self-command that lay society demanded of all men, with respect to both sexual and nonsexual behaviors, as we have already seen.

Such an interpretation of celibacy may seem prosaic, even cynical, but I think it allows us to understand most of the late medieval clergy better, as men, and to get a fairer grasp of the dilemmas in which they often found themselves. The stamp of Protestant historiography is so strong that to call attention to the clerical life as a practical business seems inevitably like an accusation of excessive worldliness and corruption, about to be swept away by the change in religion. I do not want to leave such an impression. Chaucer's simple, godly Parson was an idealization. Even the best-intentioned priest in the real world could not shun Mammon even as he sought to serve God. That endeavor depended crucially and no doubt stressfully on his adherence to standards of lay masculinity.

Thus, we should not overemphasize conflict between clergymen and laymen when in fact they shared many interests. As some examples above illustrate, it was not simply a matter of social-climbing priests groveling to lay patrons. In the late 1460s, Sir William Plumpton received a request to send venison to a clerk celebrating his first mass, the assumption being that the gesture would create a socially useful link. Distinctions between estates diminished with increasing social rank: the writer of another letter portrayed the abbot of Lilleshall as the "good master" that their correspondents were always exhorting the Plumptons themselves to be. A different abbot, in 1455, wanted to discuss various matters with John Paston I—including a church that fell under the Pastons' influence. He therefore invited Paston to dinner on his founder's name day, "trusting our communication . . . shall cause peace and pleasure to all parties."[138] Of course, these were locally powerful men, in the uppermost sliver of their respective vertical hierarchies, and they represent an extreme rather than an average example. Their interests, however, grew out of versions of the household, which undergirded lay masculinity, and this was true as well of a broader band of both laymen and clergymen.

The Rector and the Bailiff

One vivid and richly documented collision between the husbandly selves of priests and laymen occurred in the little Essex village of Bowers Gifford in 1513.[139] The conflict first surfaces in the records as a prosecution *ex officio* for assault on a cleric, namely John Baker, rector of Bowers Gifford. The defendant, Richard Rawlyns, said he had merely helped two other men to take Baker by the arm and lead him out of the house of Alan Cady, where a quarrel had escalated between the priest and one Thomas Alyn. Alyn had accused Baker of striking one of Alyn's servants. Baker himself claimed a far more severe assault, including being dragged by the shins, but his colleague William Browne, rector of Pitsea, did not corroborate this. That is the essence of what happened, but we learn far more from the details that the different parties provide.

Browne appears the most reliable and least self-interested witness, so it seems best to take the story from his deposition in the first suit, where he testified *for* the other priest, Baker.[140] Baker and Browne were on civil terms, perhaps friends, as Browne said they had entered Cady's house together. Their object was to hear news about international affairs: Baker thought that Thomas Alyn, recently returned from the royal court, might have news about the Admiral of England who had been captured beyond the sea. Alyn's greeting, however, was cold: "Ye be welcome, saving my quarrel." Baker responded that he hoped no quarrel stood between them that a mug of beer would not resolve. Alyn was not to be pacified, accusing Baker of beating "our household members and servants." (Browne editorialized that one such servant was Alyn's own; the other served William Hare, who was also present.) An argument broke out; Alyn, the priests, and their host all jumped up from the table. Alyn drew his sword, and after yet more verbiage, ordered Rawlyns, Hare, and Thomas Camper to seize Baker, lest he hurt somebody. Yet the three laymen seemed reluctant to obey (perhaps, Browne dryly suggested, they had not heard), so Alyn pulled rank: he repeated his order, this time speaking "in the name of the king, whose servant he was." At this point, comedy took over. Browne testified that the laymen had, neither violently nor maliciously, taken Baker's arm and tried to expel him. Amid Baker's struggling, they tripped over the doorsill and fell together onto the ground, finally managing to get the priest out into the high street. Alyn said that they ought to put him in the stocks, but Browne convinced them just to let him go. The stocks were not a good idea anyway; Camper told the examiner that the three impromptu henchmen could not find them.[141]

(It was after vespers, so probably dark, and one suspects the beer had been resolving quarrels before the priests even arrived.)

At the root, this was a dispute between two locally prominent men, Baker and Alyn, both of whom summoned the full formal equipment of their masculine social selves to wield against each other. The fact that Baker was a priest mattered in some ways and did not in others. All parties chose to emphasize it when it suited their purposes. It certainly mattered legally; it meant that Baker, having been grabbed by laymen, could prosecute the quarrel in an ecclesiastical court as an offense to priestly dignity. That, in turn, meant that Baker could only charge the three humbler men who had literally laid hands on him: the court never called Thomas Alyn, despite his obvious responsibility, as either respondent or witness. The laymen's counteraccusation (to judge by the answers to long-vanished questions) was that Baker had been himself guilty of an earlier assault against the servant youths. They described that assault much as witnesses might testify against an abusive husband: Baker's strokes and blows were sufficiently apparent, on John Gilbard's shins, to the point that John was useless to his master for four days thereafter; nor could he provide him any service, because he could neither walk nor get out of bed for that time.[142] They also called in question Baker's adherence to correct priestly demeanor, stressing that Baker had been carrying a sword and had been wearing secular clothing. Both were dubious points. As we have seen, English priests were at some liberty to carry arms. And no one was able to show that Baker had ever wielded his own sword otherwise than defensively, especially after Alyn had brandished his. Just as with the mug-throwing quarrel in London, everyone knew Baker was a priest; Browne identified the respondents as Baker's own parishioners. The laymen's own witness did not sound surprised at Baker's attire: John Longstroder testified that "he believes he has seen other priests going about in their sleeveless tunics, or in English 'in their jackets,' for recreation's sake, and they do not do any harm thereby, as far as he can see. But whether or not they thus committed an offence, he can neither explain nor answer, because it is a point of law."[143]

The alpha male, Thomas Alyn, confronted Baker in the terms of one husband to another, seizing on the beating of servants as a trespass on his household and his own extended self. On this point, as in his other words and actions, Alyn appears through the depositions as *officious* in the most literal sense: a man whose consciousness of his own status, his symbolic "office," determined everything he did. The servant that Baker had allegedly beaten severely was not even Alyn's own, but William Hare's. Hare and Baker had already had an argument about this; Alyn, the socially bigger man, the bailiff of Bowers Gifford, who had been at the royal court and was now the center of attention, subsumed that dispute within his own grievance against the rector. Alyn was quick to flash a sword around and to call on the language of royal authority in ordering his social inferiors, like servants, to do the physical work of apprehending Baker—in Rawlyns's account, thus: "Sirs, you know well enough Master Parson here has hurt a man, and is likely to begin a fight with me here. I am the king's officer. I charge you in the king's name to lay hands on him, to see the king's peace be kept and that the king's subjects not be hurt."[144] Note how the servant, an adolescent and otherwise a social nonperson, here at Alyn's will becomes "a man," so that beating him ceases to be an everyday matter and makes the beater a dangerous offender. (According to Browne, Alyn also warned that if they failed to obey, they would be liable for any damage Baker did: a reference well chosen to intimidate men who no doubt saw Alyn as the authority on secular law.[145]) With one exception, nobody remembered Alyn referring to Baker's priestly status in any way other than the conventional "Master Parson."

The one exception is Baker himself. Baker denied cruelly thrashing either Hare's or Alyn's servants; he had struck them, but only lightly. Moreover, he had made clear to both youths that he intended to report them to their masters, and he claimed he had in fact done so, speaking to Alyn's wife since Alyn was not at home. Both chastisement and reports had what Baker considered good cause, and here we glimpse a patchwork of clerical and lay identities, both unmistakably masculine in the terms of his society. Alyn's servant, playing tennis with other youths, had trampled some newly planted shrubs near the rectory: a matter of property. John Gilford, in contrast, had been disrespectful. To Baker's question about his absence from vespers, Gilford replied, "mocking Master John" that he had been asleep. Baker's "two or three light blows" with a juniper branch, however, derived not from this pastoral concern, but from the insolent youth's failure to take off his hat and from a rude gesture he made, turning his rear end toward Baker. Such "rudeness and presumption" offended, we may assume, Baker's sense of the respect he was due both as a priest and as a social superior; the two were, in that moment, indistinguishable. In recounting the events at Alan Cady's house, Baker stressed his own self-command: terrible things were said to him, but he kept his tongue in check and restrained himself. Again, this is entirely characteristic of legal defenses in cases of violence among laymen. He only reached for his own sword to keep the other men from taking it away from him. Baker's reference to that sword, which he preferred to call a knife, is intriguing. Baker mentioned it simply as part of his clothing. Because it was a warm night he had dressed lightly, but he thought the combination of calf-length sleeveless jacket, black tippet, and knife "for his defence" made him "properly dressed as an honest priest."[46]

The argument with Thomas Alyn, however, brought out Baker's sense of priestly distinctiveness. In Baker's memory, Alyn had told him "you rebuke and correct every man's servant at your pleasure like a proud whoreson priest." Nor was this the last: after his undignified exit from the house, Baker said, he had told the others to mark well and consider what they did, for he was their "priest and pastor." The case's final trace in the record is Baker's account of his exchange with Alyn. Baker had demanded to know of any authority they had from his ordinary to treat him like this. Alyn replied that he was a servant of the king, and that was enough for "a whoreson priest."[47] These insults appear only in Baker's own testimony. Of course it is possible that Baker, speaking to a church court, wanted to play up the disrespect he had received as a clergyman. Overall, though, Baker's identity as a priest was a matter of social privilege and authority. It belonged to him as a man, and it made him a contender with other men. His story would have surprised neither Jane Austen nor Anthony Trollope. Baker acted like a layman or like a priest, as it suited his sense of himself to do so.

Clergymen and the Household

Late medieval realities bound most clergymen to the secular code of husbandry and frequently placed them where they would conflict with laymen in the terms of husbandry, precisely at the sensitive bounds of the household. Beneficed priests, whose property responsibilities gave them the status of householders, were not the only clerics to experience this difficult dilemma. A London chaplain complained that when he sued the goldsmith William Skinnor for some money he had lent him, Skinnor responded with a malicious action of trespass, alleging that the chaplain had severely beaten a child whom Skinnor had "put unto your Orator to be taught more than two years ago." In a familiar defense, the chaplain claimed he had "never hurt nor beat the child except as a child ought to be chastised in the course of his learning."[48]

A priest would never have legitimate biological children, but that did not mean that he would never have dependents requiring governance; this example shows that his enemies could use such governance against him. The social self of a well-placed cleric, in contrast, included servants, as we have already seen, who called for prudent management, and whom he could deploy against others. The vicar of Mere (Bath and Wells diocese) went to see the abbot of Glastonbury after one of the abbot's men had beaten him and provoked "a horrible great dog" to attack him as well. His hope, that the abbot would provide "a due correction and remedy thereupon, considering that Totyn was his servant," was disappointed. The abbot answered, "When that was done, it was done in the defense of my man. And it shall cost me forty pounds before you shall do my man any wrong, for I'll have you understand I will defend him."[149] The vicar hoped to persuade the chancellor to call the abbot to account for what amounted to extorcion and irresponsible husbandry. Where a priest bore a masterly social self, he was open to judgment by husbandly standards.

Just as with laymen, husbandry had both sexual and nonsexual dimensions. A Norwich witness in 1521 ran imprudence and licentiousness together, citing the defamatory sentence: "Sir William Kenston keeps unthrifty rule in his house, and with Agnes Cootes he keeps ill rule." In a case a year earlier, some of their fellow townsmen had been unsure as to the malice of statements that Hugh Kestryn had a living son. Beyond doubt, however, were both the malice and the consequent damage of the remark that "Kestryn would have been better advised to keep his money in his purse and to bestow it on his son, rather than to spend it in any [law] suit, for it cost him 40s lately in suit to Umfrey, which he might have saved if he had been wise, and if he begin again I think he shall have small winning." The next year, the vicar of Woodkirk, Yorkshire, successfully sued a man for saying he had "fostered lechery" in his household; the defendant disowned that phrase, but admitted to saying that the vicar had sheltered an adulterous priest, and this was sufficient for the sentence to go against him.[150] Both priests and laymen were vulnerable to such accusations of "fostering" (countenancing, encouraging) sexual misconduct in their households; toward the end of the sixteenth century, they could be prosecuted merely for hosting someone who had previously committed a sexual offense.[151]

Certain insults that we have already encountered logically implied such activity. The "whoremaster" or "whoremonger," a generic conception of male sexual misconduct, evokes a perversion of responsible masculine husbandry, wherein failure adequately to rule oneself leads logically to the misrule of others, or the rule of the wrong sort of others. In 1509, Randolph Dighton and his parish priest Richard Holme agreed in the York court that Holme had publicly said that Dighton had come to his house by night and called Katherine Thorp, the priest's servant, into bed. Holme, however, denied saying that Katherine (dressed only in a shift) had let Dighton in, that

Dighton had slept with her, or that he had gotten her pregnant. At any rate, Dighton claimed to have subsequently cleared himself of any wrongdoing in the church court, upon which, he said, the vicar called him a perjurer and said he could prove it. For his part, Holme, the vicar, claimed that Dighton had publicly insulted *him*, saying, "By God's passion, thou art one whoremaster priest." Dighton countered that there was more to it: the priest had said, no doubt suggestively, "I have kept a whore in my house overlong," to which Dighton had (rather wittily) replied, "Then you are a whoremaster." The reason for all these verbal theatrics is clear from a list of questions for the witnesses: the general rumor was that Holme himself had gotten Katherine pregnant.[152] Dighton's suit therefore looks like a last-resort defense against the vicar's persistent attempts to deflect suspicion onto him. Meanwhile, Katherine, who doubtless could not afford to sue anyone, would probably agree that clergymen could be just as adept as laymen in using a woman and her reputation, like a tennis ball, to be bounced around in competitive social exchanges. Neither man, for good social reasons, wanted to be known as the father of a servant's illegitimate child. We might think that the stakes were higher for the priest because he was a priest. Yet we cannot ignore the fact that he was also the woman's master, and that violation of celibacy here also meant a violation of husbandry.

So clergymen and laymen might have had very similar interests in the household. The priests with husbandly responsibilities were often locally prominent and possibly powerful men. They were surely far fewer in number than those priests who encountered households from the outside or moved across their boundaries in possibly unsettling ways. A priest might be a trusted friend or confessor to a master or to his wife. Yet his household connections might run counter to, or at least not in perfect consonance with, the masculine responsibilities of the lay head of the household. In maintaining their own social interests and identity, that is, their livelihood, which shaped a great part of their masculinity, priests could easily find themselves in situations that compromised the interests of other men.

The problem had much to do with clergymen's real or imagined contact with women, which could be a point of inflammation in their relations with men. The head of the household was not necessarily the only one put out. John Paston III complained bitterly about the family chaplain, "the proud, peevish, and evil disposed priest to us all, Sir James," and his influence over John's mother:

Many quarrels are picked to get my brother E. and me out of her house. We don't get to bed without some scolding. Everything we do is ill done, and all that Sir James and Peacock do is well done. Sir James and I are at odds. We fell out in front of my mother saying "you proud priest" and "you proud squire," and my mother took his side, so I have pretty much worn out my welcome in my mother's house.¹⁵³

For the Paston brothers, a priest in the household alienated their mother's attention and favor. Though not literally a sexual betrayal, such disruption was certainly analogous to one, when the priest usurped the mother's affections from their accustomed objects. It represented an occupational hazard, probably often blown out of proportion in the minds of husbands and sons, but with some grounding in reality. Clerical responsibilities for confession and moral guidance involved intimate conversation. The priest who gains a seductive power over women through his access to their confidences is, of course, a stock figure of medieval literature.¹⁵⁴ The following scene, reported in 1524 at York, illustrates the husbandly anxieties about where such relationships could lead:

> Robert Erle said to John [Bell], "Brother, I have been to seek you at your house, and there I found a priest sitting with your wife, and if you knew so much about him as I hear say, you would not trust him." And then John Bell asked why. Then Robert Erle answered and said that he heard one or two say that they found Sir William [Bell, the priest] about the mason's lodge within the Minster precincts on last All Hallows Night with a wench, and that he was taken so hastily that he did not manage to tie up his codpiece.¹⁵⁵

In these connections, the problem for clerical masculinity was not that, being celibate, clergymen were considered asexual and unmanly. It was rather that they might be too sexual, unable or unwilling to keep those vows. They might also be too attractive to women, with too much access to them, and too aware of that attractiveness. Even Swanson, in the midst of his argument for the unmanliness of celibacy, has to admit that this was clergymen's primary threat in the eyes of laymen.¹⁵⁶ Once again, distinguishing reality through the masculine paranoia of laymen is difficult, but the stereotype was there. A Kensington priest named Robert Langton or Lane seems to have sued over a layman's allegation that he had told the man's wife she could do with some sex, and (in now obscure, but undeniably suggestive, terms) that he could do more for her in this respect with an inch-long candle than her husband could with a candle worth a pound.¹⁵⁷ In lay suspicion of clerical sexuality, we encounter a tangle of possible discourses. As with adulterous laymen, even where sex was the problem on the surface, material concerns were rarely far below. Clergymen's excessive sensuality and attraction to women could paradoxically imply effeminacy in itself. It also implied that they might be prone to dishonor the husbandly code of respect for property. In the 1460s, in petitioning Chancery, William Phylip claimed that a Kent priest named William Roddock had seduced his daughter and extorted money from his wife, whose wrongful arrest the priest had arranged. Phylip feared that Roddock intended "to have all their goods through such *extorcion* or to destroy utterly their child."[158] That fearsome pair of prospects went together. The mention of material loss and legal manipulation was necessary for Chancery to respond, but it was not a mere fiction; it was embedded in the sexual injury. This was literal, in the social-material value of the daughter's chastity, and also more symbolic, as the priest's sexual access siphoned off the husband's substance.

In the early 1360s, a young unmarried Yorkshire woman named Margaret, the sole daughter of Thomas de Pikworth, became pregnant by her father's servant. On learning of this, Thomas dismissed the man from his household. Subsequently, one William de Bracebridge made some outrageous allegations about Thomas: most shockingly, that Thomas knew full well that the man who had gotten Margaret pregnant was not the servant, but Thomas's own priest, William de Saperton. Thomas was covering up this scandal by bribing the servant to take the blame. Everyone, Bracebridge alleged, knew what was going on.[159]

Thomas and the priest sued Bracebridge together in 1363, though probably with different motives. For Thomas, public rumor of such a shameful affair would imply poor governance of his family and household. Since his daughter *was* undeniably pregnant, however, poor governance could not be ruled out, so the lawsuit's official version puts the best face on things by showing that Thomas administered discipline by firing the offender. Bribing a servant instead would have meant entering a relationship of trust and dependence with a social inferior, making his confidence dependent on payment. These are the classic and, in context, understandable concerns of a *paterfamilias*.

The threat to Saperton, the priest, seems cruder, less subtle, but it was not simple. Of course, he possibly faced ecclesiastical penalties, but these in practice were much a matter of discretion. More immediately, he could have cleared himself through compurgation (bringing to court a specified number of respectable men to swear to his innocence). The defamation suit really served to restore trust damaged by the allegation that Saperton had abused another man's confidence in him, as well as abusing his property (i.e., Margaret). Without proving that anything actually did happen between Saperton and Margaret Pikworth, the defamer Bracebridge drew on a common expectation that a priest in the household (or even, in this case, merely coming to the household) meant sexual trouble. For clergymen, this kind of sexual situation was especially complex because their self-command in celibacy bore directly on the respect for property expected of responsible husbands.

Because the meaning of sexual continence, self-restraint, for clergymen and husbands in this respect was at root the same, it should not surprise us that their interests could coincide as easily as they might conflict. In 1510, a priest named William Kemp sued Thomas Castell for insinuating that he had had a sexual affair with a married woman, the wife of William Radley of Orsett in Essex. Although, in fact, the husband himself was merely called as one of several witnesses for Kemp, it seems fair to allow him the primary voice in the story. On Good Friday, Radley related, Castell had confronted him in the parish churchyard and asked what Radley's wife had been doing in London on a recent Monday. Falling straight into the trap, Radley replied (in an unfortunate phrasing) that she was there taking care of some business. To this Castell replied, "A curse on such errands, for she was shut in the parson's—Master Kemp's—chamber at London, and there she was alone with him on the day after." According to Radley, nobody had been present to overhear Castell, but somehow the story got out, because Radley went on to name several other people who had called him a cuckold. Another witness verified that Radley had been called cuckold "face to face" in Orsett parish.[160]

Despite being the one who brought the suit, Kemp, the priest, seems oddly absent from the text of the depositions, aside from the defamatory statements themselves. Everyone affirmed they had heard the tale about Kemp, and that his grievance was justified. But somehow the injury to Radley, the husband, seems the more immediate and more tangible to the people in his community; we do not hear what the after effects for Kemp were said to be. (The equally slandered wife, we must note, retreats even further to the margins, the suit not admitting even her name into the record.) The situation resembles Robert Bokeland's experience in Kent a century earlier (see chapter 3). Bokeland used a woman's defamation suit to strike back at the man who insulted him; Radley rode the coattails of a defamed priest in order to avenge a similarly painful but also dubiously actionable slur. Perhaps, also, whether the slanders were actionable was not the determining factor. Kemp, the priest, seems to have been a man of some means. He is named "parson," and his tryst with Radley's wife was said to have happened in his chamber at the Charterhouse of London, while an "old bawd" named

Rose walked about in "his" garden. A parish priest with a London *pied-à-terre*, Kemp might well have been better equipped to finance a lawsuit than Radley, who described himself only as a "husbandman." The investments of both cleric and layman in an honorable masculine reputation could work together.

The sneak thief, the liar, and the whoring priest share a common defining flaw: they are all false, that most common adjective of insult. They inhabit and exploit spaces, literal or symbolic, under the visible surface of life. So, for that matter, does the father who covers up illicit sex in his household. These are not "true men." In the wider context of everyday clerical life amid laymen, with its highly gendered social roles, a cleric had more to lose, as a man, by breaking his vows of celibacy than by remaining chaste. Institutionally sanctioned chastity separated him from the subordinate discourse of masculine self-indulgence, that hypercharged embodiment prized by the young and unmarried, which I will discuss in the next chapter. But sexual activity jeopardized his place in the far more important discourse of masculine maturity, manhood, where the higher stakes lay. Touching too many sensitive nerves, sex threatened to spoil his vital connections to those other men among whom he must buy, sell, negotiate contracts, and angle for dinner invitations, and possibly, thereby, help to make a nice marriage for his sister or cousin, find a good position for his godchild, or act as respected mediator in some local dispute.

Still, the modern reader finds it hard to shake the sense that suspicion of sexual misbehavior bore more heavily on clergymen, of all ranks, than on laymen. This is, in part, true. I would still urge caution, however, in making conclusions about the masculine identity of clergymen based solely on a sense of the greater circumspection that community opinion may have required of them. The factors involved were multiple and complex, indeed contradictory, which is often the way with culture, and especially with gender.

In the masculine world, where trueness and honesty were such powerful themes, priestly lechery made a priest "false," as I have already suggested. For the rector of Ickburgh, Norfolk, there was no distinction between being a "false priest" and being a "whoremaster," words together prompting him to sue.[161] "Whoremaster" and "whoremonger" were certainly not rare insults encountered by late medieval priests. The circumstances, however, often suggest that they were not meant literally. Even when they were, nonsexual factors complicate interpretation, as with laymen. Robert and Joan Pellet's repeated defamation of the prior and canons of St. Mary's Hospital, as whoremongers and maintainers of bawds and harlots, originated in the priory's attempt to sue the couple for an outstanding debt. Similarly, the tithe dispute that led to Thomas Wybard's attack on William Richardson began with the words "whoreson and whoremonger priest with other unfitting and unlawful words and demeanor."[162] Tithes and other financial obligations meant that laypeople's assets—laymen's substance—flowed to clergymen as an everyday matter. If one saw this as a waste, it was easy to image one's resentment in the terms of irresponsible male sexuality, as did the Norfolk man who allegedly said that his priest "deals with me like 2 false whoreson priests, that would have my goods to keep their brothels on."[163]

The sensitivity was also, in other ways, peculiar to the clerical estate. Trust organized a cleric's relations with other people, and many of those others (more than for most laymen) could be female. The trust clergymen needed, especially as confessors, was particularly personal and intimate. It depended on the rather fragile fiction, cherished by all involved, that they were not exactly like other men. Speech rebounding on them as sexual slander fractured that illusion, so a cleric was well advised to be watchful for even the hint of impropriety. The priest James Boswell sued in Norwich in 1521 over the mere suggestion that he "would not leave the company of Elisabeth Oliver, but keeps with her and hangs around her suspiciously."[164] The witnesses for William Bell (he of the untied codpiece) commented: "Diverse folks say, such as Thickpeny's wife, Thomas Gregg's wife, and diverse others, that while they were disposed . . . to give him the devotion afore, they intend now to give him no more, unless he could clear himself of this crime. . . . If this were proved upon him, they would love him less, and . . . he should have no good of them."[165] Without "devotion" and "good" from others, a cleric lost significant advantage in the masculine world of social competition. And "good," of course, also meant "goods." Surely this effect concerned priests as much as the danger of actual diocesan penalties for sexual incontinence, the nature and chances of which are surprisingly difficult to discern.[166]

Violation of celibacy could, however, have more severe consequences for priests, depending on their neighbors' attitudes, and such consequences were distinct to clergymen. R. L. Storey has convincingly argued that fifteenth-century indictments of clergymen for rape were probably often a means to end consensual relationships. The indicting juries knew that the priests, unlike laymen, could not be hanged for the offense, because their punishment came from the ecclesiastical authority.[167] In about 1480, the petition of a priest from Exeter implies that a rash of such false indictments had occurred there and in "the country thereabout."[168] The further dimension that Storey does not mention (though it strengthens his case) is that these clerical concubinages could not, unlike illicit relationships between laymen and women, be resolved by marriage. Where they threatened to spoil the reputation of a marriageable woman, it was therefore in the interest of her male kin to stop them. But not all such cases worked this way. The vicar of Sutton (Wiltshire) claimed that his imprisonment for rape arose because his oppressors, who had extorted "such little goods as God had sent him," "say that they know well that if your Orator were at large, he would sue them according to the law for the taking away of the goods; therefore they boast that they will indict him of another felony with the intent that he shall not be able to come out of prison."[169] Rape was presumably a convenient "other felony" to trump up because by the 1490s, the legal system had grown accustomed to the commonplace that clergymen were inclined to it. Institutional dicta protected priests from certain penalties applying, at least theoretically, to laymen. Plainly, and ironically, they also served to make clergymen more vulnerable to a certain kind of pseudolegal regulation and helped draw special attention to their sexual behavior.

False rape indictments, of course, directly addressed sexual behavior. But we can group them with other evidence that lay society could critique the social selves of clergymen with a sexual discourse in a blunter, more immediate way than worked for laymen. English culture could understand fornication between unmarried laymen and women, even as it officially frowned on it, as part of a life-stage continuum. As I will further discuss in chapter 3, this understanding was possible from two social levels. Authorities, formal and informal, could see it as a typical failing of young men with an obvious remedy: marriage. Young men themselves could valorize sexual experience for what it meant to them and their subordinate peers. Both these points, I think, make particular sense in a society like England where young people of most social strata had such relative heterosocial freedom.

Neither frame fit priests in major orders, so it was more difficult for both clergymen and laypeople to assign masculine sexuality a place in the social self of celibate priests. And when criticizing the interpersonal transactions of priests, even within the most laymanlike aspects of their professional lives, laypeople often expressed themselves using a sexual vocabulary. When the priest William Richardson petitioned Chancery, he cited Thomas Wybard's verbal attack as "whoreson and whoremonger priest, with other unfitting and unlawful words and demeanor."[170] One wonders what the other words were, and why (particularly if they were "unlawful") Richardson chose to specify only "whoreson and whoremonger priest," particularly as Wybard did not actually accuse him of sexual misconduct. It was hurtful to call a layman a whoremaster or whoremonger, but if one really wanted to get him, one called him a thief. For clergymen, something like the reverse may have been true, even when the insult's essential significance was the same.

Blaming the Friars

To complete this part of the argument, I turn now to some literary evidence showing how social and sexual anxieties converged on the subsection of the clergy that late medieval laymen, and also some clerics themselves, loved to hate. Both had reasons to feel threatened by the mendicant orders. The texts generated by that sense of threat predictably use the theme of clerical sexuality, but in a way that also brings gender, masculinity, to the surface.

One such poem from the late fourteenth century implies quite clearly that because friars have "naught to live by," they live off real men. Friars figure here as itinerant peddlers who cater to wives "when husbands are not in."[171] Moreover, the friars depend on the wives, or they would not be living so high. The poem directly connects this to their sexual access to women. In the first stanza, friars' luxurious clothes tempt women into spending their husbands' money on them (the clothes and, by extension, the friars), so friars perform a metaphoric adultery. Moreover, the friars are cheaters, extorcioners; they sell their goods at inflated prices. The warning becomes more explicitly sexual in the third stanza, referring to the "bower" in which the friars "make masteries." The cuckoo-bird pattern gets reasserted through a reference to church politics, via a claim that the friars usurp the "service" of "priests seculars."[172] The poem shows how neatly the husbandly jealousies of laymen and secular clergy could dovetail.

Another piece of hostile testimony, from about 1490, impugns the friars' masculinity in much more clearly sexual terms: "If you let a friar of any order stay overnight with you, either he will violate your wife or your daughter, or he will prefer your son, like a strong thief. May God give such a friar pain at the gate down below!"[173] These few lines comprise only part of an antifraternal poem that in other stanzas assails the friars in conventional terms for their general corruption and hypocrisy. But this excerpt brings together several of the concerns we have seen already. The friar poses a threat to the integrity of the layman's household, and the danger to property comes through in a nuanced, though also blunt, fashion. Here we have moved one notch up on the threat scale. The danger is not seduction; once admitted into the house, the friar will take what he wants by force.

The multivalence of both English and Latin terms brings together a number of different meanings, especially in the central four lines. "Ordur" may be a pun on "order/ordure"; the two different words shared a spelling at this time. *Violare* seems most obviously to mean "rape" in the modern sexual sense. But the contemporary legal blurring between rape and ravishment or abduction makes this an unstable meaning. This instability is consequently the source of the friar's strength: wife or daughter may be raped, abducted, or "abducted"—that is, they may have run off with the friar of their own volition. Remember, the person who wrote this did not speak Latin as a first language. His use of Latin was grounded in his knowledge of English and was meant to appeal to English-speaking persons in an English legal and linguistic culture.

The same principles destabilize the reference to the layman's son, for additional reasons. Surely we cannot read "prefer" innocently when it follows so closely on the preceding references to female victims. Will the friar "prefer" the son to the women, as a sexual conquest? Or will he abduct him,[174] perhaps to force him into his own order? That possibility was well established by the late fifteenth century. Numerous claims survive of forced or deceitful enticement of boys, especially those who were underage, into religious orders, and especially into the mendicant orders. The parallel with late-twentieth-century anxieties about homosexual "recruitment" of young people, particularly male ones, is too obvious to pass up, especially given the medieval equivalence of ages of consent for marriage and for entering the novitiate.[175] Both anxieties operate on a seduction theory, with varying components of deceit and forceful coercion. In both cases, the young victim becomes, via the seductive influence of an older, dominant agent, something he would never otherwise be; there is always within this fantasy an implied moment of sudden and critical change or initiation: "They lure you in, and before you know it, you're trapped—you've become one of them." For the imagined victim of homosexual seduction (who is always, at least homosexually, a virgin), this moment comes with sexual initiation, consensual or not, which effects a magical transformation, irreversible except with great difficulty and effort: a homosexual identity solidifies around him. In the discourse of medieval fathers' hostility to friars, the corresponding dreaded moment is the forced tonsure and profession, always an element in legal claims of fraternal abduction, also requiring difficult effort (complicated and expensive litigation) to reverse. (The possibility of reversal hardly exists within the purest form of the fantasy.) Moreover, no matter how we understand it within the "acts or identities" debate, surely a sodomitical threat awaits the son within the antifraternal fantasy as well. In both cases, masculine reproductive and patrimonial potential has been diverted to unproductive ends: wasted.

Hence, the descriptive phrase *sicut ffurtam ffortis,* "like a strong thief," resonates especially loudly in this context. Unmasculine thievery, such a potent concept among laymen, here becomes assimilated to the frustration of patriarchal needs. However, most importantly, the unmasculinity has nothing to do with normative clerical celibacy; indeed, the poem recognizes its utter irrelevance, except in the breach, as an indicator of the friars' falseness. The friars' unmanliness instead consists in their disregard for masculine property. As we discover here, that property includes not only the household and its female members, but the masculine potential represented by the layman's male heirs, all of which the friars cannot be trusted not, literally, to steal. However forceful and blunt the implications of *violare,* this is still a crafty and stealthy theft, not only because it contains the possibility of seduction, but also because it involves a breach of trust between men. The poem's victim has allowed the friar to stay overnight in his house (and make no mistake: rape, abduction, or whatever, the true victim here is always the male householder).

Such evidence moves us, perhaps, toward a distinction between masculinity and manliness. We cannot simply characterize the friar's ambivalent desire, wavering between male and female objects, as "sexual"; it is the desire for what does not belong to him, which he may obtain by sexual means. However, the polysemousness of the language means we cannot keep sexual meanings out. The desire for possession, penetration, and consumption is masculine in the negative sense; it is a phallic threat posed by male individuals and an expected feature of male behavior. However, it is not manly, because when selfishly indulged, it violates the unwritten compact of mutual respect between men.

Satire on friars was not restricted to the literature of complaint. In early sixteenth-century collections of short comic stories, the friars well outnumber the other clerical orders as illustrations of greed, hypocrisy, and licentiousness: wanting the best dishes at a rich man's table, pestering housewives who flee at their approach, making lewd comments to bent-over girls.[176] The roughly contemporary *Merie Tales of Skelton* contains a less angry, but at heart no less contemptuous, story called "How Skelton handled the friar that wanted to lie with him in his inn." Here, the fictionalized poet Skelton, the hero of this collection of stories, finds himself the object of a friar's request to share the only available bed at an alehouse. Skelton reluctantly agrees, gets the friar drunk, defecates on him while he is asleep,[177] tricks him into thinking he has been mortally stabbed, and humiliates him, having him ejected from the chamber to spend the night in the barn.[178] The mean spirit of the tale seems pointless, but only if we refuse to register the rather obvious pun on "lie with"—which is just what our historical knowledge that few people slept alone in the Middle Ages *and* our ingrained habit of denying homosexual readings unless the evidence hits us in the face both push us to refuse. Here, however, social pretensions and sexual protestations intersect. Skelton's refusal depends on two status claims: that he is sufficiently substantial, a "big" enough man socially, not to have to share a bed with another man, and that he does not make a habit of "lying with" other men sexually either. The friar's response challenges both of these claims on their own terms; whether we consider the friar to have "intended" one or both is part of the ambiguity that makes the joke work. The sexual interpretation cannot be refused because there is no other way the otherwise unoffending friar can be said to have "deserved" the particular insult he receives. The reader has to sympathize with Skelton in order to laugh at the friar; something has to stop the reader from asking why Skelton did not simply refuse the request, and this same something has to close the reader's ears to the friar's protest that he too deserved lodging for his money (which, presumably, the alewife did not refuse).

That "something," obvious but unmentioned, what the masculine compact with the reader assumes is well known and therefore to be unnamed, is signaled in increasingly crude manner as the tale progresses: first a play on the words "lie with" (culminating in the veiled accusation), then an observation of the friar's nocturnal nakedness (surely unremarkable for the period, unless a point is being made), and finally the defiling of the friar's body. And why this particular choice of body function? Defecation, to borrow Camille Paglia's more universal statement about male urination, is here a form of masculine commentary, a commentary that makes more than one statement.[179] By befouling another man's body, Skelton acts out the status comment: you are not equal to me socially, you are something to be shit on. Tied up with that statement, "You are not a man as I am," is the explanatory: "because you are a sexually different man." To put it in terms that I think are not too crude for the tale's logic: who but a bugger ends up with another man's feces on his abdomen—and at the same time can be made to claim, to *admit*, that he has been "thrust in the belly"? The sodomitical meaning here is not just a matter of penetrator versus penetrated; a confluence of attitudes rejects, pushes out to the pigsty the male who presumes on another's body, or better yet, who can be suspected of that presumption because of his particular clerical status.

I say particular because Skelton, both in life and in these stories, was a cleric himself, an ordained priest who held the living of Diss in Norfolk. As a beneficed priest, he was securely in the better-off ranks of the clergy, even before becoming poet laureate. The tale takes up the status assumptions of the secular or diocesan clergy and unites those, fuelled by their antimendicant jealousies, with popular suspicion of the friars. And this animus works for the lay reader because it is expressed in a masculine language uniting clerics and laymen.

Celibacy and Gender Identity: What Was the Real Problem?

Whether or not laymen considered clergymen unmanly because of their celibacy is one question. The more pertinent, but also much more difficult, question to answer is whether the clergy themselves felt unmanly because of it. Stated less negatively, the issue is whether their gender identity was substantially different from that of laymen. Did it amount to "emasculinity"? The weight of the social evidence I rehearsed above should make us think twice about assuming any significant difference or, indeed, any significant problem in most everyday situations.

In 1473, through a servant, Margaret Paston advised her son Walter to "be not too hasty to take binding [holy] orders till he is 24 years old or more, even if he be contrarily advised, for often one regrets haste." She packed much into this eloquent recommendation. Twenty-four, of course, was the canonical age for the order of priest. At that age "or more," a young man would have achieved a basic maturity of personality still very much in development only a few years before. Margaret's word for haste was "rape," a word that also carried its modern meaning, suggesting she was most concerned about sexual misconduct, whether she was thinking of Walter's reputation or more generally the family's. She knew that, for the clerically inclined, to rush into priesthood was tempting and possible—and possibly disastrous. Her advice shows a practical faith in a young man's ability to know himself, including the strength of his own sexuality. Placing the question in the terms of trueness, Margaret concluded, "I will love him better as a good secular man than as a lewd priest."[180] By now, the man making the decision was surely as much a man, in terms of sexuality and gender identity, as he would ever be.

Some failures of celibacy probably happened in exactly the way Margaret feared. Others probably were conscious rejections of authority, which had its own value for masculinity, as I will discuss in the next chapter. We cannot learn much about masculine identity from most such cases, though, because we lack the subjective dimension of the evidence. The implication of the McNamara-Swanson-Cullum argument is that violations of celibacy happened because clergymen had internalized a lay model of masculinity centered on sexual performance, which they could only either embrace or replace with emasculinity. Such logic implies that clerics could understand manliness itself only in sexual terms. They hollowed out a place within themselves and put God there, became "emasculine," and learned to love their new state (and thought they were loving God). Or, not having managed this feat of self-evacuation, they carried around the lay sexual standard like a homing device that eventually drove them back to sexuality. This view of things fails to consider two possibilities. The first is that a certain number of clergymen had made a private accommodation (of which there could be many) between sexuality and spirituality, thereby broke the rules, and felt justified nonetheless.

The other possibility is that those who took celibacy seriously did not see it as "emasculine" but as the very essence of manliness itself. In the first two sections of this chapter, I referred to the importance of self-command in lay masculinity. The origins of the celibate ideal relate (in a somewhat extreme and ironic way) to the same ancient values of self-command, or self-control, given perhaps their most memorably eloquent formulation by Cicero. All the advantages and honors of such a life strategy in the ancient world were masculine ones; it was for men among men that they mattered. The classical ideal was moderation, not asceticism. Extreme self-denial (as opposed to control or command) was as dangerous and undesirable, possibly as unmanly, as was being ruled by lust.[181]

The Christian application of this ethic in the monastic ideal was in some ways revolutionary, because it made celibacy, a very special form of self-command, equally honorable for men and women. Culturally, though, celibacy as self-control never lost its fundamentally masculine significance. From the earliest times, women (female religious, women saints) who maintained their celibacy in the face of severe temptation or brutal threat gained praise as having overcome specifically feminine weakness, as having taken on masculine virtues and strengths.[182] More to the point, the early ascetics, up to Jerome, valorized self-denial to a competitive extreme; in effect, ascetic masculinity could be as demonstrative and quasi-phallic as under a sexual regime.[183] As Jacqueline Murray explains, regular clerics of the high and late Middle Ages also inherited a tradition of thinking about celibacy as the manliest of battles against the temptations of the flesh. Gerald of Wales argued, further, that only men who actually experienced sexual desire truly engaged in the battle. For self-control to mean something, one had to have something to control. In valorizing the fight against male lust, monastic writers like Caesarius of Heisterbach and Adam of Eynsham explicitly invoked armed combat, transmuting the desire for masculine aggression into a form that celibate men could achieve.[184]

This way of associating sexuality, self-control, and combat has not disappeared completely even from our own world. Loïc Wacquant relates how young American boxers conceive their masculinity to depend on discipline and sacrifice, particularly on sexual abstinence. Unlike the premodern clergy, these prizefighters are not supposed to be celibate all the time. Yet, as with the clergy, not everyone believes the struggle is always successful. Still, the ability to resist sexual desire when its satisfaction is inappropriate (i.e., when preparing for a fight) provides an important ideal for them, for classic reasons: sexual activity dissipates energies and passions that ought to be directed toward the (male) opponent, converted into "(homoerotic) *libido pugilistica*, the urgent desire to delve into a violent *corps-à-corps* with another man." Simultaneously, the struggle for control of sexual desire means that their sexual potential is real.[185]

The tradition Murray identifies originated at the time of the Gregorian reforms, three to four centuries before the period of my study. In addition, it was partly rooted in the desire of the regular clergy to preserve their sense of distinctiveness from secular priests, who had only just begun to give up marital sexuality. Yet, seeing celibacy, and by extension the other self-denials of monastic life, as manly in these terms was not necessarily remote from the experience of clergymen in late medieval England, though it may be difficult to establish this directly. Some of the exemplars themselves were English, such as Hugh of Lincoln. Nor was this monastic manliness incompatible with the kinds of behavior that late medieval priests, especially, had to undertake. Conrad Leyser discusses "the rise of ascetic masculinity in the early Middle Ages not as an introverted discourse of sexual anxiety, but in terms of a fiercely competitive culture of public power."[186] That culture long outlasted the early Middle Ages. Aelred of Rievaulx, who "in his *Mirror of Charity* criticized the presence of 'effeminate amusements' within monastery walls," attracted the praise of Walter Daniel for the virility of his administration.[187] The competitively masculine possibilities of asceticism were not lost even on fifteenth-century laypeople. In 1470, John Paston II invoked the story of "a holy young monk who fasted more than all the convent, and afterward hoped to be abbot for his holiness and fasting; afterward he was abbot, and then he stopped his abstinence, saying the day was come for which he had spent the evening fasting."[188] Paston was primarily making a point about hypocrisy, but the point depended on an awareness of (and a certain cynicism about) the status value of self-command. In the more ordinary world, several factors worked in combination. By the late fourteenth century, with the Gregorian and Fourth Lateran reforms well in the past, the difference in values between priests and monks had most likely flattened out. Celibate men were in the world, to a degree very rarely achieved by celibate women. Moreover, as we have just seen, male clerics' secular involvements were so significant that they had to maintain secular credit among laymen as well. Where celibacy was concerned, the masculine ethic twisted back on itself: failure to maintain a clerical ideal could diminish one's masculine social self in the lay world. Cullum does not substantiate her assertion that "celibacy and virginity were coming to be increasingly seen as feminine virtues by the later Middle Ages."[189] Even were this the case, however, the weight of learned discourse and authority on the one hand, and the persuasions of the lay world on the other, must together have outweighed "feminine" meanings.

If celibacy, properly maintained, could ease rather than complicate clergymen's relations with laymen, and could offer its own version of masculinity, did that mean that the successfully celibate clergy as a result lived lives of confident self-acceptance? Not necessarily. I would like to suggest in closing, however, that the problems may have been somewhat different from what we often assume. My first point refers to the social frame. In a world where marriage and fatherhood so importantly signified manhood, inability to marry and to produce lineal heirs may have been more sorely missed than sexual activity per se, whatever the compensations of being "married" to the church. Cullum argues that clerics in minor orders faced a difficult choice because taking major orders—necessary in order to advance in the church—meant giving up marriage, while the marital prospects of a man with a future as a parish clerk, the typical fate of one in minor orders, were not brilliant. The point is convincing, though I think Cullum overdraws the contrast between such minor clerics' limitations and the supposedly greater possibilities open to their lay peers, the urban apprentices, who faced difficulties of their own in advancement.[190]

My second point connects social, that is professional, and spiritual concerns. Far from feeling they had entered an insufficiently masculine social identity, clergymen may rather have experienced the opposite: dismay at learning that being a clergyman called for too *much* masculinity, too much competition, sycophancy, and entanglement in the sordid negotiations of everyday life. Cullum rightly calls attention to the subordination and dependency of unbeneficed clergy. Her argument that this imperiled their gender identity, however, fails to place subordination and dependency within the medieval ethic of service, which bore on laymen of all ranks as well.[191] Virginia Davis, perceiving a scholarly tendency to see late medieval clergy as "cynical careerists," warns that we must credit them with some genuine piety in order to understand why they pursued such a materially insecure vocation.[192] Even though my own discussion has emphasized the secular side of clerical life, I believe Davis's point is valid, and that it supports mine. That very piety could easily imply a desire to escape The World, or at least The City in its metaphorical sense: not just sex and money, but the load of obligations great and small to people great and small, whether kin, friends, masters, or servants. In late medieval England, the desire for such a personal divestment was bound to be disappointed. Clergymen, who as shepherds of their flock were symbolically "husbands" in that sense, needed to get along with lay husbands, and often to behave like them, and in doing so, they were men, whether they liked it or not.

※

CHAPTER THREE

Sex and Gender:
The Meanings of the Male Body

IN CHAUCER'S *Canterbury Tales*, the Reeve tells the story of Symkyn, a proud and dishonest miller cuckolded by two clever university students he had cheated.[1] The clerks also manage to deflower his daughter, whose advantageous marriage Symkyn had been at great pains in preparing. Masculinity is an obvious theme in this story, and it is a masculinity signified importantly by bodies. Symkyn's very person conveys a bodily presence suffused with pride and aggression. He carries around with him an assortment of weapons accentuating the combative, self-aggrandizing nature of this "market-beater" ("Reeve's Tale" [RT], 3936). The miller is preoccupied with maintaining and improving on the social status he sought to augment through his own marriage—to the parish priest's daughter, an obviously illegitimate woman, but nonetheless a moneyed one. A medium-sized fish in a small pond, Symkyn thrusts his limited prominence in everyone's face. Chaucer's description of Symkyn's weapons connects that pride to the precise location on the body where Symkyn, we suspect, feels it: his long cutlass *by his belt*, the fine-looking dagger *in his "pouch,"* the Sheffield knife *in his hose* (RT 3929–33). Social and corporeal masculinity here are one, and both turn out to be illusory, all in the miller's mind.

The clerks repay Symkyn's crafty thievery through their own male bodies, by a sexual humiliation. They frustrate his social goals (his daughter's marital value) and his household governance (they make his wife betray him). In the latter case, they expose false husbandry in two senses: along with governance, they make a mockery of Symkyn's sexual relation to his wife, who needs little persuasion to sleep with them. Chaucer, here, as elsewhere, does not merely parrot cultural commonplaces but plays with their implications. The clerks themselves are crafty thieves, but they are not false. They employ guile to answer guile, to "quite" it. The miller first cheated them by frustrating their efforts to monitor his milling of their grain. That grain was to feed their physical bodies; their revenge, in turn, robs Symkyn of his substance, part of his social body. Gaining the upper hand over a crafty thief, the clerks win a masculine contest fought, expressed, and symbolized in terms of bodies, and specifically genital ones. Contrary to one recent claim, no "perversion of the power of masculinity" occurs here.[2] Instead, Chaucer shows how pretension to one kind of masculinity, built on falseness, collapses when it encroaches on the social bodies of other men.

I referred to Symkyn's "corporeal masculinity" quite deliberately, because the story makes a point not about maleness but about its meaning. His body, and the accessories of weaponry that draw our attention to it, suggest not only his social gender identity, as do the physical descriptions of many of Chaucer's pilgrims. They also suggest the attitude he takes to that identity: his personal masculinity. The male body was useful to medieval writers, of course, in ways that are far more abstruse; they employed it metaphorically, for example, to portray an essential connection between masculinity and productive labor (as opposed, especially, to usury and sodomy, both of which cheat this system).[3] Yet these tropic functions represent only one rather indirect way that the male body conveyed meanings of masculinity. A historical analysis focused on both social and subjective experience needs to get closer to the meaning of physical maleness.

FROM PHYSIOLOGY TO PERSONALITY

Human beings may be more than bodies, but they are bodies, and their experience of the body—whether accepted, contested, rejected, or altered—defines them. Our perception of the world depends on our bodies: both pleasure and pain reside in them; they provide the metaphors by which we understand things outside ourselves at all levels of complexity. It is foolish to think that this has ever not been the case. In premodern Europe, a society dependent on the rhythms and vicissitudes of the natural world, the reach of the physical into the realm of mental and psychological experience must surely have been even deeper. One thing determining that experience is the sex of the body in question.

Without sex, gender threatens to float away from the individual, to become a completely social and exteriorized phenomenon. Yet, gender, even in its most plastic or "performative" formulations, makes no sense without reference to sex. As Judith Butler put it, over a decade ago:

> [If] gender is the social significance that sex assumes within a given culture . . . then what, if anything, is left of "sex" once it has assumed its social character as gender? . . . If gender consists of the social meanings that sex assumes, then sex does not *accrue* social meanings as additive properties but, rather, *is replaced by* the social meanings it takes on. . . . gender emerges, not as a term in a continued relationship of opposition to sex, but as the term which absorbs and displaces "sex."[4]

In making this comment, Butler criticized the facile association of sex with "nature" and gender with "culture," and the consequent opposition between them, in one version of feminism. Butler's words, however, serve to underscore one of my main arguments: that the meanings of gender are not only "social."

In emphasizing the relation of gender to sex, to the body, I do not intend to reject the constructed and discursive conception of gender entirely, but to place it in perspective. Such ideas are neither as all encompassing nor as exclusive of other approaches, as they often seem in the second- and thirdhand versions where most historians (and students) encounter them. If gender is a matter of meaning, then of course the meaning lies in discourse. If we seek to know the body, of course we can only do so through the epistemological systems of a given culture, past or present. Yet this makes it more, not less, urgent to consider the corporeal body in historical analysis.

The male body helped to define masculinity, first, through its appearance, which medieval theory attributed to what went on inside it. Form and appearance commented further on the character of the man; physiology implied personality. Part of form was physical maturity. One condition of manhood was having a man's body—which might or might not be a manly body, in turn reflecting its inhabitant's masculinity. The body conveyed masculinity also, both to society and to the self, through its function, what it did. Sexual acts were only the most specially charged of such functions. Together, form and function spoke back to the self, creating an embodied subjectivity.

MEDIEVAL MALENESS: FORM AND MEANING

Male bodies five hundred or a thousand years ago were much the same as today; they all had penises, they did not bear children, their breasts did not lactate, and they tended to have hair on their faces, whether preserved or removed. In other ways, those bodies differed from male bodies today: they were probably shorter and not so well nourished, and they tended not to last as long. Both sex and gender bear only partially on the matter. Female bodies also suffered from malnutrition and disease, and the additional risks of pregnancy meant that many women died young. So maleness, in itself, seems not a very promising subject. Even if someone established that the average adult male in the year 1200 had more hair on his chest than today, the fact would not open out very far to tell us much about men's experience of masculinity in society. However, if someone could show that having insufficient chest hair was socially shameful for men, that would tell us something. Facial and body hair are markers of physical maturity and might be used to establish a young man's approximate age, in a period when exact ages were not always known. That might, in turn, affect his ability to succeed to property, to be sworn into a tithing group in his village, or to serve for the first time in certain public capacities.

It would stand to reason that in a culture in which the difference between boy and man was so important, physical maturity would be one criterion. Moreover, maturation speaks directly to the historicity of bodily masculinity because of the possibility that the age of puberty varies between cultures and, moreover, between historical periods. But there were very few ways for concerns over physical maturity to leave traces in the records. The problem is not that males lack clear physical signs of maturity. Rather, there were enough other ways for people to attest to age, even without written documentation, that legal authorities did not depend on physical markers. The experience of being, for example, an apprentice or university student whose physical development had not caught up with his numerical age—a sensitive matter in adolescence and young adulthood—is hidden from us. We miss, therefore, an important perspective on gender identity.

Physical manhood involved for the individual not only social selfhood, but a sense of the body's evolving capacities, especially strength and sexuality. An early sixteenth-century tale turns on flirtation between a mature woman and a man of twenty who has, he claims, a beard more noticeable "above" than "below."[5] The distinction may be between his upper lip and his chin; it may also, given the idiom of punning innuendo, oppose facial hair to pubic hair. Either possibility (which admits the other) matches a common pattern in early male puberty. In either case, the man's sexual capacity depends on maturity. At twenty, he seems rather old even in an era of poor nutrition for this ambiguous situation to apply. It is still impossible to judge whether the late medieval audience would have found it imaginable or taken it as comic exaggeration for the sole purposes of the tale. Whatever the precise details, the possibility of mismatch between the masculinity that social intercourse might require of a young man and the reality of his physical maturity seems to me the most significant aspect.

Evidence relating exactly to these questions of embodiment (to borrow Jacqueline Murray's term) is generally difficult to find.[6] Knowing about the medieval body often means knowing only the things written about it. Most of our evidence concerning medieval attitudes to the body comes from medical discourse, which set out to describe what bodies were like—or rather, what they ought to be like. But several cautions are in order. The strong influence of tradition and the authority of the *auctor* within learned culture meant that medieval medical texts in use by the later centuries were usually recensions and redactions of originals from hundreds of years before, often coming from sources well outside the geographical area where they were in use. The *Secret of Secrets*, for example, exists in Middle English versions, but derives ultimately from an Arabic original. One can easily see how distorting such derivations are for any attempt to say something about English attitudes to the body. Outside general physiology and humoral theory, specific interpretations about the meaning of a certain hair color or distribution may be less reliable when their ultimate cultural origin is very distant. My compromise in this unhappy situation, especially since the book is not about medical treatises, has been to rely chiefly on two Middle English texts that were well known and well distributed in the late Middle Ages. These I supplement with remarks from recent scholarship on the gender norms legible in medieval medical theory, whether or not they specifically concern English sources.

The learned authorities saw both sex and gender as constitutionally determined. Constitution here refers to physiology as much as to anatomy. It predestined general sexual characteristics, but also accounted for variations within the sexes—for example, the existence of more or less masculine men, or even of women with masculine traits. In the logic of "complexion," much followed from men's greater heat, which allowed them to convert excess nutritive qualities into "seed" and body hair. Consequently, to return to my initial example, "prominent body hair not only marked the male among humans but also signified masculinity."[7] Joan Cadden, the commentator here, provides a quotable summation: "The contrast is not only between males and females but rather between the masculine and the nonmasculine, including children of both sexes as well as women. The production of beard and body hair followed from the physiological, and the links between male maturity, the growth of the beard, and the ability to produce semen created a bridge between sexual maleness and gender-linked virility."[8] "Virility" here encompasses both functional sexuality and nonsexual aspects of social masculinity. The latter qualities are themselves grounded, and detectible, in the body. By the fourteenth century, treatises on sex difference comple-mented the older humoral theory with physiognomy, which read character traits through external physical features.[9]

The Middle English texts show a combination of such influences, and they bear out the importance of maturity in defining manhood both mor-phologically and functionally. John Trevisa's Middle English translation of Bartholomew the Englishman's *De Proprietatibus Rerum* (technically an ency-clopedia, with a section on sex difference) bears the imprint of Barthol-omew's own apparent reliance on Constantinus Africanus and Aristotle. Hence, women of "hot and moist complexion" may have facial hair, and men who are "cold and dry" have "little beards." In addition, "thickness of the beard is a sign and token of heat and of substantial humor and of strength, and a certain test to know the difference between men and women." Possi-bly, then, in dubious cases, it is the amount of facial hair that marks a man. Children do not have facial hair because their "superfluity of exhalation" goes instead into growth.[10] Beards, then, are markers of both sex and gender. Indeed, Constantine-Bartholomew-Trevisa does not distinguish between those categories. He does not specifically say that the beard marks a "manly" man, except through the implicit association that strength is a manly char-acteristic. (The text later makes clear that males of all species are stronger than females.) Yet neither does he suggest that it adds anything to a woman, or that it indicates anything specifically qualitative about the inner person.

Bartholomew-Trevisa's further comments on maturity cite Aristotle and move silently from animals to humans. Trevisa points out the voice as a marker of mature masculinity: "The emission of sperm in males comes in the time when the voice changes, and that is after the age of fourteen."[11] Note that this is not so different from the modern age of male puberty. Book 6 again cites Aristotle in declaring that the voice change indicates the beginning of sexual desire ("liking of Venus"). Trevisa himself makes a rare interruption to clarify his idea of youth; he claims that *iuventus* in his source (presumably Bartholomew) is not the same as in "our common speech." Here, says Trevisa, it means adulthood, starting as early as twenty-one to as late as fifty, with the main inner range being thirty-five to forty-five. He rehearses this idea, coming from Isidore of Seville, at the beginning of book 6, which places men in *adolescencia* either narrowly from fourteen to twenty-one, or widely even up to thirty-five. Such a wide range obviously takes in much more than "adolescence" and seems to mean the time when the man is still able to accumulate strength and power, which may or may not mean actually growing. The man is sexually mature at this point. But full "strength" comes only with the next stage, *iuventus,* when the man is "at the end of his full increasing," so that he is no longer changing.[12] (This idea reflects rather well the way men's bodies actually work, as appreciable muscular growth and acquisition of a mature body shape may continue into the late twenties, well past sexual maturity and the end of long bone growth.) This discussion of age applies only to men. Women's ages are not dealt with or classified in the same way; they are classified under their roles of mother, daughter, nurse, midwife, and so on.

Because Bartholomew-Trevisa's sources reason through complexion, the possible meaning of individual body parts gets little mention beyond their relevance to sex difference. (I will discuss the comments about the male sexual organs in the next section.) Trevisa mentions breasts solely as a female feature; no mention is made of men's possibly analogous breasts. This omission makes sense given the derivation from Aristotle that one function of breasts is "to know sex and ages."[13] The Middle English *Book of Physiognomy,* a version of the *Secret of Secrets,* in contrast, as its name implies, reads the body's visible parts for their nonbodily significance. Because (judging by the features discussed) the body is assumed to be male, the text's judgments on what is good or bad in particular body parts amount to judgments on masculinity. The features discussed are not those we might necessarily expect. To be sure, we learn that shoulders are best "not fat but of a middling type," and that slim haunches and buttocks are better than fleshy ones. But more attention goes to characteristics of the head and face: "A low forehead is not manly." Small nostrils are associated with "old men" as well as "thieves and losers," while round nostrils are good.[14] The shape of the mouth can indicate "strong" and "great-hearted" men, the latter a feature assimilated to masculinity in Trevisa as well, from Constantine: "In males the hearts are large and great. Therefore, they are able to draw great quantities of spirit and of blood, and so because of this great abundance of blood, a man is bolder and hardier than a woman."[15] Men should have "nearly square" chins; round ones are "womanish." Most important, however, are the eyes, which receive very detailed attention. A "woman's look" indicates lechery, and shaking eyes signify the love of women. This is discussed amid similarities to various animals. Shifty eyes, as we might expect, signify a thief. Large red eyes are characteristic of women; however, there may be speckles in the eyes, and "if they are sanguineous, it shows manhood."[16]

The conceit of the *Secret of Secrets* is that its interpretations are meant for the instruction of princes. That fiction points us toward the text's broader relevance in decoding what the body of a man indicates about his character. As Cadden remarks, "Since being masculine or feminine entailed, *not as incidental effects but as defining characteristics*, dimensions of disposition, character, and habit, the variations [on a binary model] had to do not only with complexion and appearance but also with behaviour, including sexual conduct."[17] Physiognomy was, then, ultimately a discourse pointed toward social relations. And yet both physiognomy and complexion had other implications beyond the social. The "Book of Physiognomy" seems to warn in the end that its readings are only to be taken as a guide to inclinations, not as the last word on a man's character.[18]

The texts' respective treatments of hair are revealing in this regard. The only substantial statements about hair and gender in Bartholomew-Trevisa are those concentrating on the hair of the head. Here, following Isidore, the text asserts the propriety of distinct masculine (short, plain) and feminine (long, decorated) hairstyles: not a matter of physiology but of culture. Bartholomew-Trevisa explains why baldness afflicts men more than women (women and children have more moisture in their heads). He also claims, after Aristotle, that men who "often serve Venus" lose their hair, though it is hard to tell from the context whether this means in general, as a life pattern, or as a cause and effect. Yet little is said about male-female differences. The *Book of Physiognomy* discusses body hair alongside that of the head, drawing various meanings. It includes, however, parts of the body that would not be seen in ordinary social interactions.[19] Possibly, of course, nakedness between socially equal men was not unusual, particularly in the context of bathing and perhaps also sleeping. The latter case particularly might imply a certain mutual trust and hence a need for a reading of the body, to get at character traits that might bear on a homosocial relationship. Yet without stretching the point too far, we need to consider that the intent of such readings might not be so narrowly practical. After all, the male body that a man was likely to be able to know most closely was his own. Physiognomy could be a route toward a kind of embodied self-knowledge.

MANLINESS AND ATTRACTIVENESS

Did, however, the manliness of the medieval body have a meaning in itself? Was a manly body an attractive body? Making exact correspondences is difficult unless we have a clear idea of what we mean by attractiveness, even beauty. Perhaps a manly body was attractive because of the qualities it suggested about the inner person; attractive need not have meant sexually attractive. (The London cutlers required their apprentices to be "handsome in stature, having straight and proper limbs"—probably, as Karras suggests, "a matter of honor," but perhaps best understood as *gentilesse*, that subtle medieval combination of the mannerly and the moral.)[20] I cannot do more than touch on this large subject here, one which depends largely on literary references, though I will return to it when I deal with clothing later in this chapter. In general, however, whether medieval writers judge a male figure's appearance manly or unmanly, the discrete contribution of the physical body is almost impossible to isolate. It depends greatly on a relationship to factors both more interior and more exterior than visible flesh. The person "inside" the body on the one hand, and the clothes that cover and adorn it on the other, combine with the body itself to form a complex wherein the different elements express and influence each other. We saw this in Symkyn the miller; the other figures in the *Canterbury Tales* provide similarly variegated examples. The Monk, for example, gets a strongly corporeal description, and as Michael Sharp observes, his physical presence later draws the attention of the Host.[21] Moreover, the Monk, not the seductive Friar, is named the "manly man," even though he is rather overweight and not apparently handsome. There are several probable reasons for this, resulting from Chaucer's deliberate manipulation of stereotypes about the different failings of the two clerical orders.[22] The Monk is "manly" with reference to the phallic self-indulgence and pride signified by his well-fed body, his social confidence among men—not his apparent fondness for "venerie" (surely a pun), which would equally well apply to the Friar. The Friar's smooth-tongued guile, however, disqualifies him. "Manly" here is therefore at best an ambivalent descriptor.

Male bodies in the *Canterbury Tales* encode unmanliness more vividly than they do ideal masculinity. The Reeve's close-shaven thinness embodies crafty deceit, the Summoner's pustules a corruption bursting out from the inside. The Chaucerian *locus classicus* for the sex-gender relation, however, has to be the Pardoner. The possible ambiguity in Chaucer's treatment of this character has spawned many different readings from literary critics; most of these turn on concepts of sexuality rather than gender, and in fact add very little to a discussion of masculinity.[23] At present, we should leave aside the narrator's famous statement that the Pardoner was "a gelding or a mare" to note the other aspects of his physical description. Chaucer draws our attention to the Pardoner's hair: to its color, its smoothness and straightness, its length, and the fact that it is uncovered. (His hood is "trussed up in his wallet" [General Prologue (GP) 681].) He is also beardless, and apparently to remain so. This is decidedly an unmanly body, which comes as close as it can to femaleness without actually slipping over; Chaucer denies the Pardoner even the hint of the one facial feature that the discourse of complexion chooses to illustrate maleness.

The implications of this amalgam of features are complex. The description slips back and forth between body and clothes. Long, golden, unbound hair (which occupies more descriptive space than any other single feature) is a conventionally feminine attribute. On a woman, its connotations could be very positive in medieval terms, evoking youth, beauty, and virginity. Yet it also shades into an enduring, and enduringly criticized, feature of the very conventional attire of young men (see also below). His "wallet, in front of him in his lap," "brimful of pardons come from Rome all hot" (GP 686–87), is surely a gendered reference to the location of the Pardoner's actual masculinity. In the occupational identity that names him, he has power, even if it is not as peremptory as the Summoner's. His attempted extension of his social self through his side trade in relics, however, expresses falseness: the relics are fake (GP 700–1). As with Symkyn, objects on or about the Pardoner's body comment on it by association. His purported veil of Mary is carried in his "male": literally a pouch or bag, and thus suggestive in its meaning, but even the very word is legible as a pun.[24] Moreover, some of the objects that sustain that dishonest trade are themselves body parts, so they associatively form a false social body. They are direct analogues of the "feigned flattery and japes" (GP 705), the falseness in the Pardoner's rhetoric, which is itself part of his occupational identity and his basis for a place in the world of men. Whatever else may be implied about the Pardoner, his socially visible body expresses an essential unmanliness in terms comprehensible without any reference to sexual practice.

FROM PHALLUS TO PENIS (OR VICE VERSA?)

In 1470, John Paston II, who was serving in the army of King Edward IV, wrote a letter to his brother John III, in which he mentioned offhandedly:

> Also, a new little Torke has come along: a good-looking fellow 40 years of age. He is shorter than Manuel by a hand's width, and shorter than my little Tom by his shoulders, and smaller still above his nipple. And he has, as he himself said to the king, three or four sons, each one as tall and strapping as the king

himself. His legs are normal enough, and it is reported that his penis is as long as his leg.[25]

Obviously this fellow caught Paston's attention, and he thought him worth mentioning in a letter: not as a matter of great importance, just an interesting tidbit. And why was it so interesting? First, Torke was unusually short in stature, shorter than other small men Paston knew. Paston tries to give his reader a picture of the man's body, whose oddness seems to be a matter of proportion: the description divides his upper torso into sections, and it would seem that he was particularly compressed between his shoulders and chest. The language used makes it difficult to imagine the body precisely. Still, Torke was not hideously deformed, but a "well-visaged fellow," pleasant enough to look at; moreover, to serve in an army, even as a servant, he could not have been too much disabled.

Rhetorically, the description of Torke's abnormalities serves to set up the real surprise, the contrast with what was (surprisingly) normal about him. Despite his shortness, Paston reports, he had fathered several children—male children, at that—who were of normal, indeed admirable stature, as tall and "likely" (impressive, strapping) as the king. (Edward IV stood at least 6 ft. 3½ in., or 189 cm, tall and was considered by contemporaries, at this point, still a good-looking man, only in his late twenties in 1470.)[26] That Torke's smallness was a matter of the upper body seems to be supported by Paston's comment that he was "legged right enough"—that his legs seemed normal, at least in proportion. Like a good storyteller, Paston saves the sauciest bit for last: the rumor that Torke's genital endowment made up for whatever was lacking in the rest of his body. Paston did not begin his story by saying, "There's a guy in our company who is hung like a stud horse," which would have changed the relative importance of all the other elements. As it is, Torke's penis appears, a rumor and punch line, as the final bit of proof: that is, proof of what is both most important and most unusual. It does this by establishing emphatically that this is a *man's* body: both male and masculine. A précis of the passage through gender analysis might say: "Torke is a tiny man, with a weirdly proportioned body, and therefore we might expect him to fall short (pun intended), to be weak and unmanly, to be unable to carry himself as a man in our society among other men. But actually, he has several sons, normal and attractive sons, so he's obviously sexually capable and socially capable, in that he has secure heirs. And he didn't hesitate to say all this to the prime alpha male of them all, the king himself. So consequently, his penis must be big enough to fill in the gaps, to make the equation balance."

The discourse of letter writing, ordinary family communication about very practical and prosaic matters, allowed this passage to come to light, riding alongside more "important" information in the terms of writer (John II) and reader (John III). So one writer-reader relation (Paston to us) encloses another (John II to John III). And the fifteenth-century discourse is a one between men, a homosocial discourse. The secondhand reports, the circulation of rumors about Torke and his self-presentation, are homosocial as well. They belong to a system of communication between men in an all-male context (the military cohort), one of many such contexts where talk established reputation. Torke's body, or most of it, was on display for public comment; so were his interactions with other men. What he said to the king and, by implication, other men who outranked him, then formed part of another discursive network, which affected the way his peers and superiors saw him. Competition, and making and holding one's place in a masculine hierarchy, depended on discourse (language, speech, manner) as well as on physical conflict or sheer social and monetary advantage: a point driven forcefully home by other kinds of evidence we have seen.

Discourse bears on gender in this passage another way, following from the précis I suggested above. In the imaginative logic that Paston enters and sustains, Torke's penis—the thing that marks him most securely as physically male—is an outcome, a conclusion of the profile he has cut through checking all the right masculine boxes: soldier, husband, father, public figure (in his own small way), competitor. Hence, he is a sexually complete man as well. The little man's impressive sex organ existed, and exists, in the context of a discourse. It served to symbolize certain homosocially sustained values. Its power to do so depended, in turn, on its reference to the male body and especially Torke's unusual male body. The example nicely illustrates Judith Butler's remark: "To claim that discourse is formative is not to claim that it originates, causes, or exhaustively composes that which it concedes; rather, it is to claim that there is no *reference to* a pure body which is not at the same time a further formation of that body."[27]

Body, maleness, masculinity, penis: all these elements seem to lead toward the explanatory concept of the phallus. It is probably the most famous symbolic structure associated with the male body, imaging the idea of extension or aggrandizement of self through the penetrative capacity of the erect penis. That which is phallic, therefore, usually involves aggressive or defensive self-interest. Jacques Lacan's linguistic recasting of psychoanalysis, and the plentiful literary-cultural criticism derived from it, understand the phallus further in terms of power: a fantasy of autonomous completeness, domination, and control.[28] Both men and women may seek to possess this phallus, but, as a fantasy, it is by definition always incompletely accessible.

The phallus is a powerful image, practically unavoidable in speaking of masculinity. It provides a way of symbolizing, through the most vivid fleshly sign of maleness, certain behaviors that men often display. Associations of masculinity with aggression and physical strength, whether literal or figurative, cannot be ignored in medieval evidence; neither can their social equivalents. The masculine identity that Symkyn the miller attempts to maintain is unmistakably phallic, for example, and the phallic qualities of late medieval men's attire will feature later in this chapter. Yet the phallus is also an image highly amenable to cliché. Social masculinity involved far more than phallic self-gratification, and indeed could mean its opposite, as Chaucer shows through the same figure of Symkyn. Moreover, we need to entertain the idea that even the penis itself could have meanings that were not narrowly "phallic." The prospect of impotence, of the failure of erection, is itself a versatile metaphor, especially in modern theory and polemic seeking to expose the fragility of male dominance. However, we elide fresher readings when we assume that the penis has no symbolic meaning unless it resembles, or functions as, a phallus.[29]

Is Torke's "pintle" (the original word), revealed to us in discourse, a penis or a phallus? It is both, because the fantasized, speculative representation of it in the minds of Paston and other men involved both presence and function. There are other phalluses in this story, too. The existence of Torke's children proves his achievement of conventional penetrative sexual capacity, a normal penis. The children's sex, number, health, and size prove something else. In Paston's account, Torke's "three or four" sons, those big strapping fellows, become metonymically Torke's own phallus, as he wields them in conversation with the king as an extension of himself, to prove his own sufficient and equivalent manhood. Penetration and domination do not seem as important as social viability, which Paston then reads backward into fleshly sufficiency: phallus morphs back into penis.

I mentioned the possibility of the non-phallic penis mostly as a reminder of the bias of medieval evidence, which refers most immediately to the social sphere. The meanings closest to the surface of written evidence are those relevant to social identity. Where penises do appear, which is not often, they usually seem pretty phallic, because a phallic social significance caused the creation of the document. That does not mean, however, that the references are not meaningful at other levels as well. I take up this point about multiple levels of significance in more detail in chapter 4, using romance literature.

Establishing the significance of the literal, bodily penis is more difficult when we restrict ourselves to late medieval English evidence, even the texts specifically dealing with the body. It is perhaps not surprising that the *Book of Physiognomy* ignores the genitals, given religious-moral disapproval of attention to them. Yet even in Bartholomew-Trevisa, the emphasis is not what we might expect. The penis gets only a few lines, devoted mostly to the etymology of its Latin equivalent *veretrum*. Most attention goes to the testicles. This, too, makes sense given a physiological model in which the testicles, in contrast to the penis, produced something. After Isidore, testicles provide manly "sinew and strength"; "no man is complete without their 'testimony.'" And (after Constantine) they supply the heat that turns blood into seminal "whiteness." But they also do something else: "if they are cut off, a man's strength disappears and manly complexion changes into female complexion." Of course, "complexion" has more than one meaning. Bartholomew-Trevisa goes on to cite Aristotle, saying that if boys are gelded before puberty, no hair will grow on their bodies. If this is done after puberty, all body hair falls out "except the hair of the chest" (strangely enough), and they (no pronoun, but presumably the men themselves) become "womanish, soft and feeble of heart and body"; voices and body shape change also, the former "as the voice of women," the latter not specified. Men who are "gelded" have no beards because they have lost the "hottest member that should breed the hot humour."[30]

In one discourse, then, the testicles were more responsible for both maleness and masculinity than the penis was. Yet testicles do not seem to have supplied, in themselves, much imagery of maleness in any other kind of English evidence. The occasional allusions (as with Symkyn and the Pardoner above, and some poems I mention later in this chapter) do not indicate that they were any more important in forming the popular sense of physical masculinity. The court book of Bishop Alnwick of Lincoln in 1448 reports that a group of Huntingdonshire villagers had attacked and castrated their priest. The text's vocabulary is both suggestive and frustratingly vague: "inhumanely castrated him and cut off his manhood"; "amputating his manhood."[31] The reduplication in the phrases may refer to testicles and penis separately, or it may be simple rhetorical emphasis. We have no way of knowing what was cut off, and therefore, whatever specifically and literally embodied "manhood," in this nonmedical discourse, is hidden from us.

The significance of particular genital qualities (size, shape) for masculinity is also impossible to evaluate. Michael Solomon, discussing texts current in medieval Spain, reports that William of Saliceto's *Summa conservationis* contained a chapter on penis enlargement. Well before the age of unsolicited electronic mail, then, genital size was a concern that medical professionals might be called on to address.[32] It does not appear, though, that William's *Summa* was well known in late medieval England. In general, English literary evidence does not indicate much attention to the male genitals in themselves (especially compared to the French tales explicitly concerned with them, in which they may become actual characters).[33] To judge what this comparative silence indicates culturally—an extreme anxiety about physical manhood, or a prudish distaste, or simply a failure to find penises either funny or exciting—requires more evidence and analysis than I can provide.

One fifteenth-century lyric, however, seems to speak from inside a male body. Its diction bounces slyly and distractingly back and forth between apparently innocent description and sexual punning, and only at the end are we sure what it has described. Of the five stanzas, the first three all begin with the line "I have a gentle cock." This was probably not standard slang for "penis" in the fifteenth century.[34] The poem seems simply to be praising, perhaps as a charming joke, the nobility and beauty (comb, tail, legs, spurs) of a pet rooster: a bird who crows first thing in the morning to wake the speaker for matins, and who comes of a good pedigree. The conclusion, however, cannot be mistaken: "And every night he perches in my lady's chamber." The physical description of the "cock," then, reveals itself to be a clever combination of penile allusion and nonsexual filler. The references, while suggestive, are not anatomically precise, and this refusal to specify gives the poem its playfulness. First the cock's "comb is of red coral, / His tail is of jet"—hard red flesh at the top, black hair at the bottom? But in the next stanza, though comb is again of red coral, the tail is "of indigo"; it is a bird after all. Next, "His legs are of azure, / So gentle and so small": blue veins? But what then are the spurs, "silver up to the root"? Textual coyness aside, I think that when we consider the masculinity of the rooster (the bird that mates with a harem of hens), it is impossible to deny that this is a "cock" in the modern slang sense as well. Even "He gets me up early / To say my morning prayers" is a sly little contrast.[35] The more important point, however, is not the fact of sexual allusion, but the overall effect. Since the cock getting so much praise is the speaker's own, the poem conveys the enjoyment of an enthralled, autoerotic embodiment, dwelling on every beautiful and desirable feature. One should not generalize too broadly from one little poem. Yet because we can assume the speaker of the poem to be unproblematically male, I think it shows that pride in one's genital maleness was taken for granted in fifteenth-century masculine subjectivity—however much it violated normative religious morality.

The genital contribution to masculine identity seems, from late medieval English evidence, however, to concern function more than form. Here, again, different discourses provide contrasting impressions. Jacqueline Murray describes the range of attitudes about male sexuality through the sweep of the Middle Ages. Early medieval evidence in particular suggests a clash between the values of secular society, which valorized male sexual prowess, and those of the church. Binary opposites inherited from early theological and canonical evaluations saw women as "more subject to their bodies and to lust" than men, and also as "the source of sexual temptation." Yet the Church's theory of conjugal relations was "profoundly influenced by the secular notion of men as active initiators of sex."[36] By the late Middle Ages, medical discourse added to this dynamic a third perspective, which could see sexual activity as healthy or even necessary for men in moderation, but harmful in excess.[37]

A poem from about 1500 clearly takes the last view. The speaker addresses a "burgess," a respectable mature man, who has apparently worn himself out through too much sex. The effect of sexual excess here is evacuation. The man has lost so much substance (as his testicles' "substance is wasted and spent") that he is pale, and "there is no flesh upon thy carcass: / There is naught left but empty skin and bone." This sexual exhaustion has led to impotence, a word the poem itself uses. In good humoral logic, the testicles generate the substance whose deficiency collapses the man's physical presence. Yet the text locates sexual masculinity more importantly in the man's penis. This "sentry, who always tended to be mighty . . . in his work, now is so weary from excess, he has lost his taste for the hunt. He himself is your real accuser, for so say those that know his impotence as well as you do, my master reveller."[38]

These lines depend on the assumption that a man's sexual performance could become part of his reputation—to which the assessments of his sex partners would contribute. The poem's ostensible reproach, and its advice, apply to the sufferer's status as a "burgess," who ought to be more responsible. Yet the speaker does not make a specifically moral comment on what sounds like promiscuity; instead, he recommends patience and continence in future. The confidentially jocular tone (one man to another) undercuts the surface criticism in a wink-nudge manner. It suggests the burgess' true error was in making too plain the sexual appetite expected to lie underneath the sober social persona. As with the discourse of manly celibacy, self-control depends on there being something to control. One could overdo it, but the tone here suggests that masculinity in the eyes of peers might fall closer to the side of more rather than less sex.

Frequency was one factor in male sexual performance. We are on more treacherous ground in considering specific sexual acts, even the choice of partners. It would be pointless to rehearse here ecclesiastical condemnations of sodomy, prominent though they are in the surviving discourse of deviant sexuality. There is simply not enough evidence, of any kind, to assess social attitudes toward same-sex relations in late medieval England. During the period I am discussing, England never experienced the fervent prosecution of sodomy evident in contemporary Florence. In fact, although isolated references to cases crop up in act books here and there, we lack any full documentation of them, especially the questions, the testimony of witnesses, and the sentences. Nor was Middle English literature fond of the theme; it did not exploit it either for horror or humor, yet another difference from the Italian situation.[39] So we cannot tell whether homosexual behavior in itself made a man less manly, whether people judged by distinguishing between penetrator and penetrated, or on the basis of the ages of the parties. Where suggestions do appear, as in the antimendicant poem I quote in chapter 3, the reflection on masculinity seems to emerge from a complex of other factors.

We cannot know whether masculinity, and especially a subjective masculinity, depended on sexual performance unless we take into account the (sub)cultural and institutional conventions shaping our documents. Much of the time, for obvious reasons, evidence about male sexual performance in late medieval England is also evidence about marriage: a condition theorized and regulated by legal-religious discourses. The church frowned severely on nonprocreative sex as on that outside marriage, but it also defined sexual intercourse as the conjugal debt each spouse owed to the other.[40] I will return to such normative treatments shortly, but we should note that popular attitudes admitted other motivations for marital sex, as the injunctions against them reveal. In one of the "Merry Tales of Skelton," a rich widow claims not to care about "fooling around." Nevertheless, she rejects a prospective husband who, though otherwise worthy, has no "private members." Her reason: "I want my husband to have that with which we may be reconciled, if we have a falling-out."[41] Mere sexual dissatisfaction within marriage had no formal remedy in medieval England, and so we are denied the kind of evidence from which Thomas Foster makes an argument about sexuality in the exported English culture of seventeenth-century America. For Foster,

Puritan ideology valued women's sexual pleasure in marriage, as divorces were granted to women claiming sexual inadequacy of their husbands— regardless of procreative ability. He defines this as a discourse of "sexuality" in the modern sense, because of its attention to pleasure. What Foster does not fully emphasize is the lineage of the moralistic and advice literature he cites as discursive context. It seems to have inherited almost unchanged the definitions of Aristotelian physiology via Trevisa and Bartholomew. So the Puritan definition of marriage as a "civil contract, not a sacrament" may not be so important as Foster claims, though this and the informality of the Puritan courts probably helped make divorce easier.[42]

HUSBANDLY SEXUALITY

Status as a true husband did depend, in part, on sexual performance, and not just because of the importance of heirs. We can see this in an early-fifteenth-century poem published in 1843 under the title "Lyarde," which is the name of a worn-out old horse. Lyarde the horse is actually just a point of departure for the poem's discussion of those men who, like the horse, are "just a waster": they consume, but do not produce. Included in this lot are sexually incompetent husbands, whom the speaker sees being put to pasture in a "park" belonging to "all the wives of this land"; such men cannot fulfill their covenant to "bed and to board." (Unfortunately, some lines are damaged, or possibly censored, here.) The incompetent will be gelded and put into "that abbey" from whence no one leaves: made a "sick friar."[43]

Imagery then shades into the "market" where wives exchange feeble horses (men) for fresh; this is the "park." The poem introduces the friars as a company of men who "know how to fuck," that being the main requirement for their fellowship, as they boast. But the master of the park answers their boast: there is a friar in the losers' park, he says. The friars claim he cannot be a real "tonsured" friar. The parker answers this with a reference to friars being hanged. That results in a challenge by the friars, who charge the park, break its bounds, and free all the "sorry [excuses for] fuckers." Now, the speaker claims, the women of the land cannot be sure that they have not got such a one for a husband, and often (in bed) think they do. So these "Lyarde's men" are, the speaker claims, still very much around.[44]

Though it expresses a sexual antipathy to the friars, "Lyarde" says at least as much about the masculine value of marital sexuality. The text's incoherence and contradiction are themselves meaningful, indicating the complexity of the concerns. Sexual performance seems to be a fit measure of manliness here. Women, in the poem's imagined past, originally had the power to choose mates on that basis. The poem's implication is: "Imagine if they could? Wouldn't we all be in trouble?" The (false) friars, champion "fuckers," become foils to the sexually inadequate husbands, embodying laymen's fears not only of cuckoldry but also of women's judgment and rejection. "Lyarde" admits a general knowledge of male frailty, a knowledge that is, however, more safely protected in the present day that the speaker addresses, because the "park" no longer exists.

Without such literary material, late medieval England would provide a rather one-sided view of masculine sexual performance. The nonliterary, that is, legal, evidence about what actually went on in the marital bed tells us only about problems: malfunction rather than function. It is still invaluable evidence. Our discussion therefore continues with a couple of late-fourteenth-century suits for marriage annulment on the grounds of impotence, a canonically defined impediment. Here, the male body, brought to the surface through the mechanics of legal process, becomes a site of contention, its sexual function defining the lines of legal argument. As an institution with both private and public dimensions, marriage provides the arena wherein the law can address the relation between sex and gender.

My first example is relatively straightforward. The witnesses for Tedia Lambhird testified that she and her husband John Sanderson had been publicly married and had lived together for three years, during which time they faithfully attempted to maintain sexual relations. The couple then openly admitted that John's impotence had prevented him from ever having carnal knowledge of Tedia. These claims were, in their context, conventional. Divorce suits, though rare, had developed a standard way of setting out their issues, conforming to the strictures of canon law. The three years of marriage was a minimum to demonstrate that the couple had really given it a try and that there was an enduring problem. Even when they reported it to their clerical authority, they might well be told to wait another year. John and Tedia were no exception. They separated for more than a year, and then resumed living together to try again at the order of the dean of Holderness. The reunion brought no success. At the time of the suit, Tedia is described as a young woman of twenty-six, willing to bear children, and having expected to do so when she married John.[45]

The fact that both parties had admitted to the problem did not mean an automatic divorce. Canon law required ensuring, first, that the claim was not a fabrication by an unhappy couple with no other options, and second, that it was not a matter of mere sexual incompatibility. John must be impotent with women other than his wife. And the method employed by the court of York to show this, though having the weight of precedent and written authorities, is one for which, as Richard Helmholz commented, "no canonist prepares us."[46] The last three depositions in the file come from a trio of women who put John's claim to the test. Johanna de Wyghton provided the venue, apparently her kitchen, which she warmed with a good fire (this was November), supplying also good food and drink. Having arranged John before the fire, she testified, she "felt and took between her hands the penis of the said John," to no effect; it remained "just like the end of an empty intestine," or sausage-skin. Isabella, the second woman, had no better luck, despite additionally placing it against her own body. She reported also that John's testicles were not present in the scrotum but "contiguous with the skin of the groin just as in certain children." Along with Ellen de Hedon, who seems to have acted as an observer, they concluded that John was incapable of sexual relations with any woman.[47]

Through such testimony, such concentrated attention, John's genitals become characters, more present in the legal narrative than their owner. They attract a rich vocabulary to describe their looks (like a sausage skin, soft, no veins, black all over) and what they do or do not do. The penis "neither got wider [literally, "*dilatabat se*," widened itself] nor longer"; it "wouldn't in any way [literally, "*nullo modo voluit*," did not want to] become erect, but persisted in the same state."[48] This is a greater agency of will than is ever imputed to John himself, who does not get to "want" anything. He becomes a cipher, signified by a body part of which he is not master.[49] Can we learn anything about the masculinity of John the subject through a legal process that makes him John the object? Such interpretive questions become even more intriguing applied to my second example, bizarre and exceptional as it is.

AN INCOMPLETE HUSBAND

Here is a new story about a very old body. We know that the body's owner was named Nicholas, that he lived about 600 years ago in Lincolnshire, England, and that his father was a knight, Sir Randolph de Cantelupe. We know that when he was about twenty years old, Nicholas married a girl of thirteen, Katherine Paynell, whose father was also a knight. We know these things because when Nicholas was alive, a story was told about his body. It began when Nicholas' wife decided that his body made their marriage unsustainable, and sued him for divorce. The bones of that story lie in the

Borthwick Institute for Archives, in York, which is the archival resting place for the skeletal remains of stories told in the ecclesiastical court of the archbishop of York. Witnesses testified for Katherine; scribes and clerks wrote that testimony down, translated it from English into Latin, and shaped it into the conventional forms of the different legal documents. Thus, the lawsuit created the only remains we have of the body that set it in motion. Numerous historical actors, from Nicholas's parents to Katherine to the court staff to Nicholas himself, are in some way authors, of both story and body.

Paying attention to the role of legal procedure in forming this story, we will begin with the series of "positions and articles," or points to be proven, which Katherine's proctor drew up in April 1368. The first position was that Nicholas and Katherine had been properly married, and that they had lived together for three years, faithfully maintaining conjugal relations, Katherine not evading or preventing intercourse in any way. So far we are on relatively familiar ground. In the second article the proctor claims that Nicholas "always was and is totally impotent and incapable and naturally cold [*totaliter impotens et ineptus ac naturaliter frigidus*] so that he neither could nor can have carnal knowledge of the aforesaid Katherine nor of any other woman, nor has he ever had carnal knowledge of the same Katherine." *Impotens* signifies impotence in the modern sense, a lack of erectile function. *Ineptus* is a little subtler; it intensifies *impotens* through its medieval meaning of incapacity or inability, with lingering traces of its classical sense: foolish, awkward, "inept." *Naturaliter frigidus* did not just mean an emotional coldness, nor even a disinclination to sexual activity, as twentieth-century "frigidity" implies. As we have seen, in medieval humoral theory, with its direct connections between the body and temperament, heat was a masculine quality, and cold a feminine one. Cold was not just the absence of heat, but held its own substantive meaning. Calling a man "cold" in this sense, therefore, implied both a lack of masculine traits (energies, inclinations) and the possession of feminine ones. So wrapped up in this one clause, this one body, is a medical-technical description incorporating a judgment on the whole person: body and character, maleness and masculinity, sex and gender. But the third and most surprising article makes clear that this is not just an impotence case. "Also, he [the proctor] propounds and intends to prove that the aforesaid Nicholas was from the time of his birth, and still is, *castratus*, such that the natural organs required as tools of procreation were and are lacking. And that if the said Nicholas ever had at any time, or has, any such organs, the same organs were and are unfit, completely defective, and useless for any procreation whatsoever."[50]

An entire array of questions—about sex, language, identity, and legal argument—unravels from those two drily phrased sentences. First, just how did Katherine's proctor "intend to prove" what Nicholas did or did not have, and why his confusion on this point? What was being alleged? Was it not redundant to claim Nicholas was impotent, if he lacked a penis? Does "*a tempore nativitatis suo castratus*" mean he was born without male genitals? If so, why was no one, especially his parents, in any doubt that he was male? If it points, rather, to some postnatal injury making sexual function impossible, why did Nicholas get married at all, given that this was a canonical impediment?

These are all important questions, but before examining how the suit does or does not deal with them, we should take note of the rest of the story. No documents from Nicholas's side of the case are extant. But it seems safe to assume that he never admitted to any such defects. He launched an "exception," a challenge to Katherine's charges. This exception claimed that she had made a retraction and sworn to his carnal knowledge of her. We know this because we do have Katherine's rejoinder to the exception, in the form of a new set of positions and articles, dated about three months after the first set. What the proctor now "intends to prove" is that any confession Katherine might have given was gotten out of her by coercion, through the combined forces of her parents and "friends" and Nicholas himself. Indeed, one article claims that Nicholas forcibly confined her at his house. Katherine escaped, and persisted, though her claim did change slightly. Her replication no longer literally alleges impotence, but maintains that Nicholas's genitals, if they exist, are useless, "his penis far too weak and too short and small," and that he utterly lacks any testicles.

Comparing the witness depositions to the articles, and to each other, shows us how many episodic layers may be folded up inside the straightforward phrasing of any one account. Take that article's three years of faithful marriage, for example, which may seem a suspiciously long time for any woman to have put up with this situation. Katherine's first witness, Thomas the rector of Burton, described the marriage as follows: Nicholas and Katherine had been married at the village of Caysthorpe in Lincolnshire, four years previously, on the feast of St. Hillary. This works out to January 13, 1364. After their marriage, they lived at Caysthorpe with Katherine's parents for a year and then set up house by themselves at Nicholas's manor of Gresley, in Derbyshire, some distance away. A year after that, Katherine left Nicholas, returned to her parents, and "in the presence of this witness complained to her mother and father that she could not live with the said Nicholas, because he could not have carnal knowledge of her as a husband should of his wife, and that he did not have genitals, nor could he emit semen." Thomas says that at his mediation and in his presence, Katherine was subsequently led back to Nicholas, so that the couple could try again. Two years later, Katherine was back at her parents', this time with the clear intention to seek a divorce. So the faithful three years turns into a rather disrupted four years, though still dividing into convenient canonical units. And Thomas's testimony itself has its involutions. We may well wonder what outraged family reactions are contained in those offhand references to "mediation" and the "leading back" of Katherine. In fact, the next witness, Margery de Halton, betrayed more than she needed to of the frustration of a gentry family seeing a perhaps long-negotiated marriage falling apart because of the fancies of a willful fourteen-year-old. Margery reports that when the Paynells "compelled" their daughter by threats to tell them why she had left her husband, they did not believe her answer and said that she was a fool and did not understand what she was doing.

Amid all this drama, Nicholas himself seems to get pushed rather to the side up to this point in the story. Until his drastic reaction makes it necessary for Katherine to make a legal response, he is scarcely present as an autonomous agent. In the first part of the suit, he is more object than subject, delineated by the genitals he does or does not possess. To us, that uncertainty, the failure to show whether Nicholas was a gelding or a mare, is a definitively frustrating aspect of this case. After all, the problem of proof facing Katherine's proctor in this regard would seem to have a rather commonsense solution. But oddly enough, the court of York was better equipped to deal with the burden of proof of impotence than with the allegation of genital abnormality. The lack of canonical prescriptions to deal with an unusual situation like Nicholas's left the church court few options. At the end of July, shortly after Katherine's replication and evidence were entered, an order came down from the archdiocese, stating that there was insufficient evidence to judge the case fairly and authorizing five chaplains to compel Nicholas to appear at the archdiocesan court of York for a physical examination. We have no evidence that Nicholas ever showed up, and indeed the order does not suggest how the deputized chaplains were to make him do so. This was a general problem, not confined to the church courts, in a world before effective policing.

Adding to the suit's diminution of Nicholas's agency is the fact that it is the probing hands of his young wife that draw that body in the text. Katherine, according to Thomas, claimed that she had often felt Nicholas's genital area with her hands while he lay sleeping beside her. The girl said she could "neither feel nor find anything there [*nulla palpare nec invenire potuit*], and that the place where his genitals should be is as broad as a man's hand." I think this apparently straightforward description adds another layer to the suit's construction of Nicholas. *"Invenire,"* surely a translation from English, conveys something not very far from the idea of "carnal knowledge." Carnal knowledge, however, in the legal-linguistic convention of this time and long after, is usually something men have of women; women are the ones "known." The same applies to the use of *"invenire."* "Finding" is a masculine act.[51] Neatly, then, Thomas's statement further emasculates Nicholas, whose wife attempts to "find" and yet "finds" nothing on this therefore very dubiously male body.

With his violent reaction, however, Nicholas himself makes a dramatic entrance, and the story's details seem suddenly to snap into sharper focus. Since Katherine's having been forced to make a false retraction is at issue, the articles now stress that it was through force, threats, and fear that she was brought back to Nicholas. Thomas the rector now "remembers" there being discord on account of Nicholas's impotence within a month, or even fifteen days, after the marriage. He says that Nicholas showed him a room in his house, fitted up as a prison, where Katherine would be detained if she refused to retract her claims about him. It all converges on the scene in Nicholas's house (now become the "castle" it truly was), related by the chaplain Robert de Selby. Katherine was dragged into the house chapel crying, to be confronted by Nicholas, who greeted her, saying, "Cursed are you, woman, among all women." "You know well," he continued, "that I have the power to know you carnally, having good enough instruments of coition." "I know," answered the girl. Nicholas went on to demand that she swear to his physical integrity, and that she never leave his household without his permission or betray his confidence to anyone. And that is as far as the testimony takes us. The only subsequent event we are told of is that Katherine escaped "as soon as she could."

One needs no hypersubtle perception to see fictional elements operating even in this one small piece of testimony. Robert the chaplain has begun with a parody of the biblical annunciation scene. The words he puts in Nicholas's mouth are a malevolent inversion of the angel Gabriel's address to the Virgin Mary in Luke's gospel, also familiar as the "Ave Maria." This sets up a comment on the state of the marriage, with Katherine (a virgin despite being married) cursed for her supposed refusal to be impregnated by her husband. Katherine replies, in good Marian fashion, that she will do whatever is pleasing to Nicholas. Robert's tale casts Nicholas as the negative image not only of Gabriel but also of Joseph, Mary's husband, who in late medieval folklore often was depicted (despite the church's misgivings) as a cuckold.[52] Joseph's wife bore a child that was not his; Nicholas's wife will not bear a child that is his. Since the point of the case is that Katherine is not to blame in any way, the scene creates Nicholas as irrational and a twister of the truth, a point to which I will return. And whatever words Nicholas chose to insist on his virility at that moment, they have surely undergone some modulation of tone and vocabulary to be rendered so clinically in Latin as *"instrumenta ad coheundem."*

But here I am again, paying attention to what the text does *to* Nicholas when I set out trying to find Nicholas himself. What can we say about Nicholas the subject? As I have already suggested, making any sort of assessment of what actually happened all those years ago requires telling a new story.

The story really begins, of course, long before the case does. Sometime in the 1340s, a child was born to a landed knight. The sex of the child was perhaps not as clear as might have been wished, but there was enough indication of maleness that the baby was named Nicholas, raised and socialized as a boy, the male heir his parents had waited for. He survived the Great Plague, grew up to the appearance of adulthood, and even if his beard was a bit scanty and his voice a bit high, there was still no doubt in anyone's mind, least of all his own, that he was a man. By the time he was in his early twenties, his father was dead, and Nicholas had succeeded to the manor of Gresley. He found a wife, a girl of thirteen from a family of his class, whose family thought him a good enough match for their daughter. Katherine knew what married life involved and soon realized that something was wrong in the conjugal bed. Her tender age did not rule out her desire for, and curiosity about, an ordinary marital sex life. She was a married lady now and expected the whole package: children, the governance of a household, social standing, even affection. She knew that lacking one part (so to speak) endangered the rest. Besides, she was frightened because she had no way of understanding the body she had found with her hands. Who or what was this person she had married? She confided in the rector of Burton and in Margery, whom she had known all her life. Margery warned her not to get above herself, saying, "You're not a great lady." So Katherine stuck it out somewhat longer, but finally, perhaps on the pretext of a visit home, decided to leave for good. Her shocked family marched her straight back to her husband, who had found out what was afoot, because Thomas (as that priest admits) had told him.

Nicholas was enraged by what Katherine had revealed, and not just at the prospect of the divorce; this was well before she had commenced the actual suit. The allegations about him were both true and untrue. They were based on Katherine's observations, but they were not at all congruent with Nicholas's sense of himself. Clearly he did not, overtly at least, consider himself a sexual freak; he felt he was a man with a male body. Finding out that that body did not, in the eyes of his wife and others, entitle him to the full range of masculine roles and privileges offered by his society, was a discovery so fundamentally challenging to his self-concept that it became inadmissible. The story must be changed, suppressed, rewritten, its author locked up. More deeply, the discovery was inadmissible because it was really no discovery; the nature of the reaction shows this. Nicholas must have known he was not like other men, that he would not father a child, that the marriage would not achieve the goals at which it generally aimed among people of his class. But as we are all aware, humans often act in ways rationally out of step with what they really know about themselves, particularly when social pressures are deployed. Besides, Nicholas presumably had other assets: the manor of Gresley, for a start. Another woman might have decided that an unsatisfying sex life was a small price to pay for the security and stability offered by Nicholas, his name, and his estate. At least there would be no dying in childbirth (and suspected female infertility, unlike male impotence, was not a ground for divorce). Katherine was not that woman.

But some very different evidence suggests that Nicholas's previous experience may have led him to expect otherwise. Katherine was not Nicholas's first wife. Among the properties inventoried at Nicholas's decease were two manors that had come to him on the death of a woman named Joan, his "late wife," about whom I have not yet discovered anything further.[53] The divorce papers do not mention her for obvious reasons: they concerned only the marriage to Katherine, and of course, it was hardly in the interest of Katherine (whose side of things is all we have) to mention any previous marriage—though whether this would have been admissible evidence, I am not sure. It adds a dimension to Nicholas's reaction. Being known, openly acknowledged, as a married man enhanced a masculine gender identity. To have his status as married, indeed marriageable, threatened, correspondingly threw the possibility of true mature manhood into doubt. "But I've been married," we can hear him protest, "and Joan never complained."

One might argue that his motives were unrelated to sex and gender: greed for a rich girl's inheritance, or a connection to her influential family, or anxiety about the loss of his patrimony in default of heirs male. A decision against him, establishing a canonical impediment, would have ended this marriage and the prospect of any others. This certainly did happen to men found impotent. But Nicholas acted well before a suit was launched. Revelation and exposure were what he aimed to prevent: revelation to himself, exposure to others. After all, of what was Nicholas accused, if not the perpetration of a gigantic fraud? In making a marriage that never should have been, the suit says by implication, he had passed himself off as something he was not. It says this without ever precisely stating what he was not; whatever Nicholas lacked, he is referred to unvaryingly as "he," and no one suggests he was female. But clearly, he was not sufficiently masculine to be a man, and the fraudulence of the marriage could be taken to show this.

So Nicholas threatened and frightened his wife into swearing on the gospel that he was a real man and thus remained himself—until Katherine got away again. And there is the end of my faulty story, almost. How much more can I tell? The documents reveal that Katherine won the suit. Still of prime marrying age, she could have made another match, assuming the local notoriety of her first experience did not reflect unfavorably on her. So perhaps she lived out the life, short or long, of a married woman. Or maybe not. One hopes she was spared the lonely existence of a resented, unmarriageable daughter. It seems unlikely that the life of the cloister would have suited Katherine, but one never knows, and after all, Margery Kempe embarked on her religious career only after a sexually fulfilled marriage.

The possible futures after such a divorce are even more vague for Nicholas: certainly not remarriage, probably not the cloister. He still had his estate, for the term of his life, but that was not to last long. Less than four years after Katherine's legal victory, Nicholas died, as we learn from his inquisition post mortem. That proceeding revealed that the estate was substantial: six manors in different counties, two of them held of the king in chief (hence the inquisition), all of which passed to his brother William. But Katherine was not yet completely out of the picture. We learn that "long before his death," for as yet unknown reasons, Nicholas created three feoffees for part of the property, of which two were our friend Thomas de Vaus, rector of Burton, and a chaplain named Robert de Ketelby. The feoffees then re-enfeoffed Nicholas jointly with Katherine in the same properties.[54] So she likely retained a life interest in that part of the inheritance.

What happened after that is beyond me to say, though there are some other intriguing clues. According to some of the inquisition jurors, Nicholas died at Avignon, which was of course where the papal court was located at the time.[55] Did death overtake this incomplete husband as he was moving toward an appeal to the pope to overturn the annulment? Did Nicholas make another last-ditch effort to salvage his masculine social self? Alas, the loss of the relevant papal petitions for 1371–72 prevents us from knowing any more clearly.

To study masculinity is not the same thing as to study men, but one cannot divorce the two, especially if one is a historian. To do history means keeping in view both the human source and the textual residue, difficult sometimes to reconcile. It is undeniable that historians do their work through discourse, and that discourse, especially text, creates our subjects for us in a very real way. But to regard our historical subjects only as abstracted textual imprints not only denies them their humanity—an error in itself—but makes us run the risk of missing something important in our analysis: the degree to which human experience is grounded in the body, in the physical being, and in meanings derived from it. It is often difficult to see what is meant by insistences that "the body" is a "product" of discourse, or "created" by it. In this case, we see how the requirements of legal, religious, and medical discourses shaped the body of Nicholas that is left to us and determined how it would affect his social self in the crucial matter of marriage. But we also see the extent to which masculinity, that complex combination of self-knowledge and performance, incorporates bodies and discourses. An individual personality responds to both.

THE MALE BODY IN ACTION

We have seen how maleness and masculinity could be related in late medieval English culture: how masculinity could derive its meaning from the male body and find expression in it. The body might express masculinity through its form: its size, shape, and particular morphology. Yet as we have already seen, form was tied to function. The process of making legible meaning, which turns a sexed body into a gendered one, depends on what that body does or is expected to do.

To pursue the capacious theme of the body in action, I introduce topics about which we yet know little, less than we would like, that may long prove difficult to explore because of a lack of evidence. I say nearly as much about limitations on our historical knowledge of embodied masculinity as about the knowledge itself. Nevertheless, we need to think at least a little about how we might approach the subject, because otherwise important aspects of masculine identity go unexplored.

The general theme of self-command, which I have stressed so much already, runs through this discussion. Some young men's self-command over the body was imposed by others. Apprentices and servants were often at the mercy of their masters' power to forbid sexual relationships and control marriages. For some others, bodily governance was a more individual responsibility, but no less obligatory. The books of courtesy, which increased in popularity from the early fifteenth century, instruct boys in deportment. Their instructions focus on the correct bearing toward social superiors and attention to speech, gesture, movement, and body functions, especially at table. The insistence on governing the body is not the only reason to consider this a masculine discourse; there were, after all, also books of conduct aimed at women. But courtesy literature for boys presupposes that homosocial settings are the most important. The books say nothing (beyond occasional platitudes) about relations with women, how to speak to women, or how to behave in their presence. Their imagined requirements are for men together. (In fact, one poem advises, "avoid crowds of women as much as you can. Hate groups of women because no greater pest in the world is able to overcome a man."[56] This overt misogyny, clerical in origin, is, however, unusual in the genre.)

Courtesy books existed in both Latin and English. By the fourteenth century, boys of a middling or higher social status might encounter both kinds: the former in the classroom, where they were used in Latin grammar instruction, and the latter "in the noble households, or more particularly, in the fifteenth century, among the merchants and guildsmen."[57] Much of their instruction is neither subtle nor complex, but it covers a wide range. At one end of the scale are the cautions against total bodily license. Again, courtesy writers imagine social situations centering on mealtimes. "O sons of the great, dining with us," are the first words of *Castrianus,* a poem that was "an established part of a typical fifteenth-century education."[58] Nose picking, nose blowing, spitting, belching, and farting are to be avoided; so are improprieties directly related to food, such as meddling in the common dishes ("Do not replace in the dish what you have touched to your teeth"), or contaminating a common spoon.[59] Effectively, the boy is to avoid invading the personal space of others, or more precisely, allowing his own presence to leak into theirs. Hands, ears and nose are to be clean.[60] "You shall never lean on the table either with elbows or indolent chest" is one admonition; "You may not pick your teeth at the table" is another.[61] The self-command of courtesy books was manly not only because it was not womanish, but also because it was not childish. Thus, the boy is told not to pick his nose "like a young child."[62] Within a society increasingly interested in self-improvement, body courtesy enabled young men to make and maintain the social connections granting them a social self to improve.

Yet the self-command needed to prevent such *faux pas* goes beyond control of the grossest bodily emissions. It extends to the very way the male body moves through social space. "If you are seated by a good worthy man," warns one text, "Make sure you pay attention to this lesson: do not put your knee under his thigh. You are truly *lewed* if you do so."[63] "Lewed" in medieval parlance primarily meant "common" or "ill bred," but the modern sense it triggers is useful for our understanding. What makes one look "lewed" in the medieval sense is an unseemly, "lewd" intimacy, getting too close to another's body. The same poem advises one to give a bedmate room: "If you should happen to be lodged in bed with a companion, a master, or someone of that rank, you shall courteously ask what part of the bed he wishes to lie in. Be honorable and lie far from him; you are unwise unless you do so."[64]

Recall the tale of Skelton and the friar—a shared bed was a situation few would be able to avoid. We might think that such injunctions aim primarily at allowing a man the possibility of a certain amount of physical presence of his own, even privacy. And although premodern and modern concepts of privacy must have been rather different, invoking them is less anachronistic than historians sometimes fear, particularly those concerning gender. The importance of the outward, social face was much greater in masculine than feminine identity. As soon as one approached any measure of independence or autonomy, one assumed a masculine subject position on the gender spectrum of the era, something men were much more likely than women to achieve. So that very complement of personhood, of being recognized more as an entity in oneself than as an appendage of someone else, was a matter of masculinity. I wonder, though, whether there is more to be made of these courtesy cautions against physical presumption. Was such excessive bodily familiarity between men a recognized kind of behavior? Were these actions (knees under thighs, being close together when sharing a bed) gestures of affection permissible only among intimate friends?

I am not suggesting that such intimacies were perceived as sexual overtures, though I would not want to exclude that possibility either; we should not underestimate our historical subjects. But primarily I am thinking along the lines that Alan Bray laid out in reference to Elizabethan men of the political classes. Bray argued that the lauded, conventional expressions of male friendship in its most politically and socially crucial forms could be the same as the external appearances that might prompt accusations of, and be taken to prove, a "sodomitical" relationship (the worst). Men expected a "true" friendship to be cemented and manifested through outward signs: gestures, embraces, gifts, even bed sharing. At the same time, the possibility of sodomitical desire bubbled under the surface. In such a milieu, passionate expressions of mutual affection were almost expected or ritualized, but could be utterly poisonous also.[65] Evidence from England before the Reformation does not seem to suggest a cultural anxiety about sodomy as severe as what began in the Elizabethan era. But even if affectionate friendships among social peers did not achieve sexual expression, the very intimacy itself, and the differences and hierarchies it created among men, would have been socially sensitive, and its signs carefully watched.[66]

Note here, of course, that in the courtesy books the cautions apply only to males of a certain status. The youth must give room in bed to fellow, master, or those of like or higher degree, and must not crowd a "right good man" at table. Social inferiors receive no particular consideration; the youth, apparently, need not govern himself quite so carefully toward them. All this makes a lot of sense applied to the late medieval world of service. Social hierarchies in many cultures usually measure status, or mark status, by the degree of distance, literal space, they assume an individual to be able to claim: a nice illustration of the symbolic size of a social self. The young man who follows the rules and learns to behave properly will make the right impression among those who are able to help him get along in the world. More literal kinds of service (as opposed to being a menial servant) were involved as part of this game, too. A number of the courtesy poems I did not consult for this study consist mainly of table etiquette, which included learning to wait on a superior and execute the honorable task of carving his meat.[67] Given how many youths spent time in the household of a social superior, such knowledge was surely not restricted to the houses of the great nobles, even if it now seems most immediately to evoke that world.

The well-ruled male body, in this discourse of courtesy, does nothing excessive, nothing beyond what is strictly necessary. Its gestures are controlled, its motions moderated. They do not include pointing or beckoning, or talking with one's hands: "While you speak, do not be flamboyant; keep both hands and fingers still;" "Do not mark out your story with your fingers."[68] It should not surprise us, then, that this masculine body follows rules other evidence has taught us. It is a body that after all includes the head, especially the eyes. (The books' prescriptions for governing the head's most incorrigible part will enter our discussion presently.) The boy is to give passers-by an open and "courteous" look and speak "fair" to them: "With a stable eye look upon them properly... also, be absolutely sure you do not chatter, nor cast your sight all around the house."[69] He is to "look men in the face" and "cast not your eye aside in other place, for that is a token of wanton inconstance."[70] Of course the other end of the body can lead one into dishonor, as well. The narrating "Wise Man" of one poem advises his son to avoid the tavern, dice, and especially lechery, "For it will take charge of all your wits, and bring you into great misdeeds." One should not sit up too late or roam the town ("scandal comes of walking around late"), but go home and sleep.[71] As with the "false side-glance thief," inconstancy of heart, a wavering eye, and a wandering foot go together to indicate an inclination to vice.

In cautioning against too much late-night gadding about, the courtesy books look well beyond the supper table and seek to prescribe habits of life in the wider world. In so doing, they cross the line from manners to morals: a line probably not conceived as such in the later Middle Ages, just as it was not in the courtesy books' most obvious ancestors. Readers may well remark that there is not much distinctively "late medieval" about values of sober bodily self-governance, particularly among men of consequence. Scholarship more and less recent has established the debts of this literature to writings of classical Roman and Greek heritage, as far back as Aristotle.[72] Of these antecedents, Cicero's statements in *On Duties* are possibly the most memorably eloquent and at the same time, below the surface, the most practical minded.[73] *On Duties* covers a very wide range of social behavior; for the moment, we can note those portions obviously inherited by the courtesy literature of the Middle Ages.

Cicero's treatment of personal conduct is aimed as much at how such behavior causes one to be regarded, how it wins one honor, as whether it is good for its own sake. Or as Cicero states at his pithiest: "The greatest effect is achieved, then, by being what we wish to seem; however some advice should be given so that we might as easily as is possible be seen to be what we are" (II.44). Because of the public nature of "virtue" and "honor" in Roman society, one cannot separate Cicero's views on correct bearing, decorum, and the like from the question of how best to be as a person, which is to say, as a man. Cicero never explicitly addresses "manliness" or "unmanliness" at any length. Yet we must consider this a masculine ideal. The kind of public life Cicero really has in mind was the province of Roman men. Women of course had personal honor, but they would not have access to the kinds of interactions in which Cicero imagines these various moral and social values being acted out. When Cicero talks about a "man," he means a man, not a "person," and more specifically a man of substance, a man of the political classes.

Fifteenth-century England did not need a classical revival to make these values familiar and relevant either socially or culturally. They fit the realm's hierarchies and social customs eminently well; moreover, medieval culture generally valued originality so little that we can hardly shrink from calling them medieval simply because they resemble the products of a much earlier time. Courtesy books merely illustrate one of the many great continuities in premodern masculinity. Instructions to avoid the tavern, dice, and especially lechery show how misleading it is to separate the "moral" and "mannerly" aspects of courtesy discourse. The governance of the body is one manifestation of the ideal. For Cicero, the honourable man will "naturally" try to hide what is shameful, not refer to it, and not deploy humor that depends on it (I.104). The movements of the body and speech must be governed moderately. Cicero does not write very specifically about these things, though he advises avoiding "too effeminate a languidness in our gait" as well as excessive haste (I.131), as in general, "we should do nothing effeminate or soft, and nothing harsh or uncouth" (I.129). Voices should be "clear and attractive" (I.133), with moderate diction.

The church had its own literature on gesture which itself built on this classical heritage (quite apart from the general importance of self-restraint in the ascetic tradition). On the whole this literature probably says more specifically about gesture than the courtesy books do, though using it to draw conclusions about standards of masculinity, especially in England, and especially in the late Middle Ages, is difficult. The fullest study of medieval gesture, by J. C. Schmitt, does establish that just as in classical times, moralists denounced those whose gestures were excessive or "effeminate," the histrion and the jongleur. Most of these writers were clerics concerned with improper gesture or movement as sinful, or as temptation to sin (though eventually it came to be admitted that some forms of dance and nonritual movement could also be to the glory of God). The *Disciplina Scolarium*, of Paris around 1235, is in the same tradition. Besides the usual injunctions against disorderly student behavior, "ornatus" is a danger, extending beyond effeminate dress to "walking like a queen . . . making half-steps at a mincing pace." (Whether, as Schmitt says, "the gestures of the homosexual and the transvestite attracted the strongest sarcasm," similar evidence from late medieval England seems to be lacking.)[74]

These general standards took the form of courtesy literature in the late Middle Ages. Schmitt points out the wide diffusion of Hugh of St. Victor's *The Training of Novices* (twelfth century), with twenty-two manuscripts found in England. The treatise found its way into the hands of fifteenth-century preachers and thence to the laity. It provides an intricate analysis of the qualities and meanings of various types of gesture and movement.[75]

Proving transmission, however, is a problem. (Schmitt uses hardly any evidence from England and very little past the fourteenth century, and it all seems to be prescriptive or descriptive: monastic rules, treatises, and artistic representations.) One wishes for some demonstration of these meanings in more ordinary contexts; if only one could find court cases, for example, which turned on gesture: "he insulted me by making this sign," he "said that I walked like a woman," or the like.

Specificity of time and place is one question. The specially masculine nature of the courtesy discourse of self-command is another, because conduct books aimed at girls seem at first glance to contain many of the same instructions. Good women do not rove about; they move modestly and decorously, and they take care with household resources. Quite apart, though, from the differences (girls, e.g., are not told to look people in the eye), we might note that conduct instructions to girls never operate against the interests of women's male guardians and may (as in the case of good householding) obviously work in their favor. The honor a woman achieved, or maintained, through behaving in these ways reflected her supportive role in securing social masculinities. The "bourgeois femininity" explicated in one well-known conduct poem is surely therefore a function of an equally powerful ethic of bourgeois masculinity. Indeed, this text, voiced by a narrative mother to her daughter, requires that a wife be content with what her husband provides her, so that (as one version puts it) "he will not lose his manhood for the love of you."[76]

THE USES OF MISRULE

Do not get mixed up in misrule by any means, for he has cast good manners away from him; I have often truly observed that he has taken away manhood from many men.[77]

The normative power of the self-restraint ethic is historically visible because the realm's regulatory institutions helped to enforce it, and in so doing, they cooperated with moralist discourses. Together, these disciplining forces generated much of the documentary evidence now left to us. It can be harder to see the importance of the other model, the countervailing mode: the one which resisted discipline, sought pleasure, and took it in sexual, drunken, and violent release. In both legal and moral terms, this was misbehavior, and so it surfaces as what was punished. The incomplete nature of the evidence means that we rarely get the offenders' own view: why they did what they did, why it was important to them. Yet, particularly among young men and those in subordinate positions, this kind of riotous and self-indulgent behavior constituted a force as powerfully directive and manipulative as the sober model of later life. The association of youth and misrule was a cultural commonplace. Moreover, more than one late medieval text personified sinful youth itself in a sexed male body.[78] In the late medieval moral poem "The Mirror of the Periods of Man's Life," the real contention between virtue and vice begins at age 14, with the richest argument (the seven deadly sins arguing with the cardinal virtues) shown as connected to age 20. Here we get such warnings as "Lechery comes at a great cost; it destroys a man's natural heat." Reckless youth, naturally tending to self-indulgence, riot, and waste, needs to be chastened, reined in.[79] Among recent scholarship by medievalists in English, Ruth Mazo Karras's studies of young men, mostly about students, argue that the riotous behavior of students was essential to defining their masculinity and affirming their membership of a privileged group. The important qualities in student subculture were generosity, toughness, and sexual prowess. Karras stresses the unsupervised nature of student life and the attempts of universities to clamp down, especially regarding relations with women.[80]

The opposition between demonstrated sexual prowess on the one hand, and strict control of sexual desire on the other, as markers of masculinity, is of course an enduring pattern detectable from the earliest records of medieval society.[81] It is hard to imagine a society where young (and not so young) men, students or not, do not frequently test the legal and customary restrictions on their access to sexual pleasure. In late medieval England, young men's common problem was not that they were rigidly segregated from women, but that there was usually a long delay in their twenties before they were married. Most men experienced up to ten years of sexual maturity in which all sexual contacts posed some risk of punishment. The satisfaction derived from evading authority surely intensified the allure of the sexual experience itself; in this, premarital sex was little different from other forbidden pleasures. In turn, as with youths of other eras, the desire for, and achievement of, sexual experience surely was a sensitive and irresistible element of self-definition, the basis of overt or speculative comparison of self with peers. It grew directly out of an embodied subjectivity shaping a gender identity. So it would be very helpful for the historian to know something substantial about it.

Alas, once again the evidence lets us down. Specifically sexual misbehavior is particularly challenging to analyze with a view to masculine subjectivity. Act books, visitation records, and bishops' registers record the prosecution of people who had sex outside of marriage. Statistical analysis might tell us whether men or women were more often called before such authorities, with what frequency, and perhaps under what circumstances. We might also get a sense of whether men or women received the more severe or more frequent punishments. Valuable information, to be sure, but the sense of gender it provides is partial (in both senses of that word). It only tells us how the community of neighbors suspected one sex or the other of greater susceptibility to sexual misconduct, or how the authorities tended to assign blame for it. It does not tell us whether, for example, communities saw any difference between a promiscuous young man and an adulterous older one.

Still less, with respect to the present purpose, does it show us how subordinate men might valorize and seek out that very misbehavior. Knowing how many men were presented for fornicating with how many women is of limited use unless we know ages, trades, or something beyond names. In addition, of course, prosecutions tell us only about the people who got caught, or who caused enough scandal for their neighbors to complain. And because authorities condemned and prosecuted any form of sexual behavior outside of marriage, the record of prosecution is inescapably shaped by the normative status of marriage. It cannot illuminate the nature of desires in which marriage figured not at all. Did young men (students, apprentices, servants, or whatever) expect to have sexual experience before marriage? Did they fear that their peers would think they were unmanly and scorn them if they did not? Getting any precise idea of what the answers might be, or even how to find the answers to questions like these requires thinking almost against the evidence, looking for the side of the story which was not written down because it was in no one's interest that it be so.

Written clues do surface in some unexpected places. One would expect the late medieval schoolroom to be a fount of unambiguous disciplinary wisdom. Yet the ever-provocative *vulgaria*, Latin exercises, remaining from early-sixteenth-century London, show us how even an educational discourse could send mixed messages. The London schoolboys read clearly didactic sentences such as, "Fornication was forbidden to men both by the old law and the new," "He has brought all his heritage to naught with misrule," "Beware the company of common women that lead a shameful life," "Unclean living women strew out their breasts." And, rather surprisingly, "He kept his sister as openly as she if had been his true wedded wife," "He gropes children and maidens," and "He was never acquainted with the unnamed sin."[82] Mixed with these phrases, schoolboys also encountered statements whose impression in young minds probably went beyond the author's intentions:

"He has deflowered many women," "He was wanton and dissolute among the maidens," "He made advances to women who consulted him, and deflowered them violently," "He is about as chaste as a dog after a bitch," "He deflowered many women of great reputation," "He is a man given over to lustful dissolution," "He enticed my daughter to lechery," "He made cuckolds of many of the community," "He keeps other men's wives."[83] The obvious intent was that along with their Latin grammar, the pupils would imbibe a distinction between correct and dishonorable masculine behavior understood in terms of acts. Most of these examples, after all, were grouped under the heading "About Sins and Improper Morals." Yet sin is always as fascinating as it is repellent and must have been especially so to boys who probably had little personal sense of the activities being proscribed. Who, they might ask, is this "he" who seems to be having all the fun? The situation here is much like what confronted commentators on early penitentials, who needed to warn confessors not to put ideas in their parishioners' heads with leading questions.[84] The pedagogical purpose may have undercut the moral one. By using racy examples like these in the classroom, the schoolmaster made Latin grammar more interesting for his pupils. He also effectively acknowledged and tacitly sanctioned a youthful code of misbehavior even as he ostensibly condemned it.[85]

The pupils learning *vulgaria* were probably only on the brink of puberty. For a representation of a later stage, a contemporary lyric provides the imaginary outlook of a sexually active young man, who states in the poem's first lines: "I have a new garden, and it is just begun."[86] The speaker goes on: "In the middle of my garden stands a pear tree, and it will produce no pears but a Johnny pear [per Jenet]. The fairest maiden of this town asked me to graft her a shoot of my pear tree." The anatomical symbolism here is not subtle. Yet the garden represents not only the speaker's literal body, but also his more abstract sense of his physical embodiment, his sexually mature maleness, and beyond that, the sense of possibility that physical masculinity confers on him. This physicality feels "new" because the speaker is young, just growing into his identity as a man; that is what "is just begun." The "pear tree" signifies the young man's physical penis and also his social phallus, in terms of his potency and fertility. Its fruit, the "Johnny pear," exists to prove fatherhood, as we subsequently see: "When I had made the graft, all at her request, she gave me my fill of wine and ale. I grafted her right up in her home, and twenty weeks after that day, it was moving in her womb. Twelve months after that day, I met that same girl; she said it was a Robert pear, not a Johnny pear!" The "fairest maiden" who desires a sample of the tree repays its bearer with wine and ale; she is the solicitor here. Her subsequent pregnancy, "moving in her womb" twenty weeks later, seems the desired result of the grafting. But he gets a surprise; when the child is born the woman assigns it to a different father.

The speaker would seem to have been made something like a cuckold. But he sounds little distressed by the result, and one suspects this is precisely because the woman is *not* his wife. That brief, flippant diction indicates a sigh of relief. This is the boast of a young man who now cannot be held responsible for the pregnancy of an unmarried "maid," and who moreover gets to say what a whore she really is. Not only did she "ask for it," she slept with at least one other and never pressured the speaker to marry her. A fantasy village tart this: easy, attractive, and cling free, the wished-for version of the aloof and hard-to-win "fairest maid" the young man would more likely encounter. Inconsistent, like many fantasies, but on its own terms comprehensible; since in the chronology of the poem the speaker does not know he is not her first until the end, all is well.

In real life, the possibility of a bastard could not be passed off so easily. Richard Cely, Jr., mentioned in a letter of 1482 that "I have many thing(s) in my mind." Three days later he revealed in a second letter that a woman named Em was pregnant, presumably by Cely himself. Cely remarked that the pregnancy "weighs upon my honest repute [*honeste*]." Yet out of the letter's twenty-nine lines in the printed edition, only six and a half are devoted to this matter. Cely goes on to talk about goshawks and other such concerns, quite matter of factly. Though the Cely brothers' extramarital liaisons in Calais are beyond reasonable doubt, Cely may have reached an age when such behavior had ceased to be commonly tolerated. Perhaps, also, Em was not as easy to discount, or leave behind, as some past women. And we do know from previous letters that Richard Cely had been looking for a wife. The rules of bachelorhood ceased to apply at the point where they might impede one's accession to true husbandry.[87]

The sexual lives of subordinate men surface in one of the Paston letters also, to a degree of clarity which never illuminates the sexuality of the Paston men themselves. About 1472, Edmond Paston II wrote regretfully to his brother John III, explaining that his mother had forced him to dismiss a servant named Gregory:

> This is to let you know that my mother has caused me to put Gregory out of my service; as God is my help, I write to you the true reason why. He happened to have the lust of a knave—to fuck a whore, to put it bluntly—and so he did, in the

rabbit warren yard. By chance he was seen by two of my mother's ploughmen, who were as eager for some of that as he was, and they asked him for a piece. And, as company called for it, he did not refuse them, so the ploughmen had her all night long in their stable. And Gregory had nothing more to do with her, and as he swears, did nothing with her within my mother's place. Nevertheless, my mother thinks that he was the cause of all this business, and that there is no remedy for it but his departure.[88]

Edmond urged John to accept Gregory, whom he knew to be a valuable servant the family could not afford to lose. Gregory, one senses, was quite aware of the Pastons' dependence on him and was not above transferring his skills and loyalties to someone else. Edmond warned that "If we, between ourselves, don't help him out, I pray God that we never thrive, and I think that is what he intends for us. So I am asking you, if you are willing to have him, that you will be a better master to him for my sake, for I am as sorry to be parted from him as any man alive is to be parted from his servant. And by my troth, as far as I know, he is as true as any alive."[89]

Clearly Edmond felt that Gregory was a good man who had made a foolish sexual blunder, led by "the lust of a knave": a lust, or wish, appropriate to younger, baser, or less creditable men, such as the ploughmen who insisted on getting their share. Gregory, though called a "servant," was far above menial status; referring to his independent ways, Edmond remarked, "that gentleman is the lord of his word."[90] Gregory should have known better, but as Edmond saw fit to mention, he had enough respect for the household to keep illicit sex outside it, in the "rabbit-warren yard." The trouble arose when he allowed the ploughmen, men of truly low status, to violate Edmond's "mother's place" by bringing the "whore" into the stable overnight (it probably did not matter whether she was a paid prostitute or simply a promiscuous woman). Edmond's wry description ("as company called for it") can even be taken to suggest that Gregory's downfall followed his very gentlemanly generosity to a couple of poor men. The mother, Margaret Paston, was certainly within her rights as lady of the household to punish behavior that endangered the household's reputation. We do not know what happened to the ploughmen. Conceivably, Margaret's ire towards Gregory was even more important, because he had failed his station. The ploughmen were simply behaving like ploughmen. In any case, Edmond (unlike his mother) seemed to feel that the consequences of illicit sex should be judged according to the circumstances. Gregory's actions suggest that he, too, thought he had not given offence and felt he was entitled to sexual release, outside marriage, but within other limits.

Gregory could rationalize his misconduct into not-so-bad behavior, and Edmond's reaction shows that a man of higher rank might understand how Gregory felt and thought. Gregory was not, probably, enjoying misbehavior for its own sake. But the importance of such misrule, and of rowdier kinds, was not restricted to the young and marginal. Lyndal Roper argues against a too easy equation of ostensibly powerful disciplinary authorities with a unitary and successful social ideal. For Roper, speaking from sixteenth-century German evidence, we cannot equate the moderate and sober ideal with masculinity, because too many of the putative exemplars violated it by indulging in its opposite. Corporate rituals easily deconstructed themselves in disordered violence and drinking. Youths were not the only men prosecuted for fighting. Roper memorably concludes, "Sixteenth-century masculinity drew its psychic strength not from the dignity of the mean but from the rumbustious energy which such discipline was supposedly designed to check.... What seems at first to be uncivilized 'wildness' was in fact carefully structured by the rules of civic society. Discipline was not so much a matter of repression of the lusts as of their dramatization."[91]

Here, Roper is speaking of the guild culture: an intensely homosocial, ritualistic one, riven within itself but resistant to outside authorities. The young men she describes had no obvious use for the niceties of courtesy literature—or, perhaps more accurately, there were other situations when disobeying such conventions became just as important and essential to masculinity. To see whether the English evidence supplies anything like what underlies Roper's virtuosic interpretations would be the subject of another project. In "The Mirror of the Periods of Man's Life," the interesting twist on the portrayal of riotous youth is that its restraint does not naturally happen at any "mature" age; the subject "Man" does not repent and change his ways until his decrepit old age, beginning at sixty (the poem interestingly sees him living to be a hundred). Instead, the ages from thirty to sixty have their own complements of pride, greed, and willful refusal of charity.[92] I suspect, however, that English urban culture before 1530, even in a place as tense as London, will look rather pale and mild compared to Roper's enthusiastically gorging, brawling, guzzling, and vomiting Germans. As Merry Wiesner also implied, German apprentices and journeymen of the later sixteenth century seem to have lived under a fraught regime of regulation, not just from above, but in what was imposed and enforced by peers.[93] In contrast, Karras remarks that collective action among English journeymen was "sporadic and disorganized."[94] And in a much earlier stage of print culture, late medieval England had yet produced no discipline literature of the vivid immediacy

Roper conveys, in which criticism seems to cloak a fetishistic authorial enjoyment of what is being forbidden.[95] Nor does anything from England compare to the gangs of young rapists that disrupted Dijon and Venice in the
fifteenth century, or to Italy more generally. There, we are told, the fifteenth
century saw tighter official regulation of young men's behavior, particularly
sexual, but also an attempt to curtail the luxurious excesses in which they
might be involved, from clothing to wedding breakfasts.[96] Still, inspired to a
certain degree by Roper, I would like at least to make a start on considering
some of these problems with respect to England's less well-documented context. As I suggested in chapter 3, the kind of petty violence that will probably
tell us most about the relationship between sober and riotous masculinities
in England has not yet received adequate analysis. The chief example I have
to offer in this regard, a petition to Chancery, is probably itself unusual in
several respects, but it is a healthy chunk of text ripe for interpretation.

The case comes from York around 1475, and the petitioner is the prior
of the monastery of the Holy Trinity there. It involves some very badly
behaving monks, namely, Robert Marshall and John Garland, who "the day
after the Assumption of Our Lady dressed themselves in secular clothing
like fighting men, and went out of the place between nine and ten o'clock
at night to a place outside the city called Saint James Leyes."[97] Having thus
evaded both monastic and civic jurisdiction, the monks "met with John
Deewe, a servant and prentice at the marshal,...and there Robert, and
John Garland, challenged him and with their baselards [short swords] gave
him several strokes till they had almost struck off his left hand, as still
shows, and will to his dying day." More than one feature of this first passage
was meant to set off alarm bells in the reader's mind; the monks were not
only dressed as laymen, but were carrying short swords (not the common
little knives) with which, unprovoked, they took the offensive against a real
layman. Quite apart from the weapons issue, the adoption of secular dress
by clerics had long been a point of concern for moralist critics.[98] The prior
also claimed that on another occasion, they had entered his household and
(again with "baselards") attacked and wounded one of his servants. Such
aggression is, of course, the opposite of the innocently defensive posture
assumed by all victimized narrative subjects in Chancery petitions.

Still more horrors awaited. Both monks, we learn, were having sexual
relationships with women:

Furthermore, Robert Marshall had a man's wife in his cell...at the Convent...which woman is called Maude Standes (her husband is a glazier). And

when this became known, Robert removed her into the steeple of the church and from there she was taken out, he not remembering that she would not leave therewith. But afterward she continually accompanied him, with other evil-named and vicious women, outside the place and in suspect places by night, not keeping his observance and times of divine services within the church like a man of religion.

Marshall, apparently, indulged his sexual appetite by bringing his mistress—whose husband was a man in a respectable trade—in with him to suit his convenience. Garland took the opposite approach:

> Also, John Garland continually accompanied him in indulgence of sin with a young woman dwelling with William Marshall . . . for which he was ordered to leave her company and not to go near her . . . But he presumptuously broke his obedience, for daily & nightly he wanted to be with her, at unlawful times & places, until she was gotten out of the place. And now, as she was staying at one Nicholas Halyday's, John, by his subtle crafts, often in the middle of the night would open the church doors and go forth, climb over the walls of the said Nicolas Halyday's place, and be with her at his pleasure, whenever he wanted to.

Daily and nightly, at his pleasure, whenever he wanted to: the outrage of the narrative voice fixes on the very audacity, or presumption, of Garland's disobedience, his daring to do what and when he wished, as much as on the specific nature of the disobedient acts. An attempt to enforce monastic discipline led only to a demonstration of exactly that arrogance: "And he would not take any correction, nor obey, but presumptuously in the chapter house, he cast off his habit & went out from us, despising everyone and saying, 'Neither prior, bishop nor chancellor shall correct me.'"

From the convent's point of view, these men posed a problem of order and governance, and the petition really operates in these terms. The prior presents the monks as bursting through every containing boundary, whether their own vows, the doors of the convent, or the judgment of their chapter. Therefore, they have also lost the rule of themselves, the control of their bodily appetites on which collective monastic life depends. The church was the prime transmitter of this ancient ideal to medieval society, so this was, not surprisingly, the model of masculinity most important to clerics, though it had a social currency beyond the institutional church.

The petition invokes uncontrolled self-indulgence, characteristic of the young and unformed man, to mark the monks as unqualified for the social privileges of adulthood, one of which is the ability to engage the public structure of the law, secular or ecclesiastical. By their unmanly behavior, Garland and Marshall disqualify themselves from adult agency; they legally emasculate themselves, becoming fit subjects of the chancellor's overreaching, adult authority. At least, that is what the petition attempts to argue. For the prior, though, the strategy backfires. Recall the syntax and tone of this excerpt: the pileup of incident, the breathless recitation, the anxious cramming of details. The text's frantic prolixity is exceptional even by the standards of Chancery, where legal formality cushions endless self-interested whining. The prior's story betrays diminished authority, while his diction suggests a loss of self-control as serious as that which he imputes to the monks, because it sounds like a loss of reason. The petition ends with a plea whose desperation exceeds formal convention, begging the chancellor's intervention because the monks are "not willing to abide any man's correction but utterly despise your suppliant," especially "considering that he has no power to punish [them], and has no ordinary within the realm of England to complain to."

So this tale of monastic indiscipline is easy enough to understand from above, from the point of view of authority, and in terms of the discourse of self-command. But what about the monks themselves? They could play the prior's game, with a Chancery lawyer's help. Both men claimed, as their legal interest demanded, that the prior's story was untrue, but without otherwise addressing its content. Instead, in contrast to the petition's despairing tones, the measured, careful cadences of their response dispassionately remove the issues to the masculine arena of legal jurisdiction, claiming that "they have here, as they understand, no competent judge to hear, decide and determine the matters contained in the said bill," that "Robert Huby naming himself prior of the Holy Trinity of York is not, nor ought not, to be prior there," that "most of the business contained in the said bill is spiritual business & not determinable in this court but in spiritual court, & . . . the rest of the business is clearly determinable at the temporal law, & in those matters determinable by the common law they ought not to be made to answer without their sovereign, for all which causes they pray to be dismissed out of this court."[99] I do not know how the chancellor judged the case, but to me, the monks win this discursive shoving match. They demonstrate that they know both the law and its received rhetorical attitudes. Perhaps they simply had a better lawyer than did the hapless prior.

By any standard, Marshall and Garland probably did not belong in a convent, or arguably in holy orders at all. Still, they seem not to have thought their enactment of sensually embodied masculinity at all problematic. They appear quite unconflicted about it. They saw no reason why they should not enjoy the security and prestige of the cloister and the pleasures of women and short swords as well. Nor did they think they were exceptional. Indeed, before making his dramatic exit from the chapter house, Garland retorted, "Thomas Dernton was as evil in the same sins as he, & worse. . . . John says that the same woman . . . that he was punished for, told him that Thomas Dernton labored her greatly to have his fleshly lusts with her, and proffered her a girdle and a noble, but she loved the foresaid John so well she would not agree thereto."[100] We have, of course, no way to assess the veracity of the story. Even if, however, some ulterior motive such as a power struggle within the monastery had prompted the prior to confabulate wildly, the fact remains that someone (and not someone hostile to the regular clergy in general) thought two unapologetic, voluptuary monks were credible figures.

The fact that Marshall and Garland were clerics simply adds another layer to the statements I made about clerical masculinity in chapter 2. Men in orders, especially (one guesses) young ones, might feel the same compulsion to rebel against the rules of obedience as might students or apprentices. Monastic discipline prescribed only a suppression and sublimation of the desire for aggressive pleasure more easily satisfied in "ranging & getting up & down with swords, baselards and with other combative array." Men who needed aggression so strongly would have caused problems and run up against disciplinary authority in secular life as well, especially if they started sleeping with other men's wives. (It was not only "chivalric culture" that "did not admire a totally uncontrolled violence.")[101] Nonetheless, they existed, and we need to admit that even within a society where conforming and complying were so often vital, it could seem just as necessary not to do so, and just as satisfying not to feel guilty about it.

DRESS

The body acquires its cultural apparatus by speaking to society. In many different times and places, that declaration occurs through the medium of clothing. Medieval Europeans made many statements through their attire, regarding their wealth, rank, marital status, and occupation. Many of these, however, came from very specific, emblematic features: livery badges, tokens of pilgrimage, clerical tonsures and habits, trimmings of variously costly fur. These were very important markers, but they were also superficial, having little to do with the body beneath. It is more difficult to retrieve the role of the body itself, especially of the sexed body, in conceptualizing how medieval people viewed each other through their clothes. It is possible to argue that the body took second place to the clothes even in the matter of sexual desire, especially when dealing with literary evidence: thus, says James Schultz, Gottfried von Straßburg's figures in *Tristan und Isold* are gendered only through the interaction of their bodies and their clothing. In this text, desire does not act upon "sexed" bodies because there are not enough markers to so distinguish them. Together, clothing and body elicit either "masculine" (approaching, possessive) or "feminine" (admiring, distant) forms of desire.[102] But we need to conceptualize a less ethereal, more immediate clothed embodiment in everyday medieval life.

The late medieval context is especially intriguing to consider with respect to the specifically *masculine* meanings of the clothed body. Even the most casual viewing of late medieval manuscript illustrations, or reading of certain kinds of literature, finds that men's clothing took some extreme directions from the mid-fourteenth to the late fifteenth century: skintight hose; long, pointed shoes; padded shoulders and chests. The result was a tight body silhouette, either revealed or concealed through long flowing outer garments such as the *houppelade*. These styles did "trickle down," being discernible among the peasantry, in less elaborate versions, by the mid-fifteenth century. But extreme styles were always more a matter of the upper classes. By the very end of the fifteenth century, Piponnier and Manne suggest, aristocratic tastes had changed again, towards a plainer, less exaggerated silhouette. Such developments were not mere curiosities. Historians of costume, in fact, regard the late medieval era as a turning point in Western attire, constituting no less than the birth of fashion itself; it was the first in some centuries to show much evidence of actual change or novelty in Western costume. The high to late Middle Ages saw the beginnings of what we can now recognize as a fashion cycle, resulting from both increased infusion of wealth and materials from the East (following the Crusades) and the emergence of a wealthier nonaristocratic class that aped its social superiors.[103]

Both the form and context of late medieval attire, therefore, invite interpretation, and scholarship has recently developed the right hermeneutic tools. Clothing is legible as a semiotic "code," though as Fred Davis cautions, we risk excessive literalness in such readings. Clothing is a code of "low semanticity," not easily producing coherent statements. It depends crucially on context (occasion, audience, the social groups involved); its meanings are unstable. Yet it is, undeniably, a code at some level. Neither explanations tracing the urge for fashion to sexuality (desire for attractiveness), nor those finding it in status identity satisfactorily account for fashion phenomena.[104]

Medieval costume presents some daunting challenges to fashion theory. Evidence comes largely from manuscript illustrations, literary references, and moralist denunciations of current fashion. Such sources' ability to convey a sense of what people actually wore is suspect. Moralistic (often clerical) criticism also cannot explain why particular styles of dress were attractive to particular groups of people. Recent fashion theory and costume analysis has drawn mostly on the trends of the nineteenth and twentieth centuries to develop its conceptual framework. Costume and fashion are, of course, not the same thing, and one ought to be able to decode the clothing of an era when "fashion," the compulsory privileging of the new, was not the driving force. Yet the concept of fashion is central to current cultural studies on clothing. For these reasons, medieval costume remains comparatively undertheorized. Most works available on the subject, especially in English, are essentially descriptive; a historical approach is still largely missing. For the present purpose there is a consequent difficulty. "Fashion" has been so strongly associated with women's attire in modern times that gender analysis of costume does not quite yet have the vocabulary for a proper consideration of masculinity.

Contemporary criticism of the new men's fashions, one of our chief sources about them, tended to concentrate on two chief vices: their wasteful luxury and their degree of bodily display. Standards of responsible masculinity, predictably, played their part in such analyses, but the messages were not as clear as we might expect. The late-fourteenth-century poem known in its latest edition as "On the Times," which I have chosen as a prime example, places its condemnation of contemporary male clothing in the context of a general complaint about corruption, decay, and hypocrisy in society. Amid a familiar canvas of oppression, greed, deceit, and misgovernance, the denunciation of luxurious and outlandish fashions is predictable.[105]

Befitting a critique that targets empty pretension and wasteful consumption, the description of these fashions focuses on the discrepancy between appearance and the reality underneath, providing an outline of the body in grotesque exaggeration: wide, high collars; long spurs; long, pointed toes; shoulders "broader than ever God made" (130). Indeed, this body contains parts out of their natural place and possibly borrowed from the wrong sex. The men have "shoulders in the place of chests" (134). This is a difficult style to imagine, but corresponds perhaps to a line that varies between three main manuscripts of the poem. Two seem to turn their ire on women: "Women, lo! with wanton breasts / *procedunt arte prophana*" (161–62). But one variant has "Womanly breasts *pretendunt arte prophana*," which may still refer to the men's clothes; a recent editor suggests "something like 'with profane art they puff out their chests like women.'" The body thus represented is a fraud, and not only in its shoulders. The men so attired *"incedunt ridiculose,"* and "Little or nought in the pouch, / *pascuntur deliciose"* (126–29). A "pouch" may be a literal purse, referring to foolish expenditure on luxury; it is probably also a scrotum, in which the presence of "little or nought" signifies the essential lack collapsing all other pretensions. Thomas Hoccleve, in a poem pointedly titled "Of Pride and of Wasteful Clothing of Lords' Men, against Their Rank," emphasized the "empty purse" in a similar way, drawing attention also to the consequent lack of "land, rent, or chattel."[106]

This clothing restricts and denies natural movement and function; hose decorated up to the crotch are so tight that men cannot kneel to pray and try not even to bend over (149–55).[107] Luxury and ornament form a constricting shell that limits masculine volition. (Even if that earlier reference is indeed to women, women's excesses are of little interest beyond their power to waste resources; no one cares about the restriction of *feminine* movement and volition.) Thomas Hoccleve made similar criticisms. Servants encumbered by such clothing are as useless as women (to whom they are thus implicitly assimilated); they cannot fulfill their role in defense of their masters. By implication, real "manhood" consists in the art of war (82–84). Hoccleve is here concerned with social order: the servants of great lords seek to "counterfeit" their masters' status through aping their costume. Indeed, the lords themselves are "to blame," like irresponsible parents (39), for allowing such abuses by their servants. The richness of "apparel" signals the leanness of the male household-body; "good" is "wasted in outrageous array."[108] The household's smaller "members" thus impoverish and waste the greater. G. R. Owst's extensive survey of sermon literature suggests that generally, the satirists' chief concern with men's costume was waste, rather than indecency.[109]

But while powerful on its own terms, this critique takes no explicit account of its targets' motivations for wearing what they do. Nowhere does "On the Times" claim that such fashions make men unattractive to women. While it goes on to lampoon behavior between fashionable lovers, whose impractical outfits in winter give them messy head colds (169–82), there is no direct mention of sexual failure. We are tempted to place the poem in the ancient lineage of complaint associating effeminacy with excessive attention both to appearance and to women. Yet there is a certain resignation in the piece's tone, as if recognizing that men refuse to revise their priorities as the commentator would like. Hoccleve, too, is forced to protest vainly: he claims that popularly, lots of clothes (involving lots of cloth) signify a "lusty man," while actually, such men are debtors to the drapers who supply them (85–87).[110]

If, however, such fashions really looked so ridiculous, why did men continue to wear them? Whether we speak of tight hose and long sleeves in the fourteenth century or pierced tongues and black lipstick in the twenty-first, we cannot properly understand the meaning of bodily adornment through the words of those who do not participate in it. Once again, in the medieval case, we are left to speculate, because we lack men's comments on their own choice of particular styles. So the question becomes hypothetical, albeit worthwhile.

Decoding appearance entails considering the spectators to whom that appearance is directed. Modern experience encourages us to frame this question in terms of sexual attractiveness. We tend to think of costume as a primarily feminine concern. Popular debate, guided by feminist criticism of popular culture, has drawn much attention to the ways fashion may represent the female body to suit masculine fantasies of sexual femininity. Fashion theorists speak of the "erotic-chaste dialectic," in which the "erotic" (exposure, enhancement) and the "chaste" (concealment, de-emphasis) may exist in a constant tension in women's clothing, one always undercutting the other while simultaneously calling attention to it. The clothing of men, past or present, certainly also may depend for part of its effect on display, which seeks to elicit a sexual interest. Nevertheless, particularly in its medieval versions, men's attire requires an analysis recognizing the interdependence of sexual and nonsexual meanings in creating the power of the clothed male body's visual image.

The exaggeration of the body in men's clothes of the fourteenth century seems aggressively sexual to us, and this effect was not lost on medieval viewers either. Some of the most famous Middle English remarks on costume come from Chaucer's Parson, who decries contemporary fashions under the rubric of pride and wasteful luxury, much as do the poems I quoted earlier. To an unusual extent, though, the Parson dwells also on the body that such clothes practically force into public view through their "horrible excessive scantiness." Short jackets and coats "do not cover a man's shameful organs, with wicked intent" ("Parson's Tale" [PT] 421).[111] This scolding reference, arguably clear enough, does not suffice for the Parson, who seems to have difficulty leaving the subject of the too-obvious privates: they bulge, "swollen" so that they "seem like the malady of hernia;" under parti-colored hose, these (again) "swollen members" appear flayed or diseased (PT 424–28).

The simultaneous exposure of male buttocks draws condemnation also, but the repeated attention to genitals should give us pause, especially since (as in "On the Times") women's immodest clothing gets only a passing glance (PT 429).[112] Clearly, the voice Chaucer has created here articulates complex anxieties, cultural and personal, which deserve a fuller analysis than I can give them at present. (For one thing, the Parson's horrified, fascinated fixation on male sexual display, especially a swelling, bulging embodiment that threatens to burst forth, is analogous to the much later fetishizing of misrule described by Lyndal Roper.) Note that the Parson attributes to such indecency a wicked intent; he does not elaborate on its effects or its possible success. And while the proximate meaning of that intent may be sexual seduction, the Parson assimilates the entire topic of hypersexual male appearance to the sin of pride. Oddly enough, appreciating this gets us closer to the embodied experience of the clothing than does concentrating on sexuality itself. In the Parson's terms, what lies behind the distasteful carnality is a form of masculine pride, a thoroughly corporeal one, manifested in phallic display.[113] This aggressive pride, in which the individual self swells up to its maximum size, takes the particularly threatening form of pride in the body, a strutting arrogance confident of its own success.[114] Wanting to attract a sexual partner is only one dimension of the problem; those male genitals, "swollen" as if in arousal, signal the (auto)erotic excitement of bodily pride itself, of a fully experienced and sexual body ego. Through the Parson, Chaucer demonstrates a deep awareness of masculine embodiment and its social significance.

As I mentioned above, the Parson does not consider whether or not women in his society actually are attracted to such unsubtle display by men. This is probably an unanswerable question for the historian; moreover, I suspect that the conscious expectation of sexual success with women can have been only an ancillary aspect of the masculine experience of such fashions. The elite social classes who adopted and displayed the most extreme and sexualized styles (particularly when the styles were new) were precisely those in which women had the least independent agency to select mates. In such a setting, clothing, desire, and attraction must exist in a transgressive counterpoint to social, indeed legal, norms. We cannot conceive the masculine subject/object's relation to social context as we would a feminine one, because men's relation to the nexus of sexual commerce (for want of a better term) was and is different.

Yet we need not excise the desire to impress from the discussion entirely. Where a style comes from the elite and involves the appearance of luxury, a sexily clothed male body was also an expensively clothed one. Davis very astutely describes the tension, analogous to the "erotic-chaste dialectic," in

Western culture, between display of status and quasi-ascetic refusal of that display, which applied to premodern cultures even more starkly.[115] In late medieval England, the dynamic was not subtle. I doubt that, in ordinary secular society, much stigma attached to excessive display. The phallic exuberance of fashionable men's clothing came not only from its emphasis on the male form but also from its display of wealth, opposed to the sober and concealing attire of those men (especially clerics) whose estate demanded at least the fiction of unworldliness. Gender and social status were intertwined. By demonstrating one's wealth and social position, one displayed the clout (the size of one's social self) to which one aspired. It is hard to imagine that the prospect of wealth has ever diminished anyone's sexual attractiveness. Power and wealth, and status differences, may themselves carry an erotic charge. That last comment, of course, would apply to women too, particularly young heiresses. But two facts remain: One, although both men and women were concerned with visual social profile, clothes were still more dramatically differentiated by sex than by social class. Two, nothing suggests that femininity was judged by wealth. (The flashily dressed lady, of town or country, demonstrated the significance of the masculine self to whom she was joined.)[116]

The provocative display of men's clothing, even in its possible appeal to the female gaze, makes most sense as aggressive competition, referring to a homosocial rather than a heterosexual arena. In such a case, "sexual" meanings may very well still exist, but their function would have more to do with self-presentation: appearing masculine to other men. This does not mean that women, and their gaze, were irrelevant. Just as in battle (real or staged), women may observe and comment, and masculine competition takes place in front of them, so there can be a masculine satisfaction in passing a kind of test even when social reality makes the woman's choice a fiction.[117] Chivalric occasions, particularly tournaments, of course celebrated that fiction. The line between sexual and nonsexual meanings therefore gets blurred: if broad shoulders suggestive of physical strength are desirable, does it matter that their ostensible function is martial (homosocial) rather than to stir desire (heterosexual)?[118]

Western culture puts men's and women's bodies on display differently. Or rather, men and women are allowed different forms of display. In the late Middle Ages, men of all classes seem to have had more room for self-exposure, but the meaning of those exposures varied within a class and also changed if the occasion demanded the meeting of individuals of different status. Fashionable men could show much more explicitly the shape of their legs, groins, and arms, if they chose, and exaggerate chests and shoulders. The only area they could completely bare without covering fabric (within reason), which women could not, was the hair, for all classes. For women the dynamic was much simpler, between cover-up and more direct suggestion (which usually meant low-necked bodices). Exposure only becomes meaningful when we know the context. In late medieval terms, the exposure of a woman's body was much more sensitive, yet elite women might be more literally exposed (in convivial situations) than lower-class women. For men, the reverse was true. Elite men rarely bared any skin of torso or extremities in public, as far as we know, showing less of their literal, physical bodies than lower-class men. But they also could deploy a wider range of styles controlling the degree of exposure or concealment.

Masculinity in dress was perhaps then a demonstration of this range of meaning. The Burgundian chronicler who commented scornfully on English men's fashions in the 1460s (in terms nearly identical to those of Chaucer's Parson 80 years before) also remarked that "those who wore short dress one day wore long clothes to the ground the next day."[119] That control could produce, as a dramatic choice, a kind of clothed nudity far greater than what a woman could display. In part, the new men's fashions drew some of their masculine charge from the fact that the way they drew attention to the body was completely off-limits to women. For centuries, the prohibition on any exposure of the female body, particularly of the legs, determined the form of European women's clothing. Masculine clothed embodiment involved a consciousness of that difference, awareness that the clothes graphically symbolized men's greater social presence. The difference is the ability to suggest. Direct uncovering of the body is different from displaying a representation of it. Literal nudity, especially in the presence of a social superior, denoted poverty, debasement, humiliation, or perhaps deliberate offense. Controlled nudity, or suggestion, could, however, suggest phallic confidence and, through its association with wealth, social power.

The dynamic between erotic and chaste did not operate within the style of dress worn by any one man in late medieval England, as it might in modern or even medieval women's dress. Its oscillations were far larger, between easily distinguishable forms of male attire worn by different kinds of men. On that scale, the erotic-chaste dynamic was itself rather less important than that between worldly and unworldly, between sober and exuberant, or between mature and youthful, whether the men wearing tight hose and short jackets were twenty or forty. We can also conceive the two poles as fashion and nonfashion. The status value of novelty, of being in style, was itself new in the fourteenth century. In the late Middle Ages generally, "the dress of women changed much more slowly than that of men and it was subject to far less dramatic changes of style."[120] The consequent possibility complicating gender analysis is that being fashionable might, for the one group, accentuate masculinity, just as much as it diminished it for the other. The insistence that lavish secular styles of male appearance are "actually" effeminate is, if not as old as the hills, at least as old as the time of William Rufus, whose court was famously condemned by Orderic Vitalis and William of Malmesbury for the womanish long hair of its male adherents. An association of fashionable novelty with effeminacy is still detectable in the late fifteenth century, in the play *Mankind*, through characters representing deviations from the sober masculine ideal: fashion, excess, newfangledness, as opposed to Mankind's productive labor. Effeminacy in *Mankind* also means a lack of control, over one's body and others.[121]

But for the men who actually wore the clothes, being fashionable itself accentuated masculinity. It encompassed the other effects (cutting a figure among men, phallic pride, *possible* sexual attractiveness) shoring up a masculine self. The wearer need not even have been fully conscious of those specific aspects as such; they were all part of being, and feeling, in fashion. The claim of Chaucer's Parson, that overemphasized male bulges look diseased and disgusting, sounds like a vain attempt at aversion therapy. As Robert Bartlett comments with respect to the controversies over hairstyles at the courts of William Rufus and Henry I:

> The monastic moralists are appealing to an image of manliness that they calculate their hearers will share. They wish . . . to convince the courtly youths of the rightness of their own connotative scheme and to shame them into conformity with it. When they talk of the youthful and courtly side of male long hair they are probably sociologically accurate but when they call the young men women they are preachers. The long hair of the Anglo Normans was a self-consciously youthful, lay, aristocratic and curial style. The attack on it . . . recognised these features but did not assault them directly. Instead it tried a flanking assault by appealing to a common sexual language which would undermine the obvious attractiveness of the other connotations of long hair. . . . Long hair could mean femininity but the monastic critics had to fight to establish that meaning and, as we have seen, had limited success.[122]

Bartlett is referring to the years around 1100. By the late Middle Ages, social change meant that fashionable wear reached a constituency far broader than the small circle of the royal court, out to the ranks of peasants and wage earners.[123] Moralist condemnation of clothing came increasingly to resemble shouting into the wind; in response to the pope's ban on piked shoes in 1468, some Londoners said they would wear long pikes whether the pope wished it or not.[124] Concern over fashionable excess went beyond poems and sermons, of course, as the existence of England's late medieval sumptuary laws indicates.[125] But such laws needed repeated promulgation. They did not work, just as appeals to modesty and economy did not work, because the enhancement of the social self—the social presumption enacted when men of one rank wore clothes resembling those above them—combined powerfully with the enhancement of the embodied self in physical pride. In clothing as in so much else, we learn only half the story if we take the meanings of masculinity from the voices of authority.

THE DANGERS OF THE TONGUE

Men's use of their bodies included their use of words. A long tradition of medieval critique recognizes the treachery of the tongue and the power of malicious talk to disrupt social relations.[126] Moralist discourse often gendered excessive or malicious speech feminine, considering women to be more prone to gossip than men and less in control of their bodily impulses. In the late Middle Ages, the well-known cultural suspicion of women's speech and the gendering of words (as against "deeds") as feminine worked in concert with an increased attention to all forms of misbehavior in England after the plague, which brought individuals more under the watchful eye of community authorities. The result was that far more women than men were prosecuted for speech offenses, especially in the form of "scolding." Scolding prosecution was disposed to suspect women first because of the cultural associations of women with (disruptive) speech, but "the prosecution of so many more women than men as scolds also helped to determine cultural expectations about women's relationship to speech, expectations reflected in representations of women's words." Men were more generally expected to enact specific forms of disorderly speech: swearing (cursing) and blasphemy. Sandy Bardsley argues that in part because of their vivid metaphorical interpretation as injuries against God, these speech acts could be seen more as masculine "deeds" than feminine "words." Where men were actually prosecuted for scolding, there were often complicating factors, such as a record of other offenses or coprosecution with wives. Rarely, it seems, did men's speech alone lead them afoul of the authorities where it did not qualify as legally actionable defamation.[127]

Although suspicion of deviant speech bore more heavily on women, men were not free from the need to watch their tongues. Almshouses established in the fifteenth and early sixteenth centuries explicitly required self-regulation of speech from their prospective tenants, forbidding quarrelling, "jangling and chiding," "evil slander," scolding, and making of "debate," and this applied equally to houses where only men lived.[128] Courtesy literature pursues the same theme, cautioning against "jangling." One common courtesy poem explicitly associates "useless words" with the "crowds of women" it advises the reader to shun.[129] One is to give short answers, "for many words are very tedious to any wise man that shall give audience."[130] One should be discreet, not repeating what one has heard, and beware of telling tales one might regret later: "Take good heed if you do speak out, for you might say a word today that seven years later might be regretted."[131] Here, once again, the instructed subject is effectively learning political behavior; "The Babees Book" specifies not to talk in the lord's presence. We sense the social dangers of idle speech for men—mainly, the betrayal of secrets and possible damage to reputation. Gossip regulated reputation for men as well as women.[132]

Words were not the only utterances to be disciplined. Laughter, too, was permissible only in small doses. Brunetto Latini's admonition that a prospective mayor must not speak too often, nor laugh too loudly, "like a child or a woman," had by the fifteenth century been Anglicized in the *Liber custumarum* of London.[133] At the table, the courtesy books dictate, "never giggle, but stay sober," and in general:

> Do not laugh too often out of pleasure,
> At any sort of jest that any man makes;
> He who laughs for all to see,
> Looks like a "shrew" or a fool.[134]

Medieval discourse might warn both sexes against excessive laughter. But it enjoined women to minimize laughter for reasons, to degrees, and in ways which did not apply to men. Laughter originated in the body (feminine); women's bodies provided a ready-made metaphor with their two "mouths," making orality and femininity all the more plausible a connection; laughter could too easily go to excess, or indicate excessive emotion, frowned on since classical times. Where men are instructed not to laugh too loudly, the reasons concern congeniality, not "decency" or quasi-sexual reputation.[135] Obviously this draws on the same rationale of discreet self-command governing so much of masculine social presence.

But the embodied nature of male speech went beyond the issue of self-control. Through speech, fantasized or desired bodily experience might achieve certain effects in the social world, though not necessarily the effects the speaker wanted. The connection of speech to masculinity emerges vividly in the record where spoken words represented sexual experience. In London at the end of the fifteenth century, a man turned down by the woman he wanted to marry sought to spite her by claiming they had slept together: "Because she would not have me, therefore I said I lay with her, so that she should be loath to any other man."[136] Such a vengeful and damaging slander—really a verbal form of rape—enacted the experience the speaker could not have, turning the fantasized male body into a weapon.

The following Canterbury tale (from the nearby Kent village of Sturrey, actually) of 1415 provides a more complex example of conflict between men mediated by the honor of a woman. Witnesses for Alice Yarewell claimed she was a virgin, of blameless reputation until the day John Maldon declared, to some men gathered in John Mycham's house, that she was a common whore. Maldon said he knew of three men who had lain with her, of whom he named two. One of these was Maldon himself. The other, Richard Bokeland, was a witness in the suit, who quoted Maldon as saying that when Bokeland slept with Alice, the woman told Bokeland that he should go away and leave her in peace, because he did not know how to "do the deed." Maldon then boasted that, in contrast, Alice had lavished praise on his sexual technique, saying, "You are to be blessed, because you truly know well how to do your deed."[137]

However much this story may have amused these men, Alice surely was not laughing. Her promising marital prospects evaporated once the rumor started going around, and witnesses were quite specific about her losses: Richard Bocher, a man worth forty pounds, dropped her, as did bachelor number two, a fisherman who was "able to spend five marks per year."[138] These were tragic but unsurprising results for a woman; no wonder she sued. Yet the unpleasant episode had meaning also for masculine reputation grounded in the sexual performance of the male body.

The gathering of men in that house was a little arena, or a little stage, where they could perform the mundane comedy-dramas of socially demonstrated masculinity. John Maldon scored a few points by bragging about a sexual conquest. By using the same story to belittle Richard Bokeland, he scored a few more. No great surprises here; there is no such thing as "just a joke," and the utility of humor, especially sexual humor, to enforce interpersonal hierarchies is well known. If these were young and subordinate men, such as students or apprentices, this coarse competition would seem understandable and somehow limited in its significance. Yet they were not youths; Richard Bokeland was more than thirty, and the other witnesses were even older, which probably means Maldon was also not very young. There seems at first to have been no shame or perceived danger even for these mature men in frankly discussing illicit sexual conduct.

Even more intriguing is Richard Bokeland's response. The supposed incompetent would have had some legal grounds for a defamation suit of his own, since fornication was punishable by the church courts. Further, Maldon apparently kept telling the story all that summer (over which period, it presumably lost much of its comic value). Bokeland did not sue, but this did not mean he was untouched. He made the deliberate decision to testify against Maldon. This strategy thus covered both an actionable slur and the nonactionable but possibly more degrading insinuation of a sexual failing. Speculation about the true nature of that suggested failing is probably not very worthwhile. The more important thing to take away may be the complexity of the response, where one motive enfolds another.

Testifying on behalf of Alice Yarewell meant supporting and defending a decent woman who had been credibly and materially injured; this was the formal part of Bokeland's reaction. We need not bring "chivalry" or gallantry into the question to appreciate how important such a response could be to Bokeland's masculine social self. Not to come to Alice's aid might have offended far more ordinary group standards of solidarity and neighborliness in this small community.[139] The formal and plainly acceptable route of testifying *for* Alice also allowed Bokeland to testify *against* Maldon, providing a legal means to react to an injury that would ordinarily not have had formal redress. That injury could not be defined in the usual terms. It makes most sense as homosocial competition, in which being seen to have reacted—not to have let a challenge go unanswered—had value, as we saw in chapter 2.

John Maldon's sexual boasts were fantasies of self-enhancement, phallic both in their literal (sexual) and metaphoric (social) aspects, here given unusually unsubtle form. Expressing those desires in a form that injured other people, male or female, might bring down official retribution on the speaker, leaving a trace in the historical record. Yet for every such surviving example, there must have been countless other instances that passed with impunity. Occasion and company might require a departure from the moralists' ideal of laconic sobriety of speech. Skill in handling the tongue made the difference between successful self-aggrandizement and humiliation. Spoken words, like dynamite, might clear a space where one could build, or they might blow up in one's face. A man who fumbled became known as loose tongued, a "harlot of his tongue" in the words of one 1528 defamation suit: something that never augmented masculinity.[140] John Baker, the rector of Bowers Gifford in chapter 2, referred to the same association of ideas in his conflict with the village bailiff. Baker claimed that Thomas Alyn had said he better deserved a bridle than a straight sword: a reference to the muzzle female scolds might have to wear as punishment.[141]

The intertwining of verbal and sexual reputation becomes clear as we see how subtly reputation for sexual acts shaded into reputation for speaking about them. For example, in York diocese in 1512, Robert Kichynman sued Elizabeth Lovecock for saying that he had committed adultery with Katherine Dawson, a married woman. Kichynman claimed he had already cleared himself of this charge through compurgation. His one witness, the vicar of Leeds, deposed that both Elizabeth and a Margaret Lovecock had denied saying anything defamatory about Robert; they had insisted that Robert himself had told them about the affair. The vicar had called several other men, who declared that the women had indeed been repeating the injurious story. On their knees, Elizabeth and Margaret had made a formal apology: not to Kichynman, but to Katherine Dawson, whom they claimed still to consider a good woman. So far, so good. Everyone, including Kichynman and Katherine's husband, claimed to be satisfied and had a drink together. But matters evidently did not end there, since Kichynman decided, after all, to sue Elizabeth.[142]

Why did he change his mind? Perhaps Elizabeth, unable to resist updating the story, had gone on repeating it, adding the revelations of the vicar's informal inquest. Everyone now knew Kichynman not as an adulterer, but as a man who made up stories about his sexual conquests, at the expense of a married woman. Worse yet, his interlocutors were women, which made it gossip. This kind of injury had no easy remedy for Kichynman, for no one had directly impugned his use of speech. He had to sue as if the accusation of sexual misbehavior was what mattered. Words, audience, and falseness added up to a more unmanly kind of looseness than anything he did or did not do in bed.

In my temporally latest example, from 1532, the chantry priest Henry Taylor sued John Hole, of Aberford (near Leeds), who, he claimed, had alleged "that Sir Henry Tailior has had two children with Margaret Feldhouse or one child at the least."[143] Hole's response was to deny that he had said this, but to claim that Margaret Feldhouse had admitted to having three children by Taylor. Thus far the issues are not very interesting. More than one child by the same woman would imply a clerical concubinage of long standing, not a momentary passionate failing, and might have been more sternly regarded by the court.

But John Hole did not stop at defending himself. He made counterallegations against Taylor, asserting not only the existence of the bastard children but something even more serious: that Taylor "caused the same Margaret to destroy them with drinks & other crafts." (This seems not to have been taken seriously by the court.) The offenses of which Hole accused Taylor were principally, however, those of speech. Taylor had, Hole claimed, made more than one sexual boast: most memorably, "that he would strike [or thrust] forth the 'rod' from his trousers at a whore's arse, not letting any man stand in his way, and then might he serve God the better all the week after."[144] The scene Hole described which summed up the situation is worth quoting in its entirety:

> Sir Henry, in Easter week last past, said . . . "John Hole, why did you say that I have destroyed a child?" And the said John answered and said, "No, I said not so, but I said that I heard Margaret Feldhows [your whore][145] confess to Lionell Roger that she by your Counsel had destroyed [3] children with drinks." Then answering, the said Sir Henry, "Why, Hole, is there no more whores in this parish but she? Yes, if every whore had a prick set in her nose, few would go without in this parish."[146]

More was involved here than the punishable misbehavior, which Hole alleged to be remorselessly committed and even boasted about. Layer on layer of defamation, or possible defamation, or rather possible dangerous speech, emerges. John Hole defamed Henry Taylor by saying that he had fathered children—the only allegation dealt with by the court, according to Taylor's positions and articles. Certainly Hole wanted to paint Taylor as a man of unruled sexuality. But that lack of self-command found additional, and additionally offensive, expression in his speech, and not only its subject but its manner. Hole's quotations of Taylor are distinguished by their open, defiant vulgarity: "which as we thought was no goodly words for a priest to speak," in Hole's opinion. Here Hole displays a drawing back and distancing from words or locutions that are not necessarily criminal or even defamatory, but distasteful, "dirty." Hole held at arm's length Taylor's remark about the parish "whores," "Which we thought was a shameful saying from him that had been father confessor to many of them before. And more he said, the which I am ashamed to speak of it." The tenor of Hole's countersuit is, roughly, "He said that I said that he'd destroyed a child, which I actually know he as good as did, because he told his 'whore' on whom he'd fathered them to do so. But I never actually said he'd murdered them. All I did was report what this woman herself confessed. And he reacted to this with shameful language. So he is not only a licentious priest and one who covers up his sins through murder, but a slanderer of the women of this parish and a man of unruled language. I, on the other hand, am no slanderer but an honest man who reports what is already common knowledge, and who knows how priests ought to conduct themselves."

It is very difficult to get a clear sense of what was commonly considered foul or vulgar language in this period, which we do not imagine as given to euphemism. The sense that priests ought to be held to a higher standard in governing their speech had been articulated long before in pastoral discourse, which condemned loose and salacious talk in general as sinful.[147] The Hole case suggests that this was becoming a standard maintained by the "we" of the lay community, whose attitudes are harder to discern than those of literate clerical authors. The almost prudish reaction to the language ("I am ashamed to speak of it") seems a new thing for the court to have bothered to record. It was now in a litigant's interest to present himself as respectable and clean of speech and manner, because the court was (or might be) willing to take that into account. (In this case, it was not enough; Hole's side of the story was taken as a "confession" of defamation.) So perhaps it is not too old-fashioned to detect in this quarrel a hint of a changed climate, of the altered world to which the new religion, in 1532 just on the horizon in England, would lead over the succeeding decades. Where speech was concerned, there were puritanical people well before there were Puritans.

In effect, this case comes down to a contest of the wielding of speech, which pivoted on expectations about how different men would use words. In telling his competing story, Hole was hoping someone would believe in a priest who not only broke his vows of celibacy but took pleasure in coarse, worldly, unpriestly talk, in boasting about it. Whether Hole told complete truth or an utter fabrication, an awareness of the discourse of rebellious masculinity lies behind his story. Hole had two social stereotypes on which to draw: the licentious priest and the loose-tongued priest, and in this instance he portrayed Henry Taylor as both—indeed, as licentious in being loose tongued. The point was not just that a priest might temporarily, guiltily, yield to sexual temptation. It was that he might, with no sense of guilt, behave exactly like other men: enjoy breaking the rules, enjoy having that known, and use spoken language to enjoy it again.

Late medieval evidence, literary and legal, indicates that speech was considered to be an experience of the body and was conceived as such, not only in learned theory, but in the everyday lives of English people. In contemporary Scotland, this belief found a vivid juridical enactment, as convicted defamers had to make public statements in which they addressed their tongues, as if they were entities apart, and made explicit that the tongue had lied.[148] Although the English did not apparently go quite this far, a version of the same belief is credible from English sources. The tongue was difficult to rule, and just like the penis, whose behavior was often also beyond control, it could lead a man into unmanliness even as he tried to use it to his own advantage.

THE BODY'S role in gender is one part of a cycle or a loop. It is neither the foundation of a structure nor the product of an assembly line. Scholarship on modern masculinity realizes this. R. W. Connell provides a fine analysis of the "body-reflexive practices" demonstrated in several men's accounts of sexual experience and sport: the body interprets, serves as metaphor, directs expectations, and feeds back into the individual's assessment of society and his place in it.[149] For Connell, this is a vision of bodies "sharing in social agency."[150] To me, it corresponds nicely to what Lyndal Roper claims we need to problematize in historical scholarship: the "relation between the psychic and the physical."[151] To admit the body to a theory, not only of prescriptive or ideal gender, but of gender identity, in history, requires attention to the ways that same body provides, mediates, and symbolizes physical experience.

As Roper and Nancy Partner both point out in their different ways, a methodology attuned to exactly that problem has existed for some time.[152] From Sigmund Freud's earliest publications onward, psychoanalytic theory has placed the body close to the center of its researches. Psychoanalysis addresses the mind, to be sure, but that is a mind provoked by physical sensation, experiencing desires and conflicts in deeply sensual form, and—in the condition known to Freud as "hysteria" and today, with more precision, called "somatization disorder"—expressing its most repressed and disavowed anxieties as vivid physical symptoms.[153]

Those aspects of the body that individuals connect with sexual difference, sexual maturity, and, of course, sexual pleasure provide especially rich material in the reflexive process of gender identity. The model of gender identity that features prominently in present-day psychoanalytic theory is itself far from "essentialist." Developed between the 1960s and the 1980s by Robert Stoller, it defines core gender identity as the most basic sense of belonging to one sex or the other. As some interesting human variations show, core gender identity has reference to genital anatomy, but does not depend on it. Core gender identity is a development of very early childhood (achieved usually at 18–36 months), rooted in the child's sense of having been assigned to the correct sex by adult caregivers.[154] By this early age, infants have discovered their own bodies. The boy, for example, knows he is a boy, having preverbally agreed that he is what everyone calls him. (There is a clear, and somewhat surprising, resonance here with Butler's remark that "the subject, the speaking 'I', is formed by virtue of... assuming a sex.... The forming of a subject requires an identification with the normative phantasm of 'sex.'"[155] Stoller's core gender theory would admit both the identificatory and normative qualities, and would question the "phantasm" part only in order to specify its meaning.) The boy also knows he has a penis and that it is part of him. Yet he does not yet know that the penis is the "reason" he is a boy. That discovery comes later, as encounters with other children and increased cognitive faculties allow the boy to link anatomical difference with gender difference. It also depends on the meaning he assigns to the sensations, especially pleasurable ones, coming from his body and particularly from the genitals. Body awareness, part of "body ego," is a significant part of gender identity.[156] The theory of core gender, and the large body of contemporary work on gender based on it, therefore cannot be classified simply as either constructionist or not; it strikes a balance, ascribing a crucial influence to culture and especially to language, but making clear that even in earliest life an equilibrium exists between culture and subjectivity, mediated by the physiologically sexed body. In Stoller's own words, core gender "is the first step in the progress towards one's ultimate gender identity and the nexus around which masculinity and femininity gradually accrete. *Core gender identity has no implication of role or object relations.*"[157] The increasingly sophisticated processing of later experiences builds on core gender to produce an adult gender identity: a far more elaborate business, incorporating a wide range of influences.

To show where the concerns of historical inquiry, psychoanalysis, and the body might coincide, I will relate the following example from personal experience. This is not a commonly approved form of evidence for historians (especially of the Middle Ages), but just this once, I think it helps. In York, England, in August 1999, I was at the Borthwick Institute of Historical Research (now the Borthwick Institute for Archives) investigating the case of Nicholas de Cantilupe, described above. Midway through transcribing one of the depositions, I realized that I had been making an error. For the word *procreare* I had been writing *procurare*. The mistake was understandable. The word *procurator* appears frequently in such documents, because the *procuratores* were the proctors who represented the parties in these suits. A little farther down the parchment page, I discovered in the manuscript the word *procurare* ruled through, with *procreare* written above it in the same medieval hand. Working six hundred years apart, the anonymous court scribe and I had made the same error.

It was a very thought-provoking error. Reading and writing, like all linguistic phenomena, are functions of cognition in the brain. Their neurological basis is profound and complex, the subject of an immense body of current research. The precise relationship between "language" and "thought," and their relation to the organic structures of the brain, are still highly contentious within cognitive psychology, neurolinguistics, and psycholinguistics.[158] Yet few neuroscientists or evolutionary biologists would contest the suggestion that the brain of a fourteenth-century court copyist was, in its relatively gross anatomy, much the same as the brain of a twentieth-century graduate student. It contained the same internal structures, working together in processes of cognition and perception. Recent research excitingly suggests, however, that those brains were also different, physically different, in the same meaningful way that the brains of two people in the same household may differ: at a much finer-grained neurological level of organization. Although the founder of psychoanalysis began as a neurologist and always sought organic models to explain his theories, Freudian psychoanalysis gradually became estranged from neuropsychology. From the 1960s until very recently, the two disciplines could not have seemed further apart: psychoanalysis assumed the existence of both a conscious and an unconscious mind, while the more radical theories in cognitive science, attributing all mental phenomena to the "hardware" of the brain, suggested that the concepts of "consciousness" and "mind" were illusory.[159]

Emergent work, however, is reestablishing a link between memory, perception, and organic structure. The direct implication is a specifiable physical level of action for those phenomena that are the typical subjects of psychoanalysis. Research on the brain's amygdala suggests a biological basis of the unconscious, of the difference between conscious and unconscious memories, and of different kinds of emotional reactions to stimuli. Amygdala theory hypothesizes a division between implicit (amygdala) and explicit (hippocampal) emotional memories. The distinction helps to explain, among other things, why people can continue to have fearful reactions to certain stimuli when they no longer have conscious memories of the original trauma. Approaches from other branches of psychology, particularly conditioning theory, do not explain this central theme of psychoanalysis.[160] The distinction between implicit and explicit memory is also the subject of cognitive studies outside amygdala theory.[161] Psychoanalysts have not ignored this aspect of the mind-body connection either, suggesting that analysis works on the organic level by introducing organic changes in the brain: the word becomes literal flesh and dwells within us. Eric Kandel, who insists that "all mental processes are biological," also argues that *genetic* does not mean *immutable* or *immune to social influence.* Kandel also states, "Psychoanalysis still represents the most coherent and intellectually satisfying view of the mind." Most promisingly, analysts and cognitive psychologists are starting to tolerate each other's work and to look for mutual connections.[162]

Such developments, linking the study of mind and brain, offer a fresh alternative to that long-stale opposition between constructionist and "essentialist" views of historical subjectivity. Their refusal to award victory to either side is satisfying, in that they require a subtle and multidimensional model of the interplay between body, mind, and language (culture, discourse), which does not reduce the process to one underlying cause. This model is the very antithesis of "binary opposition" thinking; each element (biologic, psychic, social) creates and is created by the others in an endless, fluid cycle. We are well rid of simplistic imagined divisions between mind and body. These are especially ill suited to the study of subjects in pre-Cartesian Europe:

> An engagement with pre-modern society, with its magical world-view and its belief in the demonic, with its assumption that emotions can cause harm in others or its conviction that sanctity can be seen and felt in the uncorrupted body of the saint itself, offers us the chance of rethinking our own habitual classifications of mental and corporeal.[163]

Moreover, rethinking our classifications does not have to mean restricting ourselves to premodern vocabularies. Nor need we assume that modern approaches like psychoanalysis are anachronistic from the start.

It is too early to tell how historians will capitalize on the possibilities. Addressing the history of emotions, surely a matter of interiority, medievalist Barbara Rosenwein invokes cognitive psychology and social constructionism but barely mentions psychoanalysis. Moreover, she "leaves aside," with a puzzling remark, the entire area of research I have just mentioned.[164] Rosenwein is concerned to illustrate the junking of a "grand narrative" that trivialized medieval emotionality in a *longue durée* progress toward modern emotional restraint. The more general temptation, one to beware, is to look to cognitive science because one believes that it speaks in the voice of white-coated scientific authority, and that psychoanalysis does not. (Though not concerned with cognitive science, Lee Patterson's recent attack on the use of psychoanalytic theory in medieval studies aims to discredit psychoanalysis as unscientific. Patterson's critique is one-sided; moreover, empiricism is, to say the least, an odd criterion for a literary hermeneutic.)[165]

The word-substitution error that tripped up both a late medieval court recorder and me relates directly to our theme precisely because it involved language. The power of language to shape psychic subjectivity is so central to psychoanalysis that Marshall Edelson terms that discipline the "science of the symbolizing activity of the mind"; dreams, in particular, translate linguistic elements into visual and sensual representations.[166] I will return to this definition in the next chapter. My point here, though, is that if my brain is similar enough to the scribe's that we process language in the same way, surely our brains might do other things, other linguistic things, the same way as well. Recent research is beginning to suggest that in both our brains there was an organic basis for the unconscious, and hence for a formally similar array of mental phenomena. Out of those mental phenomena, we formed our respective subjectivities—both the medieval and the modern. Our gender identities in turn were part of those subjectivities. Yet our subjectivities were also historically local. The church scribe did not know he was living in the Middle Ages, and my sense of being "modern" depends in part on the fact that I know I am not living in the Middle Ages. Yet another reason our subjectivities are historical was that in the course of our historically specific lives, our brains became organically differentiated: culture and experience imprinted themselves on us. So although subjectivity and gender identity were both located in our brains, which is to say our bodies (the body does not begin at the shoulders), they were as much "constructed" as "essential."

Obviously, a history of medieval masculinity cannot document change at the level of the cerebral cortex. It can, however, allow a cyclical model (mind, body, discourse) to inspire and refresh thinking about the relation between maleness and masculine identity: a relation not defined by written ideals, but nevertheless involving them. And it can admit the historicity of male bodily experience.

———— ✳ ————

CHAPTER FOUR

Toward the Private Self:
Desire, Masculinity,
and Middle English Romance

IN THE medieval romance that bears his name, Partonope of Blois gets separated from his male kin group while hunting in the forest one day when
he is eighteen and wanders to the seashore where, for no clear reason, he
boards a mysterious ship. With that act he enters the realm of the invisible:
he can see neither the ship's crew, nor any inhabitant of the country where
it arrives, nor of the rich castle he then enters. Unknown forces have spirited
him away. Invisible beings serve him a meal, provide nice clothes, and light
his way to a luxurious bed in a castle chamber.[1]

Certainly that sounds like the beginning of something, but not of the
history of something, or at least, not the history of something we commonly
recognize. And yet I believe that the medieval romance, perhaps the nuttiest
genre in all of English literature, with its wild tales of knights' adventures
amid fabulous monsters and magical interventions at every turn, can contribute to an understanding of masculinity in history, not just in literature,
despite having apparently nothing to do with real life.

This belief will take some explaining.

THUS FAR, this book has drawn mostly on the kinds of documentary sources
familiar to the social historian. Legal records tell us what men did (or say
they did), letters what they planned to do, prescriptive texts what someone
else expected them to do, medical treatises what someone else expected their
bodies to do. But there is another dimension to personal identity, not a social
but an interior, psychological one, without which it is too easy to confuse

identity with statements of social norms and too difficult to understand why anyone did anything out of step with social norms.

Addressing this interior dimension, or frame, does not require such a total change of interpretive gears as one might think. The private and social aspects of identity are not just linked but interdependent, mutually created:

> Society... provides structured bases for the operation of the individual's defense mechanisms. Institutionalized stereotypes of the lazy, sexually potent, or vicious minority group member afford a ready-made projective system for persons who have difficulty in coming to terms with these tendencies in themselves.... Each individual tailors such institutionalized projective systems to his or her unique psychological dynamics.... It appears that no fully comprehensive theory of the ego is possible without a simultaneous theory of social organization—and vice versa.[2]

As we shall see, the social supports for particularly masculine "defense mechanisms" are not hard to find in medieval evidence.

HISTORY, FICTION, AND LITERATURE

Historians are often unsure how to use fiction in their analyses, and we engage with the techniques of literary criticism less often than literary scholars do with those of academic history. Recognizing the literary or "fictional" character of conventional nonfiction texts, as scholars from Hayden White to Natalie Zemon Davis have done, is not quite the same as working out a coherent theory of how to use "fictional" or "literary" texts for historical purposes. Most historians do not read literature naively as a direct reflection of lived reality.[3] More often, we use literature as a colorful illustrative supplement to the "real" argument a historian makes from "real" evidence. Sometimes we take it to illustrate vaguely defined "ideals" or "values," a kind of cultural wallpaper forming the backdrop to real events. Yet historians do not generally allow literature to constitute a source *in itself*: something that tells us things that "nonfiction" does not. How can a historian, who is interested in the "real," make use of a medieval romance that makes no claim on the "real"?[4]

Consider first what we take for granted when we invest the sources of social history with that claim on the real: for example, the consistory court depositions we saw earlier in this book. The historian assumes in advance that such a source is "historical," that is to say "not fictional," primarily because it emanates from one of the culture's authoritative institutions. It demands *belief* in the way a "fictional" source does not. Yet the historian's own engagement with the legal text requires its own act of belief. The very existence of the persons appearing in consistory court depositions, for example, is usually not attested by any other form of evidence. No birth certificates, or other forms of social registration, exist. Perhaps the lucky historian may find a will left by someone of the same name, who seems to have lived in the same community, but since so many medieval Englishmen had names like John Smith, establishing identity is always a matter of least uncertainty rather than most certainty.

The point is that the very act of taking such a named but otherwise unknown subject to be a *person*, to be used as evidence, does not measure up very well to any rigorous standard of argument: How can one affirm the reality of someone attested only by one scrap of parchment? Yet historians do it all the time. We can imagine easily the "factual" and "fictional" aspects of a witness deposition only because in our minds we construct this fully human subject whose motivations we presuppose: we imagine why they want to tell a story in a certain way, and so we believe in them, in their existence, even when we have no independent proof. So making the distinction between that subject and the imagined subject of a fictional story is a more artificial process than we usually acknowledge. The historian, as reader of sparse evidence, often has to create the historical subject through an act of imaginative belief, essentially the same process by which any reader of ostensible "fiction" creates a subject also, in allowing that figure to exist for reading. Reader and text in fact together create a space in which certain subjects have agency and motivation—whether we are reading fiction or nonfiction.

THE LITERARY SUBJECT

In his thoughtful study of "symbolic stories," Derek Brewer suggested that "the characters . . . are all aspects of one enveloping mind, its contradictory desires, internal conflicts and attempts to solve them. This enveloping mind is not particular to any one individual or story-teller: it is a partial model of the human mind itself expressed in the terms of the given culture."[5] Brewer suggests that "As we read, we identify ourselves with the protagonist and by sympathy with him or her 'create' or dismiss the other varied figures, because we all know the same drama."[6] Identification, however, seems too specific and narrow to describe what happens. It carries a misleading suggestion that the audience need be sympathetic to everything the protagonist does.

Therefore, in approaching romance literature as historical evidence, I envision the literary text as referring to its *literary subject* rather than its protagonist. The literary subject is the referential entity in which all the action of the story takes place. It is not a person, but a state (in the sense of both "condition" and "territory"), activated or opened up by the engagement of audience (reader or listener) and text, as when a curtain rises on stage. The literary subject exists only when both audience and text are present and interacting, and it ceases to exist when their interaction ceases. Therefore, it is transitory, but endlessly reproducible. Subject and protagonist often do coincide, because as with the dreamer of a dream, the subject's position needs to be personified, to take recognizable form. Still, the protagonist and the other figures in romance ultimately fit "inside" the literary subject.

In effect, I am suggesting that the action of romance takes place inside a kind of culturally generalized subjectivity, like Brewer's "enveloping mind." These stories, steeped in stereotype and convention, yield a baseline, common-denominator vision. Their effectiveness depends on connections to the most commonly found anxieties and fantasies, many of which cross classes and centuries. Both players and internal audience are part of the literary subject. Because the literary subject comes into existence through the agency of the (external) audience, it is through the literary subject that the text connects us to the historical subject. The literary subject gains its symbolic repertoire and its sense of priorities, its anxieties, from its society and culture; it is therefore historical rather than ahistorical. Conventional historical analysis of the culture and period of the text allows us to place the literary subject in context, to recognize the elements it chooses for the expression of its feelings and wishes.

We need textual analysis attuned to both symbolization and human psychology, however, to understand the literary subject itself, and thereby to gain additional understanding of the historical subject. And we need a framework within which to conceive both language and desire as contributing to subjectivity. Luckily, such an interpretive method exists, and its name is psychoanalysis: the theory of integrated mind "begun and established by the work of Sigmund Freud [and] refined by over a century of continuing clinical and theoretical work."[7]

This is not "psychohistory," which has gained a bad name by using psychoanalysis to explain things psychoanalysis was never meant to explain: for example, the actions and decisions of a political leader, in terms of that person's (usually very speculatively reconstructed) childhood.[8] Medieval history is out of the picture from the start, where this is concerned, because the right kinds of evidence are so obviously lacking. Nor should psychoanalytic theory fuel a search for formulas of historical causation (this culture, with these child-rearing customs, must have produced neurosis X in its men more frequently than *that* culture). Such rules become impossibly reductive and diminish all the complexity and ability to handle contradiction that give psychoanalysis its interest in the first place. These simplistic applications are also most vulnerable to the charge of anachronism in applying a theory derived from one culture to the subjects of quite different cultures.

Instead, psychoanalytic theory has to be used as Marshall Edelson defines it: the "science of the symbolizing activity of the mind."[9] Psychoanalysis concerns itself with precisely that interaction of language and desire that characterizes the dynamics of human personality. In essence, psychoanalysis theorizes the mind's capacity to *represent:* to transform mental contents into somatic, visual, or emotional form. The mind does so most intriguingly, perhaps, in dreams. Desire, in the concentrated form of a wish, motivates the dream-work: the process by which latent contents become represented in the manifest sensory form of a dream. In dreams, practically anything can represent practically anything else, but that representation is crucially dependent on language. The transformative processes of the dream-work are the same as those of figurative language (metaphor, synecdoche, metonymy). Yet those processes themselves serve the most fundamental requirements of linguistic functioning: economy, independence of meaning and representation, and other pragmatic concerns.[10] The very mental contents that the dream-work transforms are, indeed need to be, represented *linguistically.* Freud compared dreams to rebus puzzles, whose pictorial symbolic language only makes sense when we understand both their elements and the connections between them as verbal language. In other words, "Language as a symbolic system is, according to the rebus model, logically prior and indispensable to the dream as a symbolic system."[11]

Even manifestly social evidence, from waking life, provides an analogue to such a transformative product. When late medieval Englishmen hurled the insult "thief" at one another, I have argued, they did not narrowly mean "person who steals things" but "dishonestly tricky, crafty, deceptive person."[12] In psychoanalytic terms, this qualifies as a condensation: the word-concept "thief" stands for a variety of vague, overlapping meanings—themselves meaningful because of the complex concerns they represent. No one use of the word consciously registers all the different shadings at once, but they are all present. In effect, the broader complex is *unconscious.* This unconscious, where the latent content of dreams and fantasies resides, needs to be our unit of study for the private dimension of masculinity.

What kind of historical evidence would reveal this private world? Late medieval examples of the personal, confessional texts we would expect to be most revealing are virtually nonexistent (I have already noted the shortcomings of personal letters from the period).[13] Even if medieval people had kept tell-all diaries, no one analysis could ever address more than a handful of individuals. At the present stage of knowledge, we need a more general assessment, one that looks for common features and patterns rather than interesting exceptions. (Hence the title of this chapter; I can only aim to clear a path *toward* the private self.)

And so here is the crucial link. It is precisely because medieval romance claims neither to be "original" nor "realistic," because it is so stereotypical and so outlandish, that it leads us to the unconscious world of its culture. Medieval literature was produced long before the nineteenth-century Romantic or realist authorial voice, assumed then and now to be the distinctive and original expression of a highly individual subjectivity. So we know that the vision we receive in a medieval romance is even less restrictively "the author's vision" than is that of a Victorian novel. The decisions of individual, usually now unknown writers of course shape the version of a medieval work that remains to us, but that medieval work also represents the many other individual minds who received, retold, and arguably relived the stories. Literature provides a window into the unconscious level of significance. We can consider it the manifest expression of a cultural unconscious; reading it is like experiencing a dream. Freud argued that a dream is the fulfillment of a wish, but that wish may be unacceptable to the subject's conscious standards and needs to be disguised, made safe, so that the dreamer can go on sleeping. In medieval romance, the literary subject is the one the dream aims to protect, like all truly interesting dreams, by solving impossible conflicts and keeping from consciousness the knowledge of threatening truths.

But truths about what? What would be so sensitive as to require disguise in the dream of literature? And, of all literary sources, why rely on the romance?

THE ROMANCE OF MASCULINITY

Romances are my chief literary source here because they are concerned with identity—a preoccupation that has interested literary scholars for some time. A milestone work in the more modern version of such criticism is by Robert Hanning. Referring to French literature in the twelfth century, Hanning argued that the trajectory of the romance plot described the journey of a protagonist toward self-knowledge. The chivalric concerns with managing the needs for love, prowess, desire, recognized valor, and so on all pointed to this end.[14] Edmund Reiss stated in 1985 that "the search for identity, the attempt to find one's self, may be what romance is actually most about."[15] Where Reiss insisted that romance was a didactic and essentially religious form, Derek Brewer noted the "most crucial and often painful passage in our lives . . . by which we emerge from dependent childhood to independent maturity. . . . This transition, which is a universal human necessity, is almost always the subject of medieval romance."[16] Susan Crane's more social constructionist approach argues for medieval identity as a social identity, a community identity, invested in social performance of self: "As important to romances' version of masculine identity as the tension between self and society is the process of internalization by which men incorporate the constraints of community into their own identities."[17]

A literary form whose themes are so much concerned with identity seems well suited to guide us toward an understanding of subjectivity, and because the identity in question is generally a masculine one, the usefulness for understanding masculinity is obvious. It follows that the romance would attract psychoanalytic critical approaches, and so it has. Though he preferred not to emphasize it, Brewer relied heavily on psychoanalysis for his arguments about many aspects of pre-Romantic literary genres—their portrayal of a "family drama," their symbolizing strategies, and their openness to interpretation as dreams: "From one point of view it is not unreasonable to consider the whole story as a drama going on in the mind of the protagonist, who sees himself *as* protagonist, and also 'creates,' as we do in dreams, the figures who help or oppose him, basing his view of them upon his own experience and hopes of life."[18] The merging of literary and psychoanalytic visions of identity far preceded Brewer; it dates to the early years of psychoanalysis itself. Otto Rank wrote, circa 1912: "The true hero of the romance is, therefore, the ego, which finds itself in the hero."[19] Rank wrote only three years after Freud himself invoked the literary form and related it to family dynamics in his famous essay "Family Romances."[20]

My method for reading romance literature, then, has decided precedent. It is even, in one way, conservative: I work from the core psychoanalytic concepts themselves as they are handled in revised psychoanalysis, particularly in object relations, rather than the linguistic and cultural theory applications of psychoanalysis in the work of Jacques Lacan and Slavoj Žižek, recently popular among literary theorists. In seeking to allow the texts to contribute to a *historical* analysis, however, I am obliged to take an extra step, because to do so, the romances have to be about something outside themselves. More specifically, if I am to interpret literature as a dream, I need to decide whose dream it is. In what imagined unconscious do its symbolizing and transformative processes work? My answer is directly related to my earlier statements about the function of belief in reading both fiction and history, and it connects that relation of reader and text to my ability to make conclusions about a masculine self in history.

At this point, also, my interpretation parts company with the literary scholars I have just mentioned. Hanning's argument was firmly historicized; Hanning considered the patterns he described to be characteristic chiefly of the late twelfth century and no later. Such specificity made the model fit with other significant work appearing in the 1970s and 1980s concerning the literate culture of the twelfth century, and with that culture's apparently new awareness of individual identity, also assumed to be a securely dateable phenomenon.[21] Hanning guessed that the thirteenth century's developments in institutional and intellectual culture accounted for the markedly different identity concerns of the romance produced then. Moreover, Hanning's interpretations all have reference to the *protagonist,* the romance hero, the figure whose identity concerns matter: the "crisis of inner awareness" is the protagonist's crisis. Hanning went no further in proposing any wider frame of reference for the structural symbolism of romance. Meticulous and learned, his model is nonetheless restricted to the text itself. The romances are ultimately about romances. Hanning stopped short of claiming that they presented a program or a model, or of explaining how these symbolic journeys to self-knowledge might have been related to the subjectivities of people hearing them in this newly self-aware era. Even Brewer, following previous psychoanalytic critics, states clearly:

> The protagonist is central, and all must be interpreted in relation to his interests. Other characters are often "splits," substitutes and projections of various kinds, who have no effective relationship between each other independent of their relationship to the protagonist.... Brothers represent various aspects of the protagonist; witches, stepmothers and other villains are substitutes for the protagonist's view of mother and father; helpful animals much the same. Such characters may also represent how the protagonist feels toward himself.[22]

Yet from a historical standpoint, if romances refer only to their protagonists, they ultimately refer only to themselves, and this is not very useful to the historian.

As I have just explained, however, we can understand a romance as referring to its literary subject, the representative unconscious of the historical subject. And the romance helps us to understand masculine interiority because the literary subject of medieval romance is unambiguously masculine. The best way to see this is to examine an example.

ALL HER FAULT

Recall Partonope of Blois, borne away by that ghost ship. This is not a willed journey (at least, not consciously willed), and yet the text does not make it seem like a forcible abduction. Partonope is nervous and apprehensive, but not terrified. He does not try to escape. We also note that Partonope's journey takes him progressively from more open to more enclosed spaces, and the camera-like framing of the narration keeps our attention on this tunnelling and narrowing: from the open sea to the harbor of the silent city, to the gates of the town, to the castle gate, to the hall, and thence down castle corridors to the room prepared for Partonope by those invisible hands—where his curiosity, and ours, rests finally on the fireplace. Now Partonope can rest in the luxurious bed, and as you will soon see, the eroticism becomes explicit. Partonope's acquiescence to his journey feels like a submission: a giving over of the self to something that is inevitable, unknown, but possibly pleasurable. It is a kind of release. The eerie atmosphere (deserted rooms, bobbing torches, tables that seem to clear themselves) feels more magical and exciting than threatening, though the excitement, of course, contains its portion of threat.

Here I have emphasized the *affect*—the emotional charge—which as so often in dreams seems oddly inappropriate, a clue to us that all is not what it appears. This distinctive combination of arousal and danger conveys both the erotic significance of the story and the subject's anxiety about that eroticism. I have also underscored a visual symbolic pattern, the way space closes in on Partonope to draw him further inside. Combine this with what happens next. Unbeknownst to our hero, that bed belongs to an invisible woman, Queen Melior. And what follows when she decides to get into bed? Partonope is anxious about his unseen bedmate; they accidentally touch; Melior haughtily attempts to make him leave; Partonope protests his innocence; and everything lines up along a path the text assumes to be obvious to the reader. As Partonope discovers Melior's form, apprehension yields to arousal and sexual aggression:

> Then she said all meekly to him: "For the love of God, I beg you to stop." And
> at that word, he began at once to clasp her to him in his arms. And all quietly,
> then, she said "Alas!" And she began to press her knees together, and he began

to force them apart with his knees. And as all this was happening, she said "Sir, mercy!" He would not stop at that, and took no heed of her words, but snatched away her maidenhead, and gave her his. Thus they surely dallied together. He had never tried any such dalliance before. (1560-73)

Those knees, I think, clinch the matter, aligning the reader inescapably with the male and masculine experience of the episode. Not only is the passage sexually explicit, but in addition it presents the rape as *good* for Partonope, because it represents his initiation into sexual manhood; Partonope overcomes not only the woman's resistance but his own, and the return to *his* experience (he had never before tried anything like this [1573]) makes it clear that this is a significant accomplishment. Moreover, the text's pleasure in description comes more from what is done *to* Melior than what Partonope "loses" ("gave her his" is tacked on as a near afterthought). The passage gains all its motive energy from the heightening rush toward a man's sexual penetration of a woman; all the agency within it is phallic. The destination of Partonope's bewitched journey, then, is inside the body of a woman—the path along which that ship was really traveling from the moment it set sail.

Yet this disturbing moment is only the most obvious clue to the masculinity of the narrative. It turns out that Melior (despite all her tears and resistance) brought her deflowering on herself. She had heard of Partonope from afar and decided, by means of enchantments, to make him her husband. The text thus cuts the subject's desire out of the picture by reversing it, projecting it onto the female figure: Partonope did not go to a woman, the woman made him go to her. He did not know at any point what he was doing; everyone was invisible. He did not desire a woman; the woman desired *him* and *made him* have sex with her. In *Bevis of Hampton*, the princess Josian serves this purpose of inversion, too; she throws herself unambiguously at the resistant Bevis:

> "I would rather have you as my lover, with your body all naked under your tunic, than have all the gold that Christ made, and you would have your will with me!"

> "By God," said Bevis, "I'll never do that!" (1106-10)[23]

But the enchantment feature in *Partonope* makes this sexual experience seem like something the masculine subject could not escape: it is, in some sense, necessary, and yet wanting it is forbidden. *Partonope* pushes away the mere possibility of conscious desire by having Partonope not even awake to be aware of it. Such an attenuated approach to the feminine, discharging its anxious energy through visual symbols at every turn, is a particularly fine example of the distancing strategies the masculine subject employs in romance. That refusal of desire, when desire is a crucial part of the self, is most important, both for my interpretation and in terms of historical context.

THE DANGERS OF DESIRE

Throughout this book, I have shown how the social face of masculinity depended on language, on the meanings of words and the currents of spoken discourse. The last chapter illustrated the ways that men's use of language could shape their relations with others, accentuating or diminishing their social identities. Yet the determining power of language is not restricted to the realm of interpersonal communication. It plays its part, too, in the interior dimension of gender: what masculinity means in an individual personality. The many difficulties of conceptualizing the interior aspects of masculinity become a little easier when we allow an attention to language to guide us there. I have already dropped some hints about this, exploring in chapter 1, for example, the connection between social appearance and private self-image in reactions to defamation. Interiority and social construction also seem not so antipathetic when we consider how language works in a human mind. Language is a principal route between the interior and exterior aspects of the self.

Another useful concept for considering that relationship is, fittingly enough, "relation." The social self takes form through relations to others enacted in social practice, where the bonds of kinship, social class, wealth, and sex all create recognizable needs: for sustenance, support, recognition, honor. Analogously, need also shapes the private or interior self. Psychic needs—that is, what the individual subject perceives as a need—can be for many things: security or risk, intimacy or separateness, excitement or its release, supremacy or submission. As in the social sphere, need structures a relation between self and others, but the structuring happens through symbolic and internalized representations of these factors.

In the psyche, the territory of the self's interior, both relation and need surface as desire. My use of this term includes sexual or carnal desire, but is not limited to those forms. Desire is such a powerful motivating force that much of our psychic activity is devoted to experiencing, controlling, refusing, enjoying, or satisfying it. The nature of desire itself invests its object with meaning for the desiring subject and so creates a represented relation.

Desire is a very useful concept, but historical analysis has not yet capitalized on it much. The relevance to a history of gender is obvious, and particularly for masculinity, then and now. The modern understanding of masculinity, in both popular and academic discourses, also deals largely in the vocabulary of desire: Is its object male or female? Is desire only physical or emotional also? Why do men and women often seem to direct desire differently, or to believe that they do? And so on.

Medieval writers of different kinds (clerics, poets, physicians) produced their own learned and popular discourse on the sources and effects of desire. Masculinity emerges as a concern in this literature, sometimes explicitly, and often by implication, but it is always there. Wherever writers, practically always male, caution their readers against women's wiles, see woman as the more sensual or carnal sex, or align manliness with resistance to desire, the stability of a masculine identity is at issue.

The literature on "lovesickness" apprehended extreme desire by reading it through the physical body, as a medical problem. According to its principal modern historian, Mary Frances Wack, lovesickness—debilitating, ungovernable infatuation—over the course of the Middle Ages came to be considered a male problem, for bodily, constitutional, and emotional reasons. The lovesickness literature tells us how men manifested the signs of erotic excess and attempts to explain why those effects occurred. (From here to Freud and Breuer's *Studies on Hysteria* is a long way, and yet also not so far at all.) The frequent conclusion, explicit or not, was that erotic attraction was dangerous and bad for males.

Yet treatises on lovesickness fail to tell us whether men themselves feel unmanned by desire, or whether their peers consider them so. Moreover, the lovesickness literature refuses to describe clearly enough the nature of the enervating obsession, which appears to be more than the desire for sexual intercourse. It is an obsessive preoccupation with the love object, even more confusing for *not* being susceptible to precise definition. Whatever the case, medieval medical writings related the direct physiological consequences of lovesickness to the victim's obsession with a mental image of the beloved. The role of the imagination in sexual fantasy and response, as recognized in these texts, was extensive. Wack suggests that the "unmanly" nature of the symptoms of lovesickness results from the fact that they reflected "both expressing and coping with simultaneous feelings of desire and hostility."[24] Hostility toward women seen as maternal figures, often expressed quite openly in literature, might be redirected toward the self and turned into abasement. That process twisted desire into delusion, because lovesickness involved idealizing its object, which in reality was (because female) socially inferior. Lovesickness was thus a cultural symptom in which men who were socially expected to be powerful and invulnerable could allow themselves a "willed vulnerability."[25]

The scattered suggestions of medieval evidence turn out to match anthropologist Stanley Brandes's more dramatically immediate portrait of masculinity in an Andalusian town in the late 1970s. Brandes's descriptions show that little had changed in certain masculine fantasies about women in this corner of Spain since the time of the Spanish medical texts examined by Michael Solomon.[26] The conversation, jokes, and confidences of male informants suggested that women were men's repositories of all things destructive, dangerous, and to be shunned; men saw themselves as *morally* superior to women. These beliefs attributed great power to women: men considered them constitutionally stronger and longer lived, with a sexual voracity and insatiability that sapped men's strength and enabled widows to live off men's labor. As Brandes points out, in this culture men obviously project their needs and anxieties onto women, who then become (from the male point of view) the cause rather than the object of the problem.[27]

The "problem," though, is still desire. Wack's reference to the component of hostility in lovesickness guides us toward something quite important. In a discourse that assumes that both desire and sexual performance unman men, the misogynistic implications are obvious. But what does that mistrust of desire's object, woman, say about desire and ultimately about the desiring male subject? We have already noted, in a variety of sources, the pervasiveness of an image of masculinity as something that spills out, leaks away, and becomes depleted. Desire, medieval discourse tells us, is yet another force threatening to drain something out of the masculine self.

What does this imply, this idea of a self that must be guarded and shored up for fear of depletion? It implies that all relational connections with others contain some component of danger. Erotic desire signals this danger in a particularly dramatic way. Such a self—such a subjectivity—requires that identity be invested largely in self-sufficiency, in lack of connection. It is a highly boundaried version of the self, and the word to describe it is "narcissistic," a term that has passed from psychoanalysis into common currency. The narcissistic self either subsumes its objects, viewing them as extensions of itself, or disowns them utterly. It is deeply threatened by desire (because desire threatens total autonomy). The literary subject of romance, I would argue, exhibits a distinctly narcissistic masculinity, as we understand through the dream of literature, which disguises desire—inverts it, transfers it from one object to another, pretends it does not exist. Such a subject is masculine in ways that had particular meaning in the terms of its historical era.

NARCISSISTIC MASCULINITY AND
THE RAPE OF MELIOR

Classical psychoanalysis, following Freud, originally took as a normative model of selfhood the boundaried monad.[28] Beginning even during Freud's own lifetime, however, the psychoanalytic school eventually known as "object relations" began to propose an importantly different model: the healthy and harmonious self is best conceived not as an autonomous monad, but as an entity defined by relation to others, as "inexorably social and intrinsically connected."[29] Here, autonomy is a matter of degree: the extent to which the subject can retain a secure sense of self amid both dynamic relations with others (what the subject actually does in daily life with other people) *and* his or her internalized and symbolized representations of those relational structures (how the dynamics of acted-out life pass into unconscious fantasies, wishes, and emotional charges).

Object relations originated not as a complete break with Freud, but on the contrary as an offshoot from one of his own ideas, in his essay "On Narcissism." Nancy Chodorow's description of this lineage relates so well to the present discussion that it deserves quotation:

> Freud notes how libido can be directed alternately toward objects (other people) or toward the self. He calls these forms "object libido" and "ego libido," and he locates psychic wholeness in a delicate balance between them. In Freud's view here, *exclusive investment in the self with no connection to the other* creates the narcissistic neuroses and psychoses; relatedness is the sine qua non of mental health. At the same time, he warns against the opposite danger, complete investment in the object—as in *slavish unrequited love, which debases the self* and deprives it of energy.[30]

Freud's assessment of excessive object libido evidently provided the basis for Wack's diagnosis of medieval lovesickness, and it shows that narcissism and its opposite represent two extremes of the same phenomenon. Narcissism continued to figure importantly in the theorizing of object relations theorists, especially because a chief defining feature of narcissism is the inability to accord agency or autonomy to the relational other. In a different emphasis, narcissism lies at the very center of the model of the self in the strain of psychoanalysis literary critics most often deploy, that developed by Jacques Lacan, in which "the ego is constituted by narcissistic fantasies of wholeness and homogeneity that suppress awareness of the subject's heterogeneity and its existential condition of lack."[31]

In the discourse of object relations, narcissism can shape significantly both masculine and feminine identities. In the masculine case, the effects follow a pattern that will not surprise us, given the historical and anthropological examples adduced above. For Michael Diamond, "the most fertile psychoanalytic conceptualizations of masculinity stem from an appreciation of a man's striving for narcissistic completeness."[32] Lynne Layton in fact uses the term "hegemonic masculinity," now so familiar in gender studies, to describe "a model of agency that defensively splits off dependency to appear defiantly separate and independent."[33] Psychoanalytic theorists have recognized this kind of masculinity and its observable imprints in sexual behavior, relationship patterns, and psychological problems. Common examples, discussion of which is not confined to psychoanalytic discourse, are difficulty with intimacy and "relatedness," and a sexuality disconnected from emotion and other-relations, and strongly flavored with domination and control. Desire formed in this pattern is central to masculine sexuality but also threatening to masculine identity. For some Lacanian analysts, masculine sexuality can lead to abusive and exploitive behaviors because it becomes additionally fused with, or directed by, the phallic fantasy, especially as defined by Lacan.[34] However, one need not follow Lacan specifically to grasp the connection between narcissism and a readily recognizable form of masculine subjectivity: "Normative masculinity looks like phallic narcissism, where only the self and not the other is experienced as a subject."[35]

The narcissistic self manages the prospect of relation, and of having to integrate this desire for the other, by encountering the other not as a separate center but as an extension of itself: Partonope has the castle and its pleasures all to himself, and everything is done for his enjoyment alone, including the rape of Melior, onto whom the subject's narcissistic hostility is discharged—sexually, affectively, and even through humor—as the text invites the reader to laugh at the fumbles of the two bodies in the bed.

MOTHERS

The kind of desire represented and transformed in romance is not usually so transparently carnal as in *Partonope*. Medieval discourse assumed, of course, that the object of masculine desire was feminine, and romances abound with female characters whose relation to the male protagonist is problematic. Yet they are often far closer to home, requiring no magical voyages to encounter. Representations of the mother are an obvious point of departure. Contrary to popular belief, psychoanalysis is not All About Mother as the object of blame for all subsequent problems. Rather, psychoanalysis sees mothers, or mother figures, as crucially important because the mother is, from the child's earliest consciousness, the source of that which satisfies need. She is also, therefore, the focal point for the most basic desires, for sustenance and comfort, which later modulate into other forms of desire. Simultaneously the child experiences her as one who can limit or refuse those satisfactions. Need, or desire, that is unsatisfied (however justifiably) prepares the ground for one form of hostility. So, well before the subject is even aware of "erotic" or "sexual" desire, he or she has already established mother as a paradoxical source, and object, of both love and hate.

Both boys and girls experience these developments. Freud's original for-mulation of the Oedipus complex found the roots of sexuality in the desire of children for their parents. Later psychoanalysis, in both the classic and ob-ject relations versions, has elaborated and modified this central idea to place it in the broader context of changes from early infancy to adolescence, espe-cially the gradual development of the small child's sense of self as separate, apart from the mother. Yet for very young boys, an additional complication arises: a core masculine gender identity depends on a recognition and ac-ceptance, mostly unconscious, of *difference* from mother.[36] Being a gendered self, therefore, casts everything that "mother" represents into a shadowy, unsettling world the masculine subject approaches uneasily. The result, in later life, is frequently "a conflict between the urge to return to the peace of the symbiosis and the opposing urge to separate out as an individual, as a male, as masculine. In that conflict, a barrier must be raised against the impulse to merge. Much of what we see as masculinity is, I think, the effect of that struggle."[37]

In her analysis of lovesickness, Wack provides many examples of how medieval culture quite unmistakably recognized and represented the Oedi-pal drama. Indeed, the phenomenon sometimes seems to have been closer to the surface than it was in Freud's day:

> In a number of instances that fantasy was hardly unconscious; the desire for union with the mother was scarcely, or not at all, repressed or displaced. A re-markable number of medieval stories recount examples of incest between mother and son.... Even a down-to-earth bourgeois like the Menagier of Paris

saw in a man's desire for his wife a replaying of the child's desire for the woman who nourished and took care of him. If a woman makes sure her husband is well provided for, in a snug house, and couches him well between her breasts like a child, then she will surely bewitch him.[38]

As Wack sagaciously points out, this desire encompassed not only what surfaces in adult sexuality but also "a man's desire to revert to a childlike state of dependent, identifying love."[39] Desire for mother thus imperiled not only the core gender identity based on maleness, but also the broader gender identity depending on maturity, both of which intersected on the theme of autonomy and separateness.

Mothers appear in the dream of romance as focal points of both desire and rage. Some dreams are subtle; some are not. The family trouble in *Bevis of Hampton* is apparent at the most literal or obvious level: Bevis's father dies, and his mother remarries. The father who dies is aged and pious, uninterested in sex: "All day he would rather be at church than in my bedroom," says the mother with disgust (59–60). In the plot's terms, sexual dissatisfaction (61–66) is the chief reason the mother takes the lover (an emperor!), who kills her husband in a combat she engineers (67–69, 175–276), whom she subsequently marries, and who therefore becomes Bevis's stepfather (286–92). This stepfatherhood remains only a technical one, because when the seven-year-old Bevis precociously condemns mother's actions, she rejects him and casts him out unequivocally, expressing a ferocious wish for his death: " Let him hang ever so high, I don't care what death he dies, as long as he is cold!" (340–42).

A simple Oedipal interpretation referring to Bevis's natural family would see that, for the masculine (narcissistic) subject, Bevis's real father is an idealized figure. He is no obstacle to the son's expected desire for the mother. Still, something is wrong here: the father's nonrivalry is somewhat beside the point, because the resulting situation lacks an Oedipal tension. Bevis's condemnation of his mother expresses only loathing for her and all who are, not just in character but in kind, like her: "Vile whore! You ought to be torn to pieces! I think I would be very happy at that, because you have killed my father most unjustly! Alas, mother, you fair-faced one! You're fit for evil, to be a whore, to run a brothel, and have all women whore themselves for your sake" (307–10). And these, of course, are the words that prompt the mother to repudiate Bevis. By doing so, however, she sets in motion the rest of the story.

Just like Bevis's mother, his love-object, the princess Josian, is promised to a man in marriage without her consent (449–60). All the good that mother cannot personify is loaded onto Josian, who helps rather than rejects Bevis, heals him, and remains steadfastly chaste with other men. Moreover, when her father, learning of their relationship, threatens Bevis with death, Josian protects him (655–730). Not only does desire reverse itself, but the Oedipus complex appears in this triangle as a displaced reversal. In addition, mother (bad) turns into love-object (good), and subject's father (too close) turns into love-object's father (safely distanced). The conflict itself—too difficult to undo entirely—shifts its center away from the subject and resolves itself to his satisfaction.

The splitting of "mother" into good and bad, and bad in this particular form, is a recognizable pattern. In 1910, Freud wrote about men who were capable only of falling in love with women they could not have, women who also violated social norms of chastity and fidelity. He traced the pattern to childhood desire for the mother at a stage of gradual sexual discovery, culminating in an unconscious boyish conclusion that "the difference between his mother and a whore is not after all so very great, since basically they do the same thing."[40] Freud assumes a degree of boyhood consciousness of prostitution hard to credit for our own day but quite applicable to medieval England—a culture wherein, also (among the knightly classes and elsewhere), the theme of male longing for an unavailable lady was already familiar.[41]

Recall, also, Wack's adduction of women's social inferiority as an element in lovesickness. Mothers' power over sons as mothers combined with their subordination to husbands as women, together with the sharply contrasting cultural images of women as objects of desire confronting men, supplied the complicated representations of mothers surfacing in the literary subject of romance.

Possibly the worst mother in medieval romance is Matabryne, the evil dowager queen in *Cheuelere Assygne*, the famous story of the swan-knight.[42] She is not the mother of the central male character, but of his father, the king: a rather morose man, ineffectual and childless, until in one burst of fertility he fathers septuplets. Matabryne conspires to do away with these children, apparently in order to get rid of her daughter-in-law. The story aligns itself ultimately with Enyas, the one child who by accident escapes being turned into a swan. Raised by a kindly hermit, he does not even know what a mother is, but quickly turns himself into the champion and savior of his own mother, the victimized young queen, after a crash course in jousting.[43] Yet Matabryne is the most memorable character. She is devoted to Satan, and her hatred is insistent. Her utterances are hectoring, belittling.

She badgers the king to condemn his wife and reminds him that the queen is yet "unburned" (180–90).[44] In comparison, the king appears weak-willed, befuddled, and no match for his mother; he never gets a moment of righteous anger or vengeance. That falls to the boy Enyas.

Even this brief sketch gives a sense of the conflicts romance tries to manage around the mother figure. Matabryne, rather obviously, incorporates all the subject's projected hostility and anxiety. This Bad Mother is eminently undesirable. The Good Mother, the king's wife, is the one the son gets to rescue. Here is an example of splitting, which saves the subject the trouble of relating to, and integrating into his relational matrix, a complete mother who can be both good and bad. Instead, the concept "mother" has been split into two more easily managed figures: the evil, undesirable one who can be repudiated and killed off at the end, and the lovable, gentle one to whom the subject (represented by Enyas) can relate almost as a lover, the knight saving his lady. In turn, the father's utter dampness permits his dissociation from the Good Mother, for whom he is now no rival with the son-subject, and assignment instead to the Bad Mother, safely displaced by a generation from the son. The contradictions and multiple strategies here are recognizably permanent characteristics of mental life. Mother is threatening and must be kept away, but the masculine subject also cannot do without her, and so makes her as safe as possible. Jennifer Fellows has remarked that "the more active the mother's part, at least in the initiation of events, the more likely she is to be in some degree the villain of the piece."[45] I would reverse the emphasis to say that the greater the subject's hostility toward mother, and hence the need to see her as a villain, the more likely her representation in an active role. (The Good Mother of *Cheuelere Assygne* does not really *do* anything; she simply exists, as what the subject needs her to be.)

Things are not always so obvious, and villainizing Mother is not the only way to deal with her. The conflicts in *Cheuelere Assygne* remain within the family triad. *Partonope of Blois*, however, directly portrays the problem of the young male's transition from mother to a more appropriate and socially acceptable love-object. The whole middle section of the romance sees Partonope pulled back and forth between two feminine nodes: between his invisible lover Melior and Partonope's unnamed mother. The conflict arises after Partonope, depressed because he misses Melior during a visit home, confides in his mother and confesses to her that he has never seen his beloved.[46] This, more than anything else, clinches the Mother's opposition, or at least her conviction that evil enchantment is at work. Melior knows the danger Mother poses and states it succinctly: "She will use some craft whereby you'll see me against my will, and thus you'll love her better than me" (5567–69). But for Partonope, home and Mother are too tempting to resist. Duplicitous Mother advises Partonope to remain faithful to his lady and then tricks him, by means of a magic potion, into briefly falling in love with the king's niece.[47] Later, on his next visit home, she will be more forthright about her intentions, giving him a magic lantern with which to reveal Melior and touching off the poem's biggest emotional crisis.[48]

But despite all this interference, Mother is not really a villain. She is punished only through her own emotional disappointment, not through violent death as she might be, and she makes no dramatic exit. She meets her son's angry rejections with rather credible protests; her reactions make sense.[49] These developments reach the reader because they are presented in dynamic terms; the conflicts are patently acted out. Despite the role of potions and magic lanterns, the dilemma seems familiar and reasonable because it matches what we know of openly acknowledged, enacted relationship difficulties. It does not stretch our credulity to imagine mothers who disapprove of their sons' choices of romantic partners, or women who cannot get along with their mothers-in-law. This is the manifest, superficial level. Its coherence and overall reasonableness disguise, however, the fact that here, too, it is serving the subject's narcissistic needs. The romance imagines two women using rival enchantments to keep the male protagonist in their sphere of erotic influence. The balance of agency thus shifts from the masculine subject to the feminine, as the competition between these female figures masks the subject's own conflicting desires.

Even where mothers are not literally represented, they have not necessarily left the subject's psychic realm. In *Ywain and Gawain*, Ywain's access to Alundyne, the lady he rescues and eventually marries, comes only after killing her husband.[50] That fact gains additional significance because the romance makes Alundyne Ywain's social superior. Like a parent, she must be obeyed; she can lay down rules. She issues dicta and requires response. When Gawain convinces Ywain to come away with him for a time of chivalric exploits, Alundyne insists that this period is not to exceed a year. The subject's dilemma, needing to reconcile or choose between masculine and feminine options, will concern us later. For the moment, note that in the plot of *Ywain and Gawain* we find desire for mother mingling uneasily with the need to escape maternal prohibitions and restrictions. Alundyne (the rule-maker, whom Ywain gains by killing her husband) represents mother in capacities both of desire-object and authority figure. The romance condenses these into the device we have known ever since the Garden of Eden story: you can have all these good things, enjoy all these pleasures, as long as you do not do this *one* thing, do not transgress this *one* barrier.[51] But the subject's desire for autonomy, selfhood, is so strong that he breaks the one rule, causing disaster: Ywain's failure to keep to the promised schedule causes Alundyne to break off their relationship. In addition, she takes back her ring, which protected Ywain from harm during his time as an adventurous, self-seeking knight. This plot sequence dramatizes the subject's confusion about desire, how desire for Woman uncomfortably recalls desire for Mother. To help keep things straight, the romance chooses an easily decoded symbol, the ring. That ring's protective power also neatly conveys the multiplicity of desire. Here, it includes desire for safety, protection, and security, such as a child finds in mother's arms.

LOVERS INVISIBLE AND UNSPEAKABLE

We now need to consider an intriguing feature of several romances, which I think constitutes a somewhat different strategy of the narcissistic masculine subject. In *Ywain and Gawain* and *Partonope of Blois,* one of the principal pairs of lovers is literally invisible for at least part of the story. In both cases the text provides a practical reason, a manifest one, for the invisibility, but by other means leaves clues that it has a psychosexual significance.

Alundyne's protective ring is not the first important ring in the romance of *Ywain and Gawain.* Ywain gets his first sight of Alundyne while unobserved; a magic ring has turned him invisible. Given the power Alundyne herself turns out to have, it is noteworthy that this invisibility gives Ywain a temporary power over her, the power of the voyeur: itself a power entirely in the mind of the subject, as the observed object does not know about the observation, and if she or he becomes aware of it, the erotic tension in the act of observation is broken. In *Ywain and Gawain,* this voyeuristic act or scene stabilizes the masculine subject's position, satisfying the narcissistic need to see the desired other as an outgrowth of the self's desire.

The invisibility theme plays a relatively small part in *Ywain and Gawain.* In *Partonope of Blois,* however, it is rather more important. Melior and all her court are invisible to Partonope when they first meet, and Melior makes Partonope promise not to try any necromancy of his own to see her. She is to remain visually unknown to him for two and a half years, during which time he must prove himself a knight; however, all sorts of pleasures are open to him in the meantime.[52] Their relationship continues on those terms until Partonope's mother disrupts it.

When Partonope reveals her with the magic lantern, Melior's shock and disappointment are expressed in a somewhat puzzling way. *This* revelation, she claims, is her ruin: something one would have expected her to apply to the much earlier loss of her virginity and virtue outside of wedlock. The betrayal is twofold. Melior says first that by seeing her "against my will," Partonope has deprived her of all her power (5979). Then she says that the lords of her court will now see her "shame"—that is, the loss of power—and know of the secret love between her and Partonope.[53] Melior seems to imply that Partonope's invisibility meant their clandestine relationship could be kept under wraps, but she never says this specifically. Nor does it explain why Partonope must not see Melior *or anyone else*. Melior has nothing to hide about herself; she is beautiful, not a loathly lady under a spell. We might expect that the real meaning of the blindness-invisibility for the masculine subject would lie with Partonope, the male hero. Yet Melior's invisibility does not seem to force Partonope to prove his love. He appears happy to be with his unseen lady and to take on feats of knighthood for their own sake. The "practical" reason for the invisibility, therefore, is a ruse, and not a very good one, just like the parts of dreams that make perfect logical sense until the dreamer, having awakened, tries to explain them. We need to look for a deeper purpose, and there are several possibilities.

Sylvia Huot has recently addressed similar questions about two Middle French romances, both involving a trauma around the moment when a mortal seeks to see an invisible or forbidden supernatural being. Huot makes the important proviso that in both of her examples it is not the vision itself that precipitates disaster, but the "anxiety and disorientation produced by that sight."[54] Huot's interpretation follows the Lacanian theory of psychosis, wherein psychotic hallucinations express the unknowable parts of the ego surfacing in hyper-real form. Such apparitions constitute the "encounter with the unspeakable, with that which defies representation in language and challenges the very concept of an integrated, embodied self."[55] Huot's reading also depends, following Judith Butler, on "a concept of subjectivity as an ongoing process of suppressing all that must not be seen, a creation of the subject through a repudiation of that which the subject is not."[56]

Though this model is not specifically gendered, it has obvious analogies to the psychoanalytic model of narcissistic masculinity. Where a masculine identity is defined negatively, as "what is not feminine," femininity clearly amounts to "that which the subject is not." Medieval culture certainly, as we have seen, might define masculinity this way. And the idea that an inability to integrate some element of the self causes trauma is of course a core psychoanalytic concept. But our psychoanalytic interpretation of Melior's invisibility should not stop here. What is the unspeakable, unknowable, unseeable thing for the subject of *Partonope?*

Ywain, who was made invisible to escape scrutiny in the castle of his love object, hence could observe without being observed. Partonope at Melior's court finds himself in the opposite position. He cannot see anyone, is unsure who may be watching *him*, and has only Melior's word that the court cannot see him. Where Ywain was the consummate voyeur, Partonope's situation seems like a metaphor for paranoia. And this is not a groundless reference. Just such a disavowal of desire lies beneath paranoia itself in Freud's classic formulation, deriving from the famous case study of Dr. Schreber, wherein the desire being disowned was an unconscious homosexual one.[57] That is not, I think, the case with the subject of *Partonope*, and interpretation does not call for a literal diagnosis of the subject. Freud's analysis can, however, help us understand the processes at work in *Partonope*.

Early in the romance, when Melior first explains the terms of the enchantment, she says that after the allotted time has passed, "You'll see everyone, and everyone will see you" (1822). Later, in the revelation scene, she confides that she was an amateur enchantress from an early age, who liked to use magic purely for fun, to entertain the emperor (her father) and others as well. These sorceries always remained secret, however, because Melior bewitched them so "None of them would be aware of any other, for none of them would see any other" (5970–71). In other words, Melior had power, but only under certain conditions. When no one (which here seems to mean, no men) could see each other, she had control over a certain kind of knowledge.

The romance's manifest logic is that "when Melior had power, no men could see each other." If we turn that around, we reveal a pattern we have already seen: an inversion that disguises the masculine subject's desire. The protective illusion is that the invisibility is Melior's need, rather than Partonope's: that it is the feminine object who "needs" not to be seen, rather than the masculine subject who needs not to see *her*. "Seeing" represents awareness and is directly linked both to desire and to "having power." Here is a pattern analogous to Freud's vision of the paranoid subject, defensively transforming and representing threatening desires in grammatical fashion, as if changing the relationships between components in a sentence. Table 1 shows how the pattern repeats.

Story element 4 is obviously at odds with the others: How can the subject conceive its very existence both in terms of repudiating *and* acknowledging desire? It is indeed a contradiction, but not a mutual exclusion. It represents a severe conflict not easily resolved, a conflict that plays out both in the psyche and in the social world. Psychic distress surfaces even at the manifest

TABLE 1 Defensive Transformations in *Partonope of Blois*

	Story element	Manifest significance	Latent significance	Interpretation
1	Melior bewitches Partonope in order to marry him	"*She* desires *me*," i.e., "I *do not* desire her"	"*I* desire *her*"	Defensive repudiation of desire
2	Melior breaks down when revealed to Partonope's sight	"For me to see her is to undo *her*"	"For me to see her is to undo *me*"	"For me to become aware of my desire for her is to undo me": (knowledge of) desire threatens subject's cohesion
3	Melior loses her power when she becomes visible	"If she remains unseen to me, *she has* power"	"If she remains unseen to me, *I have* power"	"If I remain unaware of my desire for her, I retain my self" (restatement of interpretation 2 above)
4	It is crucial that Partonope cannot see Melior or anyone else, nor can they see him	"In order for *her* to have power, I must *not be able* to see anyone else (including her), but no one else (including her) must be able to see me, either"	"In order for *me* to have power, *I* must *be able* to see others (including her)"	"In order for me to be a subject, I must be able to desire (consciously)"

level of the text: Partonope, like Huot's protagonists, experiences a mental breakdown and flees. Clearly some kind of disintegration happens, or threatens. But we need not, indeed cannot, follow Huot literally in invoking psychosis, as she is primarily concerned with the putative subjectivities of the characters. The "problem," for the masculine literary subject, is much more quotidian than that.

The breakdown, rather, is like a further stalling strategy; the dreamer is dangerously close to waking, to consciousness of the threatening knowledge, and the dream is barely doing its job keeping him asleep. We noted this quality of the romance-dream earlier, barely keeping tension under control, in the initial sex scene. This subject's gender anxieties are very close to the surface. The subject is at a decisive psychosexual turning point, and *Partonope* expresses this more vividly than some romances by making its hero, in some respects, convincingly adolescent. The romance presents an impossible choice between two frames of relation. The subject is between dependence and autonomy or authority, in all the social and tangible meanings of those words. The narcissistic masculinity of its subjectivity also has an adolescent flavor. The subject can recognize maternal authority for what it is, and represent it literally, but needs to progress out of immature object relations, and avoid regression, in order to preserve a securely masculine and adult sense of self. (Remember, sexual desire may have been dangerous to medieval masculinity, but it was also essential, providing the libidinous energy whose management defined both self-gratifying and self-controlling forms of masculinity.) The alluring relational role of adult heterosexuality, while needed and desired, is also difficult enough to comprehend, to integrate, that it needs to be disguised. The need is so close to the surface, and so powerful, that it breaks through—causing a nightmarish disintegration, which has to be patched over at the end.

The title character of *Sir Launfal* is in a similar situation.[58] His lady, Dame Tryamour, is a fairy-lover, sexually forward, who binds Launfal in a promise never to speak of her: an agreement resembling Partonope's relationship with his invisible mistress. She helps Launfal manage the awkward position he has fallen into at Camelot. Launfal, one of Arthur's knights, has previously distinguished himself by his generosity to others. Yet the queen, who does not like him (as he dislikes her, for her promiscuity), spitefully leaves him unrewarded at her wedding feast. Launfal gets away from the court and ends up lodging with the mayor of Karlouyn, where again he swiftly runs through his resources (gifts from Arthur).

At this point Launfal meets Dame Tryamour, who lavishes riches on him. He returns to the court, whose members admire him now that he is rich, and his largesse draws Guenevere's sexual attention (631–54). After Launfal rebuffs her, Guenevere makes an insinuation of homosexual practice against Launfal, grounded in his lack of an obvious female lover. Launfal is immediately ashamed, and this drives him to break his promise to Tryamour. That lady withdraws all her favor (and Launfal's riches melt away) when he so much as *alludes* to her existence; he does not even name her. Then, for no very clear reason, she relents, decides to clear Launfal's name, and directly gives Guenevere her comeuppance: she takes away Guenevere's sight (though this is made to seem not too arbitrary because that was Guenevere's half of a bet set to Launfal).

Unlike Melior, Tryamour can be called up whenever Launfal desires it, if he just goes into a secret place. She has clear resemblances to a conscious fantasy, a daydream: Launfal can have her there whenever he wishes. So in one way she is at Launfal's "pleasure," in the medieval sense. On the other hand, she sets the rules and has the power to enforce them, and so in that sense she is not under Launfal's control. Her unexplained return seems to be at her own volition. As with Ywain and Alundyne, the narcissistic wish is to manage an other as an extension of the self. In addition, this fantasy of control is an attempt for the subject to get around the awareness that he is, in some way, under the power and control exerted by the object, and by the desire she incites. The prohibition on speaking of Tryamour, on the least acknowledgement of her existence, is not quite the same as invisibility, which is easier to understand as a form of disguising, of keeping something from consciousness. But perhaps Launfal's predicament is, actually, analogous to the situation with Partonope at Melior's court. Partonope is forbidden to see Melior because the subject must not (does not want to) see the repudiated object; anxiety condenses and reverses into prohibition. Launfal is forbidden to speak of Tryamour because the subject must not (does not want to) speak of the object, must not "name" his desire, must not represent it in language: the unconscious "retains its consistency only on the basis of a certain nonknowledge—its positive ontological condition is that something must remain nonsymbolized, that something must not be put into words."[59]

Like Partonope, Launfal must negotiate between two powerful female figures, and the romance represents this power through recognizable symbols of social masculinity. Both women hold purse strings and wield them differently to bestow a social phallus. Tryamour is generous with Launfal, where the queen is miserly. And both, in their respective ways, take that phallus away: they socially castrate Launfal. Guenevere does this spitefully and arbitrarily, first by withholding her reward and later by alleging homosexual activity; Tryamour, as a punishment for a broken promise, by withdrawing her favor and Launfal's wealth. Here is an oscillation, between a sort of Bad Mother who cannot be appeased *and* is undesirable, and a Good Mother who is conflated with the object of desire. The more real one, Guenevere, comes directly into contact with the "less real" one, Tryamour, whose existence she directly challenges Launfal to prove. The subject, in the end, cannot make this impossible conflict resolve within the context of the romance's immediate world.

Thus, two things happen. First, the Good Mother symbolically effaces the Bad Mother. She does not kill her, but blinds her. (Guenevere can no longer see Launfal, just as the subject is, in this dream world, no longer under mother's surveillance. He is freed from her.) Blinding rather than killing symbolizes additionally a distortion or displacement of the hostile wish that the subject must be protected from. Significantly also, the displacement is not only from killing to blinding, but from Launfal to Tryamour, so the subject once again does not have to "commit" this necessary but threateningly hostile deed. The other important event, at the very end of the romance, is that Launfal himself disappears, escaping into Tryamour's world with her. Saved the trouble of integrating heterosexual desire within the interior world, the subject gets an easier way out.

Medieval discourse, including romance literature, figured feminine objects both as the primary targets of masculine desire and as the fount of powerful forces threatening to dismember the masculine subject. These figurations were open and obvious, appearing floridly in the literary record, because marital and sexual relations with women extended well beyond the psychic realm and directly shaped men's social selves. But, just as we have seen that men's relations with other men were the most important context for that social selfhood, so also in the interior self the feminine other was not the only element reached by the convolutions of desire. Hostility toward, and desire for, masculine objects played a murkier but equally important part.

FATHERS UNKNOWN AND FORBIDDEN

Everybody knows about Freud's classic formulation of the Oedipus complex, but generally only remembers its hetero side: in boys, the desire for the mother that causes the boy to see the father as a rival and as the personification of punishing guilt attendant on desire. We often forget that in his mature work Freud also theorized a pattern of *same*-sex desire (of males for the father, and females for the mother) itself marking psychosexual development, particularly because the father provided the chief representation of maleness with which the male child would identify. So the father's role in masculine identity development was not a simple one, and conflict lay at the heart of it.[60] (Brewer's comment that "Freudian theory appears to over-estimate fathers, and misinterprets the killing of the father, while under-estimating the repellent nature of the fate of marrying the mother" is itself a misinterpretation and an underestimation of "Freudian theory.")[61]

Recent psychoanalytic work has begun to pay more attention to the role of fathers, just as it has shifted attention from the Oedipal to the pre-Oedipal stage in the development of gender identity.[62] We can no longer take "father" quite so simplistically as representing judgment and the threat of castration, which is the guise he assumes in most humanities applications of psychoanalysis, especially the literary criticism influenced by Jacques Lacan. Another side of father has demanded equal attention. The *pre*-Oedipal father is very much the gentle(d) male. He shelters and protects rather than nurtures as mother does, but he supports that nurturing function; he does not hinder or oppose it.[63] We are speaking here primarily of the most basic, prelinguistic effects, which do not concern "culture." The father's handling, holding, and speaking give the infant a series of sensory associations (voice register, body shape, different scents and textures) that are marked as *male*, as different from the mother, but (ideally) also soothing, comforting, and loving just as those coming from mother.[64] These very primal associations prepare the ground for desire. They also combine in their own way with the child's ongoing perception and internalization of father's *other* capacities, especially his relationship to mother, his way of managing prohibition and discipline, and his connection to the world outside the family.[65]

For the male child, identification with the father therefore must involve a complement of desire for the father. The internal contradiction, which complicates the assumption of a masculine gender identity, is that this desire has to exist in an uneasy equilibrium with two other powerful factors. The desire for, which is also the desire-to-be-like, the "father who is like me," must find its place alongside a lingering attachment to the maternal figure previously providing the earliest sense of "me." Then, at the Oedipal stage, desire conflicts with the competitive hostility experienced as the boy's desire-to-be-like, which is also a desire to *have*, confronts his wish to be rid of the father in father's relation to mother.

These theories concern the symbolic internal representation of the father figure, the qualities the subject attaches to him. The actions of individual living fathers themselves belong to a different level of object relations. So I will address the actions of actual fathers in the romances only as far as they lead us to these deeper meanings. Still, my analysis does not preclude or seek to replace more social interpretations. The idea that romance emplots young men's attempts to establish themselves in manhood by endowing themselves with property is entirely relevant to my argument.[66] That manifest level of conflict is not all, however, and it also is not severed from what lies beneath. We require only a little thought to begin to see how the acted-out mechanics of conflict over property, succession, and birthright, or the "real-world" dilemmas of the fatherless son, would work in concert with, or proceed from, less evident psychic conflicts. Jennifer Fellows, in an analysis ostensibly about mothers and sons in romance, admits both possibilities: that such stories deal with both "oedipal tensions within the family and the young hero's need to define his identity both independently of and in relation to his parents," *and* "nearer to the surface . . . a more specifically medieval concern with the definition of a son's rights in relation to those of his father in a patriarchal society."[67]

Nor is my use of romance literature invalidated by the special social milieu of its origin and application. Especially among elite social ranks, the parenting patterns of the Middle Ages would have made father's approval a much more difficult thing to earn, much more loaded with significance (at the very least, in competition with siblings), than was the case arguably either among lower ranks or in later eras, or with mother's approval. An environment where affectionate fatherly contact was rare would not necessarily eliminate it as a factor. It would rather make *all* signs of father's love, however small, even more prized and sought after, just as the subject would have even more feared father's wrath. Whether the boy seeks father's love as an embrace, roughhousing play, or approving words spoken before others, the same complement must be there. Necessary as this approval-love is (because it is another sign of successful identification), it is also, of course, threatening, just as hetero-desire is both threatening and necessary for different reasons.

The romances I analyze here all deal with the father in different degrees of explicitness, and their strategies differ as well. The texts may write the father out of existence, disguise him by splitting among other figures, or divert attention from the subject's relation to him. In discussing these romances, I move from more to less obvious material. So I begin with *Bevis of Hampton*, where a concern with fathers and sons is evident in the very surface detail and in the actual mechanics of the plot; we require little interpretive work to tease it out.

THE FATHER UNKNOWN: *BEVIS OF HAMPTON*

Bevis of Hampton is so long, so densely crammed with figures, that it is hard to distinguish much meaning amid an apparently episodic and unsubtle adventure story. Concentrating on the main figures, however, shows that there is a masculinity plot amid all the detail. The apparently rambling and overextended structure has its own significance, more significant than most of the events. *Bevis of Hampton* seems to have two endings; it does not conclude with the hero's marriage, or reunion with his lady, or regaining his patrimony. Instead it continues to a kind of coda involving Bevis's own sons and their recognition of Bevis, their father. So although Bevis is denied a reunion with his literal father, he gets it in a reversal, through his sons. The romance takes care of the necessary business, only not smoothly or seamlessly.

The familial elements in *Bevis* show that the apparent problems characteristic of the romances—the absence of fathers, their deaths, and their separation from their sons—in fact represent solutions. Viewed psychoanalytically, they protect the masculine subject from the knowledge of desire and the conflicts it entails. Naturally, in the terms of the story, the absence of his father creates motivating problems for Bevis. Yet we have to take these problems in the context of a narrative wherein Bevis does get his wish in the end.

Because Bevis's real father is dead, he cannot be "found." There can be no reunion. Instead, Bevis has to regain his inheritance and, effectively, install himself in his father's place. There is no need to "kill" the father symbolically, for he is already dead. Moreover, as Brewer comments on the tale of "Jack and the Beanstalk," "The 'true' father is dead, and in the logic of this kind of imagination is 'therefore' good."[68]

At the story's climax, however, Bevis (returned from his dangerous adventures) does literally kill his *stepfather* (3452–59). Once again, Brewer, referring to Jack, has anticipated me: "The protagonist has already killed off his father once. . . . Now, though a bit ashamed of himself . . . he justifies his continuous need to kill him by representing him as the disagreeable Giant."[69] Giants in romance can have additional significance, however, and we can go a little further than Brewer on the element of hostility toward father. The symbolism of Bevis's stepfather's death sounds like another defense. In the terms of the masculine subject, as distinct from Bevis the character, the conclusion is that "my *real* father did not desire my mother. Therefore, *the one who desires my mother* is not my real father." This conclusion is possible because identity is so overwhelmingly invested in the idea of identifying with the father. "Therefore he is not my real father, only an impostor. And because my real father is all-good, my *not-father*, that is, my mother *and* my impostor-father, must be all-bad." Why, then, does the stepfather need to be killed? It allows the subject to kill the not-real father without killing the real one. Guilt-inducing hostility at father is instead redirected at the not-father, at a figure who is enough like father to serve as the target of such hostility, but who (because he has been villainized) reflects no guilt on the subject for that aggression.[70] These all represent severe and complex defenses against the knowledge of that desire to replace the father.

As an additional compensation, Bevis gets a substitute reunion with the prime father figure: the king, who restores him to his inheritance (4296–4303). Here, social and psychological symbolism converge, showing us how loaded and how fraught the father-son relation could be. Patrimony was so central to masculine identity among the landed class that it becomes inevitably part of these identity figures. (Disinheritance could mean social castration.) But that does not mean that the point of the romance can be reduced to the acquisition of status. The image of the palimpsest has become a cliché, but it does seem appropriate here: looking from above, from the social level, we see the adherent lower layers. Bevis's sons recognize him as their own father; then, completing the process, Bevis's son Miles marries the king's daughter. Now the triangular relation between subject, mother, and father appears in a vertical rotation, turning into subject, son, and daughter, where son and daughter both link subject to the substitute, idealized, generous, nonthreatening father. So the narrative journey bringing the subject to this point of fulfillment emerges as a path of desire for a fantasized father, a father whose indispensable relation to the subject is sensitive enough to require disguise. The fantasy solution, then, is a circumvention of a most painful conflict through displacement onto other conflicts, which *look* more florid and drawn out, but are actually evasions.

BETTER THE NIGHTMARE YOU KNOW: *LYBEAUS DESCONUS*

Bevis of Hampton represented father directly and dealt with the ensuing conflicts through strategies of splitting and displacement. *Lybeaus Desconus*, in which familial fathers hardly appear, chooses an ostensibly simpler strategy of fantasizing the conflicts out of existence. Not only does the young protagonist not know who his father is; he does not really know who he himself is. He is not even quite sure what his name is, an uncertainty he expresses meaningfully: "That young man said, 'By Saint James! I don't know what my name is, fool that I am, but while I was at home, my mother in her way called me Beau-fitz [beautiful son].'"[71] The situation changes when he comes to Arthur's court, and the king gives him a new name, "Lybeaus

Desconus." The name, derived from *le bel inconnu,* means "fair unknown." Now he knows who he is, something newly defined entirely in terms of this new father figure, Arthur, and the homosocial world Lybeaus has just entered. (Note the distinction between what his mother *called him* and the *name* granted by the king.) To a certain extent, then, the romance concerns not just identity but identification. By turning his back on home and mother and joining Arthur's court, with suspicious ease, Lybeaus finds an identity, one that "consists in the recognition he wins from the court, from Arthur."[72] The signal moment, like an imprinting, occurs when Lybeaus spots a dead knight.[73] Now he has an image of the thing he must become. Becoming like the knight (except not dead) means becoming also like the other knights, imitating their behavior and acquiring their attributes. This is more or less obvious. A little less obvious, perhaps, are the reasons why the romance sets up origin in this way.

Most simply, by fantasizing an absence of any desire to know the original father, the text eliminates an entire area of conflict. Mother is easily jettisoned for the same reason. Since father is unknown, there is much less difficulty in "identifying" with the idealized nonparental father, represented by the king. Arthur, as substitute father, not only does not compete with Lybeaus for female objects, but in fact is the one to give to Lybeaus in marriage the imprisoned queen whom the hero rescues.[74] (As a queen rather than a princess, this lady is a mother figure. Thus, the romance nicely undoes the Oedipal conflict as well.) An interpretation like Jeffrey Jerome Cohen's, wherein the needs served here are those of Society and Power, would look to the sociopolitical implications: the ideal male identifies with the power figures outside of family interests. (In one of many memorable phrases, Cohen characterizes his material as "Freud's family romance, but here as written by the father, with a father's wished-for ending.")[75] It is true that *Lybeaus Desconus* argues a personal identity invested most importantly in the male peer group. Yet that argument coexists with, overarches the psychic symbolism; it does not preclude it.

For approximately the last third of its length, the previously rather episodic and unmysterious *Lybeaus Desconus* becomes stranger, more dreamlike, and this is the most significant section for the present discussion. Before he can fight the story's final battle, Lybeaus arrives with the go-between Elaine and her steward at a town where "filth and ordure" are "collected back in" rather than "thrown out."[76] In this strange place lurks humiliation rather than death: Lybeaus risks being spattered with filth if he loses the challenge of Sir Lambard, hence (according to Elaine) to be known as a coward. Lybeaus duly fights and wins. But Lambard, the loser, welcomes Lybeaus in as a preparation for the real battle with two sorcerers ("clerkys"), inside a castle that threatens to fall down and wherein the only inhabitants are minstrels who suddenly go silent.[77] Interestingly, Lybeaus only seems to feel real fear or panic after the appearance of a woman-faced monster, with "horribly big paws": "Sir Lybeaus grew faint from sweating as he sat there in his seat, as if everything were on fire; he was so terribly afraid that he thought his heart would explode, as she got closer to him."[78] The erotic suffusion of this terror is clear; Lybeaus sweats and nearly swoons as the monster-woman approaches, thinking his heart will literally burst. And what happens next? "And before Lybeaus knew it, the monster kissed and nuzzled him about the face with its mouth."[79] After this passionate and aggressive kiss, the monster suddenly turns into a naked woman ("moder naked" in one manuscript) who turns out to be the lady Lybeaus had set out to rescue. This is the climax; the rest is denouement and reward. Arthur gives Lybeaus the lady in marriage, providing the seal of patriarchal approval, and we hear nothing more about Elaine.

The conclusion of the romance thus guides the subject past an apparently diversionary battle, which appears to be only a prelude to the "real" crisis at the end. The two situations nearly complement each other. The fight with Sir Lambard, the male figure, is public, taking place outdoors, open to view. The final confrontation with the female monster occurs in a deep interior space, a dark and treacherous edifice wherein, further, ordinary rules are reversed: the structure of the building begins to undo itself, the minstrels' vibrant song is stilled, and the opponent is not only female but a monstrous cross between species. Moving from the recognizable to the bizarre, the subject seems to confront a clear hierarchy of threat. The sojourn at the town and the combat with Lambard could be defensive stalling moves, trying to put off the most fearsome encounter with the woman-monster. The romance says, in effect, "These are not threats, these other things, whatever they represent. The real threat is the disguised approach to the feminine."

This apparent logic of the nightmare, however, serves a distracting function. The actual fantasy is the location of the "real" threat in the monstrous feminine, the last-encountered obstacle whose elimination represents the climax of the plot and brings on the rewards and denouement. Complicating the interpretation, the obvious misogyny of the final confrontation bears markers we have already come to recognize, especially the projection of desire onto the feminine, here made horrible and threatening. The female monster's kiss, which transforms her from threat into love object, serves to distance the masculine subject from heterosexual desire by inverting it into the desire of an undesirable other *for* the subject. Yet these familiar features really signal the overdetermined scene's function in a larger scheme. The fantasy of making feminine figures safe and desirable operates within a simultaneous, implied one of suppressing desire for masculine objects. The one kind of fantasy does not overrule the other.

In other words, to say that the primary fantasy clears homo-desire out of the picture does not mean that hetero-desire is not simultaneously problematic or threatening. Desire is itself a problem for the "phallic, boundaried self," because it implies lack. The ultimate fantasy is to extinguish desire altogether, to be without need for relation.

As menacing as the monster encounter is, it bears an overall consistency and coherence: too much so, in fact. It may be nightmarish, but it does not seem like a real nightmare. The earlier scene leading up to the combat with Lambard, in contrast, is marked by the truncated and inscrutable bluntness of a dream. Lybeaus has no way to understand the townspeople's waste-reclamation habits, and Elaine's explanation of their shaming purpose does not bring matters any closer to conscious clarity. These puzzling features are a clue that the scene is more important than surface appearances would suggest, that something sensitive is being smoothed over.

First, note that Lambard is the steward of the lady whom Lybeaus seeks: a detail mentioned only briefly, in passing. He stands between Lybeaus and his goal, and he cannot be eluded. He must be fought. Lambard has the potential to take away Lybeaus's very identity, to strip him of the *name* he has so importantly been given. Yet he is also possibly the most knightly opponent whom Lybeaus comes across, and in the end, he turns from enemy to ally, from Unlike to Like. It is hard not to see a figure like this, recognized as Like but at the same time a forbidding prohibitor, and especially an obstacle to a heterosexual object, as combining the father's most problematic attributes for the masculine subject.

To *lose* to this figure, this self-mirroring individual, is to risk being subsumed back into the filth the town collects—its *own* filth. Manifestly, of course, this ordure stands for the stain of dishonor that Lybeaus will bear if he loses, the stink of cowardice that cannot be washed away. But the symbolic importance here goes beyond "losing distinction" or "being besmirched," because it recalls a psychoanalytic *locus classicus*. The town that gathers its own waste back in, for the pleasure of casting it out, reminds us of Freud's landmark theory of infantile sexual organization. Freud noted that young children at one stage locate pleasure in the anal zone. They employ their developing control over the retention and expulsion of feces both for physical pleasure and for the mental satisfaction of the control itself, as a resistance to the injunctions of adults.[80]

The anal stage of sexual organization is not a gendered one either in classic or contemporary psychoanalysis; both males and females experience it, and it does not influence gender identity directly. Its marked association with infancy, or immaturity, is the primary reason the imagery in *Lybeaus* is so resonant. Even a merely impressionistic interpretation can establish an association with childhood humiliations, with immaturity and therefore with not-fully-masculine boyhood, whose cultural importance I have already discussed. The humiliation Lybeaus must fight is explained to him as "cowardice," itself often considered at root a childish failing. The chief challenges Lybeaus faces in the trajectory toward his goal are deflection and arrest. After all, Lybeaus has only proceeded to the filth-gathering town after at least one serious delay with a Wrong Woman, frittering away a year with the enchantress La Dame Amoure. So, despite the Lambard-father-figure's power to extinguish the subject (a "name," a fame, being a masculine identity in purely chivalric terms), and despite the father's castrating capacity, the anxiety here is more complex than "castration."

The threat awaiting the subject at the node represented by the town is of a regression: that one will get stuck, lose one's self-boundaries to the centrifugal emission of infantile preoccupations. The fully commanded and fully known masculine self risks being tainted and obscured, pulled back and down. Humiliation, childishness, immaturity, subjection to father, guilty pleasures now "forgotten" or repressed (in a superego sense): these are all associated. The plot structure and symbolic evasions of *Lybeaus* suggest a subjectivity wherein the threat of the feminine is accepted, but other possible sources are not, raising the possibility that those others are in fact more dangerous.

FATHER FORBIDDEN, FATHER CREATED:
OF ARTHOUR AND OF MERLIN

In contrast to these first two examples, *Of Arthour and of Merlin* selects rather more drastic strategies of transformation.[81] In sections concerned with the origins of Merlin himself and of his relationship to Arthur, the romance betrays a fascinating concern to keep the father at a safe distance from the subject. Here the father is placed off-limits not only by absence, but by being made undesirable: the subject makes him a demon.

Both Arthur and Merlin are the products of illicit liaisons ultimately legitimized after the fact: rapes, to be more precise. Merlin's mother was raped in her sleep by a demon, and so Merlin's father is not only unknown to Merlin, but he is also unknown to, even unseen by, his mother. Merlin's father, even more than Bevis's, is hence unknowable; it is impermissible to *know him*. Actually, Merlin's father is unknown to him only in a partial sense. Merlin, it transpires, knows that his father was a demon; he knows what happened to his mother. He knows, too, that his existence throws his mother's into doubt, and so he uses this knowledge to protect her from the charge of fornication. But the source of his knowledge, significantly, is never revealed. And Merlin's awareness of his demonic paternity does not mean that he "knows" his father in any personal sense, nor does he express any desire to. Knowledge of the father in that way is forbidden, by the mere fact of the father's status as an entity that by definition must *not* be known, must be shunned, exorcised if necessary. In this case the character's (Merlin's) awareness stands for the subject's fantasy.

We need to examine more closely what this element of the narrative, Merlin's unwilled and in fact unconscious conception, does for the subject. We quickly find that the subject's anxiety about father is closely tied to a representation of mother, and to an inability to accept the relation between the two parental figures. Obviously, a coupling during sleep disposes toward interpretation as a dream. But instead of seeing the incubus as the *mother's* dream, we need to see the demonic coupling as the *subject's* dream, fantasy, or wish. Like a dream's protecting repression, it solves some problems of origin for the subject. It explains how he came to be, without the messy burden of human sexuality. He undeniably has a mother, who gave birth to him, but there is no need to imagine, or to deal with, a father, since the father has disappeared after impregnating mother.

We can see how this nicely evades the more famous Oedipal conflict, the "positive" one. Now there is no rival for the mother. It also leaves mother, though demonically violated, also *virgo intacta* in a sense, where the son-subject is concerned, since there has been no human intercourse. And it leaves her morally virginal too; she was *raped,* she did not seek out or want this sexual contact. Here are two main fantasies rolled into one: "My mother did not have sex with a man in order to beget me," on the one hand, and "My mother had sex, but she was raped," on the other. *Bevis* demonizes mother to protect the idealized father; in *Of Arthour and of Merlin,* the opposite seems to be happening. Merlin's first, prodigious anxiety is to protect his mother; indeed, this is his first recorded speech. Confronting the midwife who bitterly wishes he were "Far off in the sea, so that your mother could survive," the newborn Merlin proclaims, "You're lying... you old slut; Nobody will kill my mother.... I'll save her life (1038-46)".

But why a demon? After all, would not the fantasy that one was the child of an angelic coupling serve the purpose just as well and cast a rather more, in modern terms, beneficent light over the entire issue? What is gained by casting one's unknown father as an embodiment of evil? This may be a moot question. Medieval Christian culture did not envision angels as sexual beings. Nor, on balance, did it generally view what we term sexuality as a capacity of humanity with any relation to divinity or goodness. The opposition between the carnal, the "fleshly," and the spiritual was simply too stark for that.

Merlin saves his mother from the penalties for fornication by exposing the hypocrisy of the judge who would condemn her; he reveals that this justice is himself the product of adultery. Indeed, the young Merlin shows a special ability to detect past adulteries: passing a churchyard, he points out that the father mourning a dead child is not actually its father. The child's real father is in fact the priest who is singing the burial mass, and so the grieving cuckold ought really to be rejoicing: "Therefore, that fellow who is grieving for his enemy is a real fool, because the priest's issue, who never would do him any good, is dead"—a cold and unyielding assessment of the social implications of false paternity (1391-95). In turn, it is the grown Merlin who brings about the adulterous conception of Arthur between Ygrene and Uter Pendragon. Hence, in both cases, the father is a figure of the unknown, somehow unreal.

Anxiety about paternity in a property-obsessed, lineage-driven social group; the disruptive power of extramarital sexuality; the plight of the fatherless son (here, in Merlin, given a fantasy position of fantastic power)—these are obvious concerns here, but they are not the only concerns. By returning to the theme of adultery twice more in its early section, the text shows that it has not really solved the problem of the father: the subject cannot get beyond it. Instead, the subject fixates on the problem, which it identifies with its central character, Merlin, and his ability to detect adultery, and, later, his effective creation of another male character, Arthur, through causing an adulterous union. This is not simple adultery, as Ygrene *thinks* she is sleeping with her husband. In the case of Ygrene, it seems like the story wants to keep the character requisitely virtuous, as what prompts this deception is her refusal to sleep with Uter knowingly. This was the same end that Merlin achieved for his own mother by making her a nun.[82]

Forbidding the father means that the subject cannot manage the father-introject as an *integrated* element of the self. And yet the subject cannot get rid of father completely, still needing, *desiring* him in his relational capacity. The romance wants to resolve this significant conflict by keeping its idealized father pre-Oedipal, safely unsexual.[83] This representation loads all desire onto the demonized father: a hypersexualizing of masculinity, a fear of desire and splitting off of sexuality from relation, that fits the profile of narcissistic masculinity. It also characterizes medieval concepts of gendered sexuality, particularly those whose cultural imprint derives from the social strata most immediately relevant to the romances.

Yet *Of Arthour and of Merlin* is not only about the forbidden father. It is also about the demonized father. Making father into a demon does not only eliminate him as a rival; importantly, it also eliminates him (and, by extension, all that which is masculine) as an object of desire himself.

Freud repeatedly wrote of the childhood desire of males for the father as a "feminine attitude," adding in 1923, "There is scarcely one [psycho-analytic observation] which sounds so repugnant and unbelievable to a normal adult."[84] (The addition was a comment about popular attitudes, not a judgment on this pattern of desire.) Today we would question the assumption that desire for a masculine object implies femininity. Freud's equation, however, fits the conscious logic not only of his own time but of medieval England as well; recall the absence of an English homoerotic tradition. Moreover, Freud discussed such desire in his analysis of a text with certain similarities to *Of Arthour and of Merlin*: a seventeenth-century account of an Austrian painter's alleged dealings with the devil. The painter, according to the text, had fallen into a deep depression on the death of his father, and the devil appeared to him soon after. Freud argued: "With the painter's mourning of his lost father, and the heightening of his longing for him, there also comes about in him a re-activation of his long-since repressed phantasy of pregnancy, and he is obliged to defend himself against it by a neurosis and by debasing his father."[85]

We need not follow too closely Freud's deduction of an unconscious desire to bear the father a child. We may, however, read Merlin's orchestration of Arthur's conception as a fantasy of fatherhood, of being a father who is not only an authority figure but also an object of desire. In a projective transformation, the father-creator becomes the object of the created son's desire, while simultaneously experiencing that desire in reverse. But it is less threatening for the subject to figure the father position as the primary, manifest one, which also enhances the subject's own sense of power. In part, then, Merlin represents a fantasy of creating one's own father as, in a displaced way, one's own son.

Arthur is, of course, not literally Merlin's father, but he is his king. And Merlin has a kind of paternal power over Arthur, so there is also a fantasy of having the parent (father) subject to the child, rather than the reverse. How is this related to desire? In this text, the meaning seems to go beyond the obvious fact that any "created" male is a potential father. We know already who Arthur is and who he will become. We also know the part he plays in other romances. So Merlin's creation of the Ur-father, in effect, results from a compensation: lacking a father of his own, he gets around it by creating one. But why would this have to come of an adulterous union, especially when the literal mother is again tricked into it?

Given medieval cultural hostility to, or widely divergent attitudes toward, sexuality, the demonizing of the father makes perfect sense as an imprint of culture on private subjectivity. The masculine subject of this romance cannot account for origin, for the very "I am," by admitting to the sexual union of parents. It wants to deny, for all births of boys, the basic parental relationship. It cannot allow mother to desire father, and so the "real" father remains a fantasy. Mother is thus kept blameless and metaphorically chaste. But oddly, the father figure is the more protected one, by the very implied existence of the eternally absent Good Father. The text wants to split the sexual and relational aspects of masculinity. Or rather, to unpack the idea of "father," it demonizes father's sexual function while keeping his relational and affectionate role out of bounds. (Merlin's surrogate father, who is of course *not* his father, is a safely nonsexual hermit.)

Clearly, there is a connection between the absence of the human father, the subject's desire for what he has lost, the father's becoming a demon, and the demon's sexual function. This subject seems to be caught on the cusp of sexual knowledge. The subject desires the father he does not have—that is, the father he has lost, the father of his earliest days, represented here by the father Merlin never had. Yet the subject is beginning to realize what is involved in "wanting" and "having" another person, how easily one kind of desire shades into another. The subject cannot both "know" the father in his sexual relation to mother *and* "know" that he himself desires the father. (In effect, the subject is asking, "If I desire this sexual father, what then does that say about *me*?") The father he wants to have (back) is not the father he is beginning to recognize.

Evidently, a late medieval English subjectivity found it nearly impossible to reconcile sexual and relational desire. It was unmanageably difficult for masculine subjects to identify with a father both as the model of sexual masculinity and as the object of filial devotion, especially when the culture so strongly reinforced fathers' disciplinary and prohibitive roles. Few people manage to resolve this kind of conflict completely even today.

The complications do not end there. Desire itself may be dangerous for the subject, but as we have already seen, the ability *to* desire is an essential aspect of *being* a subject. And the father represents precisely that capacity. Jessica Benjamin "contends that under our present parenting arrangements, fathers symbolize a different kind of object, more of a 'mirror of desire.' . . . A father, then, is experienced . . . more as an 'other' who wants and acts to satisfy his wants."[86] One need not restrict the contention to "present parenting arrangements." Medieval society may often have gendered *carnal* desire feminine. The equally important equivalence of agency and masculinity, however, would only have reinforced what Benjamin describes—a father imago representing the potential for having wishes and achieving them.

What, then, is the forbidden knowledge threatening the subject of this romance? It is the knowledge of a father's true relation to his son. To know that relation fully, the subject must face it in its full compound of hostility, guilt, desire, and love—a dangerous mixture. The deceptive paternity of both Arthur and Merlin attempts to resolve the masculine subject's dilemma: that to know the father requires understanding ultimate sameness and utter difference in the same being.

EMPLOTTED DESIRE: *SIR PERCEVAL OF GALLES*

Sir Perceval could stand as the exemplary masculinity romance.[87] Raised in ignorance of chivalry and isolation from courts, by a mother grieving for her husband (who was cut down in knightly combat), Perceval nonetheless sets out to become a knight and to serve King Arthur. He achieves this goal despite a series of clumsy errors. So this is a clear story of masculine formation through earning one's place in a male peer group. Indeed, Perceval enters that group so successfully that in the end he escapes feminine powers entirely and dies fighting in the Holy Land: he leaves women behind and transcends all desire.

Several features are significant in this regard. One is the marked lack of struggle in Perceval's departure from mother and home. There seems not to be much consciously holding Perceval back. His mother certainly tries, keeping him ignorant of the masculine world of chivalry; she tells him that the short spear she brought from the court is something she found in the woods (193–204). But as soon as he meets some knights, he wants to be one. Never has masculine identification seemed easier; it becomes a matter of recognizing outward signs and seeking to imitate them. The first of these outward markers is, of course, the horse: the knightly super-phallus. Perceval's interest in horses is the first sign to his mother that her efforts have been in vain; she sees this as natural: "She saw him bringing home a horse, and because of that, she knew that his true nature would emerge in spite of everything" (353–56).

Why is it important for the subject that Perceval *not* know so many things to do with his father? Or rather, why are revelations of father-associations so important? What is masculine is always, in this plot, something outside the self, always elusive and unachieved, unrealized. The entire story is one long arc of desire, ultimately dealt with by obscuring and blunting desire's object, placing it far away (the Holy Land) and associating it with the least tangible figure imaginable: God.

The text's elisions and omissions signal the problematic nature of this desire. Perceval, though never having known his father, yet unconsciously wants to imitate him. Perceval seeks to be a knight without knowing why, and further, the romance does not think it is important that he know why or that we (the subject) know why. All Perceval's seeking is motivated by these unknown objects. And that unexplained desire (in its simplest sense of "wish") to be a knight yet structures the entire tale. Everything else happens because of it. Felicity Riddy comments that this romance "raises the question, what is a knight? And then supplies the answer given by many romances: he is his father's son."[88] Perceval learns bit by bit the rules of knightly life: fighting, armor, and courtesy. (He is still learning up to the climactic battle, when Gawain has to tell him to get off his horse and fight on foot.) This romance makes the problem of desire for masculine objects safe in the form of comedy. The struggle to shape the self to a form determined by desire becomes a joke.

Two encounters stand out among the episodes on Perceval's journey. Just like a dream, or a neurotic fantasy, the romance keeps putting off conflicts: they seem about to surface, but actually emerge later. Of course, this is suspense, a standard feature of narrative. But transformational processes are features of narrative too. A suspenseful effect results from deferring crises and revelations; suspense is the end, not the means. The deferral brings together the most important conflicts in gender identity *and* individual identity by splitting the attributes of central parental introjects among other figures.

The first conflict emerges in probably the most dreamlike portion of the romance. Early in his travels, Perceval, like Partonope of Blois, enters a castle where food lies ready and refreshes himself (moderately). As with Partonope, everything he finds seems to have been prepared especially for him, including a lady he finds sleeping in a chamber, to whom he is drawn (434–80). The text does not signal danger, but rather a slight erotic awareness involving a gentle compulsion. It is the same giving over as in *Partonope:* "He was not full of false pride, and he went onward to a chamber to see more marvels. He found a lady sleeping on a bed, spread with rich bedclothes; he said, 'Surely, you'll leave a token of marriage with me'" (465–72).

Within this heightened state, whose narcissistic eroticism comes in part from the implication that "all is for me," Perceval makes his first symbolically heterosexual contact. For no conscious reason that we can discern, he decides to kiss the lady and exchange the ring he wears, which he got from his mother, for the one the lady wears. Perceval substitutes one token of attachment, to mother, for one to a heterosexual object. Perceval's actions here are crucial, and yet, like his original impulse to become a knight, they are crucially *unexplained,* a sign that something important is going on.

But unlike *Partonope, Sir Perceval* is not primarily concerned with desire for feminine objects in this scene. This lady, unlike Partonope's Melior, does not cause the enchantment. She merely functions as one of the gears attenuating an approach to a conflict. Though the ring and the kiss clearly evoke marriage, several important features signal early the unreality of the bond. The lady has not consented to either kiss or ring exchange; the ring Perceval gives her was not really his to give, and it also turns out that the lady was not free to dispose of "her" ring either. Indeed, this is not the lady destined to be Perceval's wife. Her purpose here is to represent a possibility, a potentiality for Perceval. As an object, she fits entirely within the masculine subject frame: she is there for Perceval to act upon, and the romance implicitly approves of whatever he does. So in these terms, with reference to the masculine subject, her lack of consent matters only in signifying that this is not the "real" connection for Perceval.

Mother's ring is a mere token of remembrance, but the lady's has real protective power. Perceval does not at first realize that his early successes in battle may be due to that protection; he credits himself with them. The stolen ring grants Perceval protection in combat, which allows him to begin establishing a masculine chivalric identity, a fame. These powers are however less important in themselves than the fact that Perceval takes credit for them. And the reason for that is, of course, his ignorance of the ring's qualities. This ignorance is in fact full of significance. By leaving Perceval's reasons for exchanging the rings unexplained, the romance glosses over the desire that drew him to the sleeping lady. And by keeping him ignorant of the source of his newfound power, it protects the subject from the knowledge that such desire is in some way *necessary:* that it cannot be split off from masculinity. There is yet a deeper issue, however. The romance reveals the true nature of this problem by anchoring it in a symbol of heterosexual union, the ring. It recognizes the difficult and uncomfortable similarity of desire-for-mother and desire-for-woman. By splitting the objects into two figures it can set against each other, the text attempts to distinguish between them. But it defeats its own purposes by linking them through the same tangible symbol, and especially by choosing as that symbol a thing that represents heterosexual union rather obviously. (Significantly, Perceval's tale is not complete until he has given up both rings.)

Leaving Perceval's motivation unexplained further distances the subject from desire. And this is not all. The implications go beyond gender in itself, to a central constituent issue of selfhood. Perceval, not knowing that he owes his success among men to a lady, fails to distinguish himself from what is not himself. The narcissistic self, arguably, must arrogate all agency to itself in order to exist: If it happens, I made it happen; if I did not make it happen, its existence is not real. This failure to become conscious of limitations seems often to feature unhelpfully in masculine gender identity.[89] So giving up what cannot be one's own is harder than it sounds, and the romance makes it easy by concentrating these complex problems in a ring that can, in the happy ending, be returned to its rightful owner. But before that happens, Perceval encounters a different kind of conflict.

In the next important episode, Perceval defeats the Red Knight, who, unbeknownst to Perceval, killed his father. He puts on the armor of this father killer, unwittingly assuming his identity temporarily, and in consequence is mistaken for him. This is not difficult to decode. Here, the forbidden knowledge, which the romance transmutes by a familiar splitting process, is that "the one who kills my father" is "myself," that is, the masculine subject, which cannot fully exist narcissistically with father still around as a threat, yet is plagued by guilt for wanting him gone. Even more significantly, the splitting is unsuccessful: despite itself, the romance still taints Perceval (subject) by association. Again, the episode attempts to discharge painful tensions through grisly humor: Perceval does not know how properly to get a knight out of his armor (741–72). Perceval's inability to get armor off one man and put it on another (himself) signifies a further protection from, or repudiation of, the conflict with father-desire. What is the "real" reason Perceval cannot wear a man's (knight's/father's) armor? According to one set of values, or logic, it is because he is not yet a "real" knight. He has not proven himself. In the symbolic system I am invoking, the inability further puts off the knowledge of the painful conflict necessary in this scheme of identity formation. That conflict is painful because it involves severance from something that is deeply necessary to self and therefore desired. If this conflict were merely a matter of killing off a malign and threatening figure, it would be far less painful and therefore less complicated.

Thus far, my analysis of *Perceval* seems to draw us away from the theme of fathers and sons. But these torturous correspondences lead ultimately back to the central family conflict. Where mother is, there must father be also, in whatever form. And in *Sir Perceval,* the problematics of the masculine subject's hetero-desire ultimately lead to a confrontation with homo-desire in the figure of the father.

The confrontation comes about through the triangle Perceval entered in exchanging rings with the sleeping lady. Father is not quite where one might expect him to be. The male figure that Perceval kills is not his rival for the lady, that is, her husband who punishes her for losing the powerful ring. Indeed, the Knight, not the lady, was the ring's true owner, or at least its original owner. Whether or not the Black Knight's ring was literally his wedding ring, it still stands both for his marital and sexual relationship with a woman, and for his power in a broader sense, from which it cannot be separated. Perceval has thus arrogated not only the Black Knight's social masculinity but his sexual masculinity as well, and a woman is the crucial conduit for both.

Significantly, the encounter with the Black Knight can only be resolved through an encounter with the parental dyad. Suddenly the ring at issue is mother's, despite its lack of magical power to confer. Its real significance emerges with the revelation that the giant that Perceval slays had intended to give the ring as a love token to Perceval's mother, whom he desired. So in Oedipal terms, Perceval has slain the father-rival (unconsciously, so that "knowledge" never has to be dealt with). As in *Of Arthour and of Merlin,* the One Who Desires Mother must be eliminated. But *Sir Perceval,* rather than demonizing the sexual figure, cuts him off (in more ways than one) before any damage can be done. The subject gets a more direct and less subtle fantasy of eliminating father.

The giant, allowed or granted a quasi-familial relationship to mother and Perceval, is not allowed any chivalric qualities. Giants in Middle English literature have been the objects of recent critical attention most notably by Jeffrey Jerome Cohen. The most assured part of Cohen's argument interprets giants as personifying those *socially* nonintegrable aspects of masculinity that must be killed off, as giants are slain by heroes in these tales, to ensure the formation of a sufficiently civilized (compliant) *social* subject.[90] Cohen's argument is compelling, but I find it more useful to observe the same process of repudiation happening on a psychic level. The giant represents and embodies those aspects of masculinity the subject most wants to repudiate: sexual desire and brute physicality.

Particularly in a martial culture, physical strength and endurance constitute indispensable *possibilities* for the masculine subject. But they also breed insecurity. Physicality begets violence and destruction, which threaten the subject's very survival as an embodied self. Knowledge of the physical power one can wield against others means awareness that others can wield that same power against oneself, a possibility all the more inevitable when one's very *likeness* to the other power wielders is so central to masculine identity in the first place. The other side of strength and physical plenitude is its opposite: senescence, frailty, weakness, injury. Physical masculinity inescapably foreshadows its own decay. In the same way, in *Bevis of Hampton*, Ascopard the giant represents something the masculine self cannot easily integrate or accept. That is, such potentialities create unstable combinations with desire, especially alongside the knowledge of self-denial and frustration entailed by a social subjectivity. The giant's exaggerated features represent the physical dimension of masculinity, their very magnification signifying the obsessive anxiety the subject can pay to this double-edged capacity.

What, then, is a masculine subjectivity to do? Loading the physicality conflicts onto the figure of the giant allows for a fantasy solution. Physical aggression can be made useful (Ascopard is actually responsible for killing Bevis' stepfather) and then killed off. This allows the indulgence of aggressive impulses and wishes that are too threatening to the ego. (A harsh superego helps to make them threatening, by censuring and repressing them.) This defensive maneuver shows how sensitive and guilty the hostility toward father is, when the subject must take such a mediated approach even to the surrogate. All the knightly, external, social qualities instead are loaded onto the figures representing the "outside" world of men and the renunciation of domestic and heterosexual loyalties.

Yet the self cannot renounce those things without damaging consequences. Mother cannot be forgotten entirely, and the tangled associations through which the text tries to distance Perceval from her are evidence of the degree of repression and transformation required to sustain the illusion that she *can* be forgotten. The trouble with mother necessarily warps the introjection of father in consequence. Desire for mother can be displaced onto a safely unattainable object. What about desire for father?

Perhaps the Father Problem that the romance is trying unsuccessfully to resolve is the relation between different forms of desire. Identification via imitation from the outside—the learning of chivalric behavior, which Perceval does so clumsily—contains a complement of desire, because in order to see the self in the other, one must somehow desire the other. Yet the romance wants to keep identification free of desire. So it taints desire with brutality (e.g., the giant) and grossness. And it depersonalizes father to the point that he cannot be desired. But, as with the lady, the text does not quite pull it off. In trying to get Perceval away from mother, it brings him into a questionable relation to the Black Knight figure. This romance villainizes the Oedipal father while pushing the pre-Oedipal father out of the picture; Perceval himself, unlike Bevis, gets not even a surrogate. No matter how often the subject refuses desire in all these connections, desire comes back inexorably, in symbolic form.

DESIRE AND DREAD: *SIR GAWAIN AND THE GREEN KNIGHT*

Sir Gawain and the Green Knight picks up the thread of the metaplot at a later juncture.[91] This is not a romance of formation, of becoming a knight. It dramatizes, instead, the continued difficulty of managing classic conflicts in adult, mature life. The narrative's path, from the warmth of Christmas in the hall at Camelot to Gawain's wintry journey toward a climactic confrontation, all so vividly conveyed, evoke the dream or inner fantasy even in the surface details and events.

The Green Knight arrives unannounced at Camelot one Christmas. Only Gawain consents to take up the Green Knight's bizarre challenge to Arthur's court: that someone come forward to behead him. Once Gawain has duly sliced off the Knight's head, the mysterious visitor simply picks it up. Speaking through it, he charges Gawain to meet him again in a year's time, to receive the same treatment in return; he then rides off.

On his way to fulfill his bargain, Gawain finds lodging at a castle whose lord tests his fidelity to an oath. The lord appears to trust Gawain abed with his wife, who makes no secret of her sexual attraction to Gawain. Gawain negotiates this situation, evading the lady without either shaming her or betraying his host. He also refuses a ring she offers, but with a view to self-preservation accepts a magic belt with protective powers. At the agreed meeting with the Green Knight, Gawain does not shrink from the axe. But the Green Knight feints twice, and then strikes Gawain only a slight touch, nicking the skin but leaving him whole. The Green Knight then reveals that he was in fact the lord of the castle where Gawain stayed. The entire enchantment in turn was the work of Morgan le Fay, who sought to test the renown of the Round Table (and, apparently, to scare Guinevere out of her wits).

In a number of ways, the text creates the Green Knight as a figure of paternal authority rather than a chivalric equal or a peer to Gawain. It dwells on his physical presence, a matter of size and striking looks, indeed beauty: great height, broad shoulders, narrow hips, a resounding voice (135–202). He is an exemplar of maleness. Moreover, nothing the Green Knight says or does can be questioned. His original challenge is like a cruel teasing game inflicted by parent on child: hit me so that I have an excuse to hit you back. And there are no escape clauses; no additional acts of valor or heroism, it seems, will allow Gawain to keep his head. As Brewer observes: "But it is not fair, as children say, because Father is invulnerable; he can always put his head back on, while I cannot."[92]

The Green Knight's paternal features make him into the ultimate Oedipal father: the terrifying disciplinarian, who (in the subject's internalized representation of him) holds out the threat of castration as punishment for the subject's desire—directed, in Freud's classic formulation, at the mother. Since Gawain does survive, the romance appears at first to be a relatively straightforward fantasy involving the Oedipal father. The subject gets to "kill" this primal terror whose power threatens to undo the subject's very identity. At the same time, the subject is protected from the consequences of that revenge, emerging symbolically intact. Moreover, the Green Knight does not die from his decapitation, which therefore is not "real," and the subject gets to come away without the guilt spawned by hostile wishes toward the father.

The revelation that the Green Knight *is* the castle knight makes a familial interpretation yet more compelling. The forbidden love object, the Lady, tests the subject's desire (projected, as always, onto the woman). The enchantment, moreover, symbolically distances this woman from her "true" husband (the father); the Gawain-subject does not have to own this desire because not only was it all a "game," he was fooled into a misperception of the male-female relationship. Gawain escapes with only a minor injury, and the subject can recognize desire in safely disowned forms.

Certainly, these intramasculine conflicts frame the romance's plot. But to stop at a simple equation of decapitation and castration in an Oedipal scheme is to miss a great deal. First, Gawain's relation to the Green Knight reappears in displaced form at the castle. Jeffrey Jerome Cohen and Carolyn Dinshaw have concentrated on this part of the story, exploring how the clearly heterosexual tension between Gawain and the wife structures a more problematically ambiguous relation between the husband and Gawain.[93] I believe, however, that the entire castle episode itself serves to mask and diffuse the yet more sensitive complex of conflict and desire connecting Gawain and the Green Knight.

Gawain and the Green Knight enter a relationship defined, on the surface, by the rules of chivalric challenge, oath and contract. Gawain takes up the Green Knight's challenge and is bound by its terms. But this ostensibly simple reason for the sequence of events masks a strangely compulsive and inevitable-feeling bond between them. Their relationship is structured by violent acts whose violence is, further, shifted or transformed. Either they are surprising, impossible, inexplicable, or they are averted, made safe. Such transformations of the violence, in concert with the narrative's extension across its main subplot, serve to disguise those features of the relationship between Gawain and the Green Knight that are most threatening to a masculine subjectivity.

In fact, Gawain's relation to the Green Knight is shaped by dread: the inexorable threat of punishment that seems always to be waiting in the future. The Green Knight invites injury, invites killing (which turns out not to be killing), on the condition that he will get to reciprocate on an appointed day. I say "punishment" here rather than "reprisal" or "retribution" because, again, this is not a conflict between equals. And yet there is something not quite right about this punishment. The text lavishes a little too much attention on it, lingering over the vision of the Green Knight bowing down, baring his neck, the long tresses moving forward (417–20). This is borne out later in the tensions of Gawain's second meeting with the Green Knight at the Green Chapel, where Gawain finally goes to carry out his side of the agreement: there is a great buildup of fear, or at least anticipation, stretched out over two and a half stanzas, of that stroke bearing down from above (the Green Knight originally appears physically above Gawain in that second meeting). Then it is turned into a mere graze. Though Gawain is still technically injured, and bleeds, the relative effect is like a love tap, a tease (2243–71).

That last-minute reprieve is crucial. It makes all the difference, because it fulfils the outcome to which all the previous dread and inevitability have pointed. Not only does it connect the prospect of extinction—castration, if you like—with the arbitrary and inexorable will of the father, it also brings to the surface the fact that desire is the other face of dread. What is awaited, even if inescapably feared, needs only a little push to become what is expected, desired, as the feeling "Let's get it over with" expresses. Consider, as a modern example, this passage from a short story by Alice Munro. The narrator relates a childhood memory of seeing a frightening, possibly murderous, individual approach her father:

> People say they have been paralyzed by fear, but I was transfixed, as if struck by lightning, and what hit me did not feel like fear so much as recognition. I was not surprised. This is the sight that does not surprise you, the thing you have always known was there that comes so naturally, moving delicately and contentedly and in no hurry, as if it was made, in the first place, from a wish of yours, a hope of something final, terrifying.[94]

The oscillation between dread and desire, the sensual lingering over the axe blows, the pivoting alternations of power: all of these combine with that feeling of compulsion to give the violence, threatened and achieved, a perverse necessity, sadomasochistic, like that teasing game. The subject of *Sir Gawain and the Green Knight* experiences desire, comes to know it, in precisely this form: a most disconcerting, gray zone. The desire (and the dread) is for father, therefore for the prospect of his punishment, but also for the relief and pleasure when that punishment is withheld. The Green Knight is, as Brewer says, "a projection of the son's fear of himself, and also of the son's own strength, derived from a strong father."[95] Moreover, the literary subject recognizes his own hostility toward father, his wish to be free of him—and, most desperately, his fantasized representation of father's conflicting desire and hostility toward the son-subject, wherein paternal love (and love of self mirrored in the son) meets the dread of mortality and succession that the son signifies.[96] The distinctions between these possibilities blur together until they form a self-perpetuating continuum.

Like a protecting dream, the narrative aims to divert the disintegrating energy of the father-son relation. In this case, the strategy is to fold three dramas one inside the other. Gawain–Green Knight is made to enclose Gawain–Castle Knight, and in turn (and least convincingly), Morgan la Faye's "enchantment" encloses Gawain–Green Knight. This structure keeps the father and son positions manageably distant, while dispersing desire onto safely recognizable hetero-configurations. Despite the romance's best attempts, however, it cannot make father completely safe. The desire father provokes, the punishment he threatens, and the hostility he inspires together form a loop, in which the subject circles endlessly. At root, embedded in a tangle of defensive transformations, is possibly the darkest and most neurotic representation of the father-son relation in all of Middle English romance. The Green Knight's willful appearance and disappearance, his superhuman power to withstand the loss of his head, and the uncompromising tone of his utterances all place him outside the relational system comprehensible by the subject—and by "comprehensible" I mean both "understandable" and "assimilable," "capable of being integrated." The Green Knight represents aspects, possibilities, that the masculine subject must distance, lest it fail to cohere.

BEYOND NARCISSISM? *YWAIN AND GAWAIN*

On the whole, these romances present a rather unattractive view of the late medieval masculine self—signaled by a narcissistic and neurotic subject, maintaining a conflictual gender identity through complex, contradictory defenses. But if dreams represent the fulfillment of a wish, at least one romance shows that the masculine subject of romance was capable of wishing for a more balanced and integrated masculinity, one wherein fragmentation would be resolved. Freud famously stated as the aim of psychoanalysis: "Where id was, there shall ego be." Nancy Chodorow, arguing for a relational concept of the self, paraphrased the quotation: "Where fragmented internal objects were, there shall harmoniously related objects be; and where false, reactive self was, there shall true, agentic self be."[97] Freud's economical phrasing is more elegantly memorable. But Chodorow's restatement seems to describe the kind of self for which we sense a yearning in *Ywain and Gawain*.

In its essential lines, *Ywain and Gawain* follows Sir Ywain's adventures as he saves, loses, and then regains the lady Alundyne. Here, we are concerned with a small but pivotal part of the story: the conflict causing a temporary rift between Ywain and Alundyne. This estrangement comes about, not because of Another Woman, but because of a man. The homosocial interlude with Gawain costs Ywain, first, his heterosexual relation, and consequently, his sanity—his psychic coherence. In good knightly fashion, he breaks down and flees to the woods.

Gawain represents important conflicts. On a social level, there is the conflict between homosociality and heterosexuality, which Gawain voices explicitly: "A knight who leaves all his sense of chivalric adventure behind, and lies basking in his bed, when he's married a lady, is of no account"

(1457-60).[98] Truly manly knights do not loll about in bed with women, they go seeking aggression and adventure with other men: "Then men will praise you more" (1468). So here the taming of youthful masculinity, a social concern, is posed as a chivalric and moral problem; in Crane's words, it concerns "the ways in which two orientations, toward heterosexual courtship on the one hand and masculine relations on the other, occupy overlapping terrain in men's allegiances."[99] A different reading would detect anxiety, also a social one, about the possibility that homoerotic desire may deflect, replace, or otherwise subvert heteronormative energies. At the level of masculine subjectivity, however, the triangle of conflict between Ywain, Gawain, and Alundyne stands for the subject's inability to integrate erotic desire with different forms of relation in gender identity.

The object of the erotic desire may itself be a little unclear, but that uncertainty is not the main point. Gawain more importantly signifies aggression, eroticized for the subject because it is a source of pleasure. This pleasure also moves the subject away from the recognizable and troubling relational position implied by the heterosexual relation with Alundyne. To break off that relationship, as Alundyne does, solves one problem for the subject but creates others, because so many aspects of an adult masculine identity are invested in it. The consequence is a literally represented flight into illness. From this nadir of madness, Ywain ascends as a new person, rebuilding his identity piece by piece.

The crucial step in his healing, though not the last, is a climactic combat with Gawain, who (the text makes clear) does not recognize him: "If either of them had seen the other, there would have been great love between them; now this was a great marvel, that there might be such true love and great envy together in one man at the same time, as there was between the two of them then" (3519-24). The conflict here emerges in classic psychoanalytic terms: what is actually known appears unknown. Moreover, what becomes unknown is that which is most central, most defining. So the struggle that allows it to be known once more must be a painful one: "Everyone who saw that battle marveled greatly at their strength; they had never on earth seen two such evenly matched knights" (3593-96), "They had never seen such stalwart bravery. The knights gained that honor dearly. Sir Gawain wondered greatly who it was that kept fighting him, and Sir Ywain greatly respected the one who withstood him so strongly" (3599-3604). To end the conflict, the subject must reintegrate the previously disavowed part of the self, and here, reintegration occurs as the two friends are happily reconciled and reunited: "And each took the other in his arms and kissed him many times; then they were both glad and merry" (3672–74). Ywain, having changed, is no longer at risk from the temptation Gawain previously represented.

Mary Flowers Braswell is probably right that at a moral level, the romance traces Ywain's maturing out of self-involvement into caring for the welfare of others.[100] It is also more feasible, psychically, to identify with others if one's own identity is secure first. The subject needs to enter a stage wherein he can properly perceive things outside himself, see them as different from himself, and therefore relate *to* them rather than subsume or repudiate them. Some other romances, such as *Eger and Grime,* represent this reintegration even more vividly through the motif of twin brothers.[101] Crane recommends that at the level of social representation, courtship and comradeship in romance be seen as connected "rather than simply opposing."[102] The interesting thing is that this progress beyond a narcissistic masculinity is still far enough out of the subject's reach that it needs representation in the idealizing structure of literature's dream.

My readings of these romances have referred both their structure and content to the rich and contradictory representational processes of the human mind and personality. Psychoanalysis finds the *origin* of the classic templates in the relations of parent and child, and in the enduring internalized representation of those relations. Yet the fact that these conflicts and defenses characterize very early life in their pure form does not mean that the romances are just a disguised form of early childhood. Rather, these texts represent attempts to rewrite the subconsciously recognized imprints of those conflicts, to relive them in corrected form.

To turn back toward a more recognizably historical issue: the importance of the father imago in the masculine subjectivity suggested by these romances raises the issue of "patriarchy" afresh. In historically understanding the subjective meaning of masculine identity, we cannot ignore the literal importance of paternity and the symbolism of the father-son relationship. Literary evidence shows us that in its subjective dimension, the meanings of "patriarchy" go far beyond simplistic formulae of power, domination, and the repudiation of femininity.

The self-perpetuating cycle of desire and hostility inspired by the father shapes a masculine identity, as do all interior processes, in concert with the cultural vocabulary of a historical period. Premodern European culture was especially rich in father imagery. For many medievalists past and present, that imagery leads us toward the figures of the medieval church and its distinctive triangulation of God as Father, Son, and Holy Spirit, and Mary the mother of all. But the abundance of Christian symbolism in the artistic record of medieval culture, including the romances, should not blind us to the applicability of a system of nonreligious meanings, or make us think that one precedes or excludes the other.[103] To me, the romances suggest that the family drama among late medieval elites was more likely a dramatic exaggeration of Freud's twentieth-century formulation than something completely different in kind.

Relation and desire took different forms; we do not appreciate the varied texture of any subjectivity by reducing "desire" to a monolithic factor. The gendered aspect of relation—masculine (paternal) and feminine (maternal) objects—caused different conflicts expressed in different ways, giving every personality its interestingly problematic character. It is certainly worthy of some pondering that in a culture where selves were most importantly social and had meaning in relation to others, the fantasized or idealized interior self should seek to deny or repudiate relation in its very definition. That this was in addition a masculine self suggests further, we might suppose, the extent of the fragmenting and destabilizing pressures that the social world made on men, whose sense of manliness, especially in their perceived advantage over women, was so strongly invested in a social presence.

Here, I have treated literary evidence pertinent to historical subjectivity in a way that suits its nature: a fantasy genre, representing fantasies, that tells us about an aspect of the historical human condition if approached as a representation of the historical human unconscious. Historians know all about bias, distortion, elision, and outright falsification in the historical record as *conscious* acts, or as the results of conscious acts (such as bombing raids). Perhaps, given the grave consequences of such transformations, historians tend to be reluctant to admit that in other contexts the same processes can be *unconscious*. When we recognize this, we clear new paths toward a better historical understanding.

CONCLUSION

———— ✳ ————

WHAT HAS THIS HISTORIAN DONE
WITH MASCULINITY?

A group of historians, led by Karen Harvey and Alexandra Shepard, have recently weighed in the balance scholarship on the history of masculinity in Britain, and they have found it wanting. When Harvey and Shepard put together the conclusions of scholarship ranging in focus from the sixteenth to the twentieth centuries, it was hard to tell what aspects of British masculinity changed and when—never mind why. Or, as they more diplomatically put the case:

> Are there any discernible longer-term narratives of change in the history of masculinity, and to what extent do they fit within or challenge existing periodization? Long-standing debates in women's history (especially, although not exclusively, over the nature of women's work) have tackled its relationship with established chronologies. The history of masculinity, by contrast, has yet to engage with longer-term chronologies—a project that should undoubtedly be part of its further development as a field.[1]

Of course, we all know the dangers of drawing heavy demarcations across an imagined linear timeline, as if with a blunt pencil, with respect to any historical subject. This is especially true of social history, and truer still the farther back in time we go; not only was the rate of social change slower, but also our perspective blurs, as we get farther away from our present moment and position of observation. But before long, that kind of talk starts to sound like excuses. The status of masculinity as a subject of historical analysis seems a little uncertain if we have such difficulty establishing a chronology.

What does "change" mean with respect to gender, anyway? Feminist gender history concentrating on female subjects often has a clear implicit direction. Especially where we see gender as the legitimating mask of power inequalities, the history of gender becomes the history of power dynamics and, implicitly or explicitly, of women's experience in engaging them. The narrative accommodates varying degrees of both optimism and pessimism. Yet if Judith Bennett thought that the history of women displayed a depressing lack of concrete "transformation" in women's status despite superficial "change," the history of masculinity is at least as uninviting, from the point of view of narrative.[2] Just as "men's history" offers little as to political inspiration, so it often fails to display significant alterations over time. Masculinity history carries no promise of a progressive narrative of engaging "power." Nor did men's social roles pertaining to them as men change greatly, or indeed at all, until the very recent era when women began to gain access to some of them. So what is there to furnish forth a chronology?

Harvey and Shepard believe that part of the reason histories of masculinity do not connect into a legible narrative is that the historians writing them have taken incommensurate approaches. For example, according to Shepard, there is a striking difference between the men portrayed in studies of the period before 1640 and those after 1660, largely because the former studies have relied more heavily on sources that document men's household role and their patriarchal relations with women, while those of the Restoration era have turned largely to cultural (especially literary) evidence. A possibly misleading impression of change from a household masculinity to one grounded in the public sphere has resulted.[3] Problems like these have generated "a degree of dissatisfaction with the dominant emphases in much existing work. Several contributors [to this journal issue] highlight the need for a combination of approaches to enable a comprehensive account that can engage with the questions of long-term change and established chronologies."[4] Harvey and Shepard classify four such disparate approaches: analyses of patriarchal power relations, social history exploring the interaction of gender with social status or class, investigations of masculine selfhood or psychology, and cultural history focusing on representations of manliness.[5] The last category, particularly, lends itself to a disconnection from social reality and therefore from the dynamics of personal interactions. As a result, it seems that "we are witnessing a retreat from analyses of meaning alone"; that "there is a palpable dissatisfaction with an exclusively cultural approach"; that "we need to deal not just in free-floating cultural attributes, but in grounded social or psychic contexts of experience that interact with representations."[6]

Historians of masculinity appear to be realizing that no one of the four approaches Harvey and Shepard have identified can, on its own, support a satisfying analysis or contribute to a meaningful chronology. That is because each one addresses a distinctive facet of gender identity, from the social world "outside" to the psychological world "inside." Masculinity, in contrast, must be comprehended in its full complexity. Michael Roper, the most psychologically oriented contributor to Harvey and Shepard's discussion and (not, I think, coincidentally) the one who works on the most recent period of history, calls for us to "develop approaches that take full account of emotional experience, and which view it in relation to the cultural constructions and social relations of gender, *while not collapsing these various levels onto each other.*"[7] That last phrase is absolutely crucial. To make psychological, social, and cultural approaches all part of one account is to employ the "double discourse," which specifically requires that these various levels *not* be collapsed onto each other. And as far as late medieval evidence permits, that is exactly what I have aimed at in the present book.

As I see it, two versions of masculinity defined the socially performed lives of men in late medieval England. The first, which was normative and aligned with regulatory forces, embodied open honesty, with a transparent concord between the inner and outer person. It emphasized maturity, self-command, moderation: all life strategies that facilitated trust between male peers and helped to cement relations with those of higher and lower rank as well. The social self that conformed to this set of meanings depended utterly on its relation to others.

The other version—rebellious, aggressive, sensual—found its core in the individual self and especially in the male body, whence it reached outward to direct all its connections to the world around. Yet it, too, had its socially cohesive function, among male peers, in situations where a conscious defiance of normative standards was important. Self-gratifying masculinity aligned more with the cultural associations of youth, and custom assumed that a man would progress from it to the mature persona. Yet, in fact, a tension between the two kinds of masculinity continued to be important, not just between two different kinds of men, but within the same man as he related to his peers. Romance literature, beneath its surface stories of selfless heroism and sacrifice, suggests that narcissistic and self-gratifying masculinity was the more deeply buried template in which anxieties about desire and relation, to objects male and female, persisted. The human subject, after all, is capable of outward conformity and inward rebellion at the same time.

This distinction between a normative form of masculinity and a possible variety of others is hardly new. Phrased as a contrast between hegemonic and nonhegemonic masculinities, it was one of the principal contributions of R. W. Connell to the field, and is now part of the discipline's standard vocabulary.[8] I have tried to avoid the plural term "masculinities," despite its currency. The "multiplicity of masculinities" idea is uncomfortably close to that of multiple "genders." When we begin to speak of "genders" rather than "gender," we have lost sight of gender as a system of signification that people *make* and have made "genders" into reified categories to which people *belong*.

Nonetheless, Connell's distinctions redefined our understanding of the relationship of masculinity to patriarchy and power relations. Historians since have adapted Connell's ideas according to their own evidence. Shepard, for example, distinguishes "patriarchal," "subordinate," "antipatriarchal," and "alternative" codes or forms of manhood in Elizabethan and Jacobean England.[9] The patterns I observe in late medieval England look rather similar to what Shepard describes, despite some significant social and economic change between the early and late sixteenth century.

The point, however, is not only to know what (for example) patriarchal and antipatriarchal forms of masculinity looked like, as if we were writing a handbook to identify bird species. What do we do with that information, once we know it? A definitive description of hegemonic masculinity threatens to become, well, hegemonic: exercising a numbing authority over historians, flattening out subtlety and tempting us to assume that our work is done. Harvey and Shepard, however, go even farther: "Hegemonic masculinity will only be a useful category for historians if it is used to analyze relations of power, how these are subjectively experienced, and how this affects behavior rather than simply to identify dominant codes."[10]

This is a splendid prescription, promising to refine historians' concept of masculinity by combining one of the foundational concerns of gender history (relations of power) with the very constituents of gender identity: the subjective experience of maleness in concert with documented acts. Yet it is also a rather tall order, especially for anyone working on the Middle Ages, whose problems of evidence I have noted over previous chapters. How are we to do it? More urgently, since this is the conclusion to the book I wrote, have I done it?

Finding gendered meaning in the actions, disputes, and desires of men, however documented, is an act of inference and interpretation. Medieval sources are not often explicit about what appearances, deeds, or tendencies they consider manly or unmanly. Much of my analysis, therefore, has found masculinity in the ways men most often behaved, or expected each other to behave, or in what I perceive them to have wanted for themselves—all coming from the discourse they generated. Masculinity has also emerged from norms and ideals about men's bodies, about their management and uses of them, and about the governance of their desires, detectable in discourse that directly addressed them. Since historical evidence, of any kind, very rarely speaks explicitly to the questions historians ask of it, the interpretive move I have made is not really far out of the mainstream of historical methods. Using literary sources as I have, to illuminate a general historical question through a technique that looks for meanings latent in the textual surface, may seem less conventional, but it is another instance of bringing an appropriate conceptual framework to a special set of evidence.

An individual man's masculine identity consisted of his particular set of conscious *and* unconscious responses to an array of idiosyncratic *and* collective factors. Even without reference to private subjectivity, we should have no difficulty seeing the individuality of the masculine social self in late medieval England, as no two men even of the same community could possibly have experienced the same combination of relational contacts (with kin, neighbors, masters) that thus defined them. Yet, although the private self left far fainter traces in the record and is harder to document, it belongs in our analysis as well. Margaret Paston, who—using the terms of self-knowledge—urged caution about taking vows of celibacy, also wrote of her son John II, "I hope he shall ever know himself"; her husband had expressed the same sentiment, by way of reproving advice, directly to John at about the same time.[11] As Margaret's concern about the priestly life showed, sexuality was part of that self-knowledge and therefore impinged on so many parts of a masculine private and social identity (even when sexual performance was conspicuously absent) that discussing it in isolation is impractical. I have not attempted to do so.

Making this analysis measure up to Harvey and Shepard's requirement of explaining behavior according to the subjective experience of relations of power will require even more willingness to push the evidence than I have ventured here. But we can at least find a place to start by noting possible points of contact between self and society: features of late medieval England that might have made the masculine subjectivities of the era possibly characteristic of it. Attention to them allows us to historicize medieval masculine identity in its private, as well as social, dimensions.

The first of these, involving limitation more than possibility, concerns religion. Readers might think that even (or especially) in my treatment of clerics, I have portrayed a rather unspiritual, or at least indifferently pious, late Middle Ages. Surely individual men's responses to the discourse and values of western Christianity must have shaped their sense of manliness? Yet the contributions of religious values are difficult to assess with respect to a society where religious discourse was everywhere and formed the very framework of legal and regulatory attitudes. In the world of social relations, the values of honest masculinity coincided with those of Christian charity, but whether the religion produced the values is quite another question. Similarly, where the disciplining rationale of secular and religious authority amounted to the same thing, to what degree did rebellious masculinity react to one, rather than to the other?

There is another methodological dimension to the problem. Pastoral and devotional treatises do not primarily aim, for example, to tell their audiences what is manly or unmanly, but what is sinful or not sinful. Even this kind of source, moreover, is too prescriptive to form a main evidence base. Religious discourse seems to speak most clearly concerning gender where it is least occupied with the *experience* of religion. Attestations of personal religious experience, on the other hand, come from men who were literally religious: in orders. We lack evidence about the combination of gender and piety in the subjective experience of ordinary *lay*men, who would be the best test case. The really interesting question about piety and masculinity is: To what degree did ordinary men experience their efforts at fulfillment of normative masculinity as a religious, or pious, endeavor? Yet this is a question for another project.

Piety, of course, had its public and private dimensions, and its most personal aspects were exactly those most difficult for anyone other than the pious subject to understand. The private self, and the private experience of masculinity, similarly defy generalization. We can, however, bring together what we know about late medieval masculinity, about the English society around it, and about the common ground of private subjectivity suggested by literature. The narcissistic features of the fantasized subjectivity legible in romance not only are not "ahistorical"; they make more sense when we consider historical, especially social, context. (To do this we do not need to speculate pointlessly about details of infant-mother relationships we cannot ever hope to know. Whatever happened in early childhood was enough to get certain results.) English society of the late Middle Ages did nothing to counteract the narcissistic aspects of a masculine identity; rather, it reinforced them. It did so not through positive endorsement, but by applying pressures that elicited narcissism as a defense. Medieval society highly invested masculine identity in a form of social performance that demanded the appearance, and often the reality, of open honesty, yet also by sheer necessity required careful guardedness. (Perhaps more depended, materially and symbolically, on this balancing act at higher social levels. Yet even among ordinary villagers, everyday affairs would have generated similar anxieties.) Moreover, the performance took place within communities with very little privacy, where people tended to know each other's business and to make sure everyone else knew it as well, where the "common voice and fame" could make or unmake a man, and where continual compromises, deferences, and tactful silences kept one's connections in the service hierarchy intact. In such a world, maintaining a sense of self that was a self—keeping any sense of anything being one's own—was no small feat for anyone; having a social self meant being pulled in many directions at once, as if in danger of coming apart; yet one could not be a man without that experience. No wonder, then, that the idealized self of literary fantasy denied relation, connection, need, and desire.

CHRONOLOGY

In 1994, the same year John Tosh first asked what historians should do with masculinity, Lyndal Roper cautioned against attaching explanatory schemes of changes in subjectivity to the "chestnuts" of periodization, such as the Renaissance or, more pertinently here, the Reformation.[12] Yet we are left without much capacity to envision *any* form of change, large or small, if we place all external factors out of the picture. If we want our apprehension of masculinity-as-identity to be rounded and subtle, we need to consider what mutable social features are most important to gender identity.

Both the prescriptive and the subjective components of gender are, in theory, susceptible to changes over time. In both cases, change depends to some extent on external factors, but often somewhat inscrutably. This study has not documented distinctive changes between 1350 and 1530 linked to the larger historically visible social trends of this period in England. However, this does not mean that the period was insignificant in the history of masculinity. The two centuries following the Black Death, rather, show us the degree of struggle and contest prevailing in a society that had undergone major social disruptions. They encompass a social world (late medieval or midpremodern as one wishes) recognizably different in some way from what came before or after, debatable as the exact definition of "before" or "after" might be. They might prompt us to think about possible links between gender and demography.

What happens at this level? Changes in family structure, in family size, in ages of weaning; in rates of infant and maternal (postpartum) mortality; in living arrangements—whether, for example, parents and children sleep separately or together. These features influence the closeness, the amount even, of physical contact in the mother-infant relationship and frame young children's experience of sexual difference, Oedipal conflict, and the sexuality of adults. The average age of leaving home, the amount of contact with the opposite sex during adolescence and young adulthood, the degrees of freedom and autonomy for making life decisions accorded one in early adulthood, the age of admittance to community responsibilities: all these determine the nature of peer group socialization and the shape of a mature sexuality. Age at marriage and the average length of marriage influence perceptions of adult gender identity. Someone needs to write a book assessing whether or not appreciable change took place in these features, considered together and as contributing to one unitary question, in late medieval England.

Between Black Death and Reformation, the essential nature of English community life did not change enough for the socially grounded aspects of masculinity to look much different in 1530 than they had in 1350. Yet we can still entertain the possibility of some historical change, possibly quite important, even if we cannot explain all of it through neat chains of causation. Marjorie McIntosh's thesis about the regulation of misbehavior in fifteenth- and sixteenth-century England strikes me as rather important in this respect, especially when we also consider Alexandra Shepard's recent emphasis on the importance of misbehavior for masculine identity in late-sixteenth-century England.[13] The increase in surveillance, by local and regional courts, which McIntosh perceives in the mid-fifteenth century, would have coincided with the extinction of older regulatory customs such as tithing and pledging. In effect, a custom that directly connected manhood with a kind of communitarian responsibility and with explicit links with other men gave way to a system in which the more vividly apparent association between masculinity and regulatory authority was an opposition. Or, to put it more subtly, routes to normative (or, as Shepard would call it, "patriarchal") manhood became less easy to conceive, less apparent, for a wider social span of men. Where the balance of regulation swung toward institutionalized authority, rather than the self-regulation of the small group, a man's investment in manly sobriety did not decrease; indeed, depending on the effectiveness of the authorities—which, after all, were composed of one's neighbors—it became a more urgent matter. Yet it was also a *different* investment, which must have involved a different view of homosocial relations. The contrast between the cohesive force of mature manhood and that of masculine rebellion against regulatory authority might have become all the sharper.

These institutional changes are not the only ones that might be responsible for possible alterations in the texture of both social and private masculinity. Indeed, though this study has not given an impression of much change over time, the shifts it notices underscore an important point: we cannot assume that changes affecting gender came from any one part of a culture. We have already seen that the shift in the meaning of one word, "truth," in the late fourteenth century signified a much more profound cultural change that altered the very basis of knowledge underlying institutional and customary practice. Similarly, the shift in practice in the church courts' treatment of defamation in the late fifteenth century meant that people could understand injuries to reputation (and therefore reputation itself) in a different way. This surely also meant a change (if not a total one) in self-concept. Certain aspects of gender are more amenable to historical change than others, and the route from society to self is neither as direct nor as unidirectional as we sometimes think.

THE OTHER HALF

Some readers might consider this book to be as concerned with sex as with gender, in that it has primarily taken men as its subjects and discussed masculinity as something solely concerning male lives and social position. It has not, for example, much entertained the possibility that women might display something we recognize as masculinity. Given my treatment of masculinity as a set of meanings, and my assertion that sex and gender are not the same, this may give readers pause. However, particularly at this stage of scholarship, it makes sense to take evidence about men as evidence about masculinity's meanings, because for those meanings to be relevant to human subjects, we have to see them being lived out. To overdraw women's access to those meanings would produce a distorted picture, especially for medieval life; women's social disadvantage meant that they had far less opportunity to enter the interpersonal dynamic where most of the retrievable meanings of masculinity operated. In English society, men worked out masculinity most importantly among themselves; ultimately, that was where the really vital interactions and transactions took place. It was in this social sense, among men, that masculinity most literally meant "not being like a woman," because of the symbolically larger, more variegated, more flexible social self that a man could develop. Having that bigger social self was a primary determinant of one's masculine identity.

There is a common notion that masculinity and femininity are interdependent, that one depends on the other for its meaning.[14] I am somewhat doubtful about the value of this scheme of "relationality" for the era I study.[15] Given the very different status and value of maleness and femaleness in premodern society, I do not think that commensurate equivalents in medieval terms for masculinity and femininity exist. What we mean by *masculinity* corresponds best to medieval "manliness" or "manhood"—both of which blurred together maleness, desirable qualities associated with males, and humanity itself. No corresponding term existed with reference to females. "Womanly" was not the female version of "manly"; its possible positive meanings were totally different in character, in what they implied about the value of the person described. The negative meanings of unmanliness (or not-enough-manliness) often resembled negative stereotypes about women, and so it is tempting to see masculinity and femininity as opposites, or at least two halves of a whole. Yet the truth may be that these two entities overlap, disjoin, and point in different directions at different angles, like two railroad tracks that cross, join, and separate, run parallel for a while, and eventually diverge, and that this was true in the late Middle Ages as in our own era.

Yet, in contrast to *femininity*, the role of *women* in helping to define and maintain masculinity, both as human actors and as the objects of male fantasies and desires, was beyond doubt. It was not simple. Women were not just a currency of exchange, nor just the mediators who structured men's social and emotional relations with each other. Those anthropological and literary formulas describe women's role only in the most general terms, sadly reducing and caricaturing its full complexity. As mothers, English women contributed to men's gender identity in ways detectable in other eras and cultures also. Within marriage, their labor could stabilize and augment the substance of their husbands, just as their mismanagement might diminish it.[16] The choices that women made about how to behave as wives or as daughters bore directly on the social selves of the men closest to them. To a certain degree here also, late medieval England had much in common with other places and eras.

I chose the word "choices," however, to remind us that England was also somewhat distinctive. English women of the fourteenth and fifteenth centuries did not enjoy anything like sexual equality, of course, but in comparison to women in many other parts of Europe, a broad social band of them had more room to maneuver. The absence of rigid spatial sex segregation in *most* situations; the visibility and physical mobility of women in English communities, wherein their talk regulated men's reputations and also other women's; the commonness of female youths in service alongside young men; their *relative* degree of choice in selecting marriage partners; and their access to certain legal institutions in their own right—all these are one side of the picture. Despite these apparent advantages, however, most English women were still nonpersons before the common law, sanctions on their husbands' mistreatment of them were hazy at best, women's education ended earlier than that of men, and women's labor was less well rewarded (to name only a few aspects of their subjection). We should, I think, consider carefully how we might relate the values and behavioral patterns of English masculinity I have described to the status of English *women*, to the particular combination of openness and restriction that defined women's place in England.

In such a society, where women were second-class but far from social nonentities, a masculinity ideology that depended on clear distinctions between the specific places men and women could be, or the specific actions they could perform, could not exist. Here, the Mediterranean regions provide the starkest contrast with England in the European world. Both historical evidence and modern anthropology show much sharper enduring divisions between men and women in the Mediterranean, especially between the "inside" space of the family home and the "outside" space of the village square or the tavern. Men's place is "outside," with other men. The division may exist *within* a space, too: Stanley Brandes observed that in 1970s Andalusia, a man did not pick things up that had fallen to the ground.[17] Late medieval England cannot have been quite like this. While it certainly preserved distinctions between what was fitting for men and women to do, English masculinity relied less on stark oppositions (inside/outside, dominant/submissive, exuberant/modest) and more on degrees; less on performative practices (men tell only these stories, sing only these songs) and more on symbolic associations that lined up far less neatly with oppositions between male and female:

open simplicity = masculine   deviousness = unmasculine (= feminine?)
self-command = masculine   sensuality = feminine (= unmasculine?)

Part of the reason, again, must have been that women were not kept out of view in "their" places and actions, but mixed with men even though they did not meet them as peers.

So the history of masculinity will be stronger when it takes more account of women. It will, for a start, be more strongly connected to larger historiographical concerns. Consider, for example, Mary S. Hartman's provocative recent argument that the distinctive economic and social development of northwestern European society is attributable to the distinctive northwest European marriage pattern. In the late Middle Ages, Hartman claims, restraint of illicit sexual activity increased in order to protect the single working women whose contribution to the economy was so important. That restraint came not only from authorities, but also from the self-restraint of young men and women themselves, who had to adjust to the reality of late marriage: it was not the safely married patriarchs, but the bachelors who walked the line that delineated this culture, and they walked it with women at their side.[18] A young man, no matter what his male peers said, had to make room for a young woman's wishes to remain chaste and respectable, not because terrible punishment threatened from above, but because the secure foundation of the couple's own household future depended on it.

Masculinity, for these young men, did involve "relations of power," both to women and to other men. But our understanding of those power relations is incomplete if we look only for evidence of their clear enactment in forms of behavior. Hartman's thesis highlights the disjuncture between an ideal of patriarchal control of women and the more complex reality of mutual dependence. So in order to understand the masculinity of these subordinate men, we also have to consider their attitudes toward their sexual and social partners—which, for reasons of solid social history, simply could not be acted out. They had to remain fantasies, daydreams, and emotional resentments: in other words, "subjective experience." We are unlikely to find a personal diary in which a young unmarried layman in late medieval England confesses such longings and jealousies about women, friends, and masters. But we actually do not need that extraordinary document to begin rising to Harvey and Shepard's challenge. Hartman has dramatically highlighted the importance of women to that world of men—not just an economic importance, but (perhaps even "therefore"?) a psychological one too. Allowing ourselves to give ordinary men of late medieval England that psychological dimension and, yes, even to speculate about it restores the possibility of conceiving real motivations for their behavior. In turn, it makes us realize the role of gender in long-term chronologies that may have nothing to do with the well-worn milestones. We will gain a more accurate picture of historical change in the experience of the majority of ordinary European men and women.

Those will be more complex chronologies, of course. They will resemble a late Impressionist painting, where strokes of different colors look strangely discordant on close inspection and resolve into patterns only when we stand back. But first we have to do the close work; so much of the canvas is still bare.

Notes

INTRODUCTION

1. For a recent comment on this aspect of gender history, with pertinent bibliography, see Karen Harvey, "The History of Masculinity, circa 1650–1800," *Journal of British Studies* 44, no. 2 (2005): 296–97.

2. For a helpful guide to this literature, see Judith Bennett, "Medieval Women in Modern Perspective," in *Women's History in Global Perspective*, vol. 2, ed. Bonnie G. Smith (Urbana: University of Illinois Press, 2005).

3. David Gilmore, *Manhood in the Making: Cultural Concepts of Masculinity* (New Haven, Conn.: Yale University Press, 1990); R. W. Connell, *Masculinities* (Berkeley and Los Angeles: University of California Press, 1995); M. C. Gutmann, "Trafficking in Men: The Anthropology of Masculinity," *Annual Review of Anthropology* 26 (1997): 385–409.

4. Note the emphasis, for example, in John Tosh, "What Should Historians Do with Masculinity? Reflections on Nineteenth-Century Britain," *History Workshop Journal* 38 (1994): 179–202.

5. Nancy F. Partner, "The Hidden Self: Psychoanalysis and the Textual Unconscious," in *Writing Medieval History*, ed. Nancy F. Partner (London: Hodder Arnold, 2005), 42.

6. Jeffrey Jerome Cohen and Bonnie Wheeler, eds., *Becoming Male in the Middle Ages* (New York: Garland, 1997); D. M. Hadley, ed., *Masculinity in Medieval Europe* (London: Longman, 1999); Clare A. Lees, ed., *Medieval Masculinities: Regarding Men in the Middle Ages* (Minneapolis: University of Minnesota Press, 1994); Jacqueline Murray, ed., *Conflicted Identities and Multiple Masculinities: Men in the Medieval West* (New York: Garland, 1999).

7. Ruth Mazo Karras, *From Boys to Men: Formations of Masculinity in Late Medieval Europe* (Philadelphia: University of Pennsylvania Press, 2003).

8. Elizabeth Foyster, *Manhood in Early Modern England: Honour, Sex and Marriage* (London: Longman, 2000); Alexandra Shepard, *Meanings of Manhood in Early Modern England* (Oxford: Oxford University Press, 2003).

9. I have analyzed this historiographical phenomenon in detail in my "Meanings of Masculinity in Late Medieval England: Self, Body and Society" (Ph.D. diss., McGill University, 2004), 53–89.

10. George Devereux, "The Argument," in *Ethnopsychoanalysis: Psychoanalysis and Anthropology as Complementary Frames of Reference* (Berkeley and Los Angeles: University of California Press, 1978), 1-19. See also chapter 1 below.

CHAPTER ONE

1. This is the impression left by the various articles in *Fifteenth-Century Attitudes: Perceptions of Society in Late Medieval England,* ed. Rosemary Horrox (Cambridge: Cambridge University Press, 1994). See also Steven Justice, *Writing and Rebellion: England in 1381* (Berkeley and Los Angeles: University of California Press, 1994), 13-66, on the degree of peasants' familiarity with written culture in the late fourteenth century. For a cautious assessment, see Philippa Maddern, "Social Mobility," in *A Social History of England, 1200-1500,* ed. Rosemary Horrox and W. Mark Ormrod (Cambridge: Cambridge University Press, 2006), 113-33.

2. L. R. Poos, *A Rural Society after the Black Death: Essex, 1350-1525* (Cambridge: Cambridge University Press, 1991), 11-31.

3. Poos, *A Rural Society,* 159-80, 183-206; Maryanne Kowaleski, "Singlewomen in Medieval and Early Modern Europe: The Demographic Perspective," in *Singlewomen in the European Past, 1250-1800,* ed. Judith M. Bennett and Amy M. Froide (Philadelphia: University of Pennsylvania Press, 1999), 46-47; P. J. P. Goldberg, "Migration, Youth and Gender in Later Medieval England," in *Youth in the Middle Ages,* ed. P. J. P. Goldberg and Felicity Riddy (York: York Medieval Press, 2004), 86-90.

4. Christopher Dyer, *Making a Living in the Middle Ages: The People of Britain, 850-1520* (New Haven, Conn.: Yale University Press, 2002), 272-73.

5. Marjorie McIntosh, *Autonomy and Community: The Royal Manor of Havering, 1200-1500* (Cambridge: Cambridge University Press, 1986), 77; Dyer, *Making a Living in the Middle Ages,* 294.

6. See Dyer, *Making a Living in the Middle Ages,* 354-55, on possible changes in family life and inheritance patterns: "Everywhere individuals broke free from some of the constraints of family and kinship."

7. Edwin Brezette DeWindt, *Land and People in Holywell-Cum-Needingworth: Structures of Tenure and Patterns of Social Organization in an East Midlands Village, 1252-1457* (Toronto: Pontifical Institute of Mediaeval Studies, 1972); Christopher Dyer, "The English Medieval Village Community and Its Decline," *Journal of British Studies* 33 (1994): 407-29; Zvi Razi, "Family, Land, and the Village Community in Later Medieval England," *Past and Present* 93 (1981): 3-36; Zvi Razi, *Life, Marriage and Death in a Medieval Parish: Economy, Society and Demography in Halesowen, 1270-1400* (Cambridge: Cambridge University Press, 1980); J. A. Raftis, *Warboys: Two Hundred Years in the Life of an English Mediaeval Village* (Toronto: Pontifical Institute of Mediaeval Studies, 1974).

8. Judith Bennett, *Women in the Medieval English Countryside: Gender and Household in Brigstock before the Plague* (New York: Oxford University Press, 1987), 24, 37-38; Judith Bennett, *A Medieval Life: Cecilia Penifader of Brigstock, c. 1295-1344* (Boston: McGraw-Hill College, 1999), 101-2, 144; Sherri Olson, *A Chronicle of All That Happens: Voices from the Village Court in Medieval England* (Toronto: Pontifical Institute of Mediaeval Studies, 1996), 46-55.

9. Bennett, *Women in the Medieval English Countryside,* 75-76; William Hudson, ed., *Leet Jurisdiction in the City of Norwich during the XIIIth and XIVth Centuries* (Publications of the Selden Society, London: Quaritch, 1892).

10. Olson, *A Chronicle,* 46.

11. Ibid., 47; Dyer, *Making a Living in the Middle Ages,* 286.

12. The plague's effects on these aspects of marital and family life in rural society are incompletely understood: Dyer, *Making a Living in the Middle Ages,* 276-77.

13. Olson, *A Chronicle*, 176–77, 194–95; Malcolm Clark Burson, "The Early Fifteenth-Century Clergy in the Archdeaconry of Exeter: Social Origins and Roles" (Ph.D. diss., University of Toronto, 1979), 343–44; McIntosh, *Autonomy and Community*, 249, including n. 103.

14. Raftis, *Warboys*, 216–17.

15. Ian Blanchard, "Social Structure and Social Organization in an English Village at the Close of the Middle Ages: Chewton 1526," in *The Salt of Common Life: Individuality and Choice in the Medieval Town, Countryside, and Church: Essays Presented to J. Ambrose Raftis*, ed. Edwin Brezette DeWindt (Kalamazoo, Mich.: Medieval Institute Publications, 1995), 327–30.

16. Raftis, *Warboys*, 217; Marjorie McIntosh, *Controlling Misbehavior in England, 1370–1600* (Cambridge: Cambridge University Press, 1998).

17. Poos, *A Rural Society*, 210–12, 231–62; McIntosh, *Autonomy and Community*, 77; Raftis, *Warboys*, 219–20.

18. Peter Coss discusses the period under the rubric of a "crisis of authority" in "An Age of Deference," in *A Social History of England*, ed. Rosemary Horrox and W. Mark Ormrod (Cambridge: Cambridge University Press, 2006), 60–70.

19. Bruce M. S. Campbell, "The Land," in *A Social History of England*, ed. Rosemary Horrox and W. Mark Ormrod (Cambridge: Cambridge University Press, 2006), 233.

20. Rodney Hilton, "The Social Structure of the Village," in *The English Peasantry in the Later Middle Ages: The Ford Lectures for 1973 and Related Studies* (Oxford: Clarendon Press, 1975); Christopher Dyer, "Small Places with Large Consequences: The Importance of Small Towns in England, 1000–1540," *Historical Research* 75, no. 187 (2002): 8–10, 18–20.

21. P. J. P. Goldberg, "What Was a Servant?" in *Concepts and Patterns of Service in the Later Middle Ages*, ed. A. Curry and E. Matthew (Woodbridge, U.K.: Boydell Press, 2000), 7.

22. Karras, *From Boys to Men*, 124.

23. Jennifer Kermode, *Medieval Merchants: York, Beverley, and Hull in the Later Middle Ages* (Cambridge: Cambridge University Press, 1998), 81–82.

24. David Gary Shaw, *The Creation of a Community: The City of Wells in the Middle Ages* (New York: Oxford University Press, 1993), 97.

25. Sylvia Lettice Thrupp, *The Merchant Class of Medieval London, 1300–1500* (1948; repr. Ann Arbor, Mich.: University of Michigan Press, 1962), 192; Karras, *From Boys to Men*, 122.

26. Barbara Hanawalt, "'The Childe of Bristowe' and the Making of Middle-Class Adolescence," in *Bodies and Disciplines: Intersections of Literature and History in Fifteenth-Century England*, eds. Barbara A. Hanawalt and David Wallace (Minneapolis: University of Minnesota Press, 1996), 166, 170; Karras, *From Boys to Men*, 113, 116–17, 149–50; M. E. Wiesner, "Wandervogels and Women: Journeymen's Concepts of Masculinity in Early Modern Germany," *Journal of Social History* 24, no. 4 (1991): 767–82; Heather Swanson, *Medieval Artisans: An Urban Class in Late Medieval England* (Oxford: Basil Blackwell, 1989), 115; Goldberg, "Migration, Youth and Gender," 97–98.

27. See Mary S. Hartman, *The Household and the Making of History: A Subversive View of the Western Past* (Cambridge: Cambridge University Press, 2004).

28. Michael Rocke, *Forbidden Friendships: Homosexuality and Male Culture in Renaissance Florence* (New York: Oxford University Press, 1996), 120–22, 131.

29. Coss, "An Age of Deference," 71–72.

30. Dyer, "Small Places," 23.

31. E. J. Dobson, "The Etymology and Meaning of Boy," *Medium aevum* 9 (1940): 121–54.

32. This is the premise underlying the analysis in Karras, *From Boys to Men*.

33. See also chapter 3 below.

34. Barbara Hanawalt, *Growing up in Medieval London: The Experience of Childhood in History* (New York: Oxford University Press, 1993), 109–11.

35. Karras, *From Boys to Men*, 13.

36. Ibid., 109.

37. Alexandra Shepard, "Manhood, Credit and Patriarchy in Early Modern England c. 1580-1640," *Past and Present* 167 (2000): 90-102 especially.

38. Karras, *From Boys to Men*, 110, 29.

39. Horrox, *Fifteenth-Century Attitudes*, 61, 71.

40. Karras, *From Boys to Men*, 124, emphasis added.

41. Taunton, Somerset Archive and Record Service (SARS), D/D/Ca/2, pp. 102-3.

42. Neil J. Smelser and Robert S. Wallerstein, "Psychoanalysis and Sociology," in *The Social Edges of Psychoanalysis* (Berkeley and Los Angeles: University of California Press, 1999), 4.

43. Devereux, "The Argument," 3, 6-7, 12-13.

44. "The Mirror of the Periods of Man's Life, or Bids of the Virtues and Vices for the Soul of Man," in *Hymns to the Virgin & Christ, the Parliament of Devils, and Other Religious Poems, Chiefly from the Archbishop of Canterbury's Lambeth MS. No. 853*, ed. Frederick James Furnivall, Early English Text Society O.S. 24 (London: N. Trübner, 1867), 60-62, 66.

45. David Gary Shaw, *Necessary Conjunctions: The Social Self in the Middle Ages* (New York: Palgrave Macmillan, 2005), 15.

46. Shaw, *Necessary Conjunctions*, 4.

47. Catherine MacKinnon, quoted in A. Mark Liddle, "State, Masculinities and Law: Some Comments on Gender and English State-Formation," *British Journal of Criminology* 36 (1996): 361.

48. Charles Donahue, Jr., "Female Plaintiffs in Marriage Cases in the Court of York in the Late Middle Ages: What Can We Learn from the Numbers?" in *Wife and Widow in Medieval England*, ed. Sue Sheridan Walker, (Ann Arbor: University of Michigan Press, 1993), 184-85.

49. Kathleen Preston and Kimberley Stanley, " 'What's the Worst Thing? . . . ' Gender-Directed Insults," *Sex Roles* 17, no. 3/4 (1987): 209-19.

50. Richard M. Wunderli, *London Church Courts and Society on the Eve of the Reformation* (Cambridge, Mass.: Medieval Academy of America, 1981), 83-84.

51. R. H. Helmholz, ed., *Select Cases on Defamation to 1600* (London: Selden Society, 1985), xxvii, xxxii-xxxiii.

52. London Metropolitan Archives (LMA), DL/C/206, fol. 326r.

53. Thomas Andrew Green, *Verdict According to Conscience: Perspectives on the English Criminal Trial Jury, 1200-1800* (Chicago: University of Chicago Press, 1985), 30, 35. Green (42) cites the only case I know where an English jury considered verbal insult sufficient provocation, or rather considered the defendant's physical reaction as self-defense; it dates from 1324.

54. C. A. Haigh, "Slander and the Church Courts in the Sixteenth Century," *Transactions of the Lancashire and Cheshire Antiquarian Society* 78 (1975): 1-13; J. A. Sharpe, *Defamation and Sexual Slander in Early Modern England: The Church Courts at York*, Borthwick Papers, no. 58 (York: University of York, Borthwick Institute of Historical Research, 1980); L. R. Poos, "Sex, Lies, and the Church Courts of Pre-Reformation England," *Journal of Interdisciplinary History* 35 (1995): 585-607; Laura Gowing, *Domestic Dangers: Women, Words, and Sex in Early Modern London* (Oxford: Clarendon Press, 1996), 60-74.

55. LMA, DL/C/205, fol. 158v. I am grateful to Shannon McSheffrey for allowing me to consult her unpublished transcript of this deposition book.

56. LMA, DL/C/205, fols. 305r-305v.

57. This study draws on the following diocesan collections: Bath and Wells, 1505-15, 1526-9, 1530; Canterbury, 1410-21, 1449-57; Exeter, 1510-18; London, 1467-76, 1488-94, 1510-16; Norwich (Basil Cozens-Hardy and Edward Darley Stone, eds., *Norwich Consistory Court Depositions, 1499-1512 and 1518-1530* [London: Fakenham and Reading Wyman & Sons, 1938]); and York. The survival of cause papers for York diocese is much better than elsewhere, permitting a fairly even sample between 1350 and 1532. Hardly any pre-1530 depositions exist for the

dioceses of Chichester, Durham, Lichfield, and Lincoln. I hope in future to examine the remaining London depositions from the 1520s and those for the exempt jurisdiction of St. Albans after 1515.

58. Helmholz, *Select Cases on Defamation*, xxvi-xxx.

59. Ibid., xliii-xlv.

60. Sharpe, *Defamation and Sexual Slander*, 28-29; Poos, "Sex, Lies, and the Church Courts of Pre-Reformation England," 592.

61. Shaw, *Necessary Conjunctions*, 130.

62. Faramerz Dabhoiwala, "The Construction of Honour, Reputation and Status in Late Seventeenth- and Early Eighteenth-Century England," *Transactions of the Royal Historical Society*, 6th series 6 (1996): 201-13; Elizabeth Foyster, "Male Honour, Social Control and Wife Beating in Late Stuart England," *Transactions of the Royal Historical Society*, 6th series 6 (1996): 215-24; Laura Gowing, "Women, Status and the Popular Culture of Dishonour," *Transactions of the Royal Historical Society*, 6th series 6 (1996): 227-34; Garthine Walker, "Expanding the Boundaries of Female Honour in Early Modern England," *Transactions of the Royal Historical Society*, 6th series 6 (1996): 235-45; Bernard Capp, "The Double Standard Revisited: Plebeian Women and Male Sexual Reputation in Early Modern England," *Past and Present* 162 (1999): 70-100; Shepard, "Manhood, Credit and Patriarchy." Cordelia Beattie, "The Problem of Women's Work Identities in Post-Black Death England," in *The Problem of Labour in Fourteenth-Century England*, ed. J. Bothwell, P. J. P. Goldberg, and W. M. Ormrod (York: York Medieval Press, 2000), provides an analogous recent analysis of medieval evidence.

63. Canterbury Cathedral Archives (CCA), X.10.1, fol. 84r.

64. Philippa Maddern, *Violence and Social Order: East Anglia, 1422-1442* (Oxford and New York: Clarendon Press; Oxford University Press, 1992), 130.

65. CCA, X.10.1, fols. 25v-27r.

66. CCA, X.10.1, fols. 26r-27r.

67. CCA, X.10.1, fols. 25v, 26v.

68. Helmholz, *Select Cases on Defamation*, xli-ii.

69. CCA, X.10.1, fol. 102v.

70. Maddern, *Violence and Social Order*, 130.

71. Alec Reginald Myers, *London in the Age of Chaucer* (Norman: University of Oklahoma Press, 1972), 148-49.

72. Maddern, *Violence and Social Order*, 132.

73. The National Archives of the United Kingdom, Public Record Office, Kew (TNAUK: PRO), C1/46/187.

74. LMA, DL/C/206, fol. 21v.

75. LMA, DL/C/206, fol. 42r.

76. LMA, DL/C/206, fol. 42r.

77. Helmholz, *Select Cases on Defamation*, 6; Cozens-Hardy and Stone, *Norwich Depositions*, no. 54.

78. The side glance also might suggest hostile envy: J. A. Burrow, *Gestures and Looks in Medieval Narrative* (Cambridge: Cambridge University Press, 2002), 88, 98-99.

79. CCA, X.10.1, fol. 26r.

80. York, Borthwick Institute for Archives (BIA), CP.F 27/2, /4.

81. LMA, DL/C/206, fol. 152v.

82. Ibid., fol. 160r.

83. Ibid., fol. 163v.

84. Richard Firth Green, *A Crisis of Truth: Literature and Law in Ricardian England* (Philadelphia: University of Pennsylvania Press, 1999), 118.

85. CCA, X.10.1, fol. 66r.

86. Maddern, *Violence and Social Order*, 85.

87. Norman Davis, ed., *Paston Letters and Papers of the Fifteenth Century*, vol. 1 (Oxford: Clarendon Press, 1971), 225.

88. TNAUK: PRO, C1/209/37.

89. SARS, D/D/Ca/2, pp. 102-3.

90. Cozens-Hardy and Stone, *Norwich Depositions*, no. 266.

91. London Guildhall Library (LGL) 9065, fol. 243, quoted in Poos, *A Rural Society*, 84.

92. Cozens-Hardy and Stone, *Norwich Depositions*, no. 264.

93. J. Addison, quoted in Liddle, "State, Masculinities and Law," 374.

94. SARS, D/D/Ca/2, pp. 102-3.

95. See the *Oxford English Dictionary*, 2d ed. (1989), entry for "trueman."

96. Green, *A Crisis of Truth*, 1-40, especially 29.

97. Norman Davis, ed., *Paston Letters and Papers of the Fifteenth Century*, vol. 2 (Oxford: Clarendon Press, 1976), 329.

98. James M. Dean, ed., *On the Times* (Medieval Institute Publications, 1996; available at http://www.lib.rochester.edu/camelot/teams/times.htm).

99. Green, *A Crisis of Truth*, 154-64.

100. SARS, D/D/Ca/1a, p. 131.

101. Davis, *Paston Letters*, vol. 2, 199-200.

102. Edward Wilson, ed., *The Winchester Anthology* (Woodbridge, U.K.: Boydell Press, 1981), fols. 75v, 76r; William Horman, *Vulgaria*, Pollard and Redgrave Short-Title Catalogue, no. 13811 (London: 1519), fols. 65v, 66v.

103. Neil Daniel, ed., *The Tale of Gamelyn* (Ann Arbor, Mich.: University Microfilms, 1970), pp. 79-80, ll. 369-86.

104. McIntosh, *Autonomy and Community*, 195.

105. *Cymbeline*, act ii, scene 3, lines 74-76 (available at http://www.shakespeare-online.com/plays/cymbel_2_3.html). Lionel Trilling (*Sincerity and Authenticity* [Cambridge, Mass.: Harvard University Press, 1972], 4) finds the same meanings in Polonius's "To thine own self be true."

106. Trilling, *Sincerity and Authenticity*, 13, 20-25.

107. Green, *A Crisis of Truth*, 385.

108. Ibid., 378-79.

109. Jane Austen, *Pride and Prejudice* (New York: Modern Library, 1995), 30; Michael Zakim, "Sartorial Ideologies: From Homespun to Ready-Made," *American Historical Review* 106, no. 5 (2001): 1559.

110. Trilling, *Sincerity and Authenticity*, 112.

111. John Tosh, *A Man's Place: Masculinity and the Middle-Class Home in Victorian England* (New Haven, Conn.: Yale University Press, 1999), 180.

112. John Williams and Regan Taylor, "Boys Keep Swinging: Masculinity and Football Culture in England," in *Just Boys Doing Business? Men, Masculinities and Crime*, ed. Tim Newburn and Elizabeth Stanko (London: Routledge, 1994), 219.

113. Particularly book 2, X/15, XVI/23; book 3, V/9 ("One must take care not to interpret a figurative expression literally"), XXV/36 ("The various meanings of a particular thing may be either contrary or just different"), XXIX/40 ("Our Christian authors used all the figures of speech which teachers of grammar call by their Greek name of tropes"). Augustine, *De Doctrina Christiana*, trans. R. P. H. Green (Oxford: Clarendon Press, 1995), 141, 167, 171.

114. Noam Chomsky, quoted in Dan I. Slobin, *Psycholinguistics* (Glenview, Ill.: Scott, Foresman, 1971), 18; Marshall Edelson, *Psychoanalysis: A Theory in Crisis* (Chicago: University of Chicago Press, 1988), 16, 188.

115. Daniel R. Lesnick, "Insults and Threats in Medieval Todi," *Journal of Medieval History* 17 (1991): 77.

116. TNAUK: PRO, SC8/277/13830, printed in John H. Fisher, Malcolm Richardson, and Jane L. Fisher, eds., *An Anthology of Chancery English* (Knoxville: University of Tennessee Press, 1984), 232-33.

117. Natalie Zemon Davis, *Fiction in the Archives: Pardon Tales and Their Tellers in Sixteenth-Century France* (Stanford, Calif.: Stanford University Press, 1987), 3.

118. Timothy S. Haskett, "County Lawyers?: The Composers of English Chancery Bills," in *The Life of the Law: Proceedings of the Tenth British Legal History Conference, Oxford, 1991*, ed. P. Birks (London: Hambledon Press, 1993).

119. E.g., TNAUK: PRO, C1/27/274; C1/32/249; C1/38/177; C1/46/102; C1/46/174; C1/54/398; C1/240/26.

120. E.g., TNAUK: PRO, C1/77/45; C1/172/3.

121. TNAUK: PRO, C1/498/1.

122. Ibid.

123. Ibid.

124. Green, *A Crisis of Truth*, 139-48. Technically, of course, Chancery was not a common-law court, but it often had to deal with claims that had been defined for common-law pleading.

125. TNAUK: PRO, C1/46/174; C1/50/402; C1/60/175; C1/61/349; C1/66/233; C1/209/37; C1/240/26.

126. Philippa Maddern, "Honour among the Pastons: Gender and Integrity in Fifteenth-Century English Provincial Society," *Journal of Medieval History* 14 (1988): 357-71.

127. Arthur Brandeis, ed., *Jacob's Well: An English Treatise on the Cleansing of Man's Conscience*, Early English Text Society O.S. 115 (London: K. Paul Trench Trübner, 1900), 96-97.

128. Edward E. Foster, ed., *Amis and Amiloun* (Medieval Institute Publications, 1997; available at http://www.lib.rochester.edu/camelot/teams/amisfr.htm).

129. Davis, *Paston Letters*, vol. 1, 92-93, 144; Joan Kirby, ed., *The Plumpton Letters and Papers*, Camden 5th series, no. 8 (London: Cambridge University Press for the Royal Historical Society, 1996), 85, 93, 113-14, 124-25, 126-27.

130. Kirby, *Plumpton Letters*, 50.

131. Devon Record Office (DRO), Chanter MS 854, vol. 1, pp. 25-27.

132. CCA, X.10.1, fols. 93v-94v.

133. Thrupp, *The Merchant Class of Medieval London*, 18.

134. BIA, CP.G 193.

135. Ibid.

136. Ibid.

137. Cf. Shaw, *Necessary Conjunctions*, 126: "Not to act would be to settle for a debasement of your standing: and rare was the person who could act the lord and simply ignore the affair as unworthy of contradiction."

138. BIA, CP.G 193.

139. Sharpe, *Defamation and Sexual Slander*, 3-4.

CHAPTER TWO

1. David Gary Shaw, *Creation of a Community*, 205-15, 193.

2. The *Oxford English Dictionary* shows that the uses of *husband* to mean "the male head of a household" (definition I.1) are the earliest (c. 1000), and that those implying "a man joined to a woman by marriage" (I.2) are contemporary with those conveying household management (II.4, 5b) (fourteenth-sixteenth centuries). "Husbandry" is first found to mean domestic economy (definition 1) about 1290; to mean "careful management" (4a, 4b), in 1362.

3. See also Miranda Chaytor, "Husband(ry): Narratives of Rape in the Seventeenth Century," *Gender and History* 7, no. 3 (1995): 384-85.

4. *OED* entry for "poller," citing Bradshaw, *St. Werburge* I. 2401.

5. CCA, X.10.1, fol. 61v.

6. Shaw, *Creation of a Community*, 188.

7. Davis, *Paston Letters*, vol. 1, 366.

8. Ibid., 362.

9. Ibid., 470, 392; Davis, *Paston Letters*, vol. 2, 247.

10. G. R. Owst, *Literature and Pulpit in Medieval England: A Neglected Chapter in the History of English Letters and of the English People*, 2nd ed. (Oxford: Blackwell, 1961), 311.

11. Davis, *Paston Letters*, vol. 2, 293-94.

12. All text references for *Partonope of Blois* are to lines in Adam Fredrik Trampe Bödtker, ed., *The Middle-English Versions of Partonope of Blois*, Early English Text Society E.S. 109 (London: K. Paul Trench Trübner and H. Frowde, Oxford University Press, 1912).

13. Bödtker, *Partonope of Blois*, 77.

14. Daniel, *The Tale of Gamelyn*, 74-78.

15. Edward E. Foster, ed., *Sir Amadace* (Medieval Institute Publications, 1997; available at http://www.lib.rochester.edu/camelot/teams/amadacin.htm).

16. Davis, *Paston Letters*, vol. 1, 357.

17. Kirby, *Plumpton Letters*, 56-57, 59, 95.

18. Davis, *Paston Letters*, vol. 1, 356.

19. Davis, *Paston Letters*, vol. 2, 63; emphasis added.

20. Ibid., 46-47; emphasis added.

21. LMA, DL/C/206, fol. 202v; emphasis added.

22. Kirby, *Plumpton Letters*, 55.

23. Owst, *Literature and Pulpit*, 162-63, 287-307, 548-93.

24. Henry Edward Nolloth and Thomas Frederick Simmons, eds., *The Lay Folks' Catechism, Or ... Archbishop Thoresby's Instruction for the People*, Early English Text Society O.S. 118 (London: K. Paul Trench Trübner, 1901), 51, 53.

25. Nolloth and Simmons, *Lay Folks' Catechism*, 93.

26. "Speculum Vitae," in *The Vernon Manuscript: A Facsimile of Bodleian Library, Oxford, Ms. Eng. Poet. A.1*, ed. A. I. Doyle (Cambridge: D. S. Brewer, 1987), fol. 234.

27. TNAUK: PRO, C1/17/233.

28. My thanks to Faith Wallis (McGill University) for pointing out the Man of Sorrows imagery.

29. Horman, *Vulgaria*, fols. 69v, 70r; emphasis added.

30. Cozens-Hardy and Stone, *Norwich Depositions*, no. 294.

31. LMA, DL/C/206, fol. 108r.

32. TNAUK: PRO, C1/48/107.

33. Michael Johnson, "Science and Discipline: The Ethos of Sex Education in a Fourteenth-Century Classroom," in *Homo Carnalis*, ed. Helen Rodnite Lemay (Ithaca: State University of New York Press, 1987), 166. The rogue general who obsessively guards his "precious bodily fluids" and refuses to yield his "essence" to women in Stanley Kubrick's film *Dr. Strangelove* (1964) is thus in an older tradition than most viewers realize.

34. LMA, DL/C/206, fols. 299rv; emphasis added.

35. Lyndal Roper, "Blood and Codpieces: Masculinity in the Early Modern German Town," in *Oedipus and the Devil: Witchcraft, Sexuality and Religion in Early Modern Europe* (London: Routledge, 1994), 112.

36. Horman, *Vulgaria*, fols. 69rv.

37. Helmholz, *Select Cases on Defamation*, 5.

38. C. D'Evelyn, ed., *Peter Idley's Instructions to His Son* (Boston: Modern Language Association of America, 1935), 101-2.

39. D'Evelyn, *Peter Idley's Instructions*, 101-2.

40. TNAUK: PRO, C1/4/116.

41. Ruth Mazo Karras, "Two Models, Two Standards: Moral Teaching and Sexual Mores," in *Bodies and Disciplines: Intersections of Literature and History in Fifteenth-Century England*, ed. Barbara A. Hanawalt and David Wallace (Minneapolis: University of Minnesota Press, 1996), throughout the essay.

42. Shannon McSheffrey, "Men and Masculinity in Late Medieval London Civic Culture: Governance, Patriarchy, and Reputation," in *Conflicted Identities and Multiple Masculinities: Men in the Medieval West*, ed. Jacqueline Murray, 260-61. See also Shannon McSheffrey, *Marriage, Sex, and Civic Culture in Late Medieval London* (Philadelphia: University of Pennsylvania Press, 2006), esp. chapter 7.

43. McSheffrey, "Men and Masculinity," 260.

44. Ibid., 263.

45. Cozens-Hardy and Stone, *Norwich Depositions*, no. 122.

46. McSheffrey, "Men and Masculinity," 261-62.

47. LMA, DL/C/205, fol. 305r.

48. DRO, Chanter 854, vol. 1, pp. 28, 37-39, 71.

49. Matters may have been different in the lower courts, whose records are now far scarcer. In the Buckingham archdeacon's court in the 1490s, John Lake "was defamed" for committing adultery but cleared himself through compurgation. Nicholas Est sued Henry Assynden for saying that Est "wanted to have the secret thing with his wife" (E. M. Elvey, ed., *The Courts of the Archdeaconry of Buckinghamshire, 1483-1523* [Welwyn Garden City: Buckinghamshire Record Society, 1975], 99-100, 35). These cases do not provide enough circumstantial information to draw any conclusions.

50. DRO, Chanter 854, vol. 2, pp. 263-64.

51. LMA, DL/C/205, fol. 158v.

52. McSheffrey, "Men and Masculinity," 262.

53. Gilmore, *Manhood in the Making*, 30-36, 100-4.

54. Hartman, *The Household and the Making of History*, 66.

55. Cf. Karras, *From Boys to Men*, 145.

56. BIA, CP.G 56.

57. With all legal stories, there is always the possibility of deliberate confabulation, and the canonists themselves were quite aware that couples whose unhappiness did not meet the church's standards for separation or annulment might collude to make things appear worse than they were (R. H. Helmholz, *Marriage Litigation in Medieval England* [Cambridge: Cambridge University Press, 1974], 146-47). We should retain this possibility but keep it in the background. Marital dissolutions were not easy to get, and not many were granted. Fakery was more likely where annulment was the aim. I find it hard to credit in the case of separations that problems would have been made up out of whole cloth; the disadvantages of separated life were too great. A couple who was willing to forego the security of marriage (giving up its possibility perhaps for decades) enough to seek a separation must have had problems making their continued life together unbearable, in which case "collusion" and "fiction" become moot. Attention to the fictionality of historical sources does not mean assuming them all to have a deceptive intent.

58. Poos, "Sex, Lies, and the Church Courts," 588, n. 4.

59. Sara M. Butler, "The Language of Abuse: Marital Violence in Later Medieval England" (Ph.D. diss., Dalhousie University, 2001), 67-69, 208. Butler's work has now been published as *The Language of Abuse: Marital Violence in Later Medieval England* (Leiden: Brill, 2007).

60. LMA, DL/C/206, fol. 268.

61. Ibid., fol. 273.

62. Butler, "Language of Abuse", 285-86, 365-67.

63. Jacqueline Murray, "Hiding behind the Universal Man: Male Sexuality in the Middle Ages," in *Handbook of Medieval Sexuality*, ed. James A. Brundage and Vern L. Bullough (New York: Garland, 1996), 129-30.

64. LMA, DL/C/206, fol. 236.

65. Ibid., fol. 237.

66. Julian Pitt-Rivers, "Honour and Social Status," in *Honour and Shame: The Values of Mediterranean Society*, ed. J. G. Peristiany (London: Weidenfeld and Nicholson, 1965).

67. For a well-described modern example, see Stanley H. Brandes, *Metaphors of Masculinity: Sex and Status in Andalusian Folklore* (Philadelphia: University of Pennsylvania Press, 1980), 87-92, 110-14, 180-82.

68. Jeanne Ward, *Broken Bodies, Broken Dreams: Violence against Women Exposed*, ed. Lisa Ernst (Nairobi: United Nations Office for the Coordination of Humanitarian Affairs; Integrated Regional Information Networks, 2005), 135-40; Andrea Parrot and Nina Cummings, *Forsaken Females: The Global Brutalization of Women* (Lanham, Md.: Rowan & Littlefield, 2006), 173-87.

69. Judith K. Brown, Jacquelyn Campbell, and Dorothy Ayers Counts, *To Have and to Hit: Cultural Perspectives on Wife Beating*, 2nd ed. (Urbana, Ill.: University of Illinois Press, 1999). This collection, despite an impressive variety of cultural examples, ends up saying little about the reasons why men beat their wives, as opposed to the reasons women are beaten. The focus is on the women, their status and living arrangements. But even where societies with lower wife-beating rates are concerned, the attention goes to how women resist or escape. The authors do convincingly establish the impossibility of explaining the phenomenon using any one theory, whether biological, evolutionist, psychological, feminist, or sociological.

70. An example of the latter is BIA, CP.E 221, wherein a woman claimed a beating had broken her "spelbon" or ulna, the bone most likely to be injured if the victim were warding off a blow to the head.

71. Butler, "Language of Abuse", 304-5.

72. TNAUK: PRO C1/162/46, cited in Butler, "Language of Abuse," 448.

73. LMA, DL/C/206, fol. 170r.

74. Elvey, *Courts of the Archdeaconry*, 115.

75. Cozens-Hardy and Stone, *Norwich Depositions*, no. 11.

76. Ibid.

77. Ibid.

78. LMA, DL/C/206, fol. 274r: "Ricardus Elkyn nescit idonee cavere pro securitate uxoris sue propter eius demenciam et excessivam indiscrecionem." To translate *demenciam* literally as "insanity" seems inaccurate; a more literal deconstruction of the Latin, *de-menciam* as "absence of mind," gets to the spirit of it.

79. Butler, "Language of Abuse," 304-5; CCA, X.10.1, fol. 36v. On noses, see Valentin Groebner, "Losing Face, Saving Face: Noses and Honour in the Late Medieval Town," trans. Pamela Selwyn, *History Workshop Journal* 40 (1995): 1-15.

80. CCA, X.10.1, fols. 55v-56r.

81. Shaw, *Necessary Conjunctions*, 139.

82. CCA, X.10.1, fol. 56r.

83. Elvey, *Courts of the Archdeaconry*, 250, 262; McIntosh, *Autonomy and Community*, 231, 258-59; Butler, "Language of Abuse," 167.

84. Shaw, *Necessary Conjunctions*, 139, original emphasis.

85. Ibid., 139.

86. Karras, *From Boys to Men*, 118.

87. Butler, "Language of Abuse," 54.

88. Davis, *Paston Letters*, vol. 2, 59.

89. TNAUK: PRO, C1/46/80.

90. See chapter 1 above.

91. Shaw, *Necessary Conjunctions*, 136-38.

92. TNAUK: PRO, C1/48/102.

93. Charles L. Kingsford, ed., *The Stonor Letters and Papers, 1290-1483*, Camden Society 3rd series, 30 (London: Camden Society, 1919), 58.

94. Kingsford, *Stonor Letters*, 57.

95. LMA, DL/C/206, fol. 223v.

96. Ibid., fol. 222v.

97. Ibid., fol. 224v.

98. Karras, *From Boys to Men*, 133.

99. JoAnn McNamara, "The *Herrenfrage*: The Restructuring of the Gender System, 1050–1150," in *Medieval Masculinities: Regarding Men in the Middle Ages*, ed. Clare A. Lees (Minneapolis: University of Minnesota Press, 1994); Lyndal Roper, "Was There a Crisis in Gender Relations in Sixteenth-Century Germany?" in *Oedipus and the Devil: Witchcraft, Sexuality and Religion in Early Modern Europe* (London: Routledge, 1994); R. N. Swanson, "Angels Incarnate: Clergy and Masculinity from Gregorian Reform to Reformation," in *Masculinity in Medieval Europe*, ed. D. M. Hadley (London: Longman, 1999); P. H. Cullum, "Clergy, Masculinity and Transgression in Late Medieval England," in *Masculinity in Medieval Europe*, ed. D. M. Hadley (London: Longman, 1999).

100. Dyan Elliott, "Pollution, Illusion, and Masculine Disarray," in *Constructing Medieval Sexuality*, ed. Karma Lochrie, James A. Schultz, and Peggy McCracken (Minneapolis: University of Minnesota Press, 1997); Jacqueline Murray, "Mystical Castration: Some Reflections on Peter Abelard, Hugh of Lincoln and Sexual Control," in *Conflicted Identities and Multiple Masculinities: Men in the Medieval West*, ed. Jacqueline Murray (New York: Garland, 1999); Murray, "Hiding behind the Universal Man."

101. Edelson, *Psychoanalysis*, 195.

102. Burson, "Early Fifteenth-Century Clergy," 109; Nicholas Orme, "The Medieval Clergy of Exeter Cathedral: II. The Secondaries and Choristers," *Reports and Transactions of the Devonshire Association* 115 (1983): 85-100.

103. Norman P. Tanner, "The Reformation and Regionalism: Further Reflections on the Church in Late Medieval Norwich," in *Towns and Townspeople in the Fifteenth Century*, ed. John A. F. Thomson (Gloucester: Alan Sutton, 1988), 137; Shaw, *Creation of a Community*, 279, 78.

104. Margaret Bowker, *The Secular Clergy in the Diocese of Lincoln, 1495-1520* (London: Cambridge University Press, 1968), 41-42; R. N. Swanson, *Church and Society in Late Medieval England* (Oxford: Blackwell, 1989), 33-38, 50-52; Burson, "Early Fifteenth-Century Clergy," 185.

105. Swanson, *Church and Society*, 51.

106. Virginia Davis, "Preparation for Service in the Late Medieval English Church," in *Concepts and Patterns of Service in the Later Middle Ages*, ed. A. Curry and E. Matthew (Woodbridge, U.K.: Boydell Press, 2000), 50; Burson, "Early Fifteenth-Century Clergy," 182.

107. Davis, "Preparation for Service," 50. See also P. H. Cullum, "Boy/Man into Clerk/Priest: The Making of the Late Medieval Clergy," in *Rites of Passage: Cultures of Transition in the Fourteenth Century*, ed. Nicola McDonald and W. Mark Ormrod (York: York Medieval Press, 2004).

108. Swanson, *Church and Society*, 63, 64.

109. Davis, *Paston Letters*, vol. 1, 233-34.

110. Cozens-Hardy and Stone, *Norwich Depositions*, no. 167.

111. Campbell, "The Land," 205.

112. Burson, "Early Fifteenth-Century Clergy," 17, 231, 232, 234, 248, 272, 306.

113. C. E. Moreton, *The Townshends and Their World: Gentry, Law, and Land in Norfolk c. 1450-1551* (Oxford: Clarendon Press, 1992), 137.

114. Denis Brearley, "The Social, Economic, and Intellectual Life of Richard Depyng, Vicar of Fillongley (1487-1529)," in *The Salt of Common Life: Individuality and Choice in the Medieval Town, Countryside, and Church: Essays Presented to J. Ambrose Raftis*, ed. Edwin Brezette DeWindt (Kalamazoo, Mich.: Medieval Institute Publications, 1995).

115. R. B. Dobson, "Cathedral Chapters and Cathedral Cities: York, Durham, and Carlisle in the Fifteenth Century," *Northern History* 19 (1983): 27.

116. Ann J. Kettle, "City and Close: Lichfield in the Century before Reformation," in *The Church in Pre-Reformation Society*, ed. Caroline Barron and Christopher Harper-Bill (Woodbridge, 1985).

117. M. Bateson, "Archbishop Warham's Visitation of Monasteries," *English Historical Review* 6 (1891): 18-35; Joan Greatrex, "Monk Students from Norwich Cathedral Priory," *English Historical Review* 106 (1991): 555-83; Joan Greatrex, "Rabbits and Eels at High Table: Monks of Ely at the University of Cambridge, c. 1337-1539," in *Monasteries and Society in Medieval Britain: Proceedings of the 1994 Harlaxton Symposium*, ed. Benjamin Thompson (Stamford, U.K.: Paul Watkins, 1999); F. Donald Logan, *Runaway Religious in Medieval England, c. 1240-1540* (Cambridge: Cambridge University Press, 1996), 43-50, 54-63.

118. LMA, DL/C/206, fol. 80r.

119. Davis, *Paston Letters*, vol. 1, 63.

120. BIA, D/C.CP.1488/1.

121. TNAUK: PRO, C1/45/378.

122. TNAUK: PRO, C1/160/21. The abbot's strategy turned on the fact that the chancellor was also archbishop of Canterbury. Skipping the arbitration hearing set by the chancellor, the abbot supposedly got Joan cited into the archiepiscopal court of audience at the same time and subsequently obtained a sentence upon her from the Court of Arches, the highest ecclesiastical court in the realm; the petition implies that this was possible because she, being at the arbitration hearing, did not appear in the audience court. The abbot also got John imprisoned for sixteen days. His *coup de grace* was to sue the Schawes for defamation in their diocesan court at Lichfield.

123. Davis, *Paston Letters*, vol. 1, 31.

124. Burson, "Early Fifteenth-Century Clergy," 240-42; TNAUK: PRO, C1/561/58.

125. BIA, D/C.CP.1529/2.

126. Elvey, *Courts of the Archdeaconry*, 129.

127. LMA, DL/C/206, fol. 159r; "ye mantene thevys" interlineated, "Have ye putt in a theeffe to be morow masse preeste" cancelled.

128. Leonard Elliott-Binns, *Medieval Cornwall* (London: Methuen, 1955), 264.

129. CCA, X.10.1, fol. 56v.

130. A. McHardy, "The English Clergy and the Hundred Years War," in *The Church and War: Papers Read at the Twenty-First Summer Meeting and the Twenty-Second Winter Meeting of the Ecclesiastical History Society*, ed. W. J. Shiels (Oxford: Blackwell, 1983), 173-74; Cullum, "Clergy, Masculinity and Transgression," 190-91; Maddern, *Violence and Social Order*, 104-5.

131. BIA, D/C.CP.1524/12.

132. Cozens-Hardy and Stone, *Norwich Depositions*, no. 250.

133. BIA, CP.G 57.

134. Cozens-Hardy and Stone, *Norwich Depositions*, no. 167.

135. LMA, DL/C/206, fols. 31v-33r.

136. BIA, D/C.CP.1488/1.

137. Kingsford, *Stonor Letters*, part 2, 85, 152.

138. Kirby, *Plumpton Letters*, 39, 106; Davis, *Paston Letters*, vol. 2, 111-12.

139. LMA, DL/C/206, fols. 215v–216v, 225r–226r, 227r–229r, 230r–233v. Summarized in Peter Heath, *The English Parish Clergy on the Eve of the Reformation* (Toronto: University of Toronto Press, 1969), 10–12, though without much analysis. Bowers Gifford is now squeezed between the suburbs of Basildon and Southend.

140. LMA, DL/C/206, fols. 227v–228r.

141. Ibid., fol. 233r.

142. Ibid., fol. 225r.

143. Ibid.

144. Ibid., fol. 215v.

145. Ibid., fol. 228r.

146. Ibid., fols. 216v, 230rv.

147. Ibid., fols. 230rv.

148. TNAUK: PRO, C1/46/162.

149. Ibid., C1/44/213.

150. Cozens-Hardy and Stone, *Norwich Depositions*, no. 253, 16; BIA, CP.G 126.

151. Richard Helmholz, "Harboring Sexual Offenders: Ecclesiastical Courts and Controlling Misbehavior," *Journal of British Studies* 37, no. 3 (1998): 258–59, 262–63.

152. BIA, CP.G 47.

153. Davis, *Paston Letters*, vol. 1, 576–77.

154. His cultural resonance has not completely faded in our own time. The stereotype endures in the modern anticlericalism of Catholic cultures (Brandes, *Metaphors of Masculinity*, 184). An even more recent example comes from *The Sopranos*. In that television series' first season, the intense attraction between Carmela Soprano and her unusually handsome parish priest grew directly out of her desire for counseling and spiritual direction.

155. BIA, D/C.CP.1524/13.

156. Swanson, "Angels Incarnate," 169–71.

157. LMA, DL/C/206, fol. 313r.

158. TNAUK: PRO, C1/28/448; emphasis added.

159. BIA, CP.E 249.

160. LMA, DL/C/206, fols. 25v–26v.

161. Cozens-Hardy and Stone, *Norwich Depositions*, no. 251.

162. LMA, DL/C/206, fols. 60v, 61v, 107v–109r; TNAUK: PRO, C1/561/58.

163. Cozens-Hardy and Stone, *Norwich Depositions*, no. 166.

164. Ibid., no. 270.

165. BIA, D/C.CP.1524/13.

166. By 1500, at least, actual deprivation or degradation was very rare. Most often, priests were assigned penance and offerings, the point being to save clerical dignity (Heath, *English Parish Clergy*, 114–19, esp. 117).

167. R. L. Storey, "Malicious Indictments of Clergy in the Fifteenth Century," in *Medieval Ecclesiastical Studies in Honour of Dorothy M. Owen*, ed. M. J. Franklin and Christopher Harper-Bill (Woodbridge, U.K.: Boydell Press, 1995), esp. 230–31; Maddern, *Violence and Social Order*, 102–3.

168. TNAUK: PRO, C1/60/175.

169. Ibid., C1/209/37.

170. Ibid., C1/561/58.

171. This was firmly within an established satirical tradition (Jill Mann, *Chaucer and Medieval Estates Satire: The Literature of Social Classes* [Cambridge: Cambridge University Press, 1973], esp. 37–46).

172. "Song against the Friars," in *Political Poems and Songs: From the Accession of Edward III to That of Richard III*, ed. Thomas Wright (London: Rolls Series, 1861).

173. Original:

> Lat a ffreer off sum ordur,
> *tecum pernoctare*
> Odur thi wyff or thi doughtor
> *hic vult violare;*
> Or thi sun he weyl prefur
> *sicut ffurtam ffortis*
> God gyffe syche a ffreer peyn
> *in inferni portis!*
>
> James M. Dean, ed., *On the Times*

174. This is the sense given in Dean's gloss to his edition of the poem in the TEAMS online version (see previous note).

175. Logan, *Runaway Religious*, 12-15.

176. "A Hundred Mery Talys," in *Shakespeare Jest-Books: Reprints of the Early and Very Rare Jest-Books Supposed to Have Been Used by Shakespeare*, repr. ed., ed. William Carew Hazlitt (New York: Burt Franklin, 1964), 27, 72, 42.

177. The editor, W. C. Hazlitt, replaced the operative verb in the text by five asterisks, but the tale's later references to foul odor make me confident that I have not misconstrued it.

178. "A Hundred Mery Talys," 16.

179. Quoted in Allen J. Frantzen, "When Women Aren't Enough," in *Studying Medieval Women: Sex, Gender, Feminism*, ed. Nancy F. Partner (Cambridge, Mass.: Medieval Academy of America, 1993), 152.

180. Davis, *Paston Letters*, vol. 1, 370.

181. Kate Cooper and Conrad Leyser, "The Gender of Grace: Impotence, Servitude, and Manliness in the Fifth-Century West," *Gender and History* 12, no. 3 (2000): 538-39.

182. Joan Cadden, *Meanings of Sex Difference in the Middle Ages: Medicine, Science, and Culture* (Cambridge: Cambridge University Press, 1993), 206.

183. Cooper and Leyser, "The Gender of Grace," 541-42.

184. Jacqueline Murray, "Masculinizing Religious Life: Sexual Prowess, the Battle for Chastity and Monastic Identity," in *Holiness and Masculinity in the Middle Ages*, ed. P. H. Cullum and Katherine Lewis (Toronto: University of Toronto Press, 2005), 30-31. See also John H. Arnold, "The Labour of Continence: Masculinity and Clerical Virginity," in *Medieval Virginities*, ed. Anke Bernau, Ruth Evans, and Sarah Salih (Cardiff: University of Wales Press, 2003), esp. 111.

185. Loïc Wacquant, "The Prizefighter's Three Bodies," *Ethnos* 63, no. 3 (1998): 342-46, 350 n. 22.

186. Conrad Leyser, "Masculinity in Flux: Nocturnal Emission and the Limits of Celibacy in the Early Middle Ages," in *Masculinity in Medieval Europe*, ed. D. M. Hadley (London: Longman), 105.

187. Murray, "Masculinizing Religious Life," 32.

188. Davis, *Paston Letters*, vol. 1, 433-34.

189. Cullum, "Clergy, Masculinity and Transgression," 182.

190. Ibid., 192-93.

191. Ibid., 194. Cf. Karras, *From Boys to Men*, 161-62.

192. Davis, "Preparation for Service," 51.

CHAPTER THREE

1. All text references to Chaucer are to lines in Larry Dean Benson, ed., *The Riverside Chaucer*, 3rd ed. (Boston: Houghton Mifflin, 1987).

2. Daniel F. Pigg, "Performing the Perverse: The Abuse of Masculine Power in the *Reeve's Tale*," in *Masculinities in Chaucer: Approaches to Maleness in the Canterbury Tales and Troilus and Criseyde*, ed. Peter G. Beidler (Cambridge: D. S. Brewer, 1998), 54. The term "perversity" is especially misapplied here.

3. Isabel Davis, "Consuming the Body of the Working Man in the Later Middle Ages," in *Consuming Narratives: Gender and Monstrous Appetite in the Middle Ages and the Renaissance*, ed. Liz Herbert McAvoy and Teresa Walters (Cardiff: University of Wales Press, 2002); D. Vance Smith, "Body Doubles: Producing the Masculine *Corpus*," in *Becoming Male in the Middle Ages*, ed. Jeffrey Jerome Cohen and Bonnie Wheeler (New York: Garland, 1997).

4. Judith Butler, *Bodies That Matter: On the Discursive Limits of "Sex"* (New York: Routledge, 1993), 5; original emphasis.

5. "A Hundred Mery Talys," 51–52.

6. Jacqueline Murray, "'The Law of Sin That Is in My Members': The Problem of Male Embodiment," in *Gender and Holiness : Men, Women, and Saints in Late Medieval Europe*, ed. Sarah Salih and Samantha Riches (New York: Routledge, 2002).

7. Joan Cadden, *Meanings of Sex Difference in the Middle Ages: Medicine, Science, and Culture* (Cambridge: Cambridge University Press, 1993), 171–72, 181.

8. Cadden, *Meanings of Sex Difference*, 181.

9. Ibid., 186–87.

10. M. C. Seymour et al., eds., *On the Properties of Things: John Trevisa's Translation of Bartholomaeus Anglicus De Proprietatibus Rerum: A Critical Text*, (Oxford: Clarendon Press, 1975), 196.

11. Seymour, *On the Properties of Things*, 212.

12. Ibid., 290–92, 301.

13. Ibid., 233–35.

14. Mahmoud Manzalaoui, ed., *Secretum Secretorum: Nine English Versions*, Early English Text Society O.S. 276 (Oxford: Oxford University Press, 1977), 94, 105, 109, 110, 112.

15. Manzalaoui, *Secretum Secretorum*, 106; Seymour et al., *On the Properties of Things*, 306.

16. Manzalaoui, *Secretum Secretorum*, 107, 97, 96, 101, 103.

17. Cadden, *Meanings of Sex Difference*, 202, emphasis added.

18. Manzalaoui, *Secretum Secretorum*, 113.

19. Seymour et al., *On the Properties of Things*, 290; Manzalaoui, *Secretum Secretorum*, 92–93.

20. Karras, *From Boys to Men*, 119–20.

21. Michael D. Sharp, "Reading Chaucer's 'Manly Man': The Trouble with Masculinity in the *Monk's Prologue* and *Tale*," in *Masculinities in Chaucer: Approaches to Maleness in the Canterbury Tales and Troilus and Criseyde*, ed. Peter G. Beidler (Cambridge: D. S. Brewer, 1998), 173–74, 176.

22. Mann, *Chaucer and Medieval Estates Satire*, 37–46.

23. The possibility that Chaucer's description indicated that the Pardoner was homosexual in the modern sense was first voiced in the 1950s and received its most explicit statement in Monica E. McAlpine, "The Pardoner's Homosexuality and How It Matters," *Proceedings of the Modern Language Association* 95 (1980): 1–22. Since then, readings have diverged. One view foregrounds sexuality, but the advent of queer theory, and the fall from fashion of the "essentialist" term "homosexual," have taken such readings far beyond conventional terms of sex and gender. The other school reads the references to sexual deviance as metaphors for social and religious critiques. There are some strange bedfellows in the latter category: Steven F. Kruger, "Claiming the Pardoner: Toward a Gay Reading of Chaucer's Pardoner's Tale," in *Critical Essays on Geoffrey Chaucer*, ed. Thomas C. Stillinger (New York: Prentice Hall, 1998), esp. 157–60; and Robert S. Sturges, *Chaucer's Pardoner and Gender Theory: Bodies of Discourse* (New York: St. Martin's Press, 2000), 1–20, despite their authors' attention to sexual politics and their claims of radical novelty, in essence argue along the same lines as Lee Patterson, "Chaucer's Pardoner on the Couch: Psyche and Clio in Medieval Literary Studies," *Speculum* 76, no. 3 (2001): 638–80, who cites their

work in opposition to his own. One can find a bibliography of the debate in Patterson, "Chaucer's Pardoner on the Couch," 657–59.

24. The word "male" had its modern meaning in the late Middle Ages, as Bartholomew-Trevisa shows: "A male is called *masculus*" (Seymour et al., *On the Properties of Things*, 306).

25. Davis, *Paston Letters*, vol. 1, 415. I have kept the spelling "Torke" and treated the word as a surname to refer to the man as an individual. The word could also mean "a Turk," a fascinating but I think unimportant possibility that strikes me as no more probable from the evidence here.

26. Charles Ross, *Edward IV* (London: Eyre Methuen, 1974), 10.

27. Butler, *Bodies That Matter*, 10.

28. See also chapter 4 below.

29. Dana Birksted-Breen, "Phallus, Penis and Mental Space," *International Journal of Psycho-Analysis* 77 (1996): 649–51.

30. Seymour et al., *On the Properties of Things*, 261, 196.

31. A. Hamilton Thompson, *The English Clergy and Their Organization in the Later Middle Ages* (Oxford: Clarendon Press, 1947), 216–18.

32. Michael Solomon, *The Literature of Misogyny in Medieval Spain: The "Arcipreste De Talavera" and the "Spill"* (Cambridge: Cambridge University Press, 1997), 51.

33. Ruth Mazo Karras, *Common Women: Prostitution and Sexuality in Medieval England* (New York: Oxford University Press, 1996), 89.

34. The 1989 edition of the *Oxford English Dictionary* finds the earliest English mention of "cock" as "penis" in 1618, the next in the 1730s.

35. Reginald Thorne Davies, ed., *Medieval English Lyrics: A Critical Anthology* (Evanston, Ill.: Northwestern University Press, 1964), 153–54. The *OED* notes the equivalence of cock-as-penis in English to the German *Hahn*, *Hähnchen*, meaning "rooster." Those familiar with the *oeuvre* of the Rolling Stones will, of course, recall the blues classic "Little Red Rooster."

36. Murray, "Hiding behind the Universal Man," 126, 130.

37. Karras, *From Boys to Men*, 108.

38. Davies, *Medieval English Lyrics*, 260.

39. Lee Patterson makes much the same point in discussing Chaucer's Pardoner (Patterson, "Chaucer's Pardoner on the Couch," 662–63). For references about homoerotic themes in Italian literary and popular discourse from the fourteenth to sixteenth centuries, see Rocke, *Forbidden Friendships*, 95, 103, 123–24. See also Kenneth Borris, ed., *Same-Sex Desire in the English Renaissance: A Sourcebook of Texts, 1470–1650* (New York: Routledge, 2004), esp. 1–24.

40. James A. Brundage, *Law, Sex, and Christian Society in Medieval Europe* (Chicago: University of Chicago Press, 1987), esp. 358–60, also 241–42, 381–84, 505; Shannon McSheffrey, *Love and Marriage in Late Medieval London* (Kalamazoo, Mich.: Medieval Institute Publications, 1995), 6.

41. "Merie Tales of Skelton," in *Shakespeare Jest-Books: Reprints of the Early and Very Rare Jest-Books Supposed to Have Been Used by Shakespeare*, vol. 2, repr. ed., ed. William Carew Hazlitt (New York: Burt Franklin, 1964), 95.

42. T. A. Foster, "Deficient Husbands," *William and Mary Quarterly*, 3rd series 66, no. 4 (1999): 726, 730–31, 743.

43. "Lyarde," in *Reliquiae Antiquae: Scraps from Ancient Manuscripts*, repr. ed., ed. Thomas Wright and James Orchard Halliwell (New York: AMS Press, 1966), 280–82.

44. "Lyarde."

45. BIA, CP.E 105.

46. Helmholz, *Marriage Litigation*, 87–90; Jacqueline Murray, "On the Origins and Role of 'Wise Women' in Causes for Annulment on the Grounds of Male Impotence," *Journal of Medieval History* 16 (1990): 235–51.

47. BIA, CP.E 105.

48. Ibid.

49. Indeed, Goldberg has recently argued that depositions in such cases may have operated as an objectifying form of pornography: P. J. P. Goldberg, "John Skathelok's Dick: Voyeurism and 'Pornography' in Late Medieval England," in *Medieval Obscenities,* ed. Nicola McDonald (York: York Medieval Press, 2006).

50. All references to this case are to BIA, CP.E 259; the different documents in the file do not bear separate item numbers.

51. My reasoning here is guided by suggestions from Philippa Hoskin, BIA (personal communications, February 16, 2000, and October 31, 2003). The *Middle English Dictionary* gives the following senses of the Middle English "find": "to discover, find out, or learn by inspection" (definition 7); "to detect or catch someone in the act of sinning or committing an offence" (9a); "to detect or discover sin or falsehood" (9b); in hunting, "to catch sight of, or get on the trail of" (12); "to obtain or get something by seeking or effort" (13). When we add up the connotations, the sexual meanings are undeniable.

52. Rosemary Drage Hale, "Joseph as Mother: Adaptation and Appropriation in the Construction of Male Virtue," in *Medieval Mothering,* ed. John Carmi Parsons and Bonnie Wheeler (New York: Garland, 1996), 101-2, 106, 108.

53. *Calendar of Inquisitions Post Mortem and Other Analogous Documents Preserved in the Public Record Office,* vol. 13 (London: Her Majesty's Stationery Office, 1954), 76.

54. *Calendar of Inquisitions,* 78.

55. Ibid., 77.

56. "De Ingenuis," in Mary T. Brentano, *Relationship of the Latin Facetus Literature to the Medieval English Courtesy Poems,* Bulletin of the University of Kansas, Humanistic Studies 5, 2 (Lawrence: University of Kansas, 1935), 118.

57. Jonathan Nicholls, *The Matter of Courtesy: Medieval Courtesy Books and the Gawain-Poet* (Woodbridge, U.K.: D. S. Brewer, 1985), 73. Ruth Mazo Karras claims the behavior prescribed by courtesy books "is clearly aristocratic, even if others did try to emulate it" (Karras, *From Boys to Men,* 177 n. 97). Surely, however, the origin of the behavior is less important than its social reach.

58. Servus Gieben, "Robert Grosseteste and Medieval Courtesy Books," *Vivarium* 5 (1967): 71; Nicholls, *Matter of Courtesy,* 69.

59. Brentano, *Latin Facetus Literature,* 112-13, 118; Gieben, "Robert Grosseteste," 72.

60. "How the Wise Man Taught His Son," in *The Babees Book,* repr. ed., ed. F. J. Furnivall (New York: Greenwood Press, 1969), 5; Gieben, "Robert Grosseteste," 72.

61. Brentano, *Latin Facetus Literature,* 118; Gieben, "Robert Grosseteste," 72.

62. "The Boke of Curtesaye," in *The Babees Book,* repr. ed., ed. F. J. Furnivall (New York: Greenwood Press, 1969), 308. Significantly, the word here for "child" is "gyrle."

63. "The Boke of Curtesaye," 302.

64. Ibid., 307-8.

65. Alan Bray, "Homosexuality and the Signs of Male Friendship in Early Modern England," in *Queering the Renaissance,* ed. Jonathan Goldberg (Durham, N.C.: Duke University Press, 1994), 42-47.

66. Karras (*From Boys to Men,* 63) makes similar suggestions about male bonding between young knights.

67. These include *Doctrina Mensae, Dum Manducatis, Phagifacetus,* and others. Nicholls, *Matter of Courtesy,* 179-95.

68. "Stans Puer Ad Mensam," in *The Babees Book,* repr. ed., ed. F. J. Furnivall (New York: Greenwood Press, 1969), 3, 71.

69. "The Babees Book," in *The Babees Book,* repr. ed., ed. F. J. Furnivall (New York: Greenwood Press, 1969), pt. 1, 3.

70. F. J. Furnivall, ed., *Caxton's Boke of Curtesye*, Early English Text Society E.S. 3 (London: N. Trübner, 1868), 9, 13.

71. "How the Wise Man Taught His Son," pt. 1, 50.

72. Before Nicholls, the clearest statement is Brentano, *Latin Facetus Literature*, 6-9.

73. All English translations are quoted from Marcus Tullius Cicero, *On Duties*, trans. M. T. Griffin and E. M. Atkins (Cambridge: Cambridge University Press, 1991), and are cited in text by chapter and line number.

74. J. C. Schmitt, *La raison des gestes dans l'occident médiéval* (Paris: Editions Gallimard, 1990), 203-4.

75. Schmitt, *La raison des gestes*, 174-200, esp. 198-200.

76. Felicity Riddy, "Mother Knows Best: Reading Social Change in a Courtesy Text," *Speculum* 71 (1996): 77. The quotation is from the H version of the text; the E version substitutes "contenance" for "manhed" (Tauno F. Mustanoja, ed., *The Good Wife Taught Her Daughter*, vol. 2, *Annales Academiae Scientarium Fennicae* [Helsinki: Suomaliaisen Kirjallisuuden Seruan, 1948], 164, 65). Conduct books for girls were not a central source for this study, and I cannot admit to an extensive knowledge of them. Two recent studies include Kathleen Ashley and Robert L. A. Clark, eds., *Medieval Conduct* (Minneapolis: University of Minnesota Press, 2001), and Anna Dronzek, "Manners, Models, and Morals: Gender, Status, and Codes of Conduct among the Middle Classes of Late Medieval England" (Ph.D. diss., University of Minnesota, 2001).

77. "Of the Manners to Bring One to Honour and Welfare," in *The Babees Book*, repr. ed., ed. F. J. Furnivall (New York: Greenwood, 1969), pt. 1, 35.

78. Karras, *From Boys to Men*, 14; Fiona Dunlop, "Making Youth Holy: Holiness and Masculinity in the Interlude of Youth," in *Holiness and Masculinity in the Middle Ages*, ed. P. H. Cullum and Katherine Lewis (Toronto: University of Toronto Press, 2005), 192.

79. "The Mirror of the Periods of Man's Life," 61-66.

80. Ruth Mazo Karras, "Sharing Wine, Women, and Song: Masculine Identity Formation in Medieval European Universities," in *Becoming Male in the Middle Ages*, ed. Jeffrey Jerome Cohen and Bonnie Wheeler (New York: Garland, 1997); Karras, "Separating the Men from the Goats: Masculinity, Civilization, and Identity Formation in the Medieval University," in *Conflicted Identities and Multiple Masculinities: Men in the Medieval West*, ed. Jacqueline Murray (New York: Garland, 1999); Karras, *From Boys to Men*, 98.

81. Murray, "Hiding behind the Universal Man," 129-30.

82. Horman, *Vulgaria*, 61v, 64v, 65r, 113v, 68r, 68v.

83. Ibid., 64v, 67v, 68v, 73v, 78v.

84. Pierre J. Payer, *Sex and the Penitentials: The Development of a Sexual Code, 550-1150* (Toronto: University of Toronto Press, 1984), 56.

85. Cf. Karras, *From Boys to Men*, 77-78: "As Marjorie Woods has pointed out, many of the standard texts used in grammar schools to teach Latin include stories of rape."

86. All references to this poem from Davies, *Medieval English Lyrics*, 158.

87. Alison Hanham, *The Cely Letters, 1472-1488*, Early English Text Society O.S. 273 (London: Oxford University Press, 1975), 155-56.

88. Davis, *Paston Letters*, vol. 1, 635.

89. Ibid., 636.

90. Ibid., 635. I cannot accept Davis's suggestion (635) that this sentence refers to a completely different person.

91. Roper, "Blood and Codpieces," 108-9, 110, 115-16, 119-20.

92. "The Mirror of the Periods of Man's Life," 66.

93. Wiesner, "Wandervogels and Women." See also chapter 1 above.

94. Karras, *From Boys to Men*, 138, 140-41.

95. Lyndal Roper, "Drinking, Whoring and Gorging: Brutish Indiscipline and the Formation of Protestant Identity," in *Oedipus and the Devil: Witchcraft, Sexuality and Religion in Early Modern Europe* (London: Routledge, 1994).

96. Elisabeth Crouzet-Pavan, "A Flower of Evil: Young Men in Medieval Italy," in *A History of Young People in the West*, ed. G. Levi and J. C. Schmitt (Cambridge, Mass.: Belknap and Harvard University Press, 1997), esp. 187–88. Crouzet-Pavan seems somewhat undecided about the nature of this clampdown, on the one hand strenuously arguing that the persistence of young men's chivalrous associations should not fool us into thinking they had power, and on the other saying that the "system, seemingly so closed, of tutelage and mistrust of *giovani* nonetheless developed cracks in it" (220).

97. This and all subsequent references to the Holy Trinity Priory petition are to TNAUK: PRO, C1/47/256.

98. Owst, *Literature and Pulpit*, 273–96, esp. 275, 277.

99. TNAUK: PRO, C1/47/255.

100. TNAUK: PRO, C1/47/256.

101. Karras, *From Boys to Men*, 163.

102. James Schultz, "Bodies That Don't Matter: Heterosexuality before Heterosexuality in Gottfried's *Tristan*," in *Constructing Medieval Sexuality*, ed. Karma Lochrie, James A. Schultz, and Peggy McCracken (Minneapolis: University of Minnesota Press, 1997).

103. Francoise Piponnier and Perrine Mane, *Dress in the Middle Ages*, trans. Caroline Beamish (New Haven, Conn.: Yale University Press, 1998), 64–65; Anne Sutton, "Dress and Fashions c. 1470," in *Daily Life in the Late Middle Ages*, ed. Richard H. Britnell (Stroud, U.K.: Sutton Publishing, 1998), 12, 14; Fred Davis, *Fashion, Culture and Identity* (Chicago: University of Chicago Press, 1992), 58.

104. Davis, *Fashion, Culture and Identity*, 5–12.

105. Dean, *On the Times*. All text references to this poem are by line.

106. Thomas Hoccleve, "Of Pridd and of Waste Clothynge of Lordis Mene, Which Is a-Yens Her Astate," in *Queene Elizabethes Achademy*, ed. F. J. Furnivall, Early English Text Society E.S. 8 (London: N. Trübner, 1869), 106. All text references to this poem are by line.

107. Dean, *On the Times*.

108. Hoccleve, "Of Pridd," 106–7.

109. Owst, *Literature and Pulpit*, 404–11.

110. Hoccleve, "Of Pridd," 107.

111. For more on short jackets, see Owst, *Literature and Pulpit*, 404–5.

112. This is not to say that sermon satirists in general ignored women's costume and adornment in treatments of vanity (ibid., 375–404).

113. Cf. Murray, "Hiding behind the Universal Man," 133.

114. See Dunlop, "Making Youth Holy," 195.

115. Davis, *Fashion, Culture and Identity*, 191, 58–59.

116. Note the conflict between Margery Kempe and her husband over Margery's insistence on buying and wearing expensive, fashionable clothes, which suited her father's status more than that of her husband: Sandford Brown Meech and Hope Emily Allen, eds., *The Book of Margery Kempe*, Early English Text Society O.S. 212 (London: Early English Text Society, 1940), 9.

117. William Ian Miller, *The Mystery of Courage* (Cambridge, Mass.: Harvard University Press, 2000), 232–53.

118. Cf. Karras, *From Boys to Men*, 37.

119. Sutton, "Dress and Fashions c. 1470," 14.

120. Ibid., 6.

121. Robert Bartlett, "Symbolic Meanings of Hair in the Middle Ages," *Transactions of the Royal Historical Society*, 6th series 4 (1994): 50–52; Garrett Epp, "The Vicious Guise:

Effeminacy, Sodomy, and Mankind," in *Becoming Male in the Middle Ages*, ed. Jeffrey Jerome Cohen and Bonnie Wheeler (New York: Garland, 1997).

122. Bartlett, "Symbolic Meanings of Hair," 58-59.

123. Dyer, *Making a Living in the Middle Ages*, 280.

124. Sutton, "Dress and Fashions c. 1470," 17.

125. Kristen M. Burkholder, "Threads Bared: Dress and Textiles in Late Medieval English Wills," in *Medieval Clothing and Textiles*, ed. Robin Netherington and Gale R. Owen-Crocker (Woodbridge, U.K.: Boydell Press, 2005), 143-47.

126. Mark D. Johnston, "The Treatment of Speech in Medieval Ethical and Courtesy Literature," *Rhetorica* 4 (1986): 21-45; Edwin D. Craun, *Lies, Slander and Obscenity in Medieval English Literature: Pastoral Rhetoric and the Deviant Speaker* (Cambridge: Cambridge University Press, 1997).

127. Sandy Bardsley, "Scolding Women: Cultural Knowledge and the Criminalization of Speech in Late Medieval England, 1300-1500" (Ph.D. diss., University of North Carolina, 1999), 145, 150-58. Bardsley's work has now been published as *Venomous Tongues: Speech and Gender in Late Medieval England* (Philadelphia: University of Pennsylvania Press, 2006).

128. Marjorie McIntosh, *Controlling Misbehavior*, 117.

129. Brentano, *Latin Facetus Literature*, 113.

130. "The Babees Book," pt. 1, 3.

131. Furnivall, *Caxton's Boke of Curtesye*, 15; "How the Wise Man Taught His Son," 49.

132. "The Babees Book," pt. 1, 4; Susan Phillips, "'That Men May of You Seyn': Public Reputation and Private Gossip in Late Medieval Courtesy Books" (paper presented at the 36th International Congress on Medieval Studies, Kalamazoo, Mich., 2001).

133. Shaw, *Creation of a Community*, 189.

134. "Shrew" here bears the meanings both of masculine "scoundrel" and of feminine "scold" ("The Boke of Curtesye," pt. 2, 28).

135. Lisa Perfetti, *Women and Laughter in Medieval Comic Literature* (Ann Arbor: University of Michigan Press, 2003), 4-12.

136. London Guildhall Library (LGL), MS 9065, fol. 184r. I am grateful to Shannon McSheffrey for allowing me to consult her unpublished transcript of this deposition book.

137. "Benedicaris tu, quia tu scis bene facere facta tua" (CCA, X.10.1, fols. 92rv).

138. Ibid.

139. Also, of course, Bokeland may have been connected in some way to Alice's kin or their interests, giving him a more tangible reason to speak up for her; this was technically supposed to disqualify him as a witness, but the Canterbury examiner's formulaic questions on the point were even more mushily phrased than usual.

140. BIA, D/C.CP.1528/7.

141. LMA, DL/C/206, fol. 230v; Linda E. Boose, "Scolding Brides and Bridling Scolds: Taming the Woman's Unruly Member," *Shakespeare Quarterly* 42 (1991): 179-213. I thank Sandy Bardsley (personal communication, November 2, 2003) for the latter reference.

142. BIA, CP.G 59.

143. All references for this case are to BIA, CP.G 166.

144. Original: "that he would dyng the duyle furth of his breik at an hoirs ars letting for no man." "Duyle," or "dool," is northern and Scots dialect for "dowel" (rod). George Clark's suggestion (personal communication, February 13, 2003) that "duyle" may also mean "devil" is, I think, quite compatible with this reading, in more ways than one. I thank Clark (Queen's University, Kingston) and Andrew Taylor (University of Ottawa) for their help in interpreting this text.

145. Interlineated in manuscript.

146. "Prick" here most likely means "nail," "spike," or other such sharp penetrating object, mutilation of the nose being a culturally recognized punishment for a whore. But

(anatomical logic aside) the sexual connotation of "prick" in this comment went along with the others.

147. Craun, *Lies, Slander and Obscenity*, 158-62, 173.

148. Elizabeth Ewan, "'Tongue, You Lied': The Role of the Tongue in Rituals of Public Penance in Late Medieval Scotland," in *The Hands of the Tongue: Essays on Deviant Speech*, ed. Edwin Craun (Kalamazoo, Mich.: Medieval Institute Publications, 2007).

149. Connell, *Masculinities*, 62, 45-66.

150. Ibid., 60.

151. Lyndal Roper, introd. to *Oedipus and the Devil: Witchcraft, Sexuality and Religion in Early Modern Europe* (London: Routledge, 1994), 21.

152. Nancy F. Partner, "No Sex, No Gender," in *Studying Medieval Women: Sex, Gender, Feminism*, ed. Nancy F. Partner (Cambridge, Mass.: Medieval Academy of America, 1993), 138-39; Roper, introd. to *Oedipus and the Devil*, 21-22.

153. American Psychiatric Association, *Diagnostic and Statistical Manual of Mental Disorders*, 4th ed. (*DSM-IV*), 1994, §300.81.

154. Robert J. Stoller, *Presentations of Gender* (New Haven, Conn.: Yale University Press, 1985), 11-14. Psychoanalysis of the past thirty years has continually reexamined, contested, and refined Stoller's theories, and his work remains a central reference point on gender in the discipline.

155. Butler, *Bodies That Matter*, 3.

156. Phyllis Tyson and Robert L. Tyson, *Psychoanalytic Theories of Development: An Integration* (New Haven, Conn.: Yale University Press, 1990), 121, 277, 345; Stoller, *Presentations of Gender*, 12, 14.

157. Stoller, *Presentations of Gender*, 11, emphasis added.

158. Steven Pinker, *How the Mind Works* (New York: W. W. Norton, 1999), esp. 93-98.

159. Pinker, *How the Mind Works*, 131-48; Drew Westen and Glen O. Gabbard, "Developments in Cognitive Neuroscience: I. Conflict, Compromise and Connectionism," *Journal of the American Psychoanalytic Association* 50, no. 1 (2002): esp. 61-62; Edelson, *Psychoanalysis*, 125.

160. Joseph LeDoux, *The Emotional Brain: The Mysterious Underpinnings of Emotional Life* (New York: Touchstone, 1996); Westen and Gabbard, "Developments I," 81.

161. Matthew Hugh Erdelyi, *The Recovery of Unconscious Memories: Hypermnesia and Reminiscence* (Chicago: University of Chicago Press, 1996); Westen and Gabbard, "Developments I," 67-70.

162. Susan C. Vaughan, *The Talking Cure: The Science behind Psychotherapy* (New York: Putnam's, 1997); Eric R. Kandel, "A New Intellectual Framework for Psychiatry," *American Journal of Psychiatry* 155, no. 4 (1998): 464; Kandel, "Biology and the Future of Psychoanalysis: A New Intellectual Framework for Psychiatry Revisited," *American Journal of Psychiatry* 156, no. 4 (1999): 505; Westen and Gabbard, "Developments I," 78; Westen and Gabbard, "Developments in Cognitive Neuroscience: II. Implications for Theories of Transference," *Journal of the American Psychoanalytic Association* 50, no. 1 (2002): 99-134. See Edelson, *Psychoanalysis*, 122-56, for a very searching and cautionary argument about the profoundly different conceptual bases of psychoanalysis and neuroscience.

163. Roper, introd. to *Oedipus and the Devil*, 21. Roper's statement is also a criticism of the influential and strongly constructionist work of Thomas Laqueur (*Making Sex: Body and Gender from the Greeks to Freud* [Cambridge, Mass.: Harvard University Press, 1990]).

164. Barbara H. Rosenwein, "Worrying about Emotions in History," *American Historical Review* 107, no. 3 (2002): 836-37, esp. 836 n. 64.: "Although such studies suggest that the brain reacts unconsciously to stimuli, this does not challenge the foundations of cognitive theory, for the brain's response implies a kind of knowing and evaluation."

165. Patterson, "Chaucer's Pardoner on the Couch," 647–56.

166. Edelson, *Psychoanalysis*, 16.

CHAPTER FOUR

1. All text references for *Partonope of Blois* are to lines in Bödtker, *The Middle-English Versions of Partonope of Blois.*

2. Smelser and Wallerstein, "Psychoanalysis and Sociology," 4–5.

3. This is, in effect, the accusation Ralph Hanna III (a literary historian) makes against Judith Bennett (a social historian) regarding Bennett's use of references to alewives in *Piers Plowman.* Ralph Hanna III, "Brewing Trouble: On Literature and History—and Alewives," in *Bodies and Disciplines: Intersections of Literature and History in Fifteenth-Century England,* ed. Barbara A. Hanawalt and David Wallace (Minneapolis: University of Minnesota Press, 1996). See also Robert M. Stein, "Literary Criticism and the Evidence for History," in *Writing Medieval History,* ed. Nancy F. Partner (London: Hodder Arnold, 2005).

4. For more reflections on the differing claims of historical and fictional discourse on the "real" and the "true," see Hayden White, "Introduction: Historical Fiction, Fictional History, and Historical Reality," *Rethinking History* 9, no. 2/3 (2005): esp. 147–49.

5. Derek Brewer, *Symbolic Stories: Traditional Narratives of the Family Drama in English Literature* (Totowa, N.J.: Rowman & Littlefield, 1980), 24.

6. Brewer, *Symbolic Stories,* 10.

7. Partner, "The Hidden Self," 46.

8. Hans-Ulrich Wehler, "Psychoanalysis and History," *Social Research* 47 (1980): 519–36.

9. Edelson, *Psychoanalysis,* 16.

10. Ibid., 49–61, esp. 57–59.

11. Ibid., 60.

12. See above, chapter 1.

13. But see Nancy F. Partner, "Reading the Book of Margery Kempe," *Exemplaria* 3, no. 1 (1991): 29–66.

14. Robert W. Hanning, *The Individual in Twelfth-Century Romance* (New Haven, Conn.: Yale University Press, 1977).

15. Edmund Reiss, "Romance," in *The Popular Literature of Medieval England,* ed. Thomas J. Heffernan (Knoxville: University of Tennessee Press, 1985), 119.

16. Derek Brewer, "Escape from the Mimetic Fallacy," in *Studies in Medieval English Romances: Some New Approaches,* ed. Derek Brewer (Cambridge: Cambridge University Press, 1988), 8.

17. Susan Crane, *Gender and Romance in Chaucer's Canterbury Tales* (Princeton, N.J.: Princeton University Press, 1994), 27.

18. Brewer, *Symbolic Stories,* 10.

19. Quoted in Brewer, "Escape," 7.

20. Sigmund Freud, "Family Romances," in *On Sexuality: Three Essays on the Theory of Sexuality and Other Works,* ed. James Strachey (London: Penguin Books, 1977; reprint, 1991).

21. Colin Morris, *The Discovery of the Individual, 1050–1200,* Medieval Academy Reprints for Teaching, no. 19 (1972; repr., Toronto: University of Toronto Press in association with the Medieval Academy of America, 1987); Caroline Walker Bynum, "Did the Twelfth Century Discover the Individual?" in *Jesus as Mother: Studies in the Spirituality of the High Middle Ages* (Berkeley and Los Angeles: University of California Press, 1982).

22. Brewer, "Escape," 7–8.

23. All text references for *Bevis of Hampton* are to lines in Ronald B. Herzman, Graham Drake, and Eve Salisbury, eds., *Bevis of Hampton* (Medieval Institute Publications, 1999; available at http://www.lib.rochester.edu/camelot/teams/bevisfrm.htm).

24. Mary Frances Wack, *Lovesickness in the Middle Ages: The Viaticum and Its Commentaries* (Philadelphia: University of Pennsylvania Press, 1990), 151-52

25. Wack, *Lovesickness*, 161-62, 171.

26. Solomon, *Literature of Misogyny*, 49-64, esp. 52-54.

27. Brandes, *Metaphors of Masculinity*, 76-80, 84-87.

28. I must be careful here to stress that even classical psychoanalysis does not define a healthy autonomy of the individual or the self as meaning immunity from social and relational connection. But, as Chodorow has put it, classical psychoanalysis challenges "the traditional notion of the pristine individual ... without fundamental recourse to the 'outside world.'" Nancy Chodorow, "Toward a Relational Individualism: The Mediation of Self through Psychoanalysis," in *Reconstructing Individualism: Autonomy, Individuality and the Self in Western Thought*, ed. Thomas C. Heller, Morton Sosna, and David E. Wellerby (Stanford, Calif.: Stanford University Press, 1986), 202.

29. Chodorow, "Toward a Relational Individualism," 200.

30. Ibid., 200, emphasis added.

31. Lynne Layton, *Who's That Girl? Who's That Boy? Clinical Practice Meets Postmodern Gender Theory* (Northvale, N.J.: J. Aronson, 1998), 13.

32. Michael J. Diamond, "Boys to Men: The Maturing of Masculine Gender Identity through Paternal Watchful Protectiveness," *Gender and Psychoanalysis* 2 (1997): 450.

33. Layton, *Who's That Girl?* 34.

34. Stephen Frosh, *Sexual Difference: Masculinity and Psychoanalysis* (London: Routledge, 1994), 89-115.

35. Layton, *Who's That Girl?* 42.

36. Stoller, *Presentations of Gender*, 16-17, esp. 16: "There is an earlier stage ... wherein the boy is merged with mother. Only after months does she gradually become a clearly separate object.... Masculinity requires a boy in time to separate from his mother's intimacy. Femininity requires also that a girl separate from her mother, but not particularly from her mother's femininity." The exact nature of this differentiation has lately become controversial among psychoanalysts, but the idea that differentiation occurs is not in question. For a further refinement, see Michael J. Diamond, "The Shaping of Masculinity: Revisioning Boys Turning away from Their Mothers to Construct Male Gender Identity," *International Journal of Psychoanalysis* 85, no. 2 (2004): 359-79.

37. Stoller, *Presentations of Gender*, 18. Again, the term "symbiosis" has been questioned in subsequent work, but for our purposes the general idea will suffice.

38. Wack, *Lovesickness*, 154.

39. Ibid., 155.

40. Sigmund Freud, "A Special Type of Choice of Object Made by Men," in *On Sexuality: Three Essays on the Theory of Sexuality and Other Works*, ed. James Strachey (London: Penguin Books, 1977; reprint, 1991).

41. Freud, "A Special Type," 237. On the ubiquity of prostitution in England, much of it casual, and the medieval vagueness of the word "whore," see Karras, *Common Women*.

42. All text references for *Cheuelere Assygne* are to lines in Donald Lee Hoffman, ed., *The Cheuelere Assygne* (Ann Arbor, Mich.: University Microfilms, 1970).

43. Hoffman, *Cheuelere Assygne*, 141, 150-52.

44. Ibid., 125-26, 137-38.

45. Jennifer Fellows, "Mothers in Middle English Romance," in *Women and Literature in Britain*, ed. C. M. Meale (Cambridge: Cambridge University Press, 1993), 43-44.

46. Bödtker, *Partonope*, 186-91.

47. Ibid., 191-97.

48. Ibid., 220.

49. Ibid., 250-54, e.g.

50. Mary Flowers Braswell, ed., *Ywain and Gawain* (Medieval Institute Publications, 1995; available at http://www.lib.rochester.edu/camelot/teams/ywnfrm.htm).

51. Cf. Brewer on fairy tales, which the romances in many ways are: "The breaking of legitimate prohibitions, leading to suffering but eventually a fuller life, is one of the most frequent and potent elements of fairy tales" (Brewer, *Symbolic Stories*, 39).

52. Bödtker, *Partonope*, 50-53.

53. Ibid., 223-24, 228-32.

54. Sylvia Huot, "Dangerous Embodiments: Froissart's Harton and Jean D'arras's Melusine," *Speculum* 78 (2003): 400.

55. Huot, "Dangerous Embodiments," 410.

56. Ibid., 413.

57. Sigmund Freud, "Psycho-Analytic Notes on an Autobiographical Account of a Case of Paranoia," in *The Case of Schreber: Papers on Technique and Other Works*, ed. James Strachey and Alix Strachey, Standard Edition, vol. 12 (London: Hogarth Press and the Institute of Psychoanalysis, 1958), esp. 43.

58. All text references for *Sir Launfal* are to lines in Thomas Chestre, Anne Laskaya, and Eve Salisbury, eds., *Sir Launfal* (TEAMS, 1995; available at http://www.lib.rochester.edu/camelot/teams/launffrm.htm).

59. Slavoj Žižek, quoted in Huot, "Dangerous Embodiments," 416.

60. Freud, "The Ego and the Id," in *The Ego and the Id and Other Works*, ed. James Strachey, Standard Edition, vol. 19 (New York: Hogarth Press and the Institute of Psycho-Analysis, 1961), 33.

61. Brewer, *Symbolic Stories*, 12.

62. John Munder Ross, "Fathering: A Review of Some Psychoanalytic Contributions on Paternity," *International Journal of Psycho-Analysis* 60 (1979): 317-27; Dana Breen, introd. to *The Gender Conundrum: Contemporary Psychoanalytic Perspectives on Femininity and Masculinity*, ed. Dana Breen (London: Routledge, 1993); Michael J. Diamond, "Fathers with Sons: Psychoanalytic Perspectives on 'Good Enough' Fathering throughout the Life Cycle," *Gender and Psychoanalysis* 3, no. 3 (1998): esp. 248-51.

63. Diamond, "Boys to Men," esp. 446-47.

64. Ross, "Fathering," 323; Peter Blos, "Son and Father," in *The Gender Conundrum: Contemporary Psychoanalytic Perspectives on Femininity and Masculinity*, ed. Dana Breen (London: Routledge, 1993); Diamond, "Fathers with Sons," 261.

65. Ross, "Fathering," 321; Tyson and Tyson, *Psychoanalytic Theories*, 283, 288-89.

66. Susan Crane, *Insular Romance: Politics, Faith, and Culture in Anglo-Norman and Middle English Literature* (Berkeley and Los Angeles: University of California Press, 1986), 87-91. Noel Menuge has recently discussed *Bevis of Hampton* and *Gamelyn* in this respect: *Medieval English Wardship in Romance and Law* (Woodbridge, U.K.: D. S. Brewer, 2001).

67. Fellows, "Mothers," 46, 50.

68. Brewer, *Symbolic Stories*, 48.

69. Ibid.

70. The subject's hostility toward the whore-mother gets a similarly guilt-free gratification. When she realizes that Bevis's stepfather is dead, his mother flings herself off a wall and breaks her neck. Bevis's valedictory words are, "Lady, forgive me my guilt for this, I never gave you even a scratch!" (3466-67).

71. Maldwyn Mills, ed., *Lybeaus Desconus*, Early English Text Society O.S. 261 (London: Oxford University Press, 1969), 78.

72. Crane, *Gender and Romance*, 28.

73. Mills, *Lybeaus Desconus*, 76.

74. Ibid., 204.

75. Jeffrey Jerome Cohen, *Of Giants: Sex, Monsters, and the Middle Ages* (Minneapolis: University of Minnesota Press, 1999), 85.

76. Mills, *Lybeaus Desconus*, 167.

77. Ibid., 184–87.

78. Ibid., 199.

79. Ibid.

80. Sigmund Freud, "Infantile Sexuality," in *On Sexuality: Three Essays on the Theory of Sexuality and Other Works*, ed. James Strachey, rep. ed. (1977; repr. London: Penguin Books: 1991), 102–4.

81. All text references for *Of Arthour and of Merlin* to lines in O. D. Macrae-Gibson, ed., *Of Arthour and of Merlin*, vol. 1, Early English Text Society O.S. 268 (London: Oxford University Press, 1973).

82. Macrae-Gibson, *Of Arthour and of Merlin*, 91.

83. Mother's desire is only a secondary concern. The subject instead wants to keep her away from father's desire, but more because of what it proves about *father*. Bevis of Hampton's evil mother achieved the same thing by different means: since she was married to Bevis's father against her will, her own lack of desire for him effectively protects his image further for the subject.

84. Freud, "The Ego and the Id," 33; Freud, "A Seventeenth-Century Demonological Neurosis," in *The Ego and the Id and Other Works*, ed. James Strachey (New York: Hogarth Press and the Institute of Psycho-Analysis, 1961), 91.

85. Freud, "A Seventeenth-Century Demonological Neurosis," 81, 90.

86. Diamond, "Fathers with Sons," 262.

87. All text references for *Sir Perceval of Galles* are to lines in Mary Flowers Braswell, ed., *Sir Perceval of Galles* (Medieval Institute Publications, 1995; available at http://www.lib.rochester.edu/camelot/teams/percfrm.htm).

88. Felicity Riddy, "Middle English Romance: Family, Marriage, Intimacy," in *The Cambridge Companion to Medieval Romance*, ed. Roberta L. Krueger (Cambridge: Cambridge University Press, 2000), 239.

89. The psychoanalytic echo here is with the work of Irene Fast, who argues that "appropriate" gender role arises not from repudiation of all those qualities associated with the other sex, but from integrating all those assimilable with one's "own" and relinquishing to the other sex only those one cannot realistically maintain (mostly reproductive capacities). True and maladaptive "repudiation" of other-sex associations is a symptom that gender differentiation has not been successful. I. Fast, *Gender Identity: A Differentiation Model* (Hillsdale, N.J.: Analytic Press, 1984), 52–53, 63–65, 72–73; Diamond, "Boys to Men," 451, 454.

90. Cohen, *Of Giants*, 78–79.

91. All text references for *Sir Gawain and the Green Knight* are to lines in Theodore Silverstein, *Sir Gawain and the Green Knight: A New Critical Edition* (Chicago: University of Chicago Press, 1984).

92. Brewer, *Symbolic Stories*, 84.

93. Carolyn Dinshaw, "Getting Medieval: Pulp Fiction, Gawain, Foucault," in *The Book and the Body*, ed. Dolores Warwick Frese and Katherine O'Brien O'Keeffe (Notre Dame, Ind.: University of Notre Dame Press, 1997), 125–36. Cohen (*Of Giants*, 147–51) conveys Dinshaw's analysis of this romance in an earlier article and adds his own slightly differing remarks.

94. Alice Munro, "Images," in *Selected Stories* (Toronto: McClelland and Stewart, 1996), 45–46.

95. Brewer, *Symbolic Stories*, 84. In keeping with his very cautious use of psychoanalytic concepts, Brewer does not discuss father-desire at all.

96. Diamond mentions, as healthy features of fathering, the father's ability "to perceive his child as representing an opportunity for self-enhancement (i.e., increased self-love) and as being a means for attaining immortality," and the father's "projection of his special, ideal self onto his child"; moreover, "[the] oedipal father . . . must also be able to *hate* his son in a contained manner." Diamond sees the mutual longing of father and son as continuing throughout the lifespan. Diamond, "Fathers with Sons," 257-58, 278, 285-56, original emphasis.

97. Chodorow, "Toward a Relational Individualism," 198, 203.

98. Braswell, *Ywain and Gawain*.

99. Crane, *Gender and Romance*, 39.

100. Braswell, introd. to *Ywain and Gawain*.

101. Brewer, *Symbolic Stories*, 63.

102. Crane, *Gender and Romance*, 39.

103. "Criticism that turns medieval romance into allegorical stories about religion makes medieval literature sound suspiciously like modern Christian discourse. . . . Criticism of this kind inevitably finds and produces Christianity, not at the heart of medieval stories, but at their surface, where it tends . . . to take the form of pious platitudes." Ad Putter, "The Narrative Logic of *Emare*," in *The Spirit of Medieval English Popular Romance*, ed. Ad Putter and Jane Gilbert (London: Longman, 2000), 178-79.

CONCLUSION

1. Harvey and Shepard, "What Have Historians Done with Masculinity?" 275.

2. Judith Bennett, "Confronting Continuity," *Journal of Women's History* 9 (1997): 73-94.

3. Alexandra Shepard, "From Anxious Patriarchs to Refined Gentlemen? Manhood in Britain, circa 1500-1700," *Journal of British Studies* 44, no. 2 (2005): 284-87.

4. Harvey and Shepard, "What Have Historians Done with Masculinity?" 275-76.

5. Ibid., 275.

6. Ibid., 276, 280.

7. Michael Roper, "Between Manliness and Masculinity: The 'War Generation' and the Psychology of Fear in Britain, 1914-1950," *Journal of British Studies* 44, no. 2 (2005): 382, emphasis added.

8. Connell, *Masculinities*, esp. chapter 3.

9. Shepard, "From Anxious Patriarchs," 290-91.

10. Harvey and Shepard, "What Have Historians Done with Masculinity?" 278.

11. Davis, *Paston Letters*, vol. 1, 293, 127-32.

12. Roper, introd. to *Oedipus and the Devil*, 7-9, 16.

13. McIntosh, *Controlling Misbehavior*; Shepard, "Manhood, Credit and Patriarchy"; Shepard, *Meanings of Manhood*.

14. See, e.g., Hadley, introd. to *Masculinity in Medieval Europe*, 4-6; Murray, introd. to *Conflicted Identities*, x.

15. For a fuller analysis, see Neal, "Meanings of Masculinity," 37-41.

16. For a recent comprehensive study of the role of women's labor in late medieval England, see Marjorie McIntosh, *Working Women in English Society, 1300-1620* (Cambridge: Cambridge University Press, 2005).

17. Brandes, *Metaphors of Masculinity*, 99.

18. Hartman, *The Household and the Making of History*, 57-64.

Bibliography

ARCHIVAL SOURCES

Canterbury Cathedral Archives (CCA)
MS. X.10.1 (Diocese of Canterbury, consistory court deposition book, 1410–21). .

Exeter, Devon Record Office (DRO)
MS. Chanter 854, 2 vols. (Diocese of Exeter, consistory court deposition book, 1510–18).

London Metropolitan Archives (LMA)
MS. DL/C/206 (Diocese of London, consistory court deposition book, 1510–16).

London, the National Archives of the United Kingdom (TNAUK)
MSS. C1 class (petitions to the Court of Chancery, late fourteenth to early sixteenth century).

Taunton, Somerset Archive and Record Service (SARS)
MSS. D/D/Ca/1a (Judicial *acta*, 1505–15).
D/D/Ca/2 (Judicial *acta* in instance cases, 1526–29).

York, Borthwick Institute for Archives (BIA)
MSS. CP.E class (Diocesan Cause Papers, fourteenth century).
CP.F class (Diocesan Cause Papers, fifteenth century).
CP.G class (Diocesan Cause Papers, sixteenth century).
D/C.CP. class (Dean and Chapter of York Minster Cause Papers, fifteenth and sixteenth centuries).

UNPUBLISHED PRIMARY SOURCES

London Guildhall Library (LGL)
MS. 9065 (Diocese of London, consistory court deposition book, 1488–94), transcribed by Shannon McSheffrey.

London Metropolitan Archives (LMA)
MS. DL/C/205 (Diocese of London, consistory court deposition book, 1467–76), transcribed by Shannon McSheffrey.

PUBLISHED PRIMARY SOURCES

Augustine. *De Doctrina Christiana*. Translated by R. P. H. Green. Oxford: Clarendon Press, 1995.

"The Babees Book." In *The Babees Book*, edited by F. J. Furnivall, part 1, 1–8. Reprint, New York: Greenwood Press, 1969.

Benson, Larry Dean, ed. *The Riverside Chaucer*. 3rd ed. Boston: Houghton Mifflin, 1987.

Bödtker, Adam Fredrik Trampe, ed. *The Middle-English Versions of Partonope of Blois*. Early English Text Society E.S. (Extra Series) 109. London: K. Paul Trench Trübner and H. Frowde, Oxford University Press, 1912.

"The Boke of Curtesaye." In *The Babees Book*, edited by F. J. Furnivall, part 1, 297–328. Reprint, New York: Greenwood Press, 1969.

Brandeis, Arthur, ed. *Jacob's Well: An English Treatise on the Cleansing of Man's Conscience*. Early English Text Society O.S. (Original Series) 115. London: K. Paul Trench Trübner, 1900.

Braswell, Mary Flowers, ed. *Sir Perceval of Galles*. Medieval Institute Publications, 1995. Available at http://www.lib.rochester.edu/camelot/teams/percfrm.htm.

———, ed. *Ywain and Gawain*. Medieval Institute Publications, 1995. Available at http://www.lib.rochester.edu/camelot/teams/ywnfrm.htm.

Calendar of Inquisitions Post Mortem and Other Analogous Documents Preserved in the Public Record Office. Vol. 13. London: Her Majesty's Stationery Office, 1954.

Chestre, Thomas, Anne Laskaya, and Eve Salisbury. *Sir Launfal*. Medieval Institute Publications, 1995. Available at http://www.lib.rochester.edu/camelot/teams/launffrm.htm.

Cicero, Marcus Tullius. *On Duties*. Translated by M. T. Griffin and E. M. Atkins. Cambridge: Cambridge University Press, 1991.

Cozens-Hardy, Basil, and Edward Darley Stone, eds. *Norwich Consistory Court Depositions, 1499–1512 and 1518–1530*. London: Fakenham and Reading Wyman & Sons, 1938.

Daniel, Neil, ed. *The Tale of Gamelyn*. Ann Arbor, Mich.: University Microfilms, 1970.

Davies, Reginald Thorne, ed. *Medieval English Lyrics: A Critical Anthology*. Evanston, Ill.: Northwestern University Press, 1964.

Davis, Norman, ed. *Paston Letters and Papers of the Fifteenth Century*. Vol. 1. Oxford: Clarendon Press, 1971.

———, ed. *Paston Letters and Papers of the Fifteenth Century*. Vol. 2. Oxford: Clarendon Press, 1976.

Dean, James M., ed. *Freers, Freers, Wo Ye Be*. Medieval Institute Publications, 1996. Available at http://www.lib.rochester.edu/camelot/teams/freerswo.htm.

———, ed. *On the Times*. Medieval Institute Publications, 1996. Available at http://www.lib.rochester.edu/camelot/teams/times.htm.

D'Evelyn, C., ed. *Peter Idley's Instructions to His Son*. Boston: Modern Language Association of America, 1935.

Elvey, E. M., ed. *The Courts of the Archdeaconry of Buckinghamshire, 1483–1523*. Welwyn Garden City: Buckinghamshire Record Society, 1975.

Fisher, John H., Malcolm Richardson, and Jane L. Fisher, eds. *An Anthology of Chancery English*. Knoxville: University of Tennessee Press, 1984.

Foster, Edward E., ed. *Amis and Amiloun*. Medieval Institute Publications, 1997. Available at http://www.lib.rochester.edu/camelot/teams/amisfr.htm.

———, ed. *Sir Amadace*. Medieval Institute Publications, 1997. Available at http://www.lib.rochester.edu/camelot/teams/amadacin.htm.

Furnivall, F. J., ed. *Caxton's Boke of Curtesye*. Early English Text Society E.S. 3. London: N. Trübner, 1868.

Hanham, Alison. *The Cely Letters, 1472–1488*. Early English Text Society O.S. 273. London: Oxford University Press, 1975.

Herzman, Ronald B., Graham Drake, and Eve Salisbury, eds. *Bevis of Hampton*. Medieval Institute Publications, 1999. Available at http://www.lib.rochester.edu/camelot/teams/bevisfrm. htm.

Hoccleve, Thomas. "Of Pridd and of Waste Clothynge of Lordis Mene, Which Is a-Yens Her Astate." In *Queene Elizabethes Achademy*, edited by F. J. Furnivall. Early English Text Society E.S. 8. London: N. Trübner, 1869.

Hoffman, Donald Lee, ed. *The Cheuelere Assygne*. Ann Arbor, Mich.: University Microfilms, 1970.

Horman, William. *Vulgaria*. Pollard and Redgrave Short-Title Catalogue, no. 13811. London: 1519.

"How the Wise Man Taught His Son." In *The Babees Book*, edited by F. J. Furnivall, part 1, 48–52. Reprint, New York: Greenwood Press, 1969.

Hudson, William, ed. *Leet Jurisdiction in the City of Norwich during the XIIIth and XIVth Centuries*. Publications of the Selden Society. London: Quaritch, 1892.

"A Hundred Mery Talys." In *Shakespeare Jest-Books: Reprints of the Early and Very Rare Jest-Books Supposed to Have Been Used by Shakespeare*, edited by William Carew Hazlitt, 1–129. Reprint, New York: Burt Franklin, 1964.

Kingsford, Charles L., ed. *The Stonor Letters and Papers, 1290–1483*. Camden Society 3rd series, no. 30. London: Camden Society, 1919.

Kirby, Joan, ed. *The Plumpton Letters and Papers*. Camden Society 5th series, no. 8. London: Cambridge University Press for the Royal Historical Society, 1996.

"Lyarde." In *Reliquiae Antiquae: Scraps from Ancient Manuscripts*, edited by Thomas Wright and James Orchard Halliwell, 280–82. Reprint, New York: AMS Press, 1966.

Macrae-Gibson, O. D., ed. *Of Arthour and of Merlin*. Vol. 1, Early English Text Society O.S. 268. London: Oxford University Press, 1973.

Manzalaoui, Mahmoud, ed. *Secretum Secretorum: Nine English Versions*. Early English Text Society O.S. 276. Oxford: Oxford University Press, 1977.

Meech, Sandford Brown, and Hope Emily Allen, eds. *The Book of Margery Kempe*. Early English Text Society O.S. 212. London: Early English Text Society, 1940.

"Merie Tales of Skelton." In *Shakespeare Jest-Books: Reprints of the Early and Very Rare Jest-Books Supposed to Have Been Used by Shakespeare*, vol. 2, edited by William Carew Hazlitt, 3–36. Reprint, New York: Burt Franklin, 1964.

Mills, Maldwyn, ed. *Lybeaus Desconus*. Early English Text Society O.S. 261. London: Oxford University Press, 1969.

"The Mirror of the Periods of Man's Life, or Bids of the Virtues and Vices for the Soul of Man." In *Hymns to the Virgin and Christ, the Parliament of Devils, and Other Religious Poems, Chiefly from the Archbishop of Canterbury's Lambeth MS. No. 853*, edited by Frederick James Furnivall, 60–66. Early English Text Society O.S. 24. London: N. Trübner, 1867.

Mustanoja, Tauno F., ed. *The Good Wife Taught Her Daughter*. Vol. 2, *Annales Academiae Scientarium Fennicae*. Helsinki: Suomaliaisen Kirjallisuuden Seruan, 1948.

Nolloth, Henry Edward, and Thomas Frederick Simmons, eds. *The Lay Folks' Catechism, Or . . . Archbishop Thoresby's Instruction for the People*. Early English Text Society O.S. 118. London: K. Paul Trench Trübner, 1901.

"Of the Manners to Bring One to Honour and Welfare." In *The Babees Book*, edited by F. J. Furnivall. Reprint, New York: Greenwood Press, 1969.

Seymour, M. C., et al., eds. *On the Properties of Things: John Trevisa's Translation of Bartholomaeus Anglicus De Proprietatibus Rerum: A Critical Text*. Oxford: Clarendon Press, 1975.

Silverstein, Theodore. *Sir Gawain and the Green Knight: A New Critical Edition*. Chicago: University of Chicago Press, 1984.

"Song against the Friars." In *Political Poems and Songs: From the Accession of Edward III to That of Richard III*, edited by Thomas Wright, 263–68. London: Rolls Series, 1861.

"Speculum Vitae." In *The Vernon Manuscript: A Facsimile of Bodleian Library, Oxford, MS. Eng. Poet. A.1*, edited by A. I. Doyle. Cambridge: D. S. Brewer, 1987.

"Stans Puer Ad Mensam." In *The Babees Book*, edited by F. J. Furnivall, part 1, 26–27. Reprint, New York: Greenwood Press, 1969.

Wilson, Edward, ed. *The Winchester Anthology*. Woodbridge, U.K.: Boydell Press, 1981.

SECONDARY SOURCES

Arnold, John H. "The Labour of Continence: Masculinity and Clerical Virginity." In *Medieval Virginities*, edited by Anke Bernau, Ruth Evans, and Sarah Salih, 102–18. Cardiff: University of Wales Press, 2003.

Ashley, Kathleen, and Robert L. A. Clark, eds. *Medieval Conduct*. Minneapolis: University of Minnesota Press, 2001.

Bardsley, Sandy. "Scolding Women: Cultural Knowledge and the Criminalization of Speech in Late Medieval England, 1300–1500." Ph.D. diss., University of North Carolina, 1999.

Bartlett, Robert. "Symbolic Meanings of Hair in the Middle Ages." *Transactions of the Royal Historical Society*, 6th series 4 (1994): 43–60.

Bateson, M. "Archbishop Warham's Visitation of Monasteries." *English Historical Review* 6 (1891): 18–35.

Beattie, Cordelia. "The Problem of Women's Work Identities in Post-Black Death England." In *The Problem of Labour in Fourteenth-Century England*, edited by J. Bothwell, P. J. P. Goldberg, and W. M. Ormrod, 1–19. York: York Medieval Press, 2000.

Bennett, Judith. "Confronting Continuity." *Journal of Women's History* 9 (1997): 73–94.

———. *A Medieval Life: Cecilia Penifader of Brigstock, c. 1295–1344*. Boston: McGraw-Hill College, 1999.

———. "Medieval Women in Modern Perspective." In *Women's History in Global Perspective*, vol. 2, edited by Bonnie G. Smith, 139–86. Urbana: University of Illinois Press, 2005.

———. *Women in the Medieval English Countryside: Gender and Household in Brigstock before the Plague*. New York: Oxford University Press, 1987.

Birksted-Breen, Dana. "Phallus, Penis and Mental Space." *International Journal of Psycho-Analysis* 77 (1996): 649–57.

Blanchard, Ian. "Social Structure and Social Organization in an English Village at the Close of the Middle Ages: Chewton 1526." In *The Salt of Common Life: Individuality and Choice in the Medieval Town, Countryside, and Church: Essays Presented to J. Ambrose Raftis*, edited by Edwin Brezette DeWindt, 307–39. Kalamazoo, Mich.: Medieval Institute Publications, 1995.

Blos, Peter. "Son and Father." In *The Gender Conundrum: Contemporary Psychoanalytic Perspectives on Femininity and Masculinity*, edited by Dana Breen, 49–66. London: Routledge, 1993.

Boose, Linda E. "Scolding Brides and Bridling Scolds: Taming the Woman's Unruly Member." *Shakespeare Quarterly* 42 (1991): 179–213.

Borris, Kenneth, ed. *Same-Sex Desire in the English Renaissance: A Sourcebook of Texts, 1470–1650*. New York: Routledge, 2004.

Bowker, Margaret. *The Secular Clergy in the Diocese of Lincoln, 1495–1520*. London: Cambridge University Press, 1968.

Brandes, Stanley H. *Metaphors of Masculinity: Sex and Status in Andalusian Folklore*. Philadelphia: University of Pennsylvania Press, 1980.

Bray, Alan. "Homosexuality and the Signs of Male Friendship in Early Modern England." In *Queering the Renaissance*, edited by Jonathan Goldberg, 40–61. Durham, N.C.: Duke University Press, 1994.

Brearley, Denis. "The Social, Economic, and Intellectual Life of Richard Depyng, Vicar of Fillongley (1487–1529)." In *The Salt of Common Life: Individuality and Choice in the Medieval*

Town, Countryside, and Church: Essays Presented to J. Ambrose Raftis, edited by Edwin Brezette DeWindt, 485–512. Kalamazoo, Mich.: Medieval Institute Publications, 1995.

Breen, Dana. Introd. to *The Gender Conundrum: Contemporary Psychoanalytic Perspectives on Femininity and Masculinity*, edited by Dana Breen, 24–33. London: Routledge, 1993.

Brentano, Mary T. *Relationship of the Latin Facetus Literature to the Medieval English Courtesy Poems*. Bulletin of the University of Kansas, Humanistic Studies 5, 2. Lawrence: University of Kansas, 1935.

Brewer, Derek. "Escape from the Mimetic Fallacy." In *Studies in Medieval English Romances: Some New Approaches*, edited by Derek Brewer, 1–10. Cambridge: Cambridge University Press, 1988.

———. *Symbolic Stories: Traditional Narratives of the Family Drama in English Literature*. Totowa, N.J.: Rowman & Littlefield, 1980.

Brown, Judith K., Jacquelyn Campbell, and Dorothy Ayers Counts. *To Have and to Hit: Cultural Perspectives on Wife Beating*. 2nd ed. Urbana: University of Illinois Press, 1999.

Brundage, James A. *Law, Sex, and Christian Society in Medieval Europe*. Chicago: University of Chicago Press, 1987.

Brundage, James A., and Vern L. Bullough. Introd. to *Handbook of Medieval Sexuality*, edited by James A. Brundage and Vern L. Bullough, ix–xviii. New York: Garland, 1996.

Burkholder, Kristen M. "Threads Bared: Dress and Textiles in Late Medieval English Wills." In *Medieval Clothing and Textiles*, edited by Robin Netherington and Gale R. Owen-Crocker, 133–54. Woodbridge, U.K.: Boydell Press, 2005.

Burrow, J. A. *Gestures and Looks in Medieval Narrative*. Cambridge: Cambridge University Press, 2002.

Burson, Malcolm Clark. "The Early Fifteenth-Century Clergy in the Archdeaconry of Exeter: Social Origins and Roles." Ph.D. diss., University of Toronto, 1979.

Butler, Judith. *Bodies That Matter: On the Discursive Limits of "Sex."* New York: Routledge, 1993.

Butler, Sara M. "The Language of Abuse: Marital Violence in Later Medieval England." Ph.D. diss., Dalhousie University, 2001.

Bynum, Caroline Walker. "Did the Twelfth Century Discover the Individual?" In *Jesus as Mother: Studies in the Spirituality of the High Middle Ages*, 82–109. Berkeley and Los Angeles: University of California Press, 1982.

Cadden, Joan. *Meanings of Sex Difference in the Middle Ages: Medicine, Science, and Culture*. Cambridge: Cambridge University Press, 1993.

Campbell, Bruce M. S. "The Land." In *A Social History of England, 1200–1500*, edited by Rosemary Horrox and W. Mark Ormrod, 179–237. Cambridge: Cambridge University Press, 2006.

Capp, Bernard. "The Double Standard Revisited: Plebeian Women and Male Sexual Reputation in Early Modern England." *Past and Present* 162 (1999): 70–100.

Chaytor, Miranda. "Husband(ry): Narratives of Rape in the Seventeenth Century." *Gender and History* 7, no. 3 (1995): 378–407.

Chodorow, Nancy. "Toward a Relational Individualism: The Mediation of Self through Psychoanalysis." In *Reconstructing Individualism: Autonomy, Individuality and the Self in Western Thought*, edited by Thomas C. Heller, Morton Sosna, and David E. Wellerby, 197–207. Stanford, Calif.: Stanford University Press, 1986.

Cohen, Jeffrey Jerome. *Of Giants: Sex, Monsters, and the Middle Ages*. Minneapolis: University of Minnesota Press, 1999.

Cohen, Jeffrey Jerome, and Bonnie Wheeler, eds. *Becoming Male in the Middle Ages*. New York: Garland, 1997.

Connell, R. W. *Masculinities*. Berkeley and Los Angeles: University of California Press, 1995.

Cooper, Kate, and Conrad Leyser. "The Gender of Grace: Impotence, Servitude, and Manliness in the Fifth-Century West." *Gender and History* 12, no. 3 (2000): 536–51.

Coss, Peter. "An Age of Deference." In *A Social History of England, 1200–1500*, edited by Rosemary Horrox and W. Mark Ormrod, 31–73. Cambridge: Cambridge University Press, 2006.

Crane, Susan. *Gender and Romance in Chaucer's Canterbury Tales*. Princeton, N.J.: Princeton University Press, 1994.

———. *Insular Romance: Politics, Faith, and Culture in Anglo-Norman and Middle English Literature*. Berkeley and Los Angeles: University of California Press, 1986.

Craun, Edwin D. *Lies, Slander and Obscenity in Medieval English Literature: Pastoral Rhetoric and the Deviant Speaker*. Cambridge: Cambridge University Press, 1997.

Crouzet-Pavan, Elisabeth. "A Flower of Evil: Young Men in Medieval Italy." In *A History of Young People in the West*, edited by G. Levi and J. C. Schmitt, 173–221. Cambridge, Mass.: Belknap and Harvard University Press, 1997.

Cullum, P. H. "Boy/Man into Clerk/Priest: The Making of the Late Medieval Clergy." In *Rites of Passage: Cultures of Transition in the Fourteenth Century*, edited by Nicola McDonald and W. Mark Ormrod, 51–66. York: York Medieval Press, 2004.

———. "Clergy, Masculinity and Transgression in Late Medieval England." In *Masculinity in Medieval Europe*, edited by D. M. Hadley, 178–96. London: Longman, 1999.

Dabhoiwala, Faramerz. "The Construction of Honour, Reputation and Status in Late Seventeenth- and Early Eighteenth-Century England." *Transactions of the Royal Historical Society*, 6th series 6 (1996): 201–13.

Davis, Fred. *Fashion, Culture and Identity*. Chicago: University of Chicago Press, 1992.

Davis, Isabel. "Consuming the Body of the Working Man in the Later Middle Ages." In *Consuming Narratives: Gender and Monstrous Appetite in the Middle Ages and the Renaissance*, edited by Liz Herbert McAvoy and Teresa Walters, 42–53. Cardiff: University of Wales Press, 2002.

Davis, Natalie Zemon. *Fiction in the Archives: Pardon Tales and Their Tellers in Sixteenth-Century France*. Stanford, Calif.: Stanford University Press, 1987.

Davis, Virginia. "Preparation for Service in the Late Medieval English Church." In *Concepts and Patterns of Service in the Later Middle Ages*, edited by A. Curry and E. Matthew, 38–51. Woodbridge, U.K.: Boydell Press, 2000.

Devereux, George. "The Argument." In *Ethnopsychoanalysis: Psychoanalysis and Anthropology as Complementary Frames of Reference*, 1–19. Berkeley and Los Angeles: University of California Press, 1978.

DeWindt, Edwin Brezette. *Land and People in Holywell-Cum-Needingworth: Structures of Tenure and Patterns of Social Organization in an East Midlands Village, 1252–1457*. Toronto: Pontifical Institute of Mediaeval Studies, 1972.

Diamond, Michael J. "Boys to Men: The Maturing of Masculine Gender Identity through Paternal Watchful Protectiveness." *Gender and Psychoanalysis* 2 (1997): 443–68.

———. "Fathers with Sons: Psychoanalytic Perspectives on 'Good Enough' Fathering throughout the Life Cycle." *Gender and Psychoanalysis* 3, no. 3 (1998): 243–99.

———. "The Shaping of Masculinity: Revisioning Boys Turning Away from Their Mothers to Construct Male Gender Identity." *International Journal of Psychoanalysis* 85, no. 2 (2004): 359–79.

Dinshaw, Carolyn. "Getting Medieval: Pulp Fiction, Gawain, Foucault." In *The Book and the Body*, edited by Dolores Warwick Frese and Katherine O'Brien O'Keeffe, 116–64. Notre Dame, Ind.: University of Notre Dame Press, 1997.

Dobson, E. J. "The Etymology and Meaning of Boy." *Medium aevum* 9 (1940): 121–54.

Dobson, R. B. "Cathedral Chapters and Cathedral Cities: York, Durham, and Carlisle in the Fifteenth Century." *Northern History* 19 (1983): 15–44.

Donahue, Charles, Jr. "Female Plaintiffs in Marriage Cases in the Court of York in the Late Middle Ages: What Can We Learn from the Numbers?" In *Wife and Widow in Medieval England*, edited by Sue Sheridan Walker, 183-213. Ann Arbor: University of Michigan Press, 1993.

Dronzek, Anna. "Manners, Models, and Morals: Gender, Status, and Codes of Conduct among the Middle Classes of Late Medieval England." Ph.D. diss., University of Minnesota, 2001.

Dunlop, Fiona. "Making Youth Holy: Holiness and Masculinity in the Interlude of Youth." In *Holiness and Masculinity in the Middle Ages*, edited by P. H. Cullum and Katherine Lewis, 192-205. Toronto: University of Toronto Press, 2005.

Dyer, Christopher. "The English Medieval Village Community and Its Decline." *Journal of British Studies* 33 (1994): 407-29.

———. *Making a Living in the Middle Ages: The People of Britain, 850-1520*. New Haven, Conn.: Yale University Press, 2002.

———. "Small Places with Large Consequences: The Importance of Small Towns in England, 1000-1540." *Historical Research* 75, no. 187 (2002): 1-24.

Edelson, Marshall. *Psychoanalysis: A Theory in Crisis*. Chicago: University of Chicago Press, 1988.

Elliott, Dyan. "Pollution, Illusion, and Masculine Disarray." In *Constructing Medieval Sexuality*, edited by Karma Lochrie, James A. Schultz, and Peggy McCracken, 1-23. Minneapolis: University of Minnesota Press, 1997.

Elliott-Binns, Leonard. *Medieval Cornwall*. London: Methuen, 1955.

Epp, Garrett. "The Vicious Guise: Effeminacy, Sodomy, and Mankind." In *Becoming Male in the Middle Ages*, edited by Jeffrey Jerome Cohen and Bonnie Wheeler, 303-19. New York: Garland, 1997.

Erdelyi, Matthew Hugh. *The Recovery of Unconscious Memories: Hypermnesia and Reminiscence*. Chicago: University of Chicago Press, 1996.

Ewan, Elizabeth. "'Tongue, You Lied': The Role of the Tongue in Rituals of Public Penance in Late Medieval Scotland." In *The Hands of the Tongue: Essays on Deviant Speech*, edited by Edwin Craun, 115-36. Kalamazoo, Mich.: Medieval Institute Publications, 2007.

Fast, I. *Gender Identity: A Differentiation Model*. Hillsdale, N.J.: Analytic Press, 1984.

Fellows, Jennifer. "Mothers in Middle English Romance." In *Women and Literature in Britain*, edited by C. M. Meale, 41-60. Cambridge: Cambridge University Press, 1993.

Foster, T. A. "Deficient Husbands." *William and Mary Quarterly*, 3rd series 66, no. 4 (1999): 723-44.

Foyster, Elizabeth. "Male Honour, Social Control and Wife Beating in Late Stuart England." *Transactions of the Royal Historical Society*, 6th series 6 (1996): 215-24.

———. *Manhood in Early Modern England: Honour, Sex and Marriage*. London: Longman, 2000.

Frantzen, Allen J. "When Women Aren't Enough." In *Studying Medieval Women: Sex, Gender, Feminism*, edited by Nancy F. Partner, 143-70. Cambridge, Mass.: Medieval Academy of America, 1993.

Freud, Sigmund. "The Ego and the Id." In *The Ego and the Id and Other Works*, edited by James Strachey, 3-66. London: Hogarth Press and the Institute of Psycho-Analysis, 1961.

———. "Family Romances." In *On Sexuality: Three Essays on the Theory of Sexuality and Other Works*, edited by James Strachey, 217-25. 1977. Reprint, London: Penguin Books, 1991.

———. "Infantile Sexuality." In *On Sexuality: Three Essays on the Theory of Sexuality and Other Works*, edited by James Strachey, 88-126. 1977. Reprint, London: Penguin Books, 1991.

———. "Psycho-Analytic Notes on an Autobiographical Account of a Case of Paranoia." In *The Case of Schreber: Papers on Technique and Other Works*, edited by James Strachey and Alix Strachey, 3-84. London: Hogarth Press and the Institute of Psycho-Analysis, 1958.

———. "A Seventeenth-Century Demonological Neurosis." In *The Ego and the Id and Other Works*, edited by James Strachey, 67-105. London: Hogarth Press and the Institute of Psycho-Analysis, 1961.

————. "A Special Type of Choice of Object Made by Men." In *On Sexuality: Three Essays on the Theory of Sexuality and Other Works*, edited by James Strachey, 227–42. 1977. Reprint, London: Penguin Books, 1991.

Frosh, Stephen. *Sexual Difference: Masculinity and Psychoanalysis*. London: Routledge, 1994.

Gieben, Servus. "Robert Grosseteste and Medieval Courtesy Books." *Vivarium* 5 (1967): 69–74.

Gilmore, David. *Manhood in the Making: Cultural Concepts of Masculinity*. New Haven, Conn.: Yale University Press, 1990.

Goldberg, P. J. P. "John Skathelok's Dick: Voyeurism and 'Pornography' in Late Medieval England." In *Medieval Obscenities*, edited by Nicola McDonald, 105–23. York: York Medieval Press, 2006.

————. "Migration, Youth and Gender in Later Medieval England." In *Youth in the Middle Ages*, edited by P. J. P. Goldberg and Felicity Riddy, 85–99. York: York Medieval Press, 2004.

————. "What Was a Servant?" In *Concepts and Patterns of Service in the Later Middle Ages*, edited by A. Curry and E. Matthew, 1–20. Woodbridge, U.K.: Boydell Press, 2000.

Gowing, Laura. *Domestic Dangers: Women, Words, and Sex in Early Modern London*. Oxford: Clarendon Press, 1996.

————. "Women, Status and the Popular Culture of Dishonour." *Transactions of the Royal Historical Society*, 6th series 6 (1996): 227–34.

Greatrex, Joan. "Monk Students from Norwich Cathedral Priory." *English Historical Review* 106 (1991): 555–83.

————. "Rabbits and Eels at High Table: Monks of Ely at the University of Cambridge, c. 1337–1539." In *Monasteries and Society in Medieval Britain: Proceedings of the 1994 Harlaxton Symposium*, edited by Benjamin Thompson, 312–28. Stamford, U.K.: Paul Watkins, 1999.

Green, Richard Firth. *A Crisis of Truth: Literature and Law in Ricardian England*. Philadelphia: University of Pennsylvania Press, 1999.

Green, Thomas Andrew. *Verdict According to Conscience: Perspectives on the English Criminal Trial Jury, 1200–1800*. Chicago: University of Chicago Press, 1985.

Groebner, Valentin. "Losing Face, Saving Face: Noses and Honour in the Late Medieval Town." Translated by Pamela Selwyn. *History Workshop Journal* 40 (1995): 1–15.

Gutmann, M. C. "Trafficking in Men: The Anthropology of Masculinity." *Annual Review of Anthropology* 26 (1997): 385–409.

Hadley, D. M., ed. *Masculinity in Medieval Europe*. London: Longman, 1999.

Haigh, C. A. "Slander and the Church Courts in the Sixteenth Century." *Transactions of the Lancashire and Cheshire Antiquarian Society* 78 (1975): 1–13.

Hale, Rosemary Drage. "Joseph as Mother: Adaptation and Appropriation in the Construction of Male Virtue." In *Medieval Mothering*, edited by John Carmi Parsons and Bonnie Wheeler, 101–16. New York: Garland, 1996.

Hanawalt, Barbara. "'The Childe of Bristowe' and the Making of Middle-Class Adolescence." In *Bodies and Disciplines: Intersections of Literature and History in Fifteenth-Century England*, edited by Barbara A. Hanawalt and David Wallace, 155–78. Minneapolis: University of Minnesota Press, 1996.

————. *Growing up in Medieval London: The Experience of Childhood in History*. New York: Oxford University Press, 1993.

Hanna III, Ralph. "Brewing Trouble: On Literature and History—and Alewives." In *Bodies and Disciplines: Intersections of Literature and History in Fifteenth-Century England*, edited by Barbara A. Hanawalt and David Wallace, 1–18. Minneapolis: University of Minnesota Press, 1996.

Hanning, Robert W. *The Individual in Twelfth-Century Romance*. New Haven, Conn.: Yale University Press, 1977.

Hartman, Mary S. *The Household and the Making of History: A Subversive View of the Western Past.* Cambridge: Cambridge University Press, 2004.

Harvey, Karen. "The History of Masculinity, circa 1650-1800." *Journal of British Studies* 44, no. 2 (2005): 296-311.

Harvey, Karen, and Alexandra Shepard. "What Have Historians Done with Masculinity? Reflections on Five Centuries of British History, circa 1500-1950." *Journal of British Studies* 44, no. 2 (2005): 274-80.

Haskett, Timothy S. "County Lawyers? The Composers of English Chancery Bills." In *The Life of the Law: Proceedings of the Tenth British Legal History Conference, Oxford, 1991*, edited by P. Birks, 9-23. London: Hambledon Press, 1993.

Heath, Peter. *The English Parish Clergy on the Eve of the Reformation.* Toronto: University of Toronto Press, 1969.

Helmholz, Richard. "Harboring Sexual Offenders: Ecclesiastical Courts and Controlling Misbehavior." *Journal of British Studies* 37, no. 3 (1998): 258-68.

———. *Marriage Litigation in Medieval England.* Cambridge: Cambridge University Press, 1974.

———, ed. *Select Cases on Defamation to 1600.* London: Selden Society, 1985.

Hilton, Rodney. "The Social Structure of the Village." In *The English Peasantry in the Later Middle Ages: The Ford Lectures for 1973 and Related Studies*, 20-36. Oxford: Clarendon Press, 1975.

Horrox, Rosemary, ed. *Fifteenth-Century Attitudes: Perceptions of Society in Late Medieval England.* Cambridge: Cambridge University Press, 1994.

Huot, Sylvia. "Dangerous Embodiments: Froissart's Harton and Jean D'arras's Melusine." *Speculum* 78 (2003): 400-420.

Johnson, Michael. "Science and Discipline: The Ethos of Sex Education in a Fourteenth-Century Classroom." In *Homo Carnalis*, edited by Helen Rodnite Lemay, 157-71. Ithaca: State University of New York Press, 1987.

Johnston, Mark D. "The Treatment of Speech in Medieval Ethical and Courtesy Literature." *Rhetorica* 4 (1986): 21-45.

Justice, Steven. *Writing and Rebellion: England in 1381.* Berkeley and Los Angeles: University of California Press, 1994.

Kandel, Eric R. "Biology and the Future of Psychoanalysis: A New Intellectual Framework for Psychiatry Revisited." *American Journal of Psychiatry* 156, no. 4 (1999): 505-24.

———. "A New Intellectual Framework for Psychiatry." *American Journal of Psychiatry* 155, no. 4 (1998): 457-69.

Karras, Ruth Mazo. *Common Women: Prostitution and Sexuality in Medieval England.* New York: Oxford University Press, 1996.

———. *From Boys to Men: Formations of Masculinity in Late Medieval Europe.* Philadelphia: University of Pennsylvania Press, 2003.

———. "Separating the Men from the Goats: Masculinity, Civilization, and Identity Formation in the Medieval University." In *Conflicted Identities and Multiple Masculinities: Men in the Medieval West*, edited by Jacqueline Murray, 189-214. New York: Garland, 1999.

———. "Sharing Wine, Women, and Song: Masculine Identity Formation in Medieval European Universities." In *Becoming Male in the Middle Ages*, edited by Jeffrey Jerome Cohen and Bonnie Wheeler, 187-202. New York: Garland, 1997.

———. "Two Models, Two Standards: Moral Teaching and Sexual Mores." In *Bodies and Disciplines: Intersections of Literature and History in Fifteenth-Century England*, edited by Barbara A. Hanawalt and David Wallace, 123-37. Minneapolis: University of Minnesota Press, 1996.

Kermode, Jennifer. *Medieval Merchants: York, Beverley, and Hull in the Later Middle Ages.* Cambridge: Cambridge University Press, 1998.

Kettle, Ann J. "City and Close: Lichfield in the Century before Reformation." In *The Church in Pre-Reformation Society*, edited by Caroline Barron and Christopher Harper-Bill, 158–65. Woodbridge, U.K.: Boydell and Brewer, 1985.

Kowaleski, Maryanne. "Singlewomen in Medieval and Early Modern Europe: The Demographic Perspective." In *Singlewomen in the European Past, 1250–1800*, edited by Judith M. Bennett and Amy M. Froide, 38–81. Philadelphia: University of Pennsylvania Press, 1999.

Kruger, Steven F. "Claiming the Pardoner: Toward a Gay Reading of Chaucer's Pardoner's Tale." In *Critical Essays on Geoffrey Chaucer*, edited by Thomas C. Stillinger, 150–72. New York: Prentice Hall, 1998.

Laqueur, Thomas Walter. *Making Sex: Body and Gender from the Greeks to Freud*. Cambridge, Mass.: Harvard University Press, 1990.

Layton, Lynne. *Who's That Girl? Who's That Boy? Clinical Practice Meets Postmodern Gender Theory*. Northvale, N.J.: J. Aronson, 1998.

LeDoux, Joseph. *The Emotional Brain: The Mysterious Underpinnings of Emotional Life*. New York: Touchstone, 1996.

Lees, Clare A., ed. *Medieval Masculinities: Regarding Men in the Middle Ages*. Minneapolis: University of Minnesota Press, 1994.

Lesnick, Daniel R. "Insults and Threats in Medieval Todi." *Journal of Medieval History* 17 (1991): 71–89.

Leyser, Conrad. "Masculinity in Flux: Nocturnal Emission and the Limits of Celibacy in the Early Middle Ages." In *Masculinity in Medieval Europe*, edited by D. M. Hadley, 103–20. London: Longman, 1999.

Liddle, A. Mark. "State, Masculinities and Law: Some Comments on Gender and English State-Formation." *British Journal of Criminology* 36 (1996): 361–80.

Logan, F. Donald. *Runaway Religious in Medieval England, c. 1240–1540*. Cambridge: Cambridge University Press, 1996.

Maddern, Philippa. "Honour among the Pastons: Gender and Integrity in Fifteenth-Century English Provincial Society." *Journal of Medieval History* 14 (1988): 357–71.

———. "Social Mobility." In *A Social History of England, 1200–1500*, edited by Rosemary Horrox and W. Mark Ormrod, 113–33. Cambridge: Cambridge University Press, 2006.

———. *Violence and Social Order: East Anglia 1422–1442*. Oxford: Clarendon Press, 1992.

Mann, Jill. *Chaucer and Medieval Estates Satire: The Literature of Social Classes*. Cambridge: Cambridge University Press, 1973.

McAlpine, Monica E. "The Pardoner's Homosexuality and How It Matters." *Proceedings of the Modern Language Association* 95 (1980): 1–22.

McHardy, A. "The English Clergy and the Hundred Years War." In *The Church and War: Papers Read at the Twenty-First Summer Meeting and the Twenty-Second Winter Meeting of the Ecclesiastical History Society*, edited by W. J. Shiels, 171–78. Oxford: Blackwell, 1983.

McIntosh, Marjorie. *Autonomy and Community: The Royal Manor of Havering, 1200–1500*. Cambridge: Cambridge University Press, 1986.

———. *Controlling Misbehavior in England, 1370–1600*. Cambridge: Cambridge University Press, 1998.

———. *Working Women in English Society, 1300–1620*. Cambridge: Cambridge University Press, 2005.

McNamara, JoAnn. "The *Herrenfrage*: The Restructuring of the Gender System, 1050–1150." In *Medieval Masculinities: Regarding Men in the Middle Ages*, edited by Clare A. Lees, 3–30. Minneapolis: University of Minnesota Press, 1994.

McSheffrey, Shannon. *Love and Marriage in Late Medieval London*. Kalamazoo, Mich.: Medieval Institute Publications, 1995.

———. *Marriage, Sex, and Civic Culture in Late Medieval London*. Philadelphia: University of Pennsylvania Press, 2006.

——. "Men and Masculinity in Late Medieval London Civic Culture: Governance, Patriarchy, and Reputation." In *Conflicted Identities and Multiple Masculinities: Men in the Medieval West,* edited by Jacqueline Murray, 243-67. New York: Garland, 1999.

Menuge, Noel. *Medieval English Wardship in Romance and Law.* Woodbridge, U.K.: D. S. Brewer, 2001.

Miller, William Ian. *The Mystery of Courage.* Cambridge, Mass.: Harvard University Press, 2000.

Moreton, C. E. *The Townshends and Their World: Gentry, Law, and Land in Norfolk c. 1450-1551.* Oxford: Clarendon Press, 1992.

Morris, Colin. *The Discovery of the Individual, 1050-1200.* 1972. Medieval Academy Reprints for Teaching, no. 19. Toronto: University of Toronto Press in association with the Medieval Academy of America, 1987.

Munro, Alice. "Images." In *Selected Stories,* 40-49. Toronto: McClelland and Stewart, 1996.

Murray, Jacqueline, ed. *Conflicted Identities and Multiple Masculinities: Men in the Medieval West.* New York: Garland, 1999.

——. "Hiding behind the Universal Man: Male Sexuality in the Middle Ages." In *Handbook of Medieval Sexuality,* edited by James A. Brundage and Vern L. Bullough, 123-52. New York: Garland, 1996.

——. "'The Law of Sin That Is in My Members': The Problem of Male Embodiment." In *Gender and Holiness: Men, Women, and Saints in Late Medieval Europe,* edited by Sarah Salih and Samantha Riches, 9-22. New York: Routledge, 2002.

——. "Masculinizing Religious Life: Sexual Prowess, the Battle for Chastity and Monastic Identity." In *Holiness and Masculinity in the Middle Ages,* edited by P. H. Cullum and Katherine Lewis, 24-42. Toronto: University of Toronto Press, 2005.

——. "Mystical Castration: Some Reflections on Peter Abelard, Hugh of Lincoln and Sexual Control." In *Conflicted Identities and Multiple Masculinities: Men in the Medieval West,* edited by Jacqueline Murray, 73-92. New York: Garland, 1999.

——. "On the Origins and Role of 'Wise Women' in Causes for Annulment on the Grounds of Male Impotence." *Journal of Medieval History* 16 (1990): 235-51.

Myers, Alec Reginald. *London in the Age of Chaucer.* Norman: University of Oklahoma Press, 1972.

Neal, Derek. "Meanings of Masculinity in Late Medieval England: Self, Body and Society." Ph.D. diss., McGill University, 2004.

——. "Suits Make the Man: Masculinity in Two English Law Courts, c. 1500." *Canadian Journal of History* 37 (2002): 1-22.

Nicholls, Jonathan. *The Matter of Courtesy: Medieval Courtesy Books and the Gawain-Poet.* Woodbridge, U.K.: D. S. Brewer, 1985.

Olson, Sherri. *A Chronicle of All That Happens: Voices from the Village Court in Medieval England.* Toronto: Pontifical Institute of Mediaeval Studies, 1996.

Orme, Nicholas. "The Medieval Clergy of Exeter Cathedral: II. The Secondaries and Choristers." *Reports and Transactions of the Devonshire Association* 115 (1983): 85-100.

Owst, G. R. *Literature and Pulpit in Medieval England: A Neglected Chapter in the History of English Letters and of the English People.* 2nd ed. Oxford: Blackwell, 1961.

Palmer, R. C. *English Law in the Age of the Black Death, 1348-1381: A Transformation of Governance and Law.* Chapel Hill: University of North Carolina Press, 1993.

Parrot, Andrea, and Nina Cummings. *Forsaken Females: The Global Brutalization of Women.* Lanham, Md.: Rowan & Littlefield, 2006.

Partner, Nancy F. "The Hidden Self: Psychoanalysis and the Textual Unconscious." In *Writing Medieval History,* edited by Nancy F. Partner, 42-64. London: Hodder Arnold, 2005.

——. "No Sex, No Gender." In *Studying Medieval Women: Sex, Gender, Feminism,* edited by Nancy F. Partner, 143-70. Cambridge, Mass.: Medieval Academy of America, 1993.

——. "Reading the Book of Margery Kempe." *Exemplaria* 3, no. 1 (1991): 29-66.

Patterson, Lee. "Chaucer's Pardoner on the Couch: Psyche and Clio in Medieval Literary Studies." *Speculum* 76, no. 3 (2001): 638-80.

Payer, Pierre J. *Sex and the Penitentials: The Development of a Sexual Code, 550–1150.* Toronto:
University of Toronto Press, 1984.

Perfetti, Lisa. *Women and Laughter in Medieval Comic Literature.* Ann Arbor: University of Michigan Press, 2003.

Phillips, Susan. "'That Men May of You Seyn': Public Reputation and Private Gossip in Late
Medieval Courtesy Books." Paper presented at the thirty-sixth International Congress on
Medieval Studies, Kalamazoo, Mich., 2001.

Pigg, Daniel F. "Performing the Perverse: The Abuse of Masculine Power in the *Reeve's Tale.*"
In *Masculinities in Chaucer: Approaches to Maleness in the Canterbury Tales and Troilus and
Criseyde,* edited by Peter G. Beidler, 53–62. Cambridge: D. S. Brewer, 1998.

Pinker, Steven. *How the Mind Works.* New York: W. W. Norton, 1999.

Piponnier, Francoise, and Perrine Mane. *Dress in the Middle Ages.* Translated by Caroline
Beamish. New Haven, Conn.: Yale University Press, 1998.

Pitt-Rivers, Julian. "Honour and Social Status." In *Honour and Shame: The Values of Mediterranean
Society,* edited by J. G. Peristiany. London: Weidenfeld and Nicholson, 1965.

Poos, L. R. *A Rural Society after the Black Death: Essex, 1350–1525.* Cambridge: Cambridge University Press, 1991.

———. "Sex, Lies, and the Church Courts of Pre-Reformation England." *Journal of Interdisciplinary History* 35 (1995): 585-607.

Preston, Kathleen, and Kimberley Stanley. "'What's the Worst Thing? . . .' Gender-Directed
Insults." *Sex Roles* 17, no. 3/4 (1987): 209-19.

Putter, Ad. "The Narrative Logic of *Emare.*" In *The Spirit of Medieval English Popular Romance,*
edited by Ad Putter and Jane Gilbert, 157–80. London: Longman, 2000.

Raftis, J. A. *Warboys: Two Hundred Years in the Life of an English Mediaeval Village.* Toronto: Pontifical Institute of Mediaeval Studies, 1974.

Razi, Zvi. "Family, Land, and the Village Community in Later Medieval England." *Past and
Present* 93 (1981): 3-36.

———. *Life, Marriage and Death in a Medieval Parish: Economy, Society and Demography in Halesowen, 1270–1400.* Cambridge: Cambridge University Press, 1980.

Reiss, Edmund. "Romance." In *The Popular Literature of Medieval England,* edited by Thomas J.
Heffernan, 108–30. Knoxville: University of Tennessee Press, 1985.

Riddy, Felicity. "Middle English Romance: Family, Marriage, Intimacy." In *The Cambridge Companion to Medieval Romance,* edited by Roberta L. Krueger, 235–52. Cambridge: Cambridge
University Press, 2000.

———. "Mother Knows Best: Reading Social Change in a Courtesy Text." *Speculum* 71 (1996):
66-86.

Rocke, Michael. *Forbidden Friendships: Homosexuality and Male Culture in Renaissance Florence.*
New York: Oxford University Press, 1996.

Roper, Lyndal. "Blood and Codpieces: Masculinity in the Early Modern German Town." In
Oedipus and the Devil: Witchcraft, Sexuality and Religion in Early Modern Europe, 107–24.
London: Routledge, 1994.

———. "Drinking, Whoring and Gorging: Brutish Indiscipline and the Formation of Protestant
Identity." In *Oedipus and the Devil: Witchcraft, Sexuality and Religion in Early Modern Europe,*
145–67. London: Routledge, 1994.

———. Introd. to *Oedipus and the Devil: Witchcraft, Sexuality and Religion in Early Modern Europe,*
1–34. London: Routledge, 1994.

———. "Was There a Crisis in Gender Relations in Sixteenth-Century Germany?" In *Oedipus
and the Devil: Witchcraft, Sexuality and Religion in Early Modern Europe,* 37–52. London:
Routledge, 1994.

Roper, Michael. "Between Manliness and Masculinity: The 'War Generation' and the Psychology of Fear in Britain, 1914-1950." *Journal of British Studies* 44, no. 2 (2005): 343-82.

Rosenwein, Barbara H. "Worrying about Emotions in History." *American Historical Review* 107, no. 3 (2002): 821-45.

Ross, Charles. *Edward IV*. London: Eyre Methuen, 1974.

Ross, John Munder. "Fathering: A Review of Some Psychoanalytic Contributions on Paternity." *International Journal of Psycho-Analysis* 60 (1979): 317-27.

Schmitt, J. C. *La raison des gestes dans l'occident médiéval*. Paris: Éditions Gallimard, 1990.

Schultz, James. "Bodies That Don't Matter: Heterosexuality before Heterosexuality in Gottfried's *Tristan*." In *Constructing Medieval Sexuality*, edited by Karma Lochrie, James A. Schultz, and Peggy McCracken, 91-110. Minneapolis: University of Minnesota Press, 1997.

Sharp, Michael D. "Reading Chaucer's 'Manly Man': The Trouble with Masculinity in the *Monk's Prologue* and *Tale*." In *Masculinities in Chaucer: Approaches to Maleness in the Canterbury Tales and Troilus and Criseyde*, edited by Peter G. Beidler, 173-86. Cambridge: D. S. Brewer, 1998.

Sharpe, J. A. *Defamation and Sexual Slander in Early Modern England: The Church Courts at York*. Borthwick Papers, no. 58. York: University of York, Borthwick Institute of Historical Research, 1980.

Shaw, David Gary. *The Creation of a Community: The City of Wells in the Middle Ages*. New York: Oxford University Press, 1993.

———. *Necessary Conjunctions: The Social Self in the Middle Ages*. New York: Palgrave Macmillan, 2005.

Shepard, Alexandra. "From Anxious Patriarchs to Refined Gentlemen? Manhood in Britain, circa 1500-1700." *Journal of British Studies* 44, no. 2 (2005): 281-95.

———. "Manhood, Credit and Patriarchy in Early Modern England c. 1580-1640." *Past and Present* 167 (2000): 75-106.

———. *Meanings of Manhood in Early Modern England*. Oxford: Oxford University Press, 2003.

Slobin, Dan I. *Psycholinguistics*. Glenview, Ill.: Scott, Foresman, 1971.

Smelser, Neil J., and Robert S. Wallerstein. "Psychoanalysis and Sociology." In *The Social Edges of Psychoanalysis*. Berkeley and Los Angeles: University of California Press, 1999.

Smith, D. Vance. "Body Doubles: Producing the Masculine *Corpus*." In *Becoming Male in the Middle Ages*, edited by Jeffrey Jerome Cohen and Bonnie Wheeler, 3-19. New York: Garland, 1997.

Solomon, Michael. *The Literature of Misogyny in Medieval Spain: The "Arcipreste De Talavera" and the "Spill."* Cambridge: Cambridge University Press, 1997.

Stein, Robert M. "Literary Criticism and the Evidence for History." In *Writing Medieval History*, edited by Nancy F. Partner, 67-87. London: Hodder Arnold, 2005.

Stoller, Robert J. *Presentations of Gender*. New Haven: Yale University Press, 1985.

Storey, R. L. "Malicious Indictments of Clergy in the Fifteenth Century." In *Medieval Ecclesiastical Studies in Honour of Dorothy M. Owen*, edited by M. J. Franklin and Christopher Harper-Bill, 221-40. Woodbridge, U.K.: Boydell Press, 1995.

Sturges, Robert S. *Chaucer's Pardoner and Gender Theory: Bodies of Discourse*. New York: St Martin's Press, 2000.

Sutton, Anne. "Dress and Fashions c. 1470." In *Daily Life in the Late Middle Ages*, edited by Richard H. Britnell, 5-26. Stroud, U.K.: Sutton Publishing, 1998.

Swanson, Heather. *Medieval Artisans: An Urban Class in Late Medieval England*. Oxford: Basil Blackwell, 1989.

Swanson, R. N. "Angels Incarnate: Clergy and Masculinity from Gregorian Reform to Reformation." In *Masculinity in Medieval Europe*, edited by D. M. Hadley, 160-77. London: Longman, 1999.

———. *Church and Society in Late Medieval England*. Oxford: Blackwell, 1989.

Tanner, Norman P. "The Reformation and Regionalism: Further Reflections on the Church in Late Medieval Norwich." In *Towns and Townspeople in the Fifteenth Century,* edited by John A. F. Thomson, 129-47. Gloucester: Alan Sutton, 1988.

Thompson, A. Hamilton. *The English Clergy and Their Organization in the Later Middle Ages.* Oxford: Clarendon Press, 1947.

Thrupp, Sylvia Lettice. *The Merchant Class of Medieval London, 1300-1500.* 1948. Reprint, Ann Arbor: University of Michigan Press, 1962.

Tosh, John. *A Man's Place: Masculinity and the Middle-Class Home in Victorian England.* New Haven, Conn.: Yale University Press, 1999.

———. "What Should Historians Do with Masculinity? Reflections on Nineteenth-Century Britain." *History Workshop Journal* 38 (1994): 179-202.

Trilling, Lionel. *Sincerity and Authenticity.* Cambridge: Harvard University Press, 1972.

Tyson, Phyllis, and Robert L. Tyson. *Psychoanalytic Theories of Development: An Integration.* New Haven, Conn.: Yale University Press, 1990.

Vaughan, Susan C. *The Talking Cure: The Science behind Psychotherapy.* New York: Putnam's, 1997.

Wack, Mary Frances. *Lovesickness in the Middle Ages: The Viaticum and Its Commentaries.* Philadelphia: University of Pennsylvania Press, 1990.

Wacquant, Loïc. "The Prizefighter's Three Bodies." *Ethnos* 63, no. 3 (1998): 325-52.

Walker, Garthine. "Expanding the Boundaries of Female Honour in Early Modern England." *Transactions of the Royal Historical Society,* 6th series 6 (1996): 235-45.

Ward, Jeanne. *Broken Bodies, Broken Dreams: Violence against Women Exposed.* Edited by Lisa Ernst. Nairobi: United Nations Office for the Coordination of Humanitarian Affairs, Integrated Regional Information Networks, 2005.

Wehler, Hans-Ulrich. "Psychoanalysis and History." *Social Research* 47 (1980): 519-36.

Westen, Drew, and Glen O. Gabbard. "Developments in Cognitive Neuroscience: I. Conflict, Compromise and Connectionism." *Journal of the American Psychoanalytic Association* 50, no. 1 (2002): 53-98.

———. "Developments in Cognitive Neuroscience: II. Implications for Theories of Transference." *Journal of the American Psychoanalytic Association* 50, no. 1 (2002): 99-134.

White, Hayden V. "Introduction: Historical Fiction, Fictional History, and Historical Reality." *Rethinking History* 9, no. 2/3 (2005): 147-57.

Wiesner, M. E. "Wandervogels and Women: Journeymen's Concepts of Masculinity in Early Modern Germany." *Journal of Social History* 24, no. 4 (1991): 767-82.

Williams, John, and Regan Taylor. "Boys Keep Swinging: Masculinity and Football Culture in England." In *Just Boys Doing Business? Men, Masculinities and Crime,* edited by Tim Newburn and Elizabeth Stanko, 214-33. London: Routledge, 1994.

Wunderli, Richard M. *London Church Courts and Society on the Eve of the Reformation.* Cambridge, Mass.: Medieval Academy of America, 1981.

Zakim, Michael. "Sartorial Ideologies: From Homespun to Ready-Made." *American Historical Review* 106, no. 5 (2001): 1553-86.

Index